The Hedge Fund Compliance and Risk Management Guide

Founded in 1807, John Wiley & Sons is the oldest independent publishing company in the United States. With offices in North America, Europe, Australia, and Asia, Wiley is globally committed to developing and marketing print and electronic products and services for our customers' professional and personal knowledge and understanding.

The Wiley Finance series contains books written specifically for finance and investment professionals as well as sophisticated individual investors and their financial advisors. Book topics range from portfolio management to e-commerce, risk management, financial engineering, valuation, and financial instrument analysis, as well as much more.

For a list of available titles, visit our Web site at www.WileyFinance.com.

The Hedge Fund Compliance and Risk Management Guide

ARMELLE GUIZOT

John Wiley & Sons, Inc.

Library of Congress Cataloging-in-Publication Data:

Guizot, Armelle, 1972–
    The hedge fund compliance and risk management guide / Armelle Guizot.
        p.   cm.
    Includes bibliographical references and index.
    ISBN-13: 978-0-470-04357-8 (cloth)
    ISBN-10: 0-470-04357-1 (cloth)
    1. Hedge funds—United States.   2. Hedge funds—Law and legislation—United
States.   3. Risk management.   I. Title.
    HG4930.G86   2007
    332.64'5—dc22

                                                                2006013381

Printed in the United States of America.
10 9 8 7 6 5 4 3 2 1

To all of you who believed in me.

"Once you passed on the other side,
There is no one to believe anymore but a shadow future to hold onto."
—Anonymous

Contents

Preface

Someone once said knowledge is something, conscience is everything. On the one hand, I wrote this book to bring more fundamental knowledge and guidance about risks embedded in financial markets in relatively free regulatory environments, more specifically with regard to hedge funds. On the other hand, I expose the fundamental changes and awareness that risk managers have to go through to become balancing actors of a new financial system. This book is intended primarily for risk managers who are sandwiched between the duty of reporting risks to regulators, the responsibility of winning market shares in a highly competitive environment, and commonly the worry of having to preserve a job and collect a paycheck. Another readership would be regulators who need knowledge about hedge fund risks in their role sandwiched between politicians and corporate managers. This book will also be of interest to traders, students in the fields of corporate law and governance as well as business finance and economics, auditors, marketers, compliance officers, and all hedge fund investors interested in knowing more about risk. The concepts and ideas in the book will also be of interest to those in the mutual funds industry and other larger financial institutions that hold explicit and implicit risks with hedge funds as these funds grow. Finally, this book is intended to prove on a quantitative and qualitative scale how integrated hedge funds are in the markets.

I must confess to another, perhaps unconventional, reason to write this book: It is my way to add value to a risk management career that I've become somewhat disenchanted with over the past few years. It is also especially written for those who sacrificed a number of years of their lives in their attempt to "do the right thing." Writing about hedge fund hogs and hawks is to put closure to what was once considered my dream career, and to transform it via education and research.

This preamble brings insights about the overall state of the markets and where they are headed. If mathematical formulas are useful for progress and advancement, they are not necessary to hide lack of integrity and create fatter excuses for larger aberrations of financial anarchy and irresponsibility. But in many cases, greed took over.

Remember 1998 and the Long-Term Capital Management fiasco?

This book is intended to bring more clarity about hedge funds; it will

examine those that have done wrong and the majority that took advantage
of scandals to arbitrage from them. Why do we select a few hedge funds
when we know that the majority had gone out of control, especially when
it comes to monitoring risk management? No regulation is as harmful as
too much regulation. The old ways of regulating markets are no longer
sustainable due to technological progress and the massive mergers that
have changed the landscape of financial markets, the validation, and the
credibility of old-time regulatory agencies. The bureaucratic nature of the
old regulations may actually be more harmful than beneficial to the
progress and evolution of financial markets unless they adapt. But the slow
bureaucratic implementations could also help a whole new generation be
more proactive in understanding the transformed era of banking. Regulation and risk taking are balancing acts keeping returns healthy and contributing to stable financial markets and global economies over time. When
too many regulators have been cooperating for too long with management
of companies for self-interests and greed instead of the interests of the
shareholders, a system becomes more vulnerable and in need of reform. It
is even graver that systems that had failed to adequately reform and regulate on time were those promoting values of democracy and freedom. Is it
too late to promote ideals of freedom and democratic values? Or do they
not ring well with technologies or do voting rights no longer really matter?
(Or is it convenient to use technologies to hide greed and omit profound
regulations?)

The hope we hold now is that the reforms in the financial industry that
have been implemented in the past few years will really change mind-sets
and behaviors, not give shareholders another layer of lies. Let us preserve
individual democratic values while we still may and respect fundamental
laws that are about teaching individuals to be more responsible rather than
depending on governments. Let us not forget that governments are "We
the people"; let us remember that the past fundamental values are what
created the markets. Let's not make excuses for perpetuating past mistakes
and make them bigger in scope and scale than ever. Let us now begin to assume that each one of us has a role, a duty, a responsibility, and foremost
the accountability to question possible financial anarchy and not to toler-
ate financial market abuses and abnormalities.

I hope my discussion of hedge funds will demonstrate such abuses but
I will also propose some basic remedies to prevent such experiences from
taking place in the future.

Acknowledgments

To my father Jean, my mother Françoise, my brother David, my relatives, my editor and team, teachers and professors of West Virginia State University and Cornell University, my friends, industry colleagues, institutional traders, compliance officers, special lawyers, regulators, academicians, and researchers who have participated in huge progress in a few years, former managers who taught me so much, my inspiring coach who keeps me going and going, and a very special thank you to those saving the future together. Thank you for your hard work, integrity, patience, and trust.

My dedication and thoughts also go to my American friends who made my dream possible, faraway friends including operations officers, families, and unknown colleagues who have spent their lives contributing to the advancement of global financial market stabilization and integration. I love our work together. Thank you.

About the Author

Armelle Guizot has worked in risk management at various financial institutions and across different instruments since 1997. After receiving her master's degree in financial engineering from Cornell University she started as an analyst in the municipal market at Merrill Lynch in New York City. After a few months spent studying the municipal bond market and learning about the life cycle of municipal derivatives and swaps, she was transferred to the pricing verification team as an equity derivative product controller to review and validate global institutional equity derivatives trading books.

From 1998 to 1999, Guizot verified institutional traders' pricing options with respect to market efficiencies and produced the upper management report on institutional traders' profits and losses. She created a compliant library of equity derivatives trades and learned about the integration of mathematics into finance by reviewing all the traders' term sheets and legal contracts. She reviewed payoff formulas, terms, and signatures with counterparties and learned about the impact of market news on counterparties' risk exposures. She reported on the impact of the 1998 Russian crisis on the company's books and then calculated potential losses and explained risk exposures with Long-Term Capital Management.

In 1999, Guizot transferred to the largely expanding risk management department of Merrill Lynch, serving as the rate product analyst for the global interest rate product risk manager until 2001. She reported weekly commodities market news and monitored traders' limits and geographical capital allocation. After almost four years at Merrill Lynch spent learning about most products and writing a strategic business plan for upper management, Guizot went to other boutiques to learn more about other risk management profiles, models, and corporate cultures.

From 2001 to 2002, Guizot was the global commodities market risk manager at Bank of America for Asia, Europe, and the Americas. As the global market risk manager of the commodities desks, she wrote an internal risk management audit based on risk management standards she had learned at her previous shop. Given the results of her initiatives on internal audit of controls, she disagreed with standards in the commodities markets unless more infrastructures were put around a new trading desk and commodities business line.

By late 2002, she was investigating risk management in hedge funds where risk monitoring was to be reengineered and reinvented because hedge funds had weak infrastructures, no audits, and so little transparency as to mislead investors. Working in a hedge fund, she observed that risk management in hedge funds had been performed on a surface level and was applied primarily for marketing sweetener, not for true risk management purposes.

She spent most of the year 2003 at Sumitomo Mitsui Corporation in order to learn about the Japanese risk management situation and to evaluate the financial trading risk appetite in Japan.

From 2004 to 2005, Guizot researched the role of risk management in offshore asset management hubs known as tax havens. She participated in the development of operational risk management in hedge funds, mutual funds, and transfer agency lines of business. She worked with various local committees to implement banking rules regarding anti-money-laundering (AML) activities, the U.S. Patriot Act, "know your customer" (KYC) rules, and Financial Action Task Force (FATF) and Groupe d'Action Financière Sur le Blanchiment de Capitaux (GAFI) disclosures. Along with these new rules within the banking industry, she also learned about ownership of data from point to point, either geographically or between different legal entities within technological infrastructures and frameworks. She participated in the planning of data encryptions of special classified banking projects.

In 2005, she worked in the insurance captives industry and evaluated their integration into the financial markets as risk management instruments to enhance transparency between different types of risks according to the Basel Accords Revised Framework (2004).

In 2006, she started to deepen her research about global macroeconomically-related and micromarkets issues. She is also the author of *Hedge Funds and Operational Risk, China and Global Commodities Markets*, and "The Chinese Dream; The Rising Sun: China's Financial and Banking System, Economy, and Foreign Exchange and Interest Rates Risks Policies." She is also researching new ways to measure transparency and operational risks in all countries to demonstrate that global hedge funds are in fact "unhedged."

CHAPTER 1

History, Definition, and Roles of Hedge Funds

Historically, Alfred Winslow Jones created the first hedge fund in 1949 according to Caldwell (1995), and its strategy was long and short equity and leverage. In 1966, *Fortune* magazine reported higher returns (net of fees) for hedge funds than for mutual funds. Caldwell (1995) states that the Securities and Exchange Commission (SEC) counted 140 hedge funds among investment partnerships by 1968. From the late 1960s to the early 1970s, the hedge fund industry continued to grow. However, the markets suffered sizable losses also correlated to commodity crises in the late 1970s. From then until 1986, hedge funds faded out of the market until Julian Robertson's Tiger fund reported a 43 percent return during his first six years net of fees. Subsequently the Commodity Trading Advisor (CTA) was created with a similar philosophy and structure. CTAs are firms or individuals trading commodity options and futures contracts and are registered with the Commodity Futures Trading Commission (CFTC) through the National Futures Association.

Unlike in the past, a hedge fund's registration no longer reveals its business strategies and trading mandates. Many funds' strategies and products deviate from what regulatorial registration once meant and was aimed at. Long-Term Capital Management LP was registered as a commodity pool operator (CPO) and yet was trading many kinds of other derivatives products as well, such as over-the-counter (OTC) securities markets. Very much like CTAs, hedge funds have grown during the 1990s, and by 1997 hedge funds had $65 billion of assets under management. CTAs accounted for 291 funds with $17 billion in assets. Typically, management fees are about 1 to 2 percent and the incentive fee is 15 to 20 percent.

Hedge funds' growth has taken off exponentially. In 1990, there were some 610 hedge funds, and by 2000 the numbers had grown to approximately 3,873 funds worldwide. (See Figure 1.1.) Now they total about

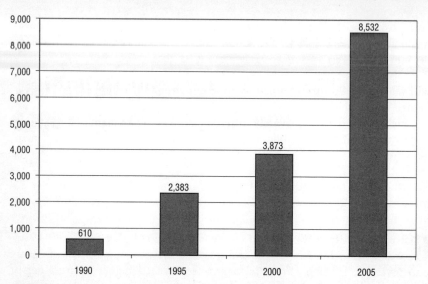

FIGURE 1.1   Number of Hedge Funds from 1990 to 2005
Source: Data from *Bloomberg Markets,* January 2006.

8,000 to 9,000. Hedge funds are created to make quick returns and to close fast, so statistics are very inaccurate as time goes along. For instance, it is estimated that only 59.5 percent of the hedge funds that were alive in 1996 were still alive by 2001. More hedge funds have been created since then, but more failures have occurred, too.

Attrition has risen at an increasing rate in parallel with the growth rate of the hedge fund industry. There are some alarming factors that need to be taken into account. For instance, in 1996, 93.8 percent of the funds alive at the beginning of the year were still alive by the end of the year. Two years later, this statistic was down to 90.9 percent. And by 2000 it was down to 87.7 percent. Yet the trend of new hedge funds rose as more investors needed to make quicker returns via alternative means, and hedge funds were the way to make up for losses from traditional types of investments. To say the least, hedge funds had loose risk management controls during those days as risk management was viewed as a cost center and a way of cutting profits short.

When Long-Term Capital Management LP collapsed in 1998, the hedge fund firm had borrowed so much money that the Federal Reserve Bank of New York helped broker a bailout to avoid an implosion that might have roiled world markets. The Long-Term Capital Management fiasco was signaling the proliferation of more fiascos to happen afterward.

Since then, hedge funds have multiplied as never before. Their number reached about 8,532 as of September 30, up 14.7 percent from 7,436 at the end of 2004 according to Hedge Fund Research.

Given past trends, some estimates forecast the hedge fund industry will reach 25,000 funds valued at approximately $4 trillion by 2013. (See Figure 1.2.)

Hedge funds are privately offered, pooled investment vehicles not widely available to the public. A professional investment management firm manages the assets. Hedge funds also refer to funds of funds. Hedge funds are not considered private equity firms, nor are they real estate funds. The growth rate of hedge funds has been phenomenal. The industry has grown from about $500 billion in assets under management in 2001 to at least $750 billion at the end of 2003. It is also estimated that having grown by more than 10 times in the past decade, its total market share could reach $1.4 trillion in 2006. (See Figure 1.3.)

Per the *Financial Times* of Monday, November 28, 2005, Morgan Stanley published a research report about large financial institutions also being involved in banks. According to the research, investment banks'

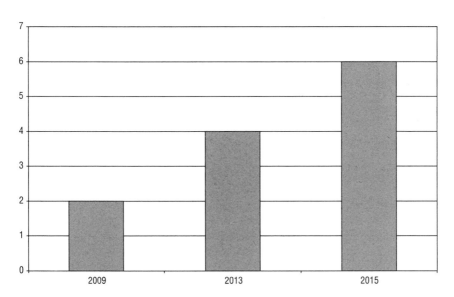

FIGURE 1.2   Forecasted Capacity of Hedge Funds in Trillions of Dollars
Source: Data from Van Hedge Fund Advisors International, LLC research, published in the Social Science Research Network in the SSRN eLibrary (www.ssrn.com).

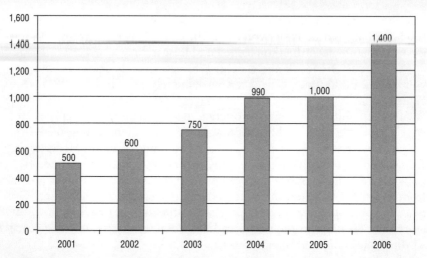

FIGURE 1.3   Asset Growth of Hedge Funds from 2001 to 2006 (Estimation) in Billions of Dollars
Source: Data from *Bloomberg Markets*, January 2006.

brokerage operations generated more than $5 billion in profits in 2005, a rise of 28 percent from 2004. Although hedge funds' returns have shrunk, the study shows that prime brokerage services have increased by 11 percent due to more hedge fund services. This understates the importance of hedge funds for investment banking because it excludes revenues from equity derivatives traded by hedge funds. Most of the hedge funds' traded instruments also go unreported as they are off-balance-sheet items. Thus, it is also estimated that the actual amount of assets in hedge funds is far greater than the amount disclosed. The total size of the hedge fund industry represents about 2 to 3 percent of the global financial markets.

It is estimated that the total of assets under management for all hedge funds in the Hedge Fund Research (www.hedgefundresearch.com) database was roughly $990 billion in January 2004, considerably less than the industry estimates of $600 billion to $1 trillion for the universe of hedge funds.

There are between 12 and 20 different hedge fund strategies. Directional funds more than doubled from 1996 to 2004 and the respective total assets under management have more than tripled. More growth is implied by the figures for market neutral and equity-focused funds. In 2004, assets under management in market neutral funds had risen to more than seven times the 1996 levels. Equity-focused funds' assets under management experienced fivefold growth.

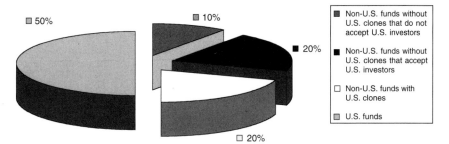

FIGURE 1.4 Global Hedge Funds Universe: U.S. and Non-U.S. Funds
Source: Data from Van Hedge Fund Advisors International, LLC.

There were about 610 hedge funds in 1990, and it is estimated there may be 10,000 of them by 2007. Some literature suggests that a number of smaller funds closed down in 2005. So all these figures remain approximations, because it is difficult to assess a full population of the live funds. Their market share distribution is: 16 percent have less than $5 million of assets under management, 29 percent between $5 million and $25 million, 32 percent between $25 million and $100 million, 19 percent between $100 million and $500 million, and 4 percent greater than $500 million.

Hedge funds make up about 10 percent of large commodity pools worldwide, about 628 of them as of 2003, worth approximately $100 million. There are 2,365 commodity pools with approximately $351 million in net assets. Eighteen of the top 25 hedge funds are operated by CPOs, while 55 of the top 100 hedge funds are operated by CPOs. About 44 of the top 100 hedge funds are registered with the CFTC as CTAs.

About 30 percent of the global hedge fund market is in Switzerland, and hedge funds are starting to develop in other European countries as well. See Figure 1.4 for an international picture of hedge funds. A specific area of development where fees are particularly high because there is still a lack of liquidity and knowledge is the real estate funds of funds in new Eastern European countries. No one knows the exactitude of these market figures.

CHAPTER 2

Trading Mandates

Depending on the sources of information regarding hedge funds, definitions and trading strategies of hedge funds vary and are somewhat inconsistent with each other except for a few of the most basic ones. This is due to the fact that hedge fund strategies have not been consistent with trading activities since their inception dates. Many trading mandates have deviated from their original strategic mission. Unlike mutual funds, hedge funds were never required to report to regulators any changes in trading and strategic mandates. Due mainly to this factor, it is difficult to assess and define exactly the asset allocations and concentrations of different strategies and what their historical evolutionary growth has been. For example, global international is one of the vague trading strategies that can overlap others such as long/short equity or global macro. According to Offshoreinvestor.com, the global international strategy can invest in either established markets or more risky emerging economies.

Bloomberg Markets reported the following asset allocations and returns by strategies as of January 2006.

CONVERTIBLE ARBITRAGE

Convertible arbitrage involves purchasing a portfolio of convertible securities, generally convertible bonds, and hedging a portion of the equity risk by selling short the underlying common stock. Certain managers may also seek to hedge interest rate exposure by selling Treasuries. The strategy benefits from three different sources: interest earned on the cash resulting from the short sales of equities, coupon offered by the bond component of the convertible, and the so-called gamma effect. The last component results from the change in volatility of the underlying equity. For this particular strategy, most managers employ some degree of leverage, ranging up to 6:1.

The average leverage is 3:1. The equity hedge ratio may range from 30 to 100 percent. The average grade of bond in a typical portfolio is BB–, with individual ratings ranging from AA to CCC. However, because the default risk of the company is hedged by shorting the underlying common stock, the risk is considerably less than the rating of the unhedged bond indicates. This strategy represents about 9 percent of the total strategies. (See Figures 2.1 and 2.2.)

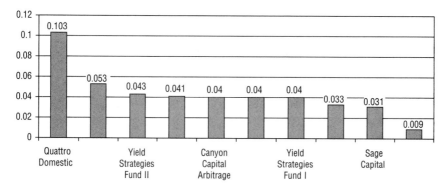

FIGURE 2.1 Largest American Hedge Funds for Convertible Arbitrage Strategy
Source: Data from *Bloomberg Markets*, January 2006.

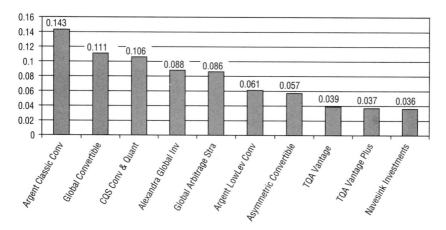

FIGURE 2.2 Largest Non-American Hedge Funds for Convertible Arbitrage Strategy
Source: Data from *Bloomberg Markets*, January 2006.

DISTRESSED SECURITIES

Distressed securities strategies invest in, and may sell short, the securities of companies where security prices have been, or are expected to be, affected by a distressed situation. This may involve reorganizations, bankruptcies, distressed sales, and other corporate restructurings. Depending on the manager's style, investments may be made in bank debt, corporate debt, trade claims, common stock, preferred stock, and warrants. Strategies may be subcategorized as high-yield or orphan equities. Leverage may be used by some managers. Fund managers may run a market hedge using Standard & Poor's (S&P) put options or put options spreads. This strategy represents about 8 percent to 11 percent of the total trading strategies. According to Bloomberg Research, since 2003 hedge funds with distressed strategies have profited a great deal from credit downgrades, bankrupted companies, and defaulted investments. Hedge Fund Research reported that junk bonds and corporate loans posted an average return of 20 percent during the three years ending September 30, 2005. Standard & Poor's reported that about 37 percent of the global companies downgraded to lower investment grade credit ratings in 2005. (See Figures 2.3 and 2.4.)

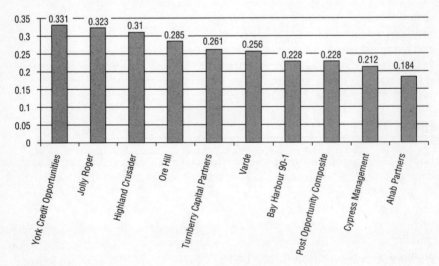

FIGURE 2.3 Largest American Hedge Funds for Distressed Strategy
Source: Data from *Bloomberg Markets*, January 2006.

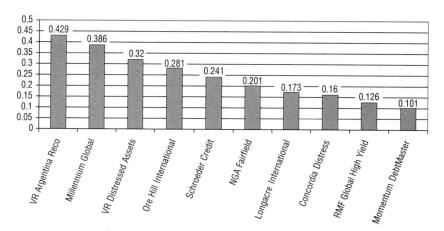

FIGURE 2.4 Largest Non-American Hedge Funds for Distressed Strategy
Source: Data from *Bloomberg Markets*, January 2006.

EMERGING MARKETS

Emerging markets funds invest in securities of companies or the sovereign debt of developing countries. Investments are primarily long. Emerging markets include countries in Latin America, Eastern Europe, the former Soviet Union, Africa, and parts of Asia. Emerging markets—global funds shift their weightings among these regions according to market conditions and manager perspectives. In addition, some managers invest solely in individual regions. For example, emerging markets—Latin America is a strategy that entails investing throughout Central and South America.

EQUITY HEDGE

Equity hedge (equity long/short) investing consists of a core holding of long equities hedged at all times with short sales of stocks and/or stock index options. Some managers maintain a substantial portion of assets within a hedged structure and commonly employ leverage. Where short sales are used, hedged assets may be comprised of an equal dollar value of long and short stock positions. Other variations use short sales unrelated to long holdings and/or puts on the S&P 500 index and put spreads. Conservative funds mitigate market risk by maintaining market exposure from zero to 100 percent. Aggressive funds may magnify market risk by exceeding 100 percent exposure and, in some instances, maintain a short exposure. In addition to equities, some funds may have limited assets invested in other types of securities. This strategy represents 34 percent of all the trading strategies and remains the single largest category with about $320 billion in assets and attracting $1.9 billion in new funds. Hedge Fund Research reported as of January 2006 that long/short equity strategy hedge funds

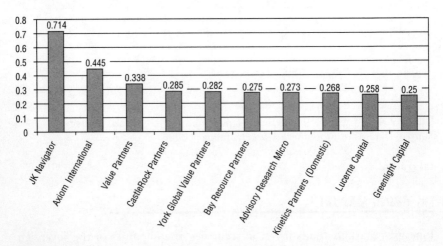

FIGURE 2.5   Largest American Hedge Funds for Long/Short Equity Strategy
Source: Data from *Bloomberg Markets*, January 2006.

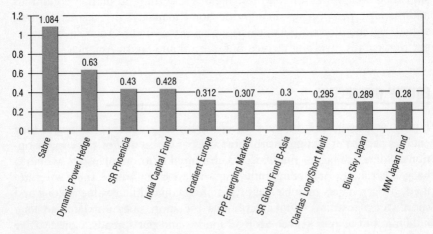

FIGURE 2.6   Largest Non-American Hedge Funds for Long/Short Equity Strategy
Source: Data from *Bloomberg Markets*, January 2006.

demonstrated an average return of 12.6 percent during the three years ended September 30, 2005, and 7.9 percent for the first nine months of that year. Although this strategy is the most common one, largely due to the flourishing of equities throughout the 1990, the strategy has been eroding since its peak, and 2005 saw its slowest year since 1997 with inflow of funds of about $9.4 billion. (See Figures 2.5 and 2.6.)

EQUITY MARKET NEUTRAL

Equity market neutral investing seeks to profit by exploiting pricing inefficiencies between related equity securities, neutralizing exposure to market risk by combining long and short positions. One example of this strategy is to build portfolios made up of long positions in the strongest companies in several industries and taking corresponding short positions in those showing signs of weakness. This strategy represents about 11 percent of the total trading strategies.

Equity Market Neutral: Statistical Arbitrage

Equity market neutral statistical arbitrage utilizes quantitative analysis of technical factors to exploit pricing inefficiencies between related equity securities, neutralizing exposure to market risk by combining long and short positions. The strategy is based on quantitative models for selecting specific stocks with equal dollar amounts comprising the long and short sides of the portfolio. Portfolios are typically structured to be market, industry, sector, and dollar neutral.

EQUITY NON-HEDGE

Equity non-hedge funds are predominately long equities, although they have the ability to hedge with short sales of stocks and/or stock index options. These funds are commonly known as stock pickers. Some funds employ leverage to enhance returns. When market conditions warrant, managers may implement a hedge in the portfolio. Funds may also opportunistically short individual stocks. The important distinction between equity non-hedge funds and equity hedge funds is that equity non-hedge funds do not always have a hedge in place. In addition to equities, some funds may have limited assets invested in other types of securities.

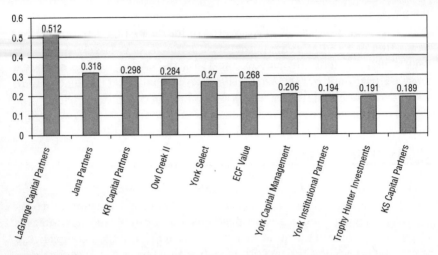

FIGURE 2.7   Largest American Hedge Funds for Event Driven Strategy
Source: Data from *Bloomberg Markets*, January 2006.

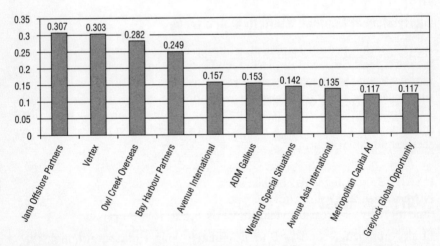

FIGURE 2.8   Largest Non-American Hedge Funds for Event Driven Strategy
Source: Data from *Bloomberg Markets*, January 2006.

EVENT DRIVEN

Event driven investing is also called "special situation" or "corporate life cycle" investing. This involves investing in opportunities created by significant transactional events, such as spin-offs, mergers and acquisitions, bankruptcy reorganizations, recapitalizations, and share buybacks. The portfolios of some event driven managers may shift in majority weighting between risk arbitrage and distressed securities, while others may take a broader scope. Instruments include long and short common and preferred stocks, as well as debt securities and options. Leverage may be used by some managers. Fund managers may hedge against market risk by purchasing S&P put options or put option spreads. This strategy represents about 7 percent of the total trading strategies. Event driven involves taking different positions in companies that are involved in transactions or are distressed in the hope of predicting the effect that the event will have on share prices. (See Figures 2.7 and 2.8.)

FIXED INCOME STRATEGIES

All fixed income strategies represent about 6 percent of the total trading strategies. Fixed income hedge funds reported an average return of 9.5 percent in the three years ended September 30, 2005, according to Hedge Fund Research. Rising U.S. interest rates have depleted fixed income funds. The push and pull of interest rates of the past two decades in the U.S. economy created an overwhelming amount of consumption based on credit to be paid by future generations. This overconsumption has been offset by new economies called new democracies.

The U.S. Federal Reserve raised interest rates in June 2004; two-year U.S. Treasury note yields climbed subsequently reaching 4.47 percent as of November 4, 2005, up from 3.07 percent at the end of 2004. At the same time the 10-year Treasury yields have risen less, to 4.66 percent from 4.22 percent, so funds that borrow money at short-term rates to buy Treasury notes make less money on their investments. The inversion of the yield curve has created more risks in the short term than in the long terms, which is inadequately representative of the geopolitical risks.

Corporate bonds are more difficult to trade profitably compared to junk bonds or high-yield securities. The inflow of capital into fixed income strategies in 2005 amounts to about $5.2 billion for the first nine months. (See Figures 2.9 and 2.10.)

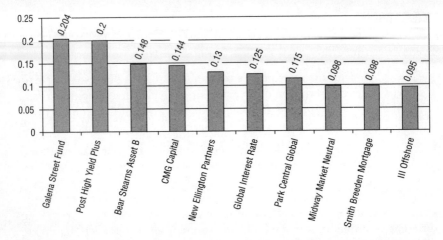

FIGURE 2.9   Largest American Hedge Funds for Fixed Income Strategy
Source: Data from *Bloomberg Markets*, January 2006.

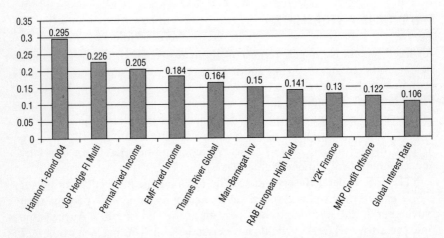

FIGURE 2.10   Largest Non-American Hedge Funds for Fixed Income Strategy
Source: Data from *Bloomberg Markets*, January 2006.

Fixed Income: Arbitrage

Fixed income arbitrage is a market neutral hedging strategy that seeks to profit by exploiting pricing inefficiencies between related fixed income securities while neutralizing exposure to interest rate risk. Fixed income arbitrage is a generic description of a variety of strategies involving investment in fixed income instruments, and weighted in an attempt to eliminate or reduce exposure to changes in the yield curve. Managers attempt to exploit relative mispricing between related sets of fixed income securities. The generic types of fixed income hedging trades include yield curve arbitrage, corporate versus Treasury yield spreads, municipal bond versus Treasury yield spreads, and cash versus futures.

Fixed Income: Convertible Bonds

Convertible bonds funds are primarily long-only convertible bonds. Convertible bonds have both fixed income and equity characteristics. If the underlying common stock appreciates, the convertible bond's value rises to reflect this increased value. Downside protection is offered because if the underlying common stock declines, the convertible bond's value can decline only to the point where it behaves like a straight bond.

Fixed Income: Diversified

Fixed income diversified funds may invest in a variety of fixed income strategies. While many invest in multiple strategies, others may focus on a single strategy less followed by most fixed income hedge funds. Areas of focus include municipal bonds, corporate bonds, and global fixed income securities.

Fixed Income: High-Yield

High-yield managers invest in non–investment grade debt. Objectives may range from high current income to acquisition of undervalued instruments. Emphasis is placed on assessing credit risk of the issuer. Some of the available high-yield instruments include extendible/reset securities, increasing-rate notes, pay-in-kind securities, step-up coupon securities, split coupon securities, and usable bonds.

Fixed Income: Mortgage-Backed

Mortgage-backed funds invest in mortgage-backed securities. Many funds focus solely on AAA-rated bonds. Instruments include: government agency, government-sponsored enterprise, private-label fixed- or adjustable-rate mortgage pass-through securities, fixed- or adjustable-rate collateralized mortgage obligations (CMOs), real estate mortgage investment conduits (REMICs), and stripped mortgage-backed securities (SMBSs). Funds may look to capitalize on security-specific mispricing. Hedging of prepayment risk and interest rate risk is common. Leverage may be used, as well as futures, short sales, and options.

GLOBAL MACRO

Global macro involves investing by making leveraged bets on anticipated price movements of stock markets, interest rates, foreign exchange, and physical commodities. Macro managers employ a top-down global approach, and may invest in any markets using any instruments to participate in expected market movements. These movements may result from forecasted shifts in world economies, political fortunes, or global supply and demand for resources, both physical and financial. Exchange-traded and

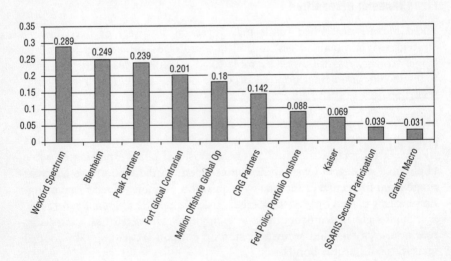

FIGURE 2.11   Largest American Hedge Funds for Global Macro Strategy
Source: Data from *Bloomberg Markets*, January 2006.

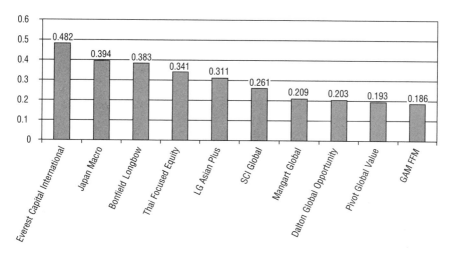

FIGURE 2.12 Largest Non-American Hedge Funds for Global Macro Strategy
Source: Data from *Bloomberg Markets*, January 2006.

over-the-counter derivatives are often used to magnify these price movements. This type of strategy, which represents about 7 percent of all strategies, aims to benefit from macroeconomic changes and developments. Macro hedge funds posted a 10.4 percent average return during the three years ended September 30, 2005. During the first nine months of 2005, this strategy reported returns of approximately 4.5 percent. (See Figures 2.11 and 2.12.)

MERGER ARBITRAGE AND RISK ARBITRAGE

Merger arbitrage, sometimes called risk arbitrage, involves investment in event driven situations such as leveraged buyouts, mergers, and hostile takeovers. Normally, the stock of an acquisition target appreciates while the acquiring company's stock decreases in value. These strategies generate returns by purchasing stock of the company being acquired and in some instances selling short the stock of the acquiring company. Managers may employ the use of equity options as a low-risk alternative to the outright purchase or sale of common stock. Most merger arbitrage funds hedge against market risk by purchasing S&P put options or put option spreads. This strategy, also called statistical arbitrage, represents 1 percent of the total trading strategies.

REGULATION D

Regulation D managers invest in Regulation D securities, sometimes referred to as structured discount convertibles. The securities are privately offered to the investment manager by companies in need of timely financing, and the terms are negotiated. The terms of any particular deal are reflective of the negotiating strength of the issuing company. Once a deal is closed, there is a waiting period for the private share offering to be registered with the Securities and Exchange Commission (SEC). The manager can only convert into private shares and cannot trade them publicly during this period; therefore the investment is illiquid until it becomes registered. Managers will hedge with common stock until the registration becomes effective and then liquidate the position gradually.

RELATIVE VALUE ARBITRAGE

Relative value arbitrage attempts to take advantage of relative pricing discrepancies between instruments, including equities, debt, options, and futures. Managers may use mathematical, fundamental, or technical analysis to determine misvaluations. Securities may be mispriced relative to the underlying security, related securities, groups of securities, or the overall market. Many funds use leverage and seek opportunities globally. Arbitrage strategies include dividend arbitrage, pairs trading, options arbitrage, and yield curve trading. These strategies represent about 10 percent of the total trading strategies.

SECTOR STRATEGIES

Sector strategies involve strategies geared toward specific sectors and industries.

Sector: Energy

Energy sector strategy focuses on investment within the energy sector. Investments can be long and short in various instruments with funds either diversified across the entire sector or specializing within a subsector, such as oil field service.

Sector: Financial

Financial sector strategy invests in securities of bank holding companies, banks, thrifts, insurance companies, mortgage banks, and various other financial services companies.

Sector: Health Care/Biotechnology

Health care/biotechnology sector funds invest in companies involved in the health care, pharmaceutical, biotechnology, and medical device areas.

Sector: Metals and Mining

Metals/mining sector funds invest in securities of companies primarily focused on mining, processing, and dealing in precious metals and other related commodities. Some funds may employ arbitrage strategies on a worldwide basis.

Sector: Real Estate

Real estate sector involves investing in securities of real estate investment trusts (REITs) and other real estate companies. Some funds may also invest directly in real estate property.

Sector: Technology

Technology sector funds emphasize investment in securities of the technology arena. Some of the subsectors include multimedia, networking, personal computer (PC) producers, retailers, semiconductors, software, and telecommunications.

SHORT SELLING

Short selling involves the sale of a security not owned by the seller; it is a technique used to take advantage of an anticipated price decline. To effect a short sale, the seller borrows securities from a third party in order to make delivery to the purchaser. The seller later returns the borrowed securities to the lender by purchasing the securities in the open market. If the seller buys the stock again at a lower price, then a profit results; if the price rises, then a loss results. A short seller must generally pledge other securities or cash with the lender in an amount equal to the market price of the borrowed securities. This deposit may be increased or decreased in response to changes in the market price of the borrowed securities.

FUND OF FUNDS

Funds of funds (FOFs) invest with multiple managers through funds or managed accounts. They do not invest in market instruments but instead take positions in selected funds based mainly on funds' historical performances and returns. They can use a diverse selection of funds or they can simply invest into one specific fund with a minority equity stake.

The strategy uses a diversified portfolio of managers with the objective of significantly lowering the risk (volatility) of investing with an individual manager. The fund of funds manager has discretion in choosing which strategies to invest in for the portfolio. A manager may allocate funds to numerous managers within a single strategy, or with numerous managers in multiple strategies. The minimum investment in a fund of funds may be lower than an investment in an individual hedge fund or managed account. The investor has the advantage of diversification among managers and styles using significantly less capital than investing with separate managers.

FOF: Conservative

FOFs classified as conservative exhibit one or both of the following characteristics: seeks consistent returns by primarily investing in funds that generally engage in more conservative strategies such as equity market neutral, fixed income arbitrage, and convertible arbitrage; exhibits a lower historical annual standard deviation than the Fund of Funds Composite index. A fund in the FOF Conservative index shows generally consistent performance regardless of market conditions.

FOF: Diversified

FOFs classified as diversified exhibit one or both of the following characteristics: invests in a variety of strategies among multiple managers; has historical annual return and/or a standard deviation generally similar to the Fund of Funds Composite index; demonstrates generally close performance and returns distribution correlation to the Fund of Funds composite index. A fund in the FOF Diversified index tends to show minimal loss in down markets while achieving superior returns in up markets.

FOF: Market Defensive

FOFs classified as market defensive exhibit one or both of the following characteristics: invests in funds that generally engage in short-biased strategies such as short selling and managed futures; shows a negative correlation to the general market benchmarks (S&P). A fund in the FOF Market Defensive index exhibits higher returns during down markets than during up markets.

FOF: Strategic

FOFs classified as strategic exhibit one or both of the following characteristics: seeks superior returns by primarily investing in funds that generally engage in more opportunistic strategies such as emerging markets, sector specific, and equity hedge; exhibits a greater dispersion of returns and higher volatility compared to the Fund of Funds Composite index. A fund in the FOF Strategic index tends to outperform the Fund of Funds Composite index in up markets and underperform the index in down markets.

COMMODITY TRADING ADVISORS

The strategy used by Commodity Trading Advisors (CTAs) is known as managed futures. This strategy essentially invests in futures contracts on financial, commodity, and currency markets around the world. Trading decisions are performed with proprietary quantitative models and technical analysis. These portfolios have embedded leverage through the derivative contracts employed. About 4 percent of managers use this type of strategy.

ROLE OF HEDGE FUND RISK MANAGER

A hedge fund manager receives assets from investors and applies trading strategies consistently with its designed trading mandate and in relation to the market. A hedge fund manager identifies inefficiencies in the market and trades on those inefficiencies in order to generate returns. The hedge fund manager searches for gaps between products and systems and leverages those gaps with arbitrage opportunities.

Other strategies represent 4 percent and multistrategies account for 8 percent of the total trading strategies. Long/short equity represents growth/value/industry geographical gap, market neutral, and short sellers. Opportunistic strategies are defined as macro and Commodity Trading Advisors.

Barra Strategic Consulting Group has performed a fund of hedge funds market survey of both investors vested in hedge funds and those who are not. Investors found hedge funds have some negative connotations, and the main concerns are lack of transparency, about 34 percent; conservative investment strategy, 22 percent; lack of understanding, 17 percent; high fees, 8 percent; liquidity, 8 percent; capacity, 5 percent; undefined marketplace, 5 percent, and volatility, 5 percent.

Due to their lightly regulated structures and markets, hedge funds have experienced some progress in improving their limitations. For example, hedge funds experience volatile returns. Hedge funds use volatility in the stock markets to produce returns, but their returns are less volatile than those of a stock market on a monthly basis. Managers use the stock market to preserve and grow capital by lowering volatility.

Hedge funds have made progress in becoming more transparent and in publishing information about risks and returns. Prior to a few years ago, hedge funds did not provide any information about the risk of their portfolios. Nowadays, investors have access to net asset values and capacity levels, although they rarely have access to pricing, mark-to-market information, models, and positions. A typical summary of market risks is given to explain profits and losses but the breakdown of them is rarely provided.

TABLE 2.1 Hedge Fund Data by Category, 1990–1997

Category	Number	Assets ($ billion)	Mean	Standard Deviation
Event Driven	120	8.6	18.9%	5.9%
Global	334	30.9	17.7%	9.4%
Global Macro	61	29.8	28.1%	16.3%
Market Neutral	201	18.0	8.6%	2.1%
Sectors	40	1.8	29.6%	15.9%
Short Sellers	12	0.5	7.0%	15.2%
Long Only	17	0.4	27.3%	15.4%

Source: Eichengreen et al. (1998).

TABLE 2.2 Asset Allocations by Strategies, 1990–1997

Strategies	Total Asset Allocations
Arbitrage	1.1%
Discretionary	26.1%
Fundamental	0.5%
Mechanical	0.2%
Pattern Recognition	0.2%
Quantitative	4.9%
Statistical	0.9%
Stochastic	0.1%
Systematic	6.7%
Technical	1.1%
Trend Following	58.1%

Source: Commodities Trading Strategies with data from Billingsley and Chance (1996).

Hedge funds are significantly leveraged. Less than 30 percent of hedge fund managers employ a leverage effect greater than 2:1, according to Van Hedge Fund Advisors International. The average leverage in hedge funds is 3:1. Leverage is one of the greatest risks in hedge funds. The failure of Long-Term Capital Management was due to greed or a 28.1 leverage ratio. The other responsible party was the large investment banks allowing hedge fund managers unlimited default coverage and unlimited leverage. Eichengreen et al. (1998) reported the data for each category in Table 2.1 from 1990 to 1997.

Commodities Trading Strategies reported the allocations of assets within the strategies in Table 2.2 from 1990 to 1997. The data comes from studies performed by Billingsley and Chance (1996).

CHAPTER 3

Performances by Strategies

Fund managers select funds mainly based on returns and performance. And in actuality, selection is based to a large extent on prior historical performances, risk-adjusted returns, and intuitive instincts, rather than on due diligence, management integrity, operational audits, and other variables that would change the landscape of the decision-making process. From a sample of 400 hedge funds, the average return for the universe in question was 13.58 percent for a given period of about four years from 1998 to 2002. Returns and performances were scattered between –2 percent and 32 percent. About 18 of the 400 funds or 4.5 percent encountered a loss, whereas 21 funds generated an annualized return in excess of 26 percent, equivalent to a total return for four years of more than 150 percent. Over 50 percent of the observed funds posted returns of between 8 percent and 20 percent while 75 percent of the universe generated returns of between 4 percent and 26 percent.

Returns among three main strategies have been studied, and it would appear that returns for long/short strategies are more scattered than for macro and arbitrage, with a range between 9 percent and 22 percent. Arbitrage has the most concentrated returns, ranging from 7 percent to 14 percent, and macro's concentrated returns are between 6 percent and 17 percent. Arbitrage/relative value strategies experience more concentrated lower annualized volatility and returns, between 0 percent and 10 percent for volatility and returns between 0 percent and 20 percent. Commodity Trading Advisors' volatility ranges between 10 percent and 30 percent while the respective returns are between 0 percent and 35 percent. Long/short strategies have been highly correlated to traditional equity indexes. For example, the correlation coefficient has been 0.7 between the long/short growth substyle and the Barra Mid Cap Growth 400 index. This overall trend has been achieved up to a certain point.

Returns in the traditional indexes have fallen in the past few years, and returns are no longer synchronized between strategies. Innovation and creativity have been displayed in the market in the sense that the external changing environments have also forced hedge fund managers to change strategies and gear asset allocations toward the most profitable classes. In eight years after 1994, long/short strategies grew consistently from 20 percent to 50 percent of the total hedge fund universe. This was very noticeable as of November 2002 when Morgan Stanley Capital International (MSCI) experienced a downturn of –16.95 percent year to date. Largest losses have been exhibited in long/short U.S. biotechnology, U.S. technology, and U.S. growth. It is also very obvious that as of September 1998, returns of different arbitrage styles were no longer synchronized and correlated.

Another example of such a trend is the comparison of the Wilshire 5000 equity index with the Hedge Fund Research (HFR) fund-weighted composite index. From 2000 to 2003, the Wilshire index lost on average 10.5 percent yearly while the HFR fund-weighted composite index gained on average 4.7 percent yearly. This is also partially due to the shifts in assets from traditional instruments and markets to more specific and sophisticated alternative investments. This flow in 2003 from traditional investments to hedge funds

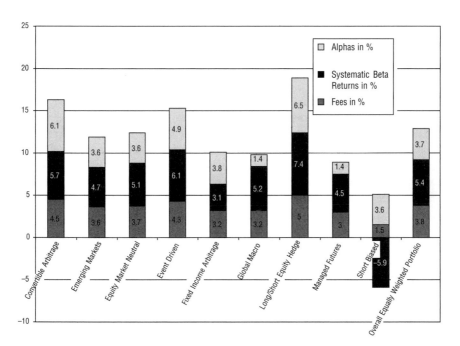

FIGURE 3.1   Sources of Hedge Fund Returns by Strategies, 1995–2004
Source: Data from *Bloomberg Markets*, January 2006.

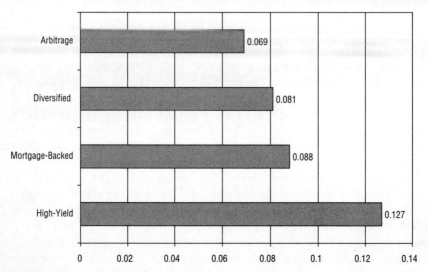

FIGURE 3.2 Average Three-Year Return for Different Strategies as of September 30, 2005
Source: Data from *Bloomberg Markets*, January 2006.

was approximately $13.82 billion according to TASS Research. This shows that the external changes in environments have been best exploited by funds of funds, and especially those performing arbitrage strategies. However, although the returns are no longer correlated with those of traditional markets, the ranges have also been narrowed in absolute terms. For example, the change in the fund of funds environment reduced the margin of rolling returns volatility for merger arbitrage managers from –10 percent to 17 percent in 1997 and from –7.5 percent to 7.5 percent in 2002. And for convertible arbitrage managers, the change in the fund of funds environment reduced the margin of rolling returns volatility from –15 percent to 13 percent in 1997 and from –7.5 percent to 8 percent in 2002.

Selection of funds is thought to be biased due to the data reliability issues and operational limitations of hedge funds. Operational losses have not been captured in hedge funds, and they have not been requested to be scrutinized by Basel Accords II and other regulatory operational mandates. Hedge fund risk managers should implement extreme value theory to model losses. Sophisticated risk management tools and methodologies are expensive and have not yet been the priority of hedge fund managers.

See Figures 3.1 and 3.2 for a breakdown in returns across different strategies.

CHAPTER 4

Geographical Areas of Hedge Fund Development

Geographically, the United States accounts for more than half of hedge fund assets worldwide with about 58 percent of the total global holdings and looks to be the most mature market. European hedge funds hold a concentration of 24 percent of the assets under management and would appear to be a new market of opportunities. Asia with currently 5 percent of the total hedge fund assets under management is expected to be the region where asset inflows will be highest. Eurekahedge, a Singapore-based research firm, showed that 60 new hedge funds have been established in Asia since the beginning of 2005, up from 15 in 2004. The most concentrated growth appears to be in Hong Kong.

In Europe, assets under management in hedge funds have increased from 14 percent in 2001 to 32 percent in 2005. In North America, the use of hedge funds has increased from 17 percent in 2001 to 21 percent in 2003 to 23 percent in 2005. In Australia, use of hedge funds rose from 2 percent in 2001 to 18 percent in 2003 to 31 percent in 2005. In Japan, hedge funds grew from 30 percent in 2001 to 41 percent in 2003 to 59 percent in 2005.

In times of market dislocations and speculative environments, hedge funds and funds of funds have flourished to take advantage of large market inefficiencies. A majority of them are established offshore in low-tax jurisdictions or low regulatory environments, such as Andorra, Angola, Aruba, Bahamas, Barbados, Belize, Bermuda, Botswana, British Virgin Islands, Cayman Islands, Cook Islands, Costa Rica, Cyprus, Dubai, Gibraltar, Guernsey, Hong Kong, Ireland, Isle of Man, Jersey, Labuan, Liechtenstein, Luxembourg, Madeira, Malta, Mauritius, Monaco, Netherlands Antilles, Nevis, Panama, Seychelles, St. Vincent and the Grenadines, Switzerland, Turks and Caicos Islands, and Vanuatu. These offshore environments have permitted high-net-worth individuals and institutional investors to create new products and financially beneficial lower tax structures or exemptions.

Ahead of their times, these safe havens where financial schemes originated have allowed specific classes of individuals to escape ordinary labor laws and regulatory, compliance, and tax environments.

A parallel example of such a development has been experienced within the insurance captive arena. Insurance captives have developed in Bermuda, where they are restricted by local regulations but there is very little transparency on what types of risks captive insurance is to cover. But the most important risks are credit risks, technological and system risks, and product-specific risks. These types of risks are described and segregated within the Basel framework. The consequence of conducting administrative accounting and offshoring in these areas is the lack of operational infrastructures and costly technological implementations.

CHAPTER 5

Integration of Hedge Funds in the Financial Markets

A ccording to Hedge Fund Research, new fund flows into hedge funds decreased to $9.4 billion in the third quarter of 2005 compared to $16.9 billion in the third quarter of 2004. The slowdown in new assets coincided with a jump in hedge fund returns, which reached 5.38 percent in the third quarter of 2005. Also note there is a similar slope between the increase in both number and returns of hedge funds and the number of futures contracts on commodities, especially those on petroleum (for example, crude oil). Standard & Poor's returned 3.61 percent for the same period and MSCI returned 6.58 percent. The HFRI Composite index measured an average overall hedge fund performance of 7.36 percent.

Attempting to beat the returns of traditional indexes, more and more institutions have invested in hedge funds, which makes their integration in the market more important. For example, according to *Bloomberg Markets* of January 2006, Bridgewater counts among its hedge fund investors the $196 billion California Public Employees' Retirement System (CalPERS), the $27 billion Pennsylvania State Employees' Retirement System, Melbourne-based National Australia Bank Limited, and the pension fund of Hartford, Connecticut–based United Technologies Corporation. It is easy to understand why lucrative hedge funds have proliferated and been successful and free of corporate governance rules. Greenwich Associates reported that in 2001, U.S. pension funds had 0.2 percent of their assets invested in hedge funds and that in 2004, pension funds rose to 0.7 percent or $37 billion of the total pension funds amounting to $5.5 trillion in assets. It is estimated that as much as $400 billion, mostly from institutions, is likely to pour into hedge funds by 2009. For example, Pennsylvania owes pensions to more than 200,000 state employees and has invested into hedge funds 22 percent of $27 billion. With increased transparency, it is easier to learn about hedge fund client profiles and to notice that many clients are government employees' retirement and pension funds or educational funds.

The hedge fund asset manager defines the trading mandate or model to follow to perform trading activities. From this initial trading system, the manager decides on the risk levels for the particular fund or strategy. This level of risk can be broadly explained or can be very specific to a product, a strategy, or a geographical market. It is linked to the capacity or size of the fund. Capital quality can be evaluated using different capital adequacy models or rating systems. This book is intended to provide hedge fund managers with new benchmarks to rate capital of funds.

The overall level of defined risk is assigned among different portfolio managers, investment strategies, or asset classes. Risk managers define a list of market-specific risks to be monitored consistently over time to report outliers, anomalies, and internal trading discrepancies with the market. This is part of the risk management function. The resulting risk information is then communicated to senior management and portfolio managers, as appropriate. Fund managers verify that funds' risk levels are acceptable within risk and capacity limits defined at the initiation of the trading mandates.

The fund manager defines investment objectives, and the trading mandate within given parameters agreed in consensus with the management board and the senior staff involved in the management of the hedge fund. They decide on the trading policies in terms of various risks, products, and markets. With those trading objectives, they define risk limits. With these goals, the team implements the proper procedures in terms of middle office operations, systems and technologies, financial statement production, compliance, and relationships with external parties such as brokers, administrative agents, auditors, and investors.

Risk management of hedge funds, very much like most recent market evolution, has quickly moved from a reactive market risk monitoring position to a proactive market and credit position to an overall responsibility of coordinating market, credit, operations, and compliance risk management. Risk managers are the main point of contact between compliance officers and market regulators in order to communicate internal risks involved in the funds and external environmental risk involving the funds. If a sizable abnormality or outlier is occurring in the funds, risk managers are liable to communicate the discrepancies to regulators so that those regulators can take appropriate actions to inform main market players. An example of this situation was the Long-Term Capital Management near collapse, where a number of competing financial institutions got together to absorb LTCM losses.

Alan Greenspan noted in October 1998 while testifying before the Committee on Banking and Financial Services:

> *. . . hedge funds do [many things] then to refine the pricing system in the United States and elsewhere, and it is that really exceptionally and increasingly sophisticated pricing system which is one of the reasons why the use of capital in this country is so efficient. . . . there is an economic value here which we not merely dismiss. . . . I do think it is important to remember that hedge funds by what they do make a contribution to this country."*

Hedge funds have changed the landscape of the market, and needless to say they will eventually be regulated as well to prevent market anarchy and to limit market abuses with regard to trading revenues available to different classes of investors. So despite the fact that hedge funds have created a great deal of market dislocation and massive bid and ask spreads for specific traded products such as commodities, the originality of hedge fund strategies has enhanced liquidity.

Hedge funds have contributed to the innovations of new financial products and to the diversification in the market. With financial engineering and product structuring, hedge funds have also promoted progress in the invention of new financial vehicles that fit individuals' needs in a timely fashion. They also act as risk absorbers in fast-paced financial technological advancements and have contributed to the creation of new markets such as derivatives of transportation of commodities or weather derivatives.

Hedge funds have forced the trading of global foreign exchange markets to be considered as a tight basket of currencies, "keeping the whole boat afloat" until geopolitical and geographical labor laws balance slowly into a common currency of exchange. This would happen simultaneously until old democracies are in line with new emerging markets through the process of globalization. Large financial institutions, government pension funds, state universities, and insurance companies have invested in hedge funds in order to make up for losses in the more traditional financial instruments.

According to the flow of funds accounts, mutual funds in 2004 held $3,697 billion of the approximately $17,204 billion (21 percent) of corporate equities. Private pension funds held another 10 percent of corporate equities. Average assets in mutual funds are now over $200 million. In a December 2003 survey of 137 U.S. defined-benefit pension plan sponsors conducted by State Street Global Advisors and Investor Force, 67 percent of the respondents indicated their intention to increase their allocations to hedge funds, and 15 percent expected their increases to be "substantial."

Most recently hedge funds have also become an integral part of other financial institutions such as pension funds, insurance companies, mutual funds, and high-net-worth private banks. From a study conducted by consulting firm Watson Wyatt Worldwide, in 12 months Schroeder's asset management division gained $440 million in hedge fund and fund of funds assets, which represents a 135 percent rise for the division. JP Morgan Asset Management saw its hedge fund assets rise by 50 percent. Morgan Stanley's fund of hedge funds assets rose 24 percent. Gottex Fund Management, the Swiss fund of hedge funds player, posted a 253 percent increase in assets under management with total assets rising to $4.07 billion. Yet national deficits have pushed politicians to request that regulators put more pressure on hedge fund managers to justify exponentially rising fees correlated with rising returns. Since 2002, hedge funds have been forced to exhibit stronger risk management infrastructures and policies. PCG Capital Partners and PCG Asset Management recorded a 1,275 percent growth in private equity fund of funds assets.

Funds of funds are a scheme allowing managers to select a diversity of fund strategies and to combine them to create new products. They are increasingly popular because their risks are hidden behind the hedge funds in which they are invested. Thus, the extra layer of funds of funds allows them to benefit from an additional lack of transparency. They counterbalance risks via a diversified approach among different funds in order not to be fully liable in any one of them.

Institutional business has $16 billion of assets invested in funds of funds. Of all the alternative assets managed for pension funds globally, 13 percent of them are allocated in funds of hedge funds. Funds of funds made up about half of new assets inflows during the year 2004 or about $81 billion, which represents about 24 percent growth in fund of hedge funds assets per year. Some 82 percent of high-net-worth assets are invested in funds of funds. Casey Quirke & Acito, a U.S. Advisory firm, predicted that U.S. institutional capital in hedge funds will increase to $300 billion over the next five years.

According to Watson Wyatt, Man Group, the world's largest hedge fund player, which has $35.5 billion in fund of hedge funds assets, has already halved its performance fees.

Hedge funds started as very small trading shops with practically no technological infrastructures and back office operations. They developed at a fast pace in the late 1990s as the dot-com firms appeared. Highly skilled traders from Wall Street left the large banks to start their own entrepreneurial shops in the form of hedge funds, and they started to innovate in trading strategies and new financial products. Hedge funds have grown exponentially since then while many dot-coms and incubators have failed. Their growth is largely due to the lack of risk management supervision and regulatory requirements. Only since 2002, when the Securities and Exchange Commission started a compliance crusade against them, have hedge funds leveraged their returns and started to invest in risk management, back office operations, and more robust technological systems. This compliance crusade was aggressively effective in the United States within a few years, but there are still many compliance and regulatory implementations to be performed outside of the United States to reestablish efficiencies in the overall market.

As of the end of 2004, hedge funds represented 13 percent of total alternative assets under management in the pension fund industry, 17 percent in the insurance companies, 44 percent in other financial institutions, 20 percent in mutual funds, and 56 percent in the high-net-worth private banking industry. (See Figures 5.1 through 5.5.) Hedge funds represented 25 percent of total investments in alternative assets in the pension fund industry, 33 percent in the insurance companies, 76 percent in other financial institutions, 35 percent in mutual funds, and 82 percent in the high-net-worth private banking industry. (See Figures 5.6 through 5.10.)

The integration of hedge funds in the new market era is even more pronounced as they account for 34 percent of the total assets of alternative managers in the entire assets universe. Hedge fund inflows are approximately 49 percent of the total net inflows in the alternative assets industry.

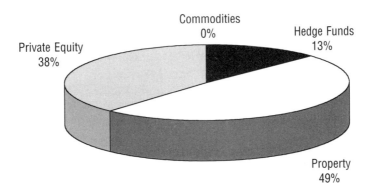

FIGURE 5.1 Alternative Assets in Pension Funds as of December 2004
Source: Data from Watson Wyatt Worldwide consulting analysis, published in *Global Alternatives*, June 2005 (www.globalinvestormagazine.com).

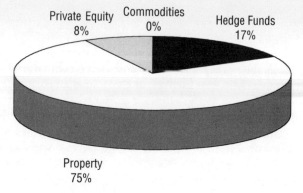

FIGURE 5.2 Alternative Assets in Insurance Industry as of December 2004
Source: Data from Watson Wyatt Worldwide consulting analysis, published in *Global Alternatives*, 2005 (www.globalinvestormagazine.com).

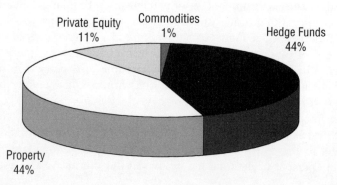

FIGURE 5.3 Alternative Assets in Other Institutions as of December 2004
Source: Data from Watson Wyatt Worldwide consulting analysis, published in *Global Alternatives*, June 2005 (www.globalinvestormagazine.com).

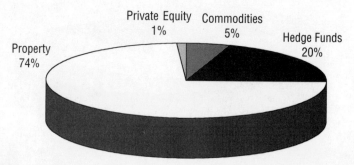

FIGURE 5.4 Alternative Assets in Mutual Fund Industry as of December 2004
Source: Data from Watson Wyatt Worldwide consulting analysis, published in *Global Alternatives*, June 2005 (www.globalinvestormagazine.com).

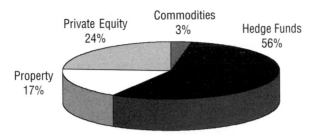

FIGURE 5.5 Alternative Assets in High-Net-Worth Clients as of December 2004
Source: Data from Watson Wyatt Worldwide consulting analysis, published in *Global Alternatives*, June 2005 (www.globalinvestormagazine.com).

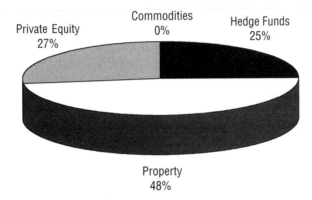

FIGURE 5.6 Total Investment in Alternative Assets for Pension Funds as of December 2004
Source: Data from Watson Wyatt Worldwide consulting analysis, published in *Global Alternatives*, June 2005 (www.globalinvestormagazine.com).

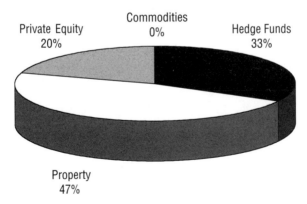

FIGURE 5.7 Total Investment in Alternative Assets for Insurance Industry as of December 2004
Source: Data from Watson Wyatt Worldwide consulting analysis, published in *Global Alternatives*, June 2005 (www.globalinvestormagazine.com).

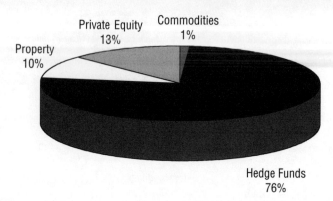

FIGURE 5.8   Total Investment in Alternative Assets for Other Institutions as of December 2004
Source: Data from Watson Wyatt Worldwide consulting analysis, published in *Global Alternatives*, June 2005 (www.globalinvestormagazine.com).

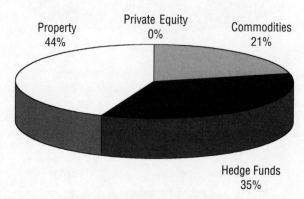

FIGURE 5.9   Total Investment in Alternative Assets for Mutual Fund Industry as of December 2004
Source: Data from Watson Wyatt Worldwide consulting analysis, published in *Global Alternatives*, June 2005 (www.globalinvestormagazine.com).

(See Figure 5.11.) This integration of hedge funds forces large companies to invest in technological and operational risk management infrastructures to monitor trading activities, so hedge funds have to improve their transparency of operations as well.

Note that what has happened over the course of hedge funds history is the gradual rise of hedge funds' capacity and trading styles. Since 1990, fi-

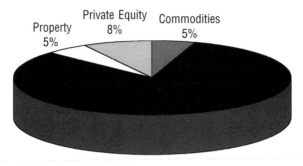

FIGURE 5.10 Total Investment in Alternative Assets for High-Net-Worth Clients as of December 2004
Source: Data from Watson Wyatt Worldwide consulting analysis, published in *Global Alternatives*, June 2005 (www.globalinvestormagazine.com).

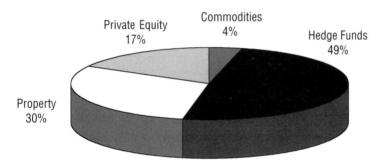

FIGURE 5.11 Net Inflows of Alternative Managers as of December 2004
Source: Data from Watson Wyatt Worldwide consulting analysis, published in *Global Alternatives*, June 2005 (www.globalinvestormagazine.com).

nancial markets have experienced a structural change during which large banks increased their technological infrastructures, but at the same time intellectual and actual capital flew out of large institutions to create hedge funds where infrastructures were practically nonexistent. However, with the hedge fund market's exponential growth comes the need for more oversight and more integration within the banking systems. Large banks have also started their own hedge fund operations to remain competitive and to restabilize the markets. Consequently, they have forced smaller hedge funds to become more robust in terms of infrastructures and operations in order for the overall market to stay afloat and competitive.

Hedge funds have also integrated global markets geographically. In Europe, the percentage of hedge funds has increased from 2001 at 14 percent to 2005 at 32 percent. In North America, the use of hedge funds has increased from 17 percent in 2001 to 21 percent in 2003 to 23 percent in 2005. In Australia, use of hedge funds rose from 2 percent in 2001 to 18 percent in 2003 to 31 percent in 2005. In Japan, hedge funds grew from 30 percent in 2001 to 41 percent in 2003 to 59 percent in 2005. Japan experienced the most phenomenal growth of hedge funds due to its deflationary economic situation from the beginning of the 1990s to 2005. Some economists argue that Japan has undergone a deflationary period of 17 years, the longest in history. During the deflationary times, Japanese banks have bought and sold debt from and to each other and cleaned up their operational infrastructures. While the Japanese economy eroded from zero interest rates to even sometimes negative interest rates, the American economy benefited from speculative credit bubbles through the rise and fall of interest rates, producing increasing amounts of credit debt in three areas: at the individual level, at the corporate level, and at the governmental level. The lack of returns in Japan from various asset classes caused erosion of assets and holdings, and this lack of revenues has forced Japan to find new sources of inflows to finance pension funds and other financial institutions. Japanese investors did not enter the hedge fund industry due to their risk aversion and conservatism but changed in the late 1990s to try to recover from prior losses—so much so that there was more interest in investing in hedge funds in Japan than in Europe and in the United States. According to Eurekahedge, Japan accounts for about 30 percent of the $70 billion in Asian funds. Man Group Financial, the largest fund in the world, is now implementing operations in Japan. Its main incentive is research for better returns. More specifically, it is estimated that more than $24 billion is now invested in Japanese funds.

Disadvantages of hedge fund implementations have been taxes and regulations. And with growing regulations and compliance for hedge funds in the United States as of February 2006, it remains to be seen whether their growth in Japan will level off, too. According to Greenwich Associates, 55 percent of Japanese institutional investors invested in hedge funds by the end of 2004 compared with 10 percent in the United Kingdom and 28 percent in the United States.

Pension funding gaps provide an example of the shift in the hedge fund industry. According to *Bloomberg Markets* as of January 2006, in 2000 221 U.S. corporate pension plans were underfunded by a total of $19.9 billion. In 2004, there were 1,108 underfunded corporate plans, supposedly covering 15 million people. The U.S. Pension Benefit Guaranty Corporation (PBGC), which guarantees the pension benefits of 44 million U.S. workers and retirees in 31,000 private plans, reported $786.8 billion in assets to meet more than $1.14 trillion in liabilities, a negative balance of $354 billion. According to the National Association of State Retirement Administrators and the National Council on Teacher Retirement, state and local pensions are underfunded by $293 billion. Richard Teitelbaum (2006) mentioned a more pertinent reality: "These gaps are particularly daunting because the 76 million U.S. baby boomers born between 1946 and 1964 are now nearing retirement age." Hedge funds are not harmful if they are better integrated into the markets with other components and if they have adequate risk management teams and tools. Yet because they did not have risk management for so long, they have provided opportunities for pension funding programs to bridge those challenging gaps.

CHAPTER 6

Hedge Fund Players

Hedge fund players are defined as the employees of the hedge funds, regulators, broker-dealers, internal and external auditors, investors, related directors and board members, compliance officers working for international regulatory agencies, rating agencies, and interested parties in communications, news, and media. Hedge funds evolved with the creation of a few jobs to perform a whole lot of tasks as the hedge funds grew in size, capacity, and risks. The job descriptions became heavier to bear and more difficult to perform. Part of the problem was the secrecy revolving around hedge funds. The secrecy of clients' names and amounts invested made it especially difficult for compliance officers, risk managers, and auditors.

The roles of the individuals within a hedge fund are well described as part of its policies and procedures. But what should be added in the description of each individual's role is the amount of or limitations to access to knowledge. Roles and job descriptions are solely at the hedge fund manager's discretion and obviously are geared to his or her level of integrity and ethics.

The roles vary depending on the size of the hedge fund. Smaller hedge funds tend to have fewer people working as a team and performing all activities together, such as a trader, an assistant, and an accountant. These types of infrastructures are subject to high levels of conflict of interest especially when price verification is to be performed independently.

Once the trader marks the book at closing of the day, a risk manager or a price verification analyst is to look at the trader's position and prices and compare the quote with the bid and ask spread of the market on the particular traded product. If there is a lack of liquidity in the market or a wide spread between the bid and the ask, the price becomes highly debatable because profits can be very substantial on a large position. For derivatives' institutional books, volumes are checked at every closing of the books, and price verification and/or risk management performs a daily mark-to-market check on traders' prices. For the past few years, this procedure has been occurring on a daily basis, but prior to 2000, marking to market on derivatives was performed manually and only at month-end.

The rise of technology and of trading complexity has also given increased opportunities in frequency and accuracy of volume pricing methodologies. The price verification analyst documents special positions of substance with various pricing sources and information. This process is a mark-to-market approach, and with technological downloads, it is feasible to perform this task daily on an entire portfolio. In the early years of hedge funds, there were very few firms able to access hedge fund portfolios to monitor traders' prices.

Another problem that arose in the hedge fund industry is the overlap of responsibilities of the same officers but for different funds. This issue came about due to the rising popularity of hedge funds. When a hedge fund reaches its capacity limits, the same hedge fund manager starts another fund under a different name. It also has been perceived that some of the hedges and trading activities have been crossing different legal entities because a few managers were sharing job duties among different funds and strategies. Conflict of interest was very high until most recently.

Very often and for too long salaries have been defined randomly and subjectively. A great way to remedy this is to implement a somewhat objective and fair mathematical formula to define the level of salary and benefits for each employee.

Because managers back default risks for hedge fund positions, they have become more sensitive to cleaner operational risk management procedures within hedge funds, and integration into the larger scope of the financial system has forced them to clarify job descriptions and segregate employees into well-defined departments. Integrity and conflict of interest have become the subjects of high-profile cases investigated by regulators since 2002. Hedge fund employees' job descriptions also help in defining the roles and the quality of work and relationships with third parties. If a hedge fund manager does not hire the appropriate qualitative employees to perform the accounting, risk management, and compliance function, it is difficult for regulators and external auditors to fulfill their duties as well.

Hedge fund employees are duly responsible for communicating the appropriate risks to regulators, investors, international compliance officers, rating agencies, internal and external auditors, and finally market news and media personnel. The hedge fund manager works in the interests of the hedge fund and its employees as well as those of the investors. Risks pertaining to trading and strategic activities as well as performance are to be communicated to third parties. Investment decisions and risk levels are considered by both investors and hedge fund managers and risk managers.

It is the hedge fund manager's duty to enhance communication responsibility internally and externally. The content of communication is well defined within hedge fund policies. It is part of the liability agreement between investors and hedge fund management about potential losses. Due diligence is also performed by the broker to ensure that a hedge fund's exposures with brokers' accounts are within reasonable responsibility limits.

As of 2002, hedge fund managers work to provide more transparency to third parties. Since the appearance of many compliance cases, transparency has become an issue and many investors have to accept liability before investing in hedge funds, in exchange for more transparency and explanations of risk exposures in the funds. The responsibilities are carried to other third parties such as regulators and external auditors. In some cases, a hedge fund manager hires an outside lawyer in addition to the internal compliance department.

The hedge fund manager has a responsibility to act in the interests of the hedge fund and of investors. The hedge fund manager is to communicate risk exposure positions and investment strategies to investors. Investors are to understand risks as clearly as possible. The level of risk information communicated to investors is to be described in the agreement between the investors and the hedge fund manager. Until the late 1990s, very few investors had access to risk exposures. Sizable investors are being communicated with about risks within the hedge fund.

The hedge fund's investment objectives and strategies enhance the ability of investors to form appropriate expectations as to the hedge fund's performance and therefore facilitate a good match between investor and investment product. The hedge fund manager therefore seeks to ensure that appropriate disclosures are prepared for dissemination to investors on a timely basis (without compromising proprietary information regarding the hedge fund's positions). Material changes are to be disclosed promptly as appropriate.

The hedge fund manager and the risk manager prepare risk and performance reports to provide to investors. Investment reports are also dispatched to the media and other marketing firms. Investment disclosures include daily profit and loss reports, as well as monthly and quarterly reports explaining overall risk exposure changes. These reports sometimes also provide pricing information. Net asset value changes and financial statements analysis can also be included. Any extraordinary purchases are inserted in the disclosures. Capital measures, changes in capacity, and capital limits are reported. Reporting of liquidity changes due to redemptions and subscriptions are also included in the reports. Connections and relationships are also to be indicated to notify investors and other third parties of any conflicts of interest. Internal auditors are to be responsible for the overall reports being made open to the public and third parties. Internal auditors are to communicate all issues to the external auditors as well as compliance and risk management departments.

CHAPTER **7**

Hedge Fund Risk Types

Pricing risk is one of the most important risks, and engenders many other risks such as liquidity, credit, leverage, technology, systems, operational, regulatory, and compliance risks.

PRICING AND NET ASSET VALUATION RISK

Product control or risk management verifies derivatives position sizes on a daily basis. The product controller also verifies that prices of all derivatives products are reasonable compared with the market or within the bid and ask margin. For nonderivatives products, market quotes are usually provided and the hedge fund trader would be within the reasonable limits of quote providers. This task can now be performed on a daily basis with automated downloads of traders' prices and brokers' quotes.

The hedge fund manager defines policies and procedures for detailed calculations of net asset value (NAV). These calculations are based on generally accepted accounting principles (GAAP), international accounting standards (IAS), and Financial Accounting Standards Board (FASB). Policies are reported fairly, consistently, and reasonably. All data can be verified in a reasonable manner and validated. Prices are verifiable so that profits and losses can be explained within appropriate levels of reasonableness. All calculations regarding net asset valuations are to be fair, consistent, and reasonable.

The International Association of Financial Engineers created a new committee to implement new guidelines for best practices valuation procedures, according to Metzger et al. (2004). Many researchers have noted that smoothing of returns was consistently practiced in hedge funds in order to gain from consistent returns to create accumulated financial reserves for periods that are not so lucratively rewarding. Return smoothing patterns are correlated with lower volatility, lower market beta, higher Sharpe ratio, and positive serial correlation.

The risk manager calculates and verifies accuracy of prices independent of the trading function to the extent practicable. To that end, a manager seeks to rely on price quotes from external sources whenever it is practicable and cost-effective to do so, and to establish policies for determining the value of assets for which appropriate external price quotes are not reasonably available. The valuation of portfolio positions for NAV purposes will be used to determine the prices at which investors subscribe to or redeem from the fund. Accordingly, a hedge fund manager is to be consistent and fair to both subscribing and redeeming investors to the extent practicable and make appropriate disclosures of circumstances in which practices may necessarily deviate from this standard in a material way. Pricing policies and procedures of net asset values have to be performed in a reasonable manner and fairly. The net asset value is to be calculated based on GAAP.

Markets have experienced illiquidity for longer-term options or thinly traded products so that hedge fund managers have used different sources of prices in order to come up with their own prices. Some hedge fund managers have taken the median, while others have considered an average of the prices or performed a mathematical fitting distribution given the points to determine a more accurate price. Still others extrapolate the fitting points linearly or attempt to bootstrap in order to obtain a mark-to-market figure more adequately with the corresponding term structure.

Research has shown that the more illiquid the market, the more room there is to manipulate and smooth returns. Chandar and Bricker (2002) found that managers of closed-end mutual funds use accounting discretion to manage fund returns around a passive benchmark. Getmansky, Lo, and Makarov (2004) demonstrated that beta was higher and consistent with illiquidity and smoothed returns. The compliance issue with illiquidity is not so much due to the fact that managers take advantage of illiquidity in the market by arbitraging or trading on pricing gaps; it is more due to the fact that they do not disclose the risks linked to the illiquidity gaps.

Liquidity risk is directly correlated with credit risk. Consequently, illiquid trades performed with counterparties expose the hedge fund investors, the broker, and the counterparty to further market risks. When markets are illiquid and are assessed to be more illiquid over the longer terms, traders reformulate their collateral credit agreements with scenarios of potential credit downgrades. Researchers such as Watts and Strogatz (1998), Watts (1999), Bookstaber (1999, 2000), and Kao (2000) have provided ideas, concepts, and measures to link illiquidity to credit exposures and to disclose consequential losses in scenario analysis.

Calculation of net asset values accounts for the value of the financial instruments in the portfolio. This value is equal to the realized profit made or loss incurred between the time the financial instrument was bought and the time it was sold. The total value of the instrument is equal to the trading profit or loss plus accruals of interest, dividends, and other receivables and fees, expenses, and other payables.

Hedge funds refer to GAAP and to international accounting standards to define "fair value" in determining the value of an investment or instrument. Under FASB Financial Accounting Standard No. 107, financial assets' and liabilities' "fair value" represents the value of reasonable exchange under typical sales conditions.

Due to the number of compliance cases arising since 2002, many hedge funds have hired compliance and risk managers to define in detail in the agreement between hedge fund managers and investors what means are used to calculate "fair reasonable value" of a transaction in an illiquid market. It is difficult between two parties to agree on a fair value if the market is illiquid or irrational or presents disparate pricing opportunities. This type of detail is fundamental as traders have mishedged and hedge funds have found themselves compelled to reimburse investors. So, investors and hedge fund advisers tend to agree on how to define the quantifiable basis on which investors can recover losses.

Pricing of sophisticated trades and exotic payoff formulas are explained in detail in the documentation agreements prior to submitting them to auditors for review. Hedge fund traders close their books and mark to market the trades daily. A price verification policy is described as part of the risk management objective. Hedge fund managers have a responsibility to provide pricing policies and procedures for trading strategies and instruments.

Hedge fund risk managers have a responsibility and a duty to verify independently the reasonableness of traders' prices and have to report any abnormalities or outliers from the bid and ask prices or "efficient market range or level." If a trade's price is found to be outside the "normal and reasonable" market boundaries, the risk manager is to report justifications for such a trade. The risk manager has to document the risks involved in such trades and to report them to auditors and, if investigated, to the regulators.

Data prices and news systems are implemented to capture trade prices and company information for the traders' positions and trading strategies. Bloomberg, Telerate, Bridge, and Reuters are among the best-known data providers. Accurate procedures for the data collection process should be included as part of the pricing task.

Hedge fund managers have policies for illiquid instruments and structured products that are not liquid. Due to the size of the trading books, the price verification reviewer might have to perform special technical downloads to compare the hedge fund traders' quotes with those of the brokers.

Any large variances and discrepancies between the parties are investigated, reported to management, and documented. These large differences can be due to human error as the trader might misenter the price or the brokers' quote might have been erroneously reported. Or they can be due to technical operational problems when a system did not choose the correct instruments or product codes.

If the difference is large but there is no human or technical error, then the error comes from an illiquid market or a product's specific risks. These positions tend to be over-the-counter trades. In these cases, specialized brokers and market makers provide the hedge fund manager with quotes to capture fair market value of the product, which can be a sophisticated, complex derivatives or structured product. Such a product usually requires a higher level of attention and awareness from risk management and price verification reviewers, as these products can be subject to model risks.

Due to the complexity of their payoff formulas and traded markets, they may require financial reserves or insurance. These particularities of payoff formulas and information on bid and ask spreads are highlighted in the fund's risk management procedures and policy. Mathematical algorithms to determine an instrument's prices are typically independently validated by a quantification expert. The quantitative conditions and payoff formulas are also validated with the technology in which the hedge fund monitors the complicated trade's positions.

Although Sarbanes-Oxley is not enforced as of yet in hedge funds, it requires that specific structured and complex trades calculated and maintained in Excel spreadsheets are to be limited and well documented. The risks of such complicated trades are to be replicated into the technology system. The hedge fund manager might highlight a limitation on the number of model trades and the size of such trades, and might also define a limitation by trading strategies depending on which category the structured trade belongs to. Spreadsheet models are considered operational flaws to infrastructural rating quality of hedge funds. Specific models for hedge funds are not technologically compliant because of the ranges in price volatility.

Extreme values are not always accurately modeled in trading technological systems. Pricing model technological testing has been rarely performed as of yet in the hedge fund world. So, if a hedge fund manager can validate prices via an independent pricing databank, granular risks get captured at a minimal level. Larger hedge funds have infrastructure to monitor model risk management.

Pricing data are verified by two independent individuals in risk management or in price verification. Internal auditors check price reliability, consistency, and reasonableness over time. They review daily, weekly, monthly, and quarterly pricing reports to verify any abnormal pricing historical trends in conjunction with capacity. They also compare different downloads from various pricing sources to evaluate market liquidity and variances. The variances between vendors can define the market's reasonableness.

A trade's fair value is based on closing price of an exchange or other relevant market price publicly advertised and published via data pricing vendors, financial newspapers, and brokers. Complex trades on structured debt or highly illiquid long-term trades cannot be priced via those sources. These trades' fair market values are quoted and estimated from counterparties or competitors, and/or validated via the internal model quantification professionals. It is difficult to assess quotes from competitors and in case of potential litigation, substantial validation measures can be requested.

As part of the policy, the hedge fund manager defines in detail the level of pricing validation that needs to be performed with the names of the individuals responsible for trading, pricing, verification of trade prices, timing and frequency details of pricing, and the other objective independent parties involved in the verification of prices such as internal and external auditors. Technological validations have become an important part of pricing models' policies. Yet, broadly, smaller hedge funds do not have the technology to accurately capture risk exposures of complex and sophisticated trades.

Hedge funds' official net asset values are issued from the hedge fund administrative financial statements. The income statement reports expense, trading profit and loss, and revenues from fees. A report describes subscriptions and redemptions to determine the fund's capacity levels in conjunction with market liquidity trends. Net asset values are provided in official internal financial statements that are produced by the fund accountants or the administrative agents in the offshore locations. Only in very rare cases are these reports fully reconciled with net asset value calculations from onshore operations.

From a trading perspective, positions from the onshore business are supposed to replicate the ones of the offshore business. Net capital values can be traceable and equivalent. Any large discrepancies should be explained in a weekly and/or monthly risk management report, but rarely are. Risk management in hedge funds rarely gets involved with explanations of intraday market movements and risk calls with their offshore traders. They are more in consistent discussion with investors and internal parties to review daily net asset values and quarterly financial statements. They report on top concentration risks with a broad market view.

Risk management is operationally sound if there is accurate reconciliation of net asset values and profits and losses reports between the brokers' reports and the traders' positions and price reports. Infrastructural operations are sound if there are reconciliations between brokers' realized and unrealized profits and losses reports with administrative fund accounting operations, most particularly for commodities, foreign exchange, and specific derivatives transactions. Finally, for reconciliations to be completed, a reconciliation report to show variances and discrepancies between traders' positions and prices and those of the hedge fund's accounting department to produce net asset value calculations is recommended as well.

One of the major operational risk problems that have been encountered since 2002 is a lack of information and transparency between brokers and hedge fund managers. Some hedge fund managers act as traders and therefore do not need sophisticated levels of operational links as they have smaller operations and less bureaucracy. The hedge fund manager implements policies and procedures to evaluate risk monitoring valuation methodologies for financial risk management and for operational risk management.

Risk managers describe procedures on price discounting to approximate risk reviews. Also, risk management can use alternative means of valuation such as quoted bids or offers prices to execute trades. With the many different trading strategies they apply, hedge funds are now faced with most risks that financial institutions face except they have more freedom to explain, manage, and justify the levels of these risks.

Risk management for hedge funds in the 1990s has been primarily market focused. With technological progress and the dot-com bubble bursting, hedge funds' risk management has also become concentrated in credit risk especially with the increasing level of distressed and high-yield debt sectors. Arbitrage opportunities in the credit market have enhanced liquidity risks. With growth in capacity and infrastructure, hedge funds have added a new type of risk: operational.

Market risk primarily involves products' and companies' specific risks. Market risk is measured at a root level by the marked-to-market quotes of the traders. These market efficiency marks determine alpha, beta, delta, gamma, vega, and theta risk exposures of the trades. Market risks have matured and are well integrated within the credit risk levels of the overall financial framework.

Credit risk is the risk of being exposed to a distressed and defaulting counterparty. The credit quality of the counterparty can decrease in critical market risk conditions. Rating agencies evaluate creditworthiness of a company and they rate the company in terms of its vulnerability and resistance to market conditions. Any downgrades in ratings affect the credit levels and collateralized asset valuations of a company and its ability to repay debt to counterparties.

Liquidity risk is the ability to cover for sudden short-term losses and critical changes in the capacity of the fund. Capacity levels are directly affected by the redemptions and subscriptions and the ability to have access to short-term cash management. Recently, risk managers and members of the risk-monitoring functions have started to integrate different types of risks with each other. In the 1990s, risks in hedge funds were evaluated separately and they were quantifiably segregated and isolated. Correlation effects were difficult to quantify, and there were few models able to capture dynamic risk management features and products as an integral part of the market.

MARKET RISK MANAGEMENT

Market risk involves interest rates, commodities, equities, foreign exchange, sovereign bonds, corporate bonds, distressed debt products, high-yield products, mortgage and loan instruments, and derivatives of these asset classes. Thanks to hedge funds, we are now able to assess the relationships and correlations between each of these products. With massive transformations technologically and in risk management concepts, market participants can also witness the ineffectiveness of using Greeks such as alpha, beta, delta, and theta to measure risks and their inefficiencies at preventing market risk crises. Greeks are the consequences of mark-to-market prices. Mark-to-market prices are the initial risks defining all risks in the portfolio. Companies' news affects the markets and prices as well as external environment phenomena. Hedge fund risk managers review market risks by strategy, by individual subfunds, and by integrating all funds and strategies as aggregate total market risk.

Market risk is described by categories such as asset class, by type of instruments used, by geographic region, by industry sector, and by top concentrated positions. Risk managers implement a consistent framework for measuring the risk of loss for a portfolio as a whole or as subparts depending on the granular level of transparency for the risk strategy and/or transaction information. Market risk has been measured with methodologies such as value at risk.

In order to evaluate market risk, it is necessary to obtain granular-level information on all transaction data. For each subtrading strategy and fund, and for each product, all positions, prices, trade dates, volatility, correlation factors, and so on should be downloaded from the hedge fund traders and checked with the brokers' reports. The trade information downloads or trades blotter are then captured into the risk management database, where they are recorded by time stamps and historical dates. From this database are derived value at risk calculations, stress testing scenarios, Monte Carlo simulations, and other more sophisticated models' experimentations. Large hedge funds have such infrastructures and systems, but many smaller ones do not and must rely on brokers' reports to visualize hedge fund risks. From this high-level superficiality of risk management access, major parts of infrastructural risk management still remain hidden and provoke inherent implicit risks.

Due to the lack of regulation, risk managers have had choices in the way they wanted to communicate risks to investors qualitatively and quantitatively. Best risk management practices include confidence and trust. But if the risk managers are not themselves informed of all risks or aware of them, they cannot prevent crises. The role of the hedge fund's risk manager is to review traders' positions versus limits and traders' prices versus market boundaries to generate risk factors.

Risk factors are supposed to measure risks and returns for individual funds and for the aggregate fund with all investment strategies combined. Factors are calculated depending on the quantitative models used. They take into consideration market rates and prices, credit spreads, volatilities, correlation between products, and sometimes strategies.

Hedge fund risk managers understand that risk measurement tools such as value at risk are not completely adequate to calculate different risk strategies. Value at risk is useful to replicate standard risks without extreme value theories and conditions. If extreme conditions are added to historical simulations, value at risk tends to become inadequate and replaced by extreme value theoretical models. Value at risk uses historical prices and volatilities to monitor trends in losses and capital charges. Due to its weaknesses in capturing correlations—especially in markets such as commodities, for example—it is combined with other means of measurement such as stress testing and scenario analysis.

In more robust and perfectionist firms, a combination of methodologies can be used to compare results and assess a weighted average of them. This trend has appeared as a result of the large structural architectural changes the markets have undergone the past few years. The hedge fund risk manager uses a combination of value at risk, stress tests, and backtesting to monitor risk exposures.

A hedge fund risk manager performs stress tests to evaluate a portfolio's results under specific conditional circumstances such as what-if scenarios by applying fictional or realistic parameters to traders' positions. The risk manager applies stress testing on a portfolio by simulating market conditions on the whole portfolio or on specific positions. The risk manager changes parameters used in the market risk model to magnify their effects. The hedge fund risk manager can change parameters such as prices, rates, and volatilities and assess results ahead of trading in real time. The simulated scenarios' values differ from the data used as inputs in the base-case market risk model. Stress testing involves parallel and nonparallel shifts of the yield curves. Stress testing consists of simulating changes in underlying price movements and evaluating consequent exposures in terms of delta, gamma, and vega. Scenarios can also be volatility shifts over the term structure of an option and evaluation of the impact on the trader's total book's position. Simulated market conditions usually attempt to replicate and apply realistic crisis conditions.

Another form of methodology used for regulators to monitor profits and losses with risk limits assessed by value at risk is called back-testing. The risk manager applies back-testing to the portfolio by comparing the distribution of profits and losses with the limits set by the market risk model. Very few hedge funds use this methodology, and more institutional risk managers have applied it as part of regulatory requirements.

An alternative form of back-testing is to compare forecasted budgetary limits set by traded products, strategies, and trading portfolios with their actual moving average profits and losses. As a risk manager of global markets for a bank commodities business line, I used to question aggressive changes in budgetary limits multiple times in a year, and it cost me my job. Effectively, in a time of loose regulations, budgetary limits were consistently increasing with upward trends and so was the volatility of profits and losses. In those days, I thought naively that risk managers were paid to protect shareholders.

Back-testing involves a limit in frequency and in severity. The frequency limit is the cap put on the number of times the profit and loss can be greater in absolute value than the value at risk limit or the limit set by the market risk management model. The severity is the dimension or magnitude in absolute value by which profit and loss can exceed the market risk range limit. For institutional trading books, back-testing limits excesses can be in the order of three per year with temporary exceptions. Any over the limits circumstances are documented and reported to regulators. Such risk management mechanisms can be used to produce a case to upper management to change the risk management models, methodology, strategy, or system. Market risk reports recording profits and losses from market information and changes in hedge funds are issued every month.

Hedge funds by their size, growth, and profits appear in financial newspapers on a daily basis. Their influence on the corporate governance landscape through political networks, nepotism, special clubs, and financial stakes of large positions of corporations on their books has not only changed traditional financial markets but has also contributed to a new way of reforming the industry. According to the risk center staff of the Global Association of Risk Professionals (GARP), hedge funds' gains in November 2005 came primarily from market risks or mark-to-market volatility pricing except for short sellers and convertible arbitrage managers.

Hedge funds have continued to perform and make lucrative gains. The Greenwich-Van Global Hedge Fund Index (GVGHFI) gained 2.0 percent as of November 2005. Hedge fund index provider Greenwich-Van reported profits up by 1.2 percent. The GVGHFI's year-to-date profits are up by 7.0 percent compared to 5.3 percent for the Morgan Stanley Capital International (MSCI) World Equity Index, 4.9 percent for the S&P 500, 3.9 percent for the Russell 2000, and 2.6 percent for the NASDAQ. The convertible arbitrage fund is the only fund for which Greenwich-Van reported negative returns. Futures managers on foreign exchange products gained the most profits with a 5.4 percent rise, primarily due to their position in dollar strengthening against the European and Asian currencies. Other gains came from holding long Nikkei positions, and still another part of the gains was made from holding long positions on commodities such as metals and benefiting from rising metals prices.

The Greenwich-Van Aggressive Growth Index reported the second-best performance with a return of 2.9 percent. This equity-based index benefited from overall increases in the stock market, a positive outlook prior to holiday sales, and a strong economy. Economic data reported strong productivity increases coupled with reasonable inflation and favorable labor costs. These macroeconomical indicators are consistent with broad equity rallies. Equity derivatives have also shown stronger profits.

The Greenwich-Van Emerging Markets Index returned 2.3 percent, and it is the leading substrategy index on a year-to-date basis with a return of 12.4 percent. Emerging markets hedge fund managers have reported strong profits for the past three years due to a high-liquidity environment coupled with low interest rates in the United States. Due to tighter controls in those markets and the convergence standard requirements for capital (for example, Basel Accord), emerging markets are expected to be less volatile and report less strong and lucrative profits. The Greenwich-Van Global Short Selling Index consists of managers with a dedicated short bias, thus they suffered the biggest loss, falling by 4.6 percent due to rising equity markets on net short positions.

The Greenwich-Van Global Hedge Fund Index rose to a value of 13,269.85 in November 2005. This index had an initial value of 1,000 at January 1, 1988. Over its 17-year and 11-month history, it generated a net compound annualized return of 15.5 percent, compared to a 12.0 percent compound annualized return for the S&P 500. The Greenwich-Van Composite Investable Index gained 1.2 percent and is up 4.7 percent for the year 2005. The Investable Index achieved an annualized return of 11.2 percent versus an annualized return of 11.3 percent for the GVGHFI since the Investable Index's inception. Its correlation to the GVGHFI of 0.96 and beta of 0.95 demonstrate the Investable Index's ability to represent the broader hedge fund universe. For comparison purposes, the S&P 500 gained 3.8 percent, the MSCI World Equity Index gained 3.1 percent, the Nikkei 225 rose

9.3 percent, and the Dow Jones Europe Stoxx Index gained 0.3 percent in November. The Lehman Brothers Aggregate Bond Index gained 0.4 percent.

LIQUIDITY RISK

Funding liquidity is the ability of a hedge fund risk manager to have immediate cash resources or reserves in case of market liquidity problems. Liquidity risk is the risk of not being able to sustain short-term funding. Innovative products such as very long-term traded instruments or sophisticated products are usually issued in illiquid markets due to the originality of the trades. To achieve liquidity consistency and adequacy, a hedge fund risk manager must verify at all times that the hedge fund's asset values are always properly hedged and are not exposed to potential downgrading of credit rating or defaulting counterparties.

Hedge funds need brokers to settle trades and therefore are more exposed to brokers' internal risks of defaulting. Since large brokers are more robust and sustainable in credit risks, hedge funds are more likely to resist credit dryouts and liquidity problems. Yet hedge funds' growth in number and in profits has also enhanced the emancipation of their legal structures. There are some hedge funds that do not have brokers to settle and clear trades.

Liquidity adequacy and consistency can be best monitored with the proper level of financial reserves and financing activities of the funds. Short-term and long-term balance sheet financing can be performed with financial dynamic hedging. Risk management verifies that cash is properly managed and that all transactions are captured. Funds' liquidity depends largely on cash flows into the funds and out of the funds.

Liquidity levels are directly related to capacity of the fund—that is, the pool of cash brought by investors to be made available to various trading strategies. The levels of liquidity fluctuate with redemptions and subscriptions. Redemptions are basically withdrawals of shares, and subscriptions are deposits of shares. The mutual fund industry is characterized by this concept as well. Because hedge funds have been geared more to high-net-worth investors, the rules to move material amounts are stricter and might impose fees for early withdrawals. Liquidity risk is directly correlated to credit risk, downgrading of ratings, and lowering of collateral assets' valuations.

Hedge funds have not been as vigilant as institutional banks about their credit risk exposures because their brokers have taken on credit risks for the hedge fund managers. Yet hedge funds managers have to be the pioneers in creating new sophisticated and innovative trading strategies. The originality and rarity of the trading strategies have created lack of liquidity in specialized market areas. So, it would be more logical to assess liquidity and credit risks rather than ignore them and assume that sizable brokers can handle all the risks.

Risk managers monitor the stability of the funds' cash flows from and to the onshore and the offshore accounts. In ideal hedge funds where risks are transparent and clearly managed, reconciliations of cash flows between onshore and offshore accounts are supposed to be performed by the accounting or finance department. However, because most hedge funds' accounting departments have been implemented as offshore operations, local laws tend to require hiring minimum-wage local labor to price net asset values of derivatives and sophisticated products.

Risk managers now have to estimate cash availability at all times and assume worst-case scenarios in order to keep minimum liquidity stable. They evaluate investor redemption and subscription levels and historical fluctuations. Risk managers assess liquidity requirements with cash flows and short-term funding. In large financial institutions, hedge fund risk managers use repurchase agreements trading to sustain the short-term financing interest of the company. Hedge fund risk managers simulate scenario stress tests to evaluate the consequences of potential changes in unusual market conditions. When entering a contract with a risk counterparty, a hedge fund risk manager has to precisely describe the terms of each asset's collateralized value. In risky conditions, risk managers purchase insurance to cover different types of risks, and liquidity reserves can be added as part of a policy. Asness, Krail, and Liew (2001) found that hedge funds invest more in illiquid exchange-traded assets or difficult-to-price over-the-counter securities and thus they have greater discretion in marking the portfolio's value at the end of the month to derive the fund's net asset value. Hedge fund compensation schemes with high-water mark provisions give managers an incentive to smooth returns by marking portfolios to less than actual value in a month with much larger returns to create reserves for months having losses.

COUNTERPARTY CREDIT RISK

When hedge fund regulations were not as tight and funds did not have to be registered, most hedge funds assumed that their direct creditworthiness was taken care of and covered by the larger financial institutional broker. Risk managers used to assume that the hedge fund's counterparty default potential was the broker's direct exposure and that the hedge fund was implicitly exposed. But with financial markets' instability and hedge fund regulation growing, credit risk exposures have become a direct concern. This is also due to the fact that some hedge funds do not have brokers to settle and clear trades.

The risk manager now has a responsibility to verify daily credit risk exposures with all counterparties. Hedge funds are exposed to defaulting counterparties and the downgrading of their creditworthiness. They monitor daily collateral asset values given market and credit conditions.

Hedge funds are also now more tuned to obtain credit ratings in order to attract quality counterparties. The higher the credit rating of the counterparty, the cheaper the cost of capital. Hedge fund risk managers monitor creditworthiness of the counterparties in case they default, and the hedge funds have to buy new hedges or remain short. Hedge funds can buy credit protection against potential defaults of counterparties. Captive insurance provides insurance coverage for credit risks and/or technology risks mostly, but recently has started covering all the risks involved within the Basel framework. Hedge fund risk managers can also enter legal contractual agreements to highlight collateral arrangements with the counterparty and arrange the ability to make and respond to collateral calls. Margin calls are detailed in agreements with conditional situations and financial barriers. For each downgrade in credit rating or margin call, an agreed amount is set on agreement to pay for credit depletion and/or for degrading collateral assets' valuations.

LEVERAGE

Leverage has been one of the most significant risks that hedge funds have encountered. Leverage is the level of borrowing risk the risk manager can sustain. The average leverage level of a hedge fund is about 3 to 1. This signifies that the total portfolio equals three times the investors' capital. Long-Term Capital Management (LTCM)'s leverage was 28 to 1, meaning that LTCM had borrowed as much as 28 times what investors had initially provided to start the fund.

Leverage is directly correlated with market, credit, and liquidity risks. Risk-based leverage measures the debt ratio of a fund's portfolio. Since the late 1990s, hedge fund risk monitors have managed risks together as a whole by integrating market, credit, counterparty, and leverage risks. Managing each risk alone is not enough, and it creates an incorrect risk representation if each risk is isolated and treated independently from the other risks. Market risk implies credit risks, and credit risks imply liquidity risks. All these risks combined impact liquidity. By considering all the risks together, new models can be applied to all of them simultaneously. Models to replicate and measure risks in extreme market conditions are extreme value theory and various types of factor models based on different nuanced methodologies. Leverage is the level of borrowing that is still sustainable to resist highly stressed market conditions and extreme events. Leverage is the uncovered amount of margins sustainable enough to survive extreme market conditions. Leverage was historically at its highest in 1997 and 1998, but reached a secondary peak in 2000 when equities were at their maximum. The more risk that is taken, the more the potential returns. And so greater leverage amplifies returns, but it also increases the risk exposures to investors and those to counterparties.

Risk managers also monitor accounting-based leverage. Leverage is often hidden in hedge funds, as it is not reported on balance sheets. In hedge funds it arises from off-balance-sheet derivative positions. Analysis on leverage trends has been more challenging due to lack of data because hedge funds do not provide much information. Not until recently have hedge funds provided information on leverage levels to outsiders. In 2003 and 2004 very little information was given on portfolio allocations and breakdowns of assets. It has been difficult to fit hedge funds' asset distributions to models because hedge funds shift exposures more often than do mutual funds. The level of transparency is also higher in the mutual fund industry than in the hedge fund industry. Because balance sheets and financial statements are prepared in the offshore locations, the levels of qualitative information are not as high as if accounting was performed in highly specialized market areas.

Another type of leverage is a time-varying indicator of leverage. According to a paper from the Bank for International Settlements from March 2005, there are two types of time-varying leverage. Balance sheet leverage refers to outright borrowing. The hedge fund assumes borrowing of debt and plays the market with debt to attempt to multiply returns faster and greater than its required debt payments. Instrument leverage refers to off-balance-sheet positions as derivatives, futures, and structured products. Realized profits can be obtained quickly and at exponential rates without cash investments by simply betting on the underlying asset's price movements. Profits or losses come from first derivative delta, the second derivative gamma, Vega positions of the options, and rho (interest rates). Large positions can also be profitable with time and theta, or cost of carry of the large derivative position.

Based on Hedge Fund Research (HFR) databases' information, Bank for International Settlements studies show that the range of leverage across all strategies has narrowed from 1997 to 2004, from 6 to 12 to 2.4 to 3.5. The lowest average leverage over time was generally experienced for the market neutral arbitrage strategy. See Table 7.1.

A way to model leverage is to build a formula using correlation coefficients by trading strategies. The model uses linear and nonlinear regression to best fit the performance of a portfolio with its set of underlying risk factors. The portfolio return can be written as the weighted average of the returns on the individual assets with the weights being the share of total funds invested in each asset class:

$$R_t = w_1 F_t^1 + w_1 \times F_t^2 + \ldots + w_k F_t^k$$

TABLE 7.1 Global Hedge Funds—Use of Leverage as of December 2004

Hedge Fund Strategy	Use No Leverage	Low < 2:1	High > 2:1
Aggressive Growth	20%	60%	20%
Emerging Markets	20%	50%	30%
Equity Market Neutral	15%	50%	35%
Event Driven	15%	60%	25%
Income	35%	30%	35%
Macro	10%	30%	60%
Market Neutral Arbitrage	10%	25%	65%
Market Timing	55%	35%	10%
Multi-Strategy	10%	50%	40%
Opportunistic	10%	60%	30%
Short Selling	30%	40%	30%
Value	20%	60%	20%
Total Sample	20%	50%	30%

Source: Van Hedge Fund Advisors International, LLC research.

where w is the weight given to the asset class (or trading strategies or products), F is the return on the asset class (or return on trading strategies or products), and k is the number of known assets. The total return is the linear sum of the weighted averaged returns by categories. A fully vested fund with all capital being allocated in different strategies, products, and/or asset classes has the sum of the weights equal to 100 percent. This is the most simple and linear way to use weighted averages to evaluate a portfolio's return. When weights are not known, they can be estimated in the form of correlation coefficients and/or regression coefficients. One of the model's weaknesses comes from the fact that analysts do not know the entire population of the securities in the portfolio. Some trades are so exotic they may be kept on a separate Excel spreadsheet, and not always included in the calculations of the entire portfolio. So regression coefficients can only be interpreted as exposures of the fund to the market risk factors. The regression is estimated with a constant term capturing the value of active management and considering only asset classes' returns, strategies, or products that are greater than the risk-free rate. A portfolio characterized with long and short positions has a regression estimated using returns in excess of the risk-free rate for both the dependent and independent variables:

$$(R_t - r_t^f) = \alpha + \beta_1 (F_t^1 - r_t^f) + \ldots + \beta_k (F_t^k - r_t^f) + \varepsilon_{I,t}$$

where R is designated for each type of asset class or trading strategy, r is the risk-free minimum and less than the return on the asset class, and β is the regression factor or correlation coefficient between the asset classes' returns and those differential returns from the risk-free rate. The total return of the portfolio is the sum of the returns on the asset classes:

$$R_t = -\lambda r_t^f + (1 + \lambda) \times (w_1 \times F_t^1 + \ldots + w_k F_t^k)$$

The weights are the allocations of the overall investment in each illiquid asset. Negative coefficients account for leverage. Short positions are also considered as leveraged positions. Short positions create downside risks with unlimited coverage. And the combination of both types of leverage increases the speed of the returns or the sensitivity of fund returns to the returns on the market factors. The coefficient reflecting the gamma (λ) or speed of both leverages is equivalent to $\Sigma \beta_i = (1 + \lambda) \xi \Sigma_i w_i = (1 + \lambda) \xi$ (with inclusion of positive and negative regression coefficients).

OPERATIONAL RISK

Operational risk involves losses that are not due to market risks and not due to credit risks but rather arise from human error, internal and external failed processes, unlinked systems, new technologies, megamergers, and/or inadequate environments. Operational risk consists of collecting claims and information on losses into a centralized database. It consists of updating the status of products until they are resolved and closed. Operational risk databases serve as a summary to be given to auditors and regulators to make them aware of infrastructural and architectural database progress. As projects are being taken cared of, they are closed.

Unlinked systems and gaps between technological frameworks create losses from unreconciled transaction flows. Operational risk management consists in linking systems in order to reestablish flow transactions and reconcile balances. A fundamental example of operational losses is also due to unknown and unevaluated losses incurred when offshoring operations to other locations. During this process of establishing new technologies in different countries data is lost. Data losses are difficult to assess in quantity and in quality.

It is also extremely difficult to find appropriate models to replicate the loss distributions. Since the late 1990s, large financial institutions have collected loss data into centralized databases in order to attempt to predict future patterns and quantify past losses' distributions and trends. Insurance companies have been the best representatives of quantifying operational risk loss distributions because they record historical data of claim losses by industries over time. They have databases of operational risk losses and trends for each industry in order for these industries to become more proactive in dynamic financial risk management practices. Insurance companies' mathematical distributions of claims and losses over time can serve as the best estimators to predict and forecast future trends given past historical data.

A representative in each department of an institution is designated to report to the main operational risk manager on all the unfinished projects and issues. Operational risk establishes adequate internal controls and review procedures to reconnect systems and technological frameworks to smooth reconciliations and financial transactions. Gaps between systems, people, and geographical locations can be monitored on a regular basis—daily, weekly, monthly, or quarterly—to investigate historical trends and abnormalities. Reports with key risk indicators and formulas measure outliers and abnormal trends.

The process of successful operational risk management in Japan is a clear example. During almost 16 years of deflationary economical trends, Japanese banks had bought debt from each other and while proceeding in megamergers and restructuring, they cleaned up internal infrastructures and architectures.

Strategically some geographical markets no longer trade specific products while other geographical areas trade exclusively interest rate products. With cleaner infrastructures and more focused strategical trading plans, communication among local, national, and international regulators is clearer and more integral, and transparency is optimum. Global corporations experience megamerger restructuring while operational risk processes have been as efficient.

The overall European infrastructural financial system is experiencing fragmentation and segregation. This market is quite embryonic in terms of enacting adequate legislation and standardizing structures. One of the main issues affecting hedge funds in Europe in operational risk is processing. There is as yet very little standardization compared to the United States in terms of trade processing, trade instructions, cutoff fees, or prospectuses. The funds industry in Luxembourg is still very fragmented because most funds have had specialized rules geared toward customized clients. So the process of standardization of prospectus, classes, and subclasses within the transfer agency business (the administration and management of banking lines of the fund industry) is extremely difficult to achieve. Hedge funds are now starting to appear in France and Germany and some of the Nordic countries, and their operational and compliance integrations are more challenging than those in offshore areas.

More slowly than in other markets, technological advancements and progresses have contributed to ease the integrations of fund accounting transactions, subscriptions, and redemptions within transfer agency business. Technological operational advancements include business-to-business (B2B) platforms such as Vestima from Clearstream and Fundsettle from Euroclear. With these applications, all funds' trades go through them to clear and settle trades and other various transactions. There are new large local consolidators in Spain, Italy, and Germany and new developments from the Society for Worldwide Interbank Financial Telecommunication (SWIFT). The emergence of distribution platform standardization applies to Undertakings for the Collective Investment Transferable Securities (UCITS) and other regulated products. Hedge funds are not subject to these new regulations and systems. Specific rules apply to hedge funds depending on the countries such as Germany. Hedge funds are rarely perceived on these platforms because they are only just starting to appear in Continental Europe.

The Swiss hedge fund market is advanced but this does not necessarily mean that it is fully compliant operationally. Some hedge funds in Switzerland do not have brokers' links and do not automate trade settlements and clearance. In Luxembourg, processing hedge fund distribution is very manual, entailing many errors, and the cost of processing hedge fund transactions remains very high compared to the standardized UCITS.

Processing of hedge fund trades is more complicated because the fund administrators responsible for shareholder registrations and fund accounting are in the offshore locations where technologies are difficult to integrate and more expensive to implement. Hedge funds' operational integrations are also more complicated because their strategies are more innovative and original than those of traditional mutual funds. Funds of funds have been more popular because of their legal structure. Their popularity is mainly due to the extra layer of funding that prevents transparency and direct liability to investors. The fact that funds allocate less than 50 percent in equity shares prevents the holder from being liable for losses from the funds but allows the holder to still benefit from the high returns. The lack of fast developments of hedge funds in Continental Europe has been due to the very high minimum initial subscriptions, which keep out small retail investors. The usual minimum requirement is USD 500,000.

In line with operational and process risk, reconciliation risk is important for clean infrastructure and capital adequacy allocation.

Some operational problems come from the lack of reconciliations between different parties involved in the reporting of risk exposures by brokers, hedge fund managers, and offshore operations. Some hedge fund managers choose not to have brokers and operate solely for their own accounts. (See Table 7.2.)

When it comes to choosing a prime broker, hedge funds consistently report that their most important selection criteria are client service, trading capacities, and financing repurchase agreement (repo) capabilities. From

TABLE 7.2 Examples of Funds That Did Not Have Brokers as of Late 2004

Group or Fund Name	Assets	Strategy	Launch Date	Target Returns	Manager Information
Forsyth Partners, Forsyth Global Property Fund	$2.1m as of 01/05	Property, derivatives, and FOF	12-Apr	NA	Manager worked for UK independent financial adviser
Forsyth Partners, Forsyth Commodities Fund	$6.5m as of 01/05	Commodities, commodities-related securities, futures, and derivatives	12-Apr	NA	Same
Protected Commodities Accelerator II	NA	Commodities fund with full capital protection	1-May	10% over 10-year agreement; closed fund	NA
PFB Guaranteed FTSE Hedge Fund Index	NA	FOF with leverage exposure to FTSE Hedge Directional Index	1-May	14.3% annualized over 7 years	NA
Prima Opportunity Fund	$12m as of 01/05	FOF and event driven focused	1-May	10% to 12%	Prima Capital Fund manager active since 1993
AXA IM, AXA Futures II Portfolio	€9.73m as of 11/04	CTA systematic and diversified	11-Apr	Euribor +800 to 1,200 basis points annually	Manager experienced 7 years in CTA
RMF Investment Management and Man RMF Commodities Strategy	$457.7m	Commodities-related strategies	11-Apr	11% to 14%	Fund manager is also head of RMF research department
SEB Asset Management and SEB Global Hedge	$55m as of 12/04	Multistrategy allocation	11-Apr	LIBOR+400 to 800 basis points	NA

Fund	Assets	Strategy	Date	Target return	Notes
GRIPS Absolute	€4m	Multistrategy allocation	11-Apr	8%–10% up to €250m in capacity	NA
Alpha Horizon and Valor Gamma Fund	$4.8m	Multistrategy allocation	12-Apr	10%–15%	Partner and director of IMF
Aptus Capital and Aptus Capital Offshore Fund	$2m as of 12/04	Long/short equities with focus on small- and midcap stocks	12-Apr	15%–20%	10 years of experience
Platinum Portfolio	NA	Multistrategy fixed income fund of hedge funds	12-Apr	+10% annual and +5% volatility annual up to $500m	NA
Dexion Capital and Financial Risk Management	£83m	FOF 80% directional trading strategies and 20% relative value	11-Apr	7% to 12% per year net of fees	Most risk management oriented in the UK
Bank Leu and Leu Absolute World Strategy	CHF 50m allocated among 3 funds as of 11/04	Worldwide investments; managed on an absolute basis; classified under Swiss law as a public traditional fund without any special risk	11-Apr	LIBOR + 400 to 500 basis points; open-ended fund	11 years of experience
Hermes Pension Management—Hermes Absolute Return	£500m as of 11/04	Multistrategy for pension funds and funds of pension funds	11-Apr	LIBOR + 350 basis points up to £2 billion	NA
Pegasus Research and Pegasus World Equity Fund of Funds	NA	Funds of funds	10-Apr	20% above MSCI World index	NA
BFT Gestion and BFT Multistrategy Hebdo	€10.3m as of 10/04	A large and diversified portfolio of alternative strategies, euro-dominated instruments	9-Apr	Euribor +150 to 350 basis points and volatility 250 to 450 basis points	Located in France and Ireland

Source: Hedge Fund Review, February 2005 and www.yahoofinance.com.

2004 to 2005 the proportion of hedge fund respondents citing capital introduction as an important factor in evaluating prime brokers doubled from 7 percent to 14 percent. Effectively, prime brokers have been competing to get hedge fund business not only for the fees but also for the attraction of new capital to be used for self-financing activities. By providing prime brokerage services to hedge funds, brokerage firms have generated higher fees and created somewhat of a conflict of interest with hedge funds.

Hedge funds have outsourced infrastructural risks, back office operations, and risk management reporting procedures to brokerage firms. Yet there is very little due diligence and operational risk management that link brokerage risk management operations to those of the hedge funds. In this sense, hedge funds' reconciliation reports between brokerage operations and internal funds' calculations are seldom performed and practically nonexistent. This is where gaps do exist and operational weaknesses become very convenient to hide clean flow of capital. Moreover, calculations of fees are yet to become more objective and more transparent to justify independence between hedge funds and brokerage firms.

The minimum but very seldom applied reconciliations are such special interentity reconciliations reporting between:

1. Brokers' prices and positions reports with administrative fund accounting reports.
2. Fund accounting net asset value backtracking with traders' positions and prices.
3. Traders' pricing reports with brokers' pricing reports.

Reconciliations should also be performed between the onshore and the offshore accounts. Very often, positions on both sides are supposed to be replicated or similarly hedged. Reconciliation processes between various internal operations entities have not been adequately performed.

Most hedge funds do not reconcile operations and financial flows from the brokers' reports to the traders' positions and prices reports. There are no reconciliations from the offshore operations reports with the hedge funds' accounting departments. And finally, there are no reconciliations between the offshore operations reports and the brokers. There are technological feeds coming from one source, but to maintain clean order of operations, there should be three-way feeds to perform the three-way reconciliations. Another reason such controls are not in place is because offshore locations must hire local individuals who seldom have the qualifications to understand the derivatives strategies and/or never had experience in pricing options or other structured products.

Operational risk management if appropriately implemented should work with the hedge funds' risk managers, brokers, and offshore resources to set up links and connections with systems and check financial transactions via key risk indicators. Key risk indicators highlight any abnormalities over history. Risk managers and auditors have access to key risk indicators and monitor their trends.

The internal audit ensures that hedge fund operations run within reasonable measures. The audit reports any gaps and material abnormalities to external auditors and regulators. Risk management is in close contact with auditors in order to maintain reasonableness in the smoothing of overall operations. Audits can be of financial and operational nature and they can also be regulatory. Local, national, and international mandates, forms, and rules are to be completed by the audit, risk management, and compliance departments. They depend on the markets of interest.

COMPLIANCE, REGULATORY, LEGAL, AND GOVERNANCE RISK

The hedge fund manager creates a management environment that provides for compliance with all rules and regulations applicable to its business operations. The risk manager takes steps to implement internal and external auditing resources in order to verify that operations and legal and compliance infrastructures are sound and reasonable. The hedge fund manager hires appropriate resources such as prime brokers, administrators, attorneys, compliance officers, auditors and accountants, technology officers, and risk managers to ensure that all operations are compliant with local and other regulations.

Hedge fund risk managers apply new legislation with regard to anti-money-laundering activities, soft dollar practices, insider trading and market manipulation, U.S. Patriot Act, regulatory practices such as Sarbanes-Oxley, Basel Accords compliance, "know your customer" rules, and other local regulations. Although hedge funds were not required to comply with all these regulations, they are subject to minimum standards and have to register with the Securities and Exchange Commission as of February 2006.

Hedge fund risk managers have responsibility for reporting to the appropriate regulators the different levels of risks and explaining open operational risk issues. Operational risk in smaller hedge funds is practically nonexistent but is practiced in the largest, most mature U.S. hedge funds. The hedge fund manager is responsible for filing and reporting to all appropriate regulatory agencies. A compliance officer usually works with the risk manager to maintain necessary regulatory, legal, and compliance levels. The risk manager describes and reports trading rules and restrictions, confidentiality requirements, policies designed to ensure compliance with applicable securities, commodities, and related laws such as market timing, insider trading, and market manipulations. Compliance policies are regularly updated, and the internal audit department verifies on a quarterly basis that all departments' operations are sound and reasonable. Most recently, all department heads have been required to sign off on the status and progress of issues regarding their departments. Background checks and clearance are required for all members of the hedge funds dealing with new procedures on anti-money-laundering regulations.

Failing to conduct proper operational risk management can cause the hedge fund to lose a significant amount of capital and be subject to much reputational risk. A sound and proper way to enforce ethical, clean, and transparent corporate governance practices in a hedge fund is to implement these very basic guidelines:

- Every hedge fund should have an independent board chairman, and two-thirds of each fund's directors should be independent.
- Every fund should have a chief compliance officer responsible for controls and oversight who reports directly to the board.
- Every fund should make full disclosure of all fees and costs, and the board chair and compliance officer should be required to make Sarbanes-Oxley certification that such costs are fully disclosed and negotiated in the interests of shareholders.
- Every board should have an independent audit committee based on Sarbanes-Oxley standards and disclose insider transactions, compensation for sales of fund shares, directed brokerage arrangements, and compensation to senior investment company management.

A hedge fund's basic guidelines with regard to compliance and internal control auditing policies and procedures ought to include the following. Very much like private equity firms, hedge funds have not been required to be audited by external or by internal control teams. This is a major way hedge funds have gone against the main fundamental law of the markets. And despite the new requirement of registration to the SEC as of 2006, auditing on a superficial level to inform investors and to avoid massive frauds still lacks efficiency and importance. In the later chapters we reveal how audits have an impact on the way reported returns are being smoothed, produced, or manipulated. More specifically, Bollen and Krepely (2005) or Liang (2002) proved that audits have an impact on the ratings and the survivorship bias of the hedge funds.

A hedge fund is to formulate a clear definition of its trading strategies, products, and geographical markets. In this policy statement, the manager has to describe capital adequacy levels, capacity objectives over time, and constraints and limits for various risks. In order to evaluate adequate capital levels, the following chapters describe different methodologies to rate capital according to various criteria.

Some hedge funds have one limit as an aggregate and describe parameters and guidelines on position sizes and concentration exposures. More sophisticated hedge funds provide several limits for concentration risks or top risk positions in terms of Greeks (delta, gamma, vega, etc.). Sophisticated hedge funds can also have limits or capacity allocation by strategies. If they do not provide limits on measures such as alpha or beta, they tend to disclose historical trends. Advanced risk management policies and procedures of certain hedge funds also provide limits on the number of sophisticated trades. They might also have limits in geographical markets. So, once the hedge fund manager has asserted all these variables, he or she can clearly define policies and procedures in relationship with the fund's investment strategies. Then, budgets are allocated to recruit adequate resources in human capital and systems to monitor market, credit, and operational risk levels. An internal risk management works in conjunction with finance, accounting, and audit functions to verify that all risk variables defined in the procedures are reviewed and appropriately controlled. Audits with accurate testing provide accuracy of valuations, precise accounting of asset allocations among legal entities, and prevention of liquidity issues. Feffer and Kundro (2003) note that one of the most recurrent frauds has been misappropriation of investments, and they describe it as the act of creating or causing the generation of reports and valuations with false and misleading information.

A hedge fund manager implements risk monitoring practices to describe management goals, policies, and procedures. The policy definition highlights management involvement in the hedge fund's trading activities. It provides information to prevent and alleviate conflict of interests, internal and external. Best practices guidelines are described as a framework on policies, code of conduct, internal ethics, and access to related third parties besides hedge funds personnel and investors. This is also an information guideline on internal expenses, internal policies on intellectual property, and confidentiality agreements. The management policy statement presents information on market, credit, and operational risks. It describes the different roles for each department such as finance, accounting, auditing, marketing, research, compliance, and risk management.

The hedge fund manager attempts to implement practices in terms of controls, limit monitoring, and capital by strategies, by funds, and by asset classes. Risk monitoring consists of verifying appropriate and reasonable levels of investors' capital with respect to initial strategic limit agreements.

Any changes in mandates or capacity of the funds are to be reported and documented to traders, risk management, and the hedge fund manager. If significant and material, they are reported to the main clients and investors as well.

A hedge fund manager's senior management and board of directors have monthly or quarterly meetings to communicate trading risk activities and operational risk issues. Appointments of board members and directors are to be performed based on voting rights of investors. In many cases, key figures in hedge funds (and large corporations) are appointed using nepotism and old boys' clubs. Slim are the hopes for a system based on merit.

Directors and board members are made fully aware of the infrastructural weaknesses within the hedge funds and the types of risk management problems. These problems and issues became better communicated after 2002 when hedge fund risk management became more relevant. Before then, the board of directors and upper management were only made aware of the overall risks on a broad macro level. Since 2002, hedge fund risk management has become more granular and is communicated in more detail.

Risk managers attend board meetings. The risk management department produces reports to provide descriptions of the largest and most concentrated positions by strategies, asset classes, and markets. Described risks are then compared with set limits and benchmark levels. Any material changes of risks are explained.

From the beginning of hedge fund risk management history, only top positions in size and risk were reported. For example, the alpha of the portfolio was clearly defined and the beta as well, but very little information was given on pricing, models, and liquidity of the traded products within the market. Various pricing sources have been kept confidential or proprietary. Mark-to-market pricing, with described Greek positions such as delta, gamma, and vega on derivatives transactions, considered to be the fundamental basis of true risk, has been performed on a monthly basis and seldom reported to investors. Stochastic and dynamic risk management was performed only in sophisticated larger hedge funds.

Pricing was not performed on a daily basis at hedge fund managers because risk management departments lacked human resources and skilled intellect. The infrastructures to perform mark-to-market verification on a daily basis were difficult to achieve. Banks, however, had by 2002 the capabilities of practicing mark-to-market verification and strict risk management controls on a daily basis because they had the automated and technological infrastructures. So, pricing liquidity gaps and dislocations appeared in the market with particular modern trends. These infrastructural changes forced the overall market to become more uniform again and to stabilize itself.

Any changes in risk management limits, procedures, and reporting are disclosed at management meetings and to the board of directors. Typical explanations consist of reporting actual static risks and comparing these with historical trends.

Third-party services providers are to be implemented and linked appropriately to the hedge fund. For example, a typical problem incurred in the hedge fund industry is lack of brokerage or partial brokerage. In some cases, trades issued by the hedge fund traders are not settled through a brokerage firm. Another service required by the hedge fund is an external auditor. Most hedge funds are subject to the local regulators and have to file the appropriate forms. Another third-party service provider is the custodian who is going to hold assets. In most cases, a hedge fund manager hires an internal compliance officer and an external lawyer to protect officers against potential lawsuits. Another type of service to obtain might be insurance. Hedge funds can purchase insurance to protect against certain types of risks such as operational risk. Until recently, hedge funds have purchased insurance to protect officers but not to protect investors against potential losses.

The job descriptions of third-party responsibilities and roles are to be well defined and appropriately documented in agreement between the hedge fund manager and the third-party service providers. The process employed for selecting service providers and monitoring their performance is to be reviewed on a regular basis.

The risk management department assumes the risk monitoring function on different levels. Risk management collects data from the hedge fund traders' positions and prices and downloads them from the brokers' reports. Risk management personnel verify accuracy of the data by comparing reports from the brokers' accounts with the hedge fund traders' raw reports. Any discrepancies are to be reported. Due to the complexity of some trades, a few models cannot be replicated into the trading systems and complicated trades do not always get captured into the brokers' reports. Operational risk problems are incurred within hedge funds' systems. Hedge funds do have best operational risk policies, and thus many gaps and unreconciled connections between hedge funds and third parties' outsourced service providers (such as prime brokers, fund administrators, etc.) exist. Risk management ensures that trades are reported and that data is accurate. Prices and positions are to be accurately checked.

Risk management reports directly to the board of directors and owners of the fund. Management gets informed about high-level risks, but these days, upper management often does not have the technical skills to understand quantitative risk positions. Hedge fund management is unusually the main capital provider as a starting point of the fund. Sometimes, the hedge fund manager is also the main trader of the hedge fund. But most of the upper management team is made up of individuals who can provide the financial resources but rarely the intellectual expertise. To the extent appropriate, risk analysis with respect to a particular investment strategy is to be performed independently of portfolio management personnel responsible for that strategy so that trading activities and operations may be effectively supervised and compliance with trading policies and risk limits can be controlled.

Risk management implements appropriate internal controls to produce risk reports on a regular basis. Most mark-to-market reports used to be performed monthly, but given levels of automation, marking to market is now performed daily and sometimes intraday to monitor pricing volatility and intraday gains and losses. Another important type of report is the daily profits and losses report. This report is obtained from hedge fund traders and compared to brokers' reports to verify the accuracy of prices and positions.

Risk management verifies that value at risk or risk limits are respected. Profits and losses are also compared to value at risk limits via back-testing checks. These exercises are performed to make sure that risk systems capture significant exposures on a timely basis and that the risk exposures are realistic and consistent with market movements. A typical example occurred with commodities markets where highly volatile profits and losses were difficult to explain, and there were no limits on budgetary guidelines implemented in any of the large commodity companies. Hedge funds have been very aggressive as well in trading commodities because of the lucrative and unregulated markets. The number of financial futures derivatives contracts rose in correlation with the prices of basic commodities. Some of the complicated derivatives models have not been sustainable for highly volatile changes in prices of such commodities. Technological systems had reached their limits to measure risks for complicated models such as swaptions on crude oil and other commodities derivatives.

MODEL RISK

Operational risk management losses can be mathematically modeled with an extreme value theory (EVT) more accurately as it provides a standard tool to analyze risk in the extremes. Value at risk methodology used to be the standard way of modeling risks of all types in large institutions and then hedge funds. Value at risk used to be more applicable toward the end of the twentieth century when most return distributions were normalized, and risks were known and controllable. Now that hedge funds' return distributions are unconventionally shaped, hedge fund risk managers are forced to apply new fitted customized distributions very much like actuaries in the insurance industry trying to mathematically best fit return trends and patterns.

Since 2002, many new ideas and models primarily from academia have come to markets to bring more sense to the latest market developments. Embrechts, Kluppelberg, and Mikosch developed the block maxima method in 1997. Focardi and Fabozzi employed the peak over threshold method in 2003. The block maxima methodology describes the limiting distribution of the maximum of a sequence of independent, identically distributed random variables with common distribution F. The generalized extreme value (GEV) distribution regroups three fundamental types of extreme value limit laws:

Type I (Gumbel or thin-tailed class): $A(x) = \exp\left(^{-e^{-x}}\right)$ with $-\infty \leq x \geq +\infty$

Type II (Frechet or heavy-tailed class): $\Phi_\alpha(x) = 0$, for $x \leq 0$ and $= \exp(-x^{-y})$ for $x > 0$, $y > 0$

Type III (Weibull or short-tailed class): $\psi_\alpha(x) = \exp - (-x)^y$ for $x \leq 0$ and $= 1$ for $x > 0$, $y > 0$

Timing is not appropriately represented in this model as the maximum value is computed over a block or subperiod of a given size n.

In 1975, Pickands demonstrated that the generalized Pareto distribution (GPD) is a limiting distribution for the distribution of the excesses. This function is also mostly used in actuarial insurance modeling to predict best fits of insurance loss distributions.

Given $F(y) = \text{GPD}_{\varepsilon,\sigma}(y)$ for u tending to ∞, the Pareto distribution is defined as:

$$\text{GDP}_{\varepsilon,\sigma}(y) = 1 - \left\{\left[1 + \left(\frac{\xi}{\sigma}\right)y\right] \wedge \left(\frac{-1}{\xi}\right)\right\} \text{ for } \xi \neq 0$$

And

$$\text{GDP}_{\xi,\sigma}(y) = [1 - e \wedge (^{-y/\sigma})] \text{ for } \xi = 0$$

And ξ and σ are scale and shape parameters, respectively. The mean of this distribution exists if $\xi < 1$ and the variance is $\xi < \frac{1}{2}$; more generally, the kth moment exists if $\xi < 1/k$.

Carol Alexander and Anca Dimitriu (2004) found the following models' theories with regard to fund selection and optimal allocations. There are five different factor models to estimate the alpha of a hedge fund:

1. The base case model is the simplest and most general representation of fund returns as a direct function of underlying asset classes, equities, and bonds.
2. The broad fundamental factor model employs indexes to capture the performance of the main asset classes, and other factors representing specific types of nonlinear strategies such as market timing, volatility trading, equilibrium trading, commodities, foreign exchange, and futures derivatives.
3. The multifactor model is based on hedge fund indexes.
4. The statistical factor model uses factors' portfolios replicating the first four components.
5. The general model is net of fees' excess return on a fund on a monthly basis.

The base case or simplest model is a linear function based on the returns of two asset classes—equities and interest rate products. Indexes used to proxy both asset classes are the Wilshire 5000 and the Lehman Government or Credit Intermediate indexes. For this model, the average total variance of fund excess returns is about 27 percent. Eighty percent of the funds have a relationship with the Wilshire 5000 excess returns (average beta is 0.3) and 38 percent of the funds lagged Wilshire excess returns. The bond index returns are significant for only 20 percent of funds. The average alpha is positive and significant for 48 percent of funds and significant for only three funds. The distribution of alphas has a mean of 7 percent and is skewed convex up. (See Table 7.3.)

The broad fundamental factor model accounts for excess above returns on traditional indexes to monitor asset performances for each strategy. Alexander and Dimitriu (2004) followed researchers such as Sharpe in 1992, Schneeweis and Spurgin in 1996, Agarwal and Naik in 2002, and others. We include in the broad fundamental factor model equity indexes such as the Wilshire 5000, S&P 500 Growth and Value, and S&P MidCap and Small-Cap to capture differences in equity investment styles; MSCI World index excluding the United States to account for the investment opportunities outside the United States; and MSCI Emerging Markets index to capture the emerging markets investment opportunities as a separate asset class. Bond indexes are Lehman Government, Lehman Credit Bond, Lehman High Yield, and Lehman Mortgage Backed Securities. The Fed trade used a foreign exchange rate index to measure currency risk. The Goldman Sachs commodity index is used to capture commodities risk. (See Table 7.4.)

TABLE 7.3 Base Case Model or Simplest Linear Bootstrapping Model to Measure Returns between Two Asset Classes

	All Funds	Convertible Arbitrage	Distressed Securities	Emerging Markets	Equity Hedge	Equity Market Neutral	Equity Non-Hedge	Event Driven	Fixed Income	FOF	Market Timing	Managed Futures	Merger Arbitrage	Sectors
Alpha	0.62 100%	0.64 100%	0.44 100%	1.11 100%	0.75 100%	0.38 100%	0.65 100%	0.6 100%	0.32 100%	0.48 100%	0.7 100%	0.93 100%	0.35 100%	0.8 100%
Wilshire 5000	0.38 80%	0.04 50%	0.22 76%	0.78 100%	0.61 83%	0.21 65%	0.76 95%	0.39 95%	0.23 65%	0.19 81%	0.07 80%	-0.23 61%	0.1 50%	0.6 100%
Lagged Wilshire 5000	0.12 38%	0.05 40%	0.15 76%	0.44 50%	0.17 30%	0 15%	0.28 42%	0.1 45%	0.07 35%	0.06 62%	NA 0%	-0.15 28%	0.06 75%	0.35 5%
Lehman Bond	-0.25 20%	0.13 60%	-0.4 12%	NA 0%	-0.68 25%	-0.15 19%	0.45 5%	-0.2 5%	0.09 18%	-0.46 29%	-0.52 20%	1.15 17%	-0.17 25%	0.14 16%
First Year Rep Dummy	0.32 24%	1.42 60%	-0.16 12%	-3.68 8%	-0.18 25%	2.25 19%	-1.39 11%	-0.53 40%	0.79 35%	-0.1 29%	1.61 20%	2.36 28%	NA 0%	-2.15 11%
R^2	0.27	0.2	0.16	0.23	0.32	0.19	0.39	0.32	0.3	0.28	0.24	0.13	0.11	0.29

Source: Data from G. Amin and H. Kat, "Welcome to the Dark Side: Hedge Fund Attrition and Survivorship Bias over the Period 1994–2001," working paper, Case Business School, 2003; *Journal of Alternative Investments* 6, 57–73. Data also published in the Social Science Research Network in the SSRN eLibrary. Art changed and altered by the author. Statistical data also overlapping with the paper from Carol Alexander and Anca Dimitriu, "The Art of Investing in Hedge Funds: Fund Selection and Optimal Allocations," ISMA Centre, University of Reading, working paper, 2004. Data also published in the Social Science Research Network in the SSRN eLibrary.

TABLE 7.4 Fundamental Factor Model Estimation Results

	All Funds	Convertible Arbitrage	Distressed Securities	Emerging Markets	Equity Hedge	Equity Market Neutral	Equity Non-Hedge	Event Driven	Fixed Income	FOF	Market Timing	Managed Futures	Merger Arbitrage	Sectors
Alpha	0.55 / 100%	0.81 / 100%	0.63 / 100%	1.35 / 100%	0.58 / 100%	0.4 / 100%	0.4 / 100%	0.57 / 100%	0.36 / 100%	0.51 / 100%	0.62 / 100%	0.34 / 100%	0.47 / 100%	0.57 / 100%
W 5000	0.62 / 18%	0.04 / 10%	0.18 / 6%	1.14 / 50%	0.82 / 21%	NA / 0%	0.84 / 42%	0.64 / 5%	0.26 / 29%	0.28 / 21%	0.36 / 20%	0.69 / 6%	NA / 0%	0.63 / 21%
SP500g	0.23 / 7%	0.12 / 20%	NA / 0%	NA / 0%	0.29 / 2%	0.29 / 31%	NA / 0%	NA / 0%	-0.08 / 6%	0.01 / 2%	0.23 / 33%	NA / 0%	NA / 0%	0.52 / 5%
SP500v	0.22 / 7%	-0.01 / 20%	0.29 / 12%	0.21 / 8%	0.32 / 2%	0.26 / 15%	0.47 / 5%	0.09 / 5%	0.08 / 6%	-0.31 / 4%	NA / 0%	NA / 0%	NA / 0%	0.45 / 26%
MD400	0.4 / 10%	NA / 0%	0.4 / 6%	0.24 / 25%	0.46 / 21%	0.1 / 4%	0.58 / 11%	0.31 / 15%	NA / 0%	0.15 / 6%	0.15 / 7%	NA / 0%	0.04 / 25%	1.01 / 11%
SC600	0.39 / 38%	0.09 / 10%	0.15 / 47%	0.45 / 8%	0.55 / 47%	0.34 / 15%	0.81 / 37%	0.37 / 70%	0.29 / 24%	0.22 / 62%	0.33 / 7%	NA / 0%	0.07 / 75%	0.76 / 37%
MSCIW EXUS	0 / 9%	0.09 / 10%	-0.08 / 6%	0.13 / 8%	0.19 / 6%	-0.01 / 8%	0.41 / 16%	NA / 0%	0.04 / 6%	0.05 / 4%	NA / 0%	-0.25 / 50%	NA / 0%	0.16 / 5%
MSCI EMF	0.18 / 20%	0.07 / 20%	0.17 / 24%	0.56 / 67%	0.18 / 21%	0.04 / 12%	0.21 / 16%	0.15 / 5%	0.14 / 12%	0.09 / 31%	0.06 / 20%	-0.22 / 6%	NA / 0%	0.1 / 11%
LEH Gov	0.25 / 6%	0.88 / 10%	NA / 0%	NaN / 0%	0.3 / 4%	0.41 / 12%	0.66 / 5%	NA / 0%	0.11 / 6%	-0.22 / 4%	-0.69 / 13%	1.12 / 6%	NA / 0%	0.41 / 16%
LEH Credit	-0.21 / 6%	0.09 / 20%	-0.23 / 24%	NA / 0%	-0.33 / 6%	NA / 0%	NA / 0%	-0.47 / 10%	0.03 / 6%	-0.22 / 6%	NA / 0%	NA / 0%	-0.1 / 25%	NA / 0%
LEH HY	0.09 / 24%	0.2 / 30%	0.27 / 65%	-0.46 / 8%	-0.11 / 23%	-0.06 / 12%	0.1 / 21%	0.26 / 30%	0.17 / 6%	0.08 / 17%	0.12 / 27%	0.4 / 22%	0.03 / 50%	-0.02 / 37%

LEH MBKD	-0.2 / 5%	NA / 0%	-0.65 / 6%	NA / 0%	NA / 0%	NA / 0%	NA / 0%	0.19 / 5%	0.27 / 18%	-0.39 / 10%	NA / 0%	0.05 / 11%	NA / 0%	-1.11 / 5%
FX	-0.45 / 11%	0.08 / 10%	NA / 0%	NA / 0%	-0.48 / 8%	-0.18 / 8%	-0.77 / 16%	-0.51 / 5%	-0.23 / 12%	0.02 / 8%	NA / 0%	-0.65 / 67%	NA / 0%	-0.41 / 16%
GSCI Com	0.02 / 19%	-0.03 / 10%	-0.13 / 12%	0.17 / 42%	-0.01 / 8%	-0.06 / 12%	-0.03 / 26%	0.08 / 15%	-0.01 / 12%	0.05 / 23%	0.08 / 20%	-0.18 / 39%	-0.07 / 25%	0.27 / 26%
LW 5000	0.13 / 18%	0.03 / 10%	0.11 / 18%	0.19 / 8%	0.14 / 28%	0.14 / 4%	0.25 / 26%	0.09 / 25%	0.08 / 18%	0.07 / 17%	-0.27 / 7%	0.38 / 6%	0.05 / 50%	0.21 / 21%
SC600^2	0 / 39%	-0.01 / 60%	-0.01 / 53%	-0.02 / 33%	0.01 / 36%	0 / 50%	0 / 42%	-0.01 / 25%	0 / 41%	0 / 35%	0.01 / 33%	0.01 / 50%	0 / 25%	0.01 / 26%
LEH HY^2	0.01 / 28%	-0.04 / 40%	0.02 / 47%	0 / 33%	-0.02 / 26%	0.02 / 19%	0.13 / 37%	0 / 5%	0.01 / 35%	-0.02 / 19%	-0.01 / 40%	0.04 / 33%	-0.01 / 50%	0.01 / 37%
VIX	0 / 27%	0 / 20%	0 / 18%	-0.01 / 25%	0 / 30%	0 / 38%	0 / 11%	0 / 15%	0 / 6%	0 / 27%	0 / 27%	0 / 61%	0 / 25%	0 / 32%
DISP	0.56 / 29%	NA / 0%	0.63 / 18%	-0.95 / 25%	1.97 / 45%	-1.09 / 23%	1.59 / 26%	-0.88 / 20%	0.4 / 12%	0.44 / 33%	-6.18 / 13%	-2.95 / 17%	-1.37 / 25%	1.41 / 58%
First Year Rep Dummy	0.43 / 25%	0.92 / 50%	0.23 / 24%	-1.39 / 17%	0.05 / 28%	1.55 / 23%	-1.33 / 11%	0.48 / 40%	0.75 / 35%	0.15 / 29%	1.41 / 20%	3.52 / 11%	NA / 0%	-0.44 / 16%
R^2	0.36	0.27	0.29	0.36	0.42	0.24	0.49	0.43	0.38	0.39	0.26	0.22	0.23	0.42

Source: Data from G. Amin and H. Kat, "Welcome to the Dark Side: Hedge Fund Attrition and Survivorship Bias over the Period 1994–2001," working paper, Case Business School, 2003; *Journal of Alternative Investments* 6, 57–73. Data also published in the Social Science Research Network in the SSRN eLibrary. Art changed and altered by the author. Statistical data also overlapping with the paper from Carol Alexander and Anca Dimitriu, "The Art of Investing in Hedge Funds: Fund Selection and Optimal Allocations," ISMA Centre, University of Reading, working paper, 2004. Data also published in the Social Science Research Network in the SSRN eLibrary.

Alexander and Dimitriu (2004) also included in the regressions the squared excess returns of the main indexes. Additionally, two factors are included capturing specific strategies: the change in the equity implied volatility index (VIX) to account for volatility trades such as Schneeweis and Spurgin (1996) and the price distribution as a leading indicator of price equilibrium trading strategies such as Alexander and Dimitriu (2003). According to the broad fundamental factor model, the average number of significant factors for individual funds was 2.5 and the regression was found to be 36 percent. This is supposed to be considered the best model to evaluate emerging markets, equity derivatives, event driven, convertible bonds, financial, and technology sectors. The MSCI Emerging Markets index was significant for 20 percent of the funds. Using this model, alpha is the largest number for emerging markets and financial sector funds, and the model reveals a negative alpha for funds investing in emerging Asian markets, convertible arbitrage, relative value, and short selling.

Alexander and Dimitriu (2004) also describe the results of the hedge fund indexes model for nonlinear exposures to traditional asset classes. This approach regroups funds into categories. It uses the relevant group index to explain fund returns. The average results in about 46 percent of the variance in fund excess. The average is 37 percent for equity market neutral strategy and 60 percent for equity non-hedge funds, event driven, funds of funds, and technology funds. Reviewing funds individually, 17 percent of the funds had a negative alpha; these funds are equity non-hedge, event driven, and some sectors. Some 11 percent of the funds had positive and significant alpha; these funds are emerging markets group, fixed income strategies, market timing, and managed futures.

Fung and Hsieh (1997c) discovered the statistical model. This model uses component factors for each portfolio: diversified strategies including funds of funds and equity funds, managed futures fund, equity market neutral, technology funds, and equity market neutral funds. Only diversified strategies' fund shows a linear regression with fundamental factors averaging 0.79 and a regression with hedge funds' indexes averaging 0.89. (See Table 7.5.)

All the other portfolio factors do not have linear patterns and prove significant distortions. Alexander and Dimitriu (2004) asserted that hedge fund indexes can be interpreted as style factors rather than location factors capturing fundamental factors. An equally weighted index is less volatile. The inclusion of equity market neutral funds in three of the four portfolios shows that the funds in the category are more heterogeneous, with lower correlations with each other. The low dependency of higher-order principal components to traditional asset classes is due to dynamic trading strate-

TABLE 7.5 Statistical Factor Model Estimation Results

	All Funds	Convertible Arbitrage	Distressed Securities	Emerging Markets	Equity Hedge	Equity Market Neutral	Equity Non-Hedge	Event Driven	Fixed Income	FOF	Market Timing	Managed Futures	Merger Arbitrage	Sectors
Alpha	-0.21	0.56	0.36	0.34	-0.57	0.01	-1.09	-0.15	0.3	-0.07	0.27	-0.92	0.31	-0.65
	100%	100%	100%	100%	100%	100%	100%	100%	100%	100%	100%	100%	100%	100%
PC1	0.6	0.08	0.51	1.8	0.93	0.16	1.17	0.8	0.3	0.39	0.06	-0.18	0.13	1.12
	79%	50%	88%	100%	85%	46%	95%	100%	65%	92%	87%	28%	75%	89%
PC2	0.19	0.03	0.06	0.27	-0.07	0.15	0.05	0.15	0.02	0.17	0.09	1.86	0	0.04
	39%	20%	18%	33%	34%	46%	42%	30%	35%	44%	33%	94%	0%	37%
PC3	-0.02	-0.07	-0.34	-1.37	0.28	0.03	0.06	-0.24	-0.19	0.06	-0.06	0.18	-0.04	0.16
	44%	20%	47%	58%	45%	42%	37%	65%	35%	50%	33%	33%	25%	37%
PC4	0.16	0.02	-0.17	0.21	0.24	0.16	0.59	0.14	-0.07	0.02	0.37	0.24	0.04	0.23
	29%	10%	18%	17%	36%	38%	53%	35%	18%	25%	20%	22%	25%	37%
First Year Rep Dummy	0.21	0.85	0.49	0.39	0.33	0.29	0.27	-0.16	0.24	0	0.51	0.51	-0.15	-0.45
	23%	60%	12%	8%	30%	31%	16%	25%	35%	21%	13%	11%	0%	16%
R^2	0.39	0.17	0.23	0.33	0.47	0.22	0.49	0.46	0.32	0.46	0.33	0.52	0.12	0.46

Source: Data from G. Amin and H. Kat, "Welcome to the Dark Side: Hedge Fund Attrition and Survivorship Bias over the Period 1994–2001," working paper, Case Business School, 2003; *Journal of Alternative Investments* 6, 57–73. Data also published in the Social Science Research Network in the SSRN eLibrary. Art changed and altered by the author. Statistical data also overlapping with the paper from Carol Alexander and Anca Dimitriu, "The Art of Investing in Hedge Funds: Fund Selection and Optimal Allocations," ISMA Centre, University of Reading, working paper, 2004. Data also published in the Social Science Research Network in the SSRN eLibrary.

gies, derivatives, and style switching. An example of such a case is market timing. This strategy positively correlates with market uptrends and negatively correlates with market downtrends.

Alexander and Dimitriu (2004) mentioned what other researchers such as Lhabitant and Learned (2002) found when volatility decreases or becomes weaker, and as the number of funds increases in fixed income arbitrage, convertible arbitrage, and event driven strategies. They performed those findings on a total sample size of 6,985 funds. Very few hedge funds do go into this level of detail for the risk management monitoring of their different strategies.

In recent years hedge fund research has promoted progress in quantifying the correlations between different markets and products. Hedge funds have served to be risk management vehicles to microscopically view detailed strategies in correlations with traditional and new markets and new instruments to bridge them. Alexander and Dimitriu (2004) implemented "a mean variance maximum information ratio optimization of a minimum variance optimization but the lack of accuracy in the individual alpha estimates resulted in lower out of sample information ratios for the mean variance portfolios than for the minimum variance portfolios and the portfolios were less stable than the ones constructed based on minimum variance." Rather than optimizing on less accurate estimates, one is better off selecting funds based on alphas and then running the optimization on only the covariance matrix. For each of the models, the return on the portfolio alpha is calculated. Alpha then allows a selection of funds and minimum variance implementation. Many researchers have found and demonstrated different factor models. (See Table 7.6.)

Nonfactored models are also used more by some larger financial firms. Ackermann, McEnally, and Ravenscraft (1999); Brown, Goetzmann, and Ibbotson (1999); Agarwal and Naik (2000b); and Liang (2000) are researchers who have found a one-factor model. Fung and Hsieh (1997c), Schneeweis and Spurgin (1996), Liang (2001), Agarwal and Naik (2000 a, b, c, d), and Edwards and Caglayan (2001 a, b) have created fundamental and statistical multifactor models.

Alexander and Dimitriu (2004) also developed a comparison of alphas from different previous factor models. They concluded from the research on different models that there are material differences from one model to another and that no one model should be considered as a benchmark or reference model due to the biases surrounding its making. (See Table 7.7.)

The disagreement shows disparate alphas ranging between –2.5 percent and 7 percent yearly. Alpha gets higher at the level of individual funds. However, alpha shows some pattern or logic for individual funds having at least one positive alpha estimate; in 30 percent of cases there is perfect

TABLE 7.6 HFRI Factor Model Estimation Results

	All Funds	Convertible Arbitrage	Distressed Securities	Emerging Markets	Equity Hedge	Equity Market Neutral	Equity Non-Hedge	Event Driven	Fixed Income	FOF	Market Timing	Managed Futures	Merger Arbitrage	Sectors
Alpha	-0.12 100%	0.18 100%	-0.34 100%	0.34 100%	-0.24 100%	-0.12 100%	-0.58 100%	-0.56 100%	0.02 100%	-0.01 100%	0.02 100%	0.56 100%	-0.07 100%	-0.31 100%
Convertible Arbitrage	0.27 25%	0.89 50%	-0.25 6%	1.84 33%	0.3 2.5%	0.12 12%	-0.32 11%	0.39 25%	0.42 47%	0.11 29%	0.07 33%	-0.27 28%	-0.06 75%	-0.74 11%
Regulation D	-0.03 27%	-0.01 50%	0 29%	-0.42 42%	0.18 2.5%	-0.08 12%	-0.32 26%	-0.04 15%	-0.06 53%	0.1 27%	0.02 40%	-0.69 11%	0.06 25%	0.05 26%
Relative Value	-0.34 28%	NA 0%	-1.48 6%	-1.64 50%	-0.6 23%	-0.24 35%	-0.39 21%	-0.04 35%	0.09 41%	-0.42 27%	0.5 33%	-0.76 33%	-0.86 25%	0.59 37%
Distressed Securities	0.39 30%	0.23 30%	1.3 100%	3.39 17%	-0.4 26%	-0.12 15%	0.12 26%	1.01 60%	-0.65 18%	0.17 33%	0.83 7%	-0.61 28%	0.11 25%	-0.95 11%
Emerging Markets (Total)	0.33 22%	-0.03 30%	-0.2 18%	1.44 100%	-0.02 8%	0.19 15%	0.15 21%	0.29 35%	0.04 29%	0.21 17%	-0.1 33%	-0.26 11%	-0.13 25%	-0.1 16%
Equity Hedge	0.68 21%	-0.25 20%	-0.12 12%	NA 0%	1.19 40%	0.98 12%	1.1 11%	0.46 10%	NA 0%	0.47 31%	0.39 13%	-0.58 22%	-0.13 25%	1.03 21%
Equity MN	0.29 24%	-0.36 20%	-0.43 18%	1.56 8%	0.05 30%	1.08 58%	0.81 21%	0.06 10%	-0.27 18%	0.18 21%	-0.25 27%	NA 0%	NA 0%	-0.06 37%
Equity Non-Hedge	0.75 16%	-0.2 10%	0 12%	-0.25 8%	1.13 19%	0.51 15%	1.14 68%	0.42 15%	0.37 12%	0.19 4%	0.34 13%	0.71 6%	0.08 25%	0.78 11%
Event Driven	-0.13 23%	NA 0%	-0.65 18%	-1.65 42%	0.34 11%	-0.04 15%	0.18 16%	0.56 50%	-0.02 12%	0.17 27%	-0.69 20%	-1.31 33%	0 75%	0.23 26%
Fixed Income	-0.18 34%	0.61 40%	-0.54 47%	NA 0%	0.49 34%	-1.68 19%	-0.15 32%	-0.08 35%	-0.45 53%	-0.63 38%	0.08 33%	-2.44 17%	0.15 50%	0.95 47%

(Continued)

TABLE 7.6 (*Continued*)

	All Funds	Convertible Arbitrage	Distressed Securities	Emerging Markets	Equity Hedge	Equity Market Neutral	Equity Non-Hedge	Event Driven	Fixed Income	FOF	Market Timing	Managed Futures	Merger Arbitrage	Sectors
Convertible Arbitrage	-0.01 20%	-0.19 20%	0.2 35%	0.86 8%	-0.2 17%	0.59 4%	-0.2 26%	0.13 20%	0.19 35%	0.13 23%	0.08 7%	-0.43 33%	NA 0%	-0.3 11%
Fixed Income HY	0.03 26%	NA 0%	0.07 35%	-0.26 42%	-0.13 19%	0.24 15%	0.96 16%	-0.75 30%	0.78 47%	-0.05 23%	-0.27 40%	0.05 28%	0.02 50%	0.09 26%
Fixed Income Arbitrage	-0.09 25%	0.26 10%	-0.22 41%	-0.57 25%	0.13 25%	-0.3 19%	-0.49 26%	-0.41 35%	0.35 35%	0.16 19%	0.41 33%	-1.02 11%	0.53 25%	-0.37 32%
Fixed Income Diversified	0.27 34%	-0.4 30%	0.66 35%	0.76 25%	-0.59 23%	0.37 19%	0.78 16%	0.3 15%	0.46 41%	0.17 48%	-0.8 33%	1.55 83%	-0.19 50%	-0.48 37%
Fixed Income MBKD	-0.09 28%	-0.51 20%	0.02 29%	-0.42 33%	-0.25 34%	0.37 19%	0.14 11%	0.08 20%	0.19 47%	0.19 29%	-0.36 33%	-0.22 28%	-0.2 50%	-0.67 26%
FOF	0.22 30%	0.07 20%	0.04 18%	-1.34 8%	-0.21 23%	-0.55 8%	-0.66 26%	-0.49 20%	0.63 65%	0.63 65%	0.08 13%	1 50%	NA 0%	-0.36 42%
Market Timing	0.08 34%	-0.05 40%	-0.14 41%	0.24 17%	0.14 38%	0.05 31%	-0.08 42%	0.12 25%	0.05 37%	0.05 37%	0.41 67%	-0.87 17%	NA 0%	0.46 26%
Macro	0.31 28%	NA 0%	0.12 18%	-0.6 25%	0.19 26%	0.23 27%	0.34 21%	0.32 25%	0.12 23%	0.12 23%	0.47 33%	1 72%	0.04 25%	0.23 37%
Short Sell	0.04 31%	0.22 10%	-0.04 35%	-0.69 8%	-0.03 36%	0.09 15%	0.08 37%	0.03 35%	0.11 37%	0.11 37%	0.24 47%	0.23 39%	NA 0%	-0.23 32%
Merger Arbitrage	0.6 30%	0.25 10%	0.51 18%	2.24 42%	0.89 32%	0.57 23%	1.29 32%	0.24 50%	-0.06 31%	-0.06 31%	0.89 20%	0.52 6%	0.8 100%	0.66 37%

	1	2	3	4	5	6	7	8	9	10	11	12	13	14
Sector (Total)	-0.02 / 13%	0.1 / 30%	-0.05 / 35%	-0.55 / 25%	0.3 / 13%	-0.13 / 8%	-0.03 / 11%	0.24 / 15%	-0.05 / 8%	-0.05 / 8%	NA / 0%	0.76 / 6%	NA / 0%	-0.54 / 16%
Energy	0.05 / 30%	0 / 40%	0.06 / 6%	0.12 / 8%	0.04 / 32%	-0.07 / 35%	0.07 / 32%	0.02 / 45%	0.01 / 23%	0.01 / 23%	0.02 / 13%	0.27 / 44%	NA / 0%	0.11 / 58%
Financial	-0.03 / 31%	-0.04 / 10%	-0.14 / 24%	-0.13 / 25%	0.02 / 36%	0.1 / 15%	-0.16 / 47%	0.06 / 35%	-0.03 / 37%	-0.03 / 37%	-0.07 / 33%	-0.2 / 50%	-0.06 / 25%	0.2 / 32%
Health Care/ Biotechnology	-0.02 / 24%	0.01 / 30%	-0.11 / 12%	-0.04 / 25%	0.02 / 13%	-0.1 / 54%	-0.1 / 21%	0.01 / 30%	0.03 / 23%	0.03 / 23%	-0.19 / 13%	-0.32 / 28%	0.02 / 50%	0.39 / 32%
Real Estate	0.1 / 20%	-0.01 / 40%	-0.51 / 12%	0.44 / 17%	-0.16 / 17%	0.41 / 12%	0.33 / 32%	0.13 / 5%	0.07 / 21%	0.07 / 21%	0.56 / 27%	-0.61 / 6%	-0.11 / 50%	0.15 / 32%
Technology	0.37 / 7%	NA / 0%	0.17 / 12%	NA / 0%	0.41 / 9%	-0.05 / 8%	0.53 / 5%	NA / 0%	0.07 / 2%	0.07 / 2%	0.38 / 13%	NA / 0%	NA / 0%	0.67 / 26%
Sector Miscellaneous	0.06 / 22%	0.01 / 30%	-0.1 / 12%	0.81 / 8%	0.16 / 23%	-0.11 / 15%	0 / 16%	-0.06 / 30%	-0.03 / 23%	-0.03 / 23%	-0.16 / 13%	0.32 / 39%	0.09 / 50%	0.01 / 42%
First Year Rep Dummy	0.46 / 28%	0.9 / 40%	0.42 / 35%	NA / 0%	0.52 / 34%	0.81 / 27%	-1.15 / 21%	0.3 / 30%	-0.02 / 27%	-0.02 / 27%	1.14 / 27%	1.99 / 39%	NA / 0%	-0.69 / 32%
R^2	0.58	0.42	0.56	0.58	0.6	0.37	0.62	0.66	0.67	0.67	0.51	0.47	0.54	0.68

Source: Data from G. Amin and H. Kat, "Welcome to the Dark Side: Hedge Fund Attrition and Survivorship Bias over the Period 1994–2001," working paper, Case Business School, 2003; *Journal of Alternative Investments* 6, 57–73. Data also published in the Social Science Research Network in the SSRN eLibrary. Art changed and altered by the author. Statistical data also overlapping with the paper from Carol Alexander and Anca Dimitriu, "The Art of Investing in Hedge Funds: Fund Selection and Optimal Allocations," ISMA Centre, University of Reading, working paper, 2004. Data also published in the Social Science Research Network in the SSRN eLibrary.

TABLE 7.7   Average Fund Alphas

	Alpha	P-Value
Base Case Model	0.689	0
Broad Fundamental Factor Model	0.5103	0
Hedge Fund Index Model	0.0057	0.3967
Statistical Factor Model	−0.2787	0.0031

Source: Data from G. Amin and H. Kat, "Welcome to the Dark Side: Hedge Fund Attrition and Survivorship Bias over the Period 1994–2001," working paper, Case Business School, 2003; *Journal of Alternative Investments* 6, 57–73. Data also published in the Social Science Research Network in the SSRN eLibrary. Art changed and altered by the author. Statistical data also overlapping with the paper from Carol Alexander and Anca Dimitriu, "The Art of Investing in Hedge Funds: Fund Selection and Optimal Allocations," ISMA Centre, University of Reading, working paper, 2004. Data also published in the Social Science Research Network in the SSRN eLibrary.

agreement between all models in terms of alpha's sign. Jagannathan and Ma (2003) show that imposing upper and lower bounds on the weights is equivalent to shrinking the covariance matrix toward zero.

According to what Alexander and Dimitriu (2004) found, all performance measures favor the portfolio where hedge funds are selected using the alphas from the statistical factor model. This produces a portfolio of hedge funds with the highest average annual information ratio of 6.91 and the lowest turnover of 12 percent semiannually. Using the methodology of the statistical factor model, Alexander and Dimitriu used two five-year timing periods (1993–1997 and 1998–2002) and a sample of 92 funds for the first period and a sample of 214 funds for the second. Then the researchers applied two mathematical distributions: the random correlations and the empirical correlations. The random correlation has a Gaussian distribution centralized on zero. The empirical correlation is centered on a positive value. Correlations in hedge funds rise more in more volatile periods. (See Table 7.8.)

The left tail of the empirical correlation distribution shows a good fit with the random correlation distribution. The observed positive correlations are less likely to be random; the 95 percent confidence interval for the random cross correlations is (−.27, .27) in both periods. (See Tables 7.9 through 7.11.)

TABLE 7.8 Correlations and Probability of Agreement between Different Models' Alphas

Correlations	Two-Index Model	Fundamental Factor Model	Multifactor HFRI Model	Statistical Factor Model
Two-Index Model	1	0.7382	0.3993	0.271
Fundamental Factor Model		1	0.3927	0.5067
Multifactor HFRI Model			1	0.45
Statistical Factor Model				1

Source: Data from G. Amin and H. Kat, "Welcome to the Dark Side: Hedge Fund Attrition and Survivorship Bias over the Period 1994–2001," working paper, Case Business School, 2003; *Journal of Alternative Investments* 6, 57–73. Data also published in the Social Science Research Network in the SSRN eLibrary. Art changed and altered by the author. Statistical data also overlapping with the paper from Carol Alexander and Anca Dimitriu, "The Art of Investing in Hedge Funds: Fund Selection and Optimal Allocations," ISMA Centre, University of Reading, working paper, 2004. Data also published in the Social Science Research Network in the SSRN eLibrary.

TABLE 7.9 Correlation Rank by Model Type

Rank Correlation	Two-Index Model	Fundamental Factor Model	Multifactor HFRI Model	Statistical Factor Model
Two-Index Model	1	0.6804	0.3466	0.1941
Fundamental Factor Model		1	0.3175	0.456
Multifactor HFRI Model			1	0.43338
Statistical Factor Model				1

Source: Data from G. Amin and H. Kat, "Welcome to the Dark Side: Hedge Fund Attrition and Survivorship Bias over the Period 1994–2001," working paper, Case Business School, 2003; *Journal of Alternative Investments* 6, 57–73. Data also published in the Social Science Research Network in the SSRN eLibrary. Art changed and altered by the author. Statistical data also overlapping with the paper from Carol Alexander and Anca Dimitriu, "The Art of Investing in Hedge Funds: Fund Selection and Optimal Allocations," ISMA Centre, University of Reading, working paper, 2004. Data also published in the Social Science Research Network in the SSRN eLibrary.

TABLE 7.10 Performance of Portfolios Selected Using Alphas from Different Factor Models and Optimized to Have Minimum Variance

	Base Case Model	Fundamental Factors Model	HFR Indexes Model	Statistical Factor Model	All Factor Models	Equally Weighted
Annual Return	8.28	8.15	9.44	8.94	9.06	10.44
Annual Volatility	1.35	1.34	1.7	1.29	1.51	6.89
Skewness	0.3	0.06	0.1	0.22	0.49	-0.07
Excess Kurtosis	-0.08	-0.03	0.24	-0.34	0.35	1.91
Information Ratio	6.15	6.06	5.56	6.91	5.99	1.51
Turnover	6.3	7.13	7.66	4.94	7.02	4.2

Source: Data from G. Amin and H. Kat, "Welcome to the Dark Side: Hedge Fund Attrition and Survivorship Bias over the Period 1994–2001," working paper, Case Business School, 2003; *Journal of Alternative Investments* 6, 57–73. Data also published in the Social Science Research Network in the SSRN eLibrary. Art changed and altered by the author. Statistical data also overlapping with the paper from Carol Alexander and Anca Dimitriu, "The Art of Investing in Hedge Funds: Fund Selection and Optimal Allocations," ISMA Centre, University of Reading, working paper, 2004. Data also published in the Social Science Research Network in the SSRN eLibrary.

TABLE 7.11 Performance of Portfolios Selected Using Alphas from Different Factor Models and Optimized to Have Maximum Information

	Base Case Model	Fundamental Factors Model	HFR Indexes Model	Statistical Factor Model	All Factor Models	Equally Weighted
Annual Return	9.24	8.55	10.39	8.98	NA	10.44
Annual Volatility	1.86	1.81	1.97	1.44	NA	6.89
Skewness	0.71	0.01	0.57	0.5	NA	-0.07
Excess Kurtosis	0.57	1.92	0.46	0.1	NA	1.91
Information Ratio	4.97	4.73	5.28	6.22	NA	1.51
Turnover	8.99	9.77	7.05	7.59	NA	4.92

Source: Data from G. Amin and H. Kat, "Welcome to the Dark Side: Hedge Fund Attrition and Survivorship Bias over the Period 1994–2001," working paper, Case Business School, 2003; *Journal of Alternative Investments 6, 57–73*. Data also published in the Social Science Research Network in the SSRN eLibrary. Art changed and altered by the author. Statistical data also overlapping with the paper from Carol Alexander and Anca Dimitriu, "The Art of Investing in Hedge Funds: Fund Selection and Optimal Allocations," ISMA Centre, University of Reading, working paper, 2004. Data also published in the Social Science Research Network in the SSRN eLibrary.

Alexander and Dimitriu (2004) also developed another model using the dynamic strategies and market timing using the Markov switching model. One way of testing for the presence of dynamic strategies is to estimate switching models for the relationship between the strategy returns and the relevant asset class returns. Regime switching models provide a systematic approach to modeling multiple breaks and regime shifts in the data-generating process. Regime shifts are considered to be stochastic rather than deterministic events. To test the existence of switching relationships, the authors specify a simple Markov switching model with two states for the relationship of the returns on PC2–PC4 portfolios and the major asset classes. They use single-factor switching models rather than multifactor in order to avoid the assumption that the switching times are the same for strategies applied to different asset classes.

In the general form of the estimated model, the regression intercept, slope, and variance of the error term are dependent. Hamilton (1994) developed the following regression model:

$$Y_t = z_t \, \beta_{S,\,t} + \varepsilon_{S,\,t}$$

where Y_t = the vector of the statistical factor returns

z_t = the matrix of explanatory variables

x_t represents the fundamental return

β = the vector of state-dependent regression coefficients or vectors going sideways to the left 1 and 2 respectively

S,t = the inert state variable

ε = the vector of the state-dependent disturbances or vertical straight vectors 1 and 2 respectively, assumed normal with state-dependent variable

The transition probabilities for the two states are assumed to follow a first-order Markov chain, to be represented by a 2×2 matrix and to be constant over time. Each portfolio's correlation was then tested with indexes and interpreted as evidence of dynamic strategies given the differences of signs indicating switches between long and short positions or showing a material slope coefficient in an asset class. The authors of the tests show that the PC4 portfolio has a positive and strong relationship with Wilshire5000 index returns in the second regime. Similar types of relationships have been identified also for the other two portfolios (PC2 and PC3). The returns of all PC2–PC4 portfolios have regime-switching relationships with the returns of the Goldman Sachs Commodity index and S&P SmallCap index, and PC2 and PC4 portfolios also have switching relationships with the returns of the Wilshire5000. According to Alexander and Dimitriu (2004), the Markov switching models for PC2–PC4 portfolios show the corresponding statistical results. (See Table 7.12.)

TABLE 7.12 Markov Switching Models for Given Portfolios with Respect to Market Indexes

Model		Beta Vector 1 to the Right	Beta Vector 2 to the Right	Horizontal Vector 1	Horizontal Vector 2	P_{11}	P_{22}	Vertical Vector 1	Vertical Vector 2
PC2/SCI	Coefficient	0.3589	1.097	-6.681	3.022	0.7394	0.8467	0.7034	1.9718
	Standard error	0.1332	0.2387	2.6801	4.8432	0.4317	0.3563	0.4055	0.2712
	Z-statistic	2.6937	4.5953	-2.4928	0.62	1.71	2.37	1.73	7.27
	P-value	0.0071	0	0.0127	0.5326	0.0868	0.0175	0.0828	0
PC2/SC600	Coefficient	0.4401	1.2313	-2.3525	-12.36	0.7994	0.8257	0.9032	1.9845
	Standard error	0.1543	0.3232	3.2286	5.4138	0.3933	0.4301	1.6491	0.3401
	Z-statistic	2.85	3.81	-0.73	-2.28	2.03	1.92	0.55	5.83
	P-value	0.0043	0.0001	0.4662	0.0224	0.0421	0.0549	0.5839	0
PC2/W5000	Coefficient	0.4684	1.2472	-5.3136	-12.85	0.7686	0.8055	0.8688	1.9682
	Standard error	0.1556	0.3516	3.4508	5.7183	0.4633	0.4677	1.1965	0.3283
	Z-statistic	3.01	3.55	-1.54	-2.25	1.66	1.72	0.73	6
	P-value	0.0026	0.0004	0.1236	0.0246	0.0972	0.085	0.4678	0
PC3/GSCI	Coefficient	0.4742	1.2345	0.4623	4.6786	0.9387	0.9859	0.6223	1.4258
	Standard error	0.1089	0.1369	2.1775	2.2343	0.5143	0.3099	0.2243	0.2323
	Z-statistic	4.36	9.02	0.21	2.09	1.83	3.18	2.77	6.14
	P-value	0	0	0.8319	0.0363	0.068	0.0015	0.0055	0
PC3/SC600	Coefficient	0.8394	1.2777	1.4383	31.3582	0.9465	0.8991	1.0072	1.3529
	Standard error	0.115	0.2566	2.1758	7.7152	0.3195	0.3452	13.9138	0.4904
	Z-statistic	7.3	4.98	0.66	4.06	2.96	2.6	0.07	2.76
	P-value	0	0	0.5086	0	0.0031	0.0092	0.9423	0.0058
PC4/GSCI	Coefficient	0.9112	1.2406	-7.6743	6.1992	0.8843	0.861	0.8179	1.7135
	Standard error	0.118	0.276	2.2306	5.9722	0.3285	0.3619	0.5302	0.3649
	Z-statistic	7.72	4.49	-3.44	1.04	2.69	2.38	1.54	4.7
	P-value	0	0	0.0006	0.2993	0.0071	0.0173	0.1229	0
PC4/SC600	Coefficient	0.7488	3.813	11.4778	-37.684	0.9409	0.412	0.9578	0.9389
	Standard error	0.0854	0.5134	1.9607	16.172	0.1817	0.9257	1.6571	4.5243
	Z-statistic	8.77	7.43	5.85	-2.33	5.18	0.45	0.58	0.21
	P-value	0	0	0	0.0198	0	0.6563	0.5633	0.8356
PC4/W5000	Coefficient	1.3653	0.9038	-15.4912	17.293	0.9583	0.9893	0.8197	1.2662
	Standard error	0.1413	0.1498	3.1131	4.1038	0.2946	0.48	0.542	0.2984
	Z-statistic	9.66	6.03	-4.98	4.21	3.25	2.06	1.51	4.24
	P-value	0	0	0	0	0.0011	0.0393	0.1304	0

Source: Data from Carol Alexander and Anca Dimitriu, "Markov Switching Models for PC2-PC4 Portfolios," table in "The Art of Investing in Hedge Funds: Fund Selection and Optimal Allocations," January 2004, Electronic Public Social Science Research Network Library (www.ssrn.com).

In conclusion, it is difficult to have an adequate model that satisfies all the features of hedge fund risks. Traditional performance measures such as the Sharpe ratio do not account for hedge fund risks, and they poorly inform investors about risk-adjusted performance. Multifactor models give a good estimate of alpha, but they fail to properly account for the specific characteristics of hedge funds (dynamic and nonlinear exposure to risk factors). Glosten and Jagannathan's (1994) contingent claim approach attempted to capture nonlinear exposure to risk factors through the use of options. (See Tables 7.13 through 7.18.)

TABLE 7.13 Comparison of Betas or Market Correlation Coefficients from Multinomial Model over Given Time Period

Variable	Liquidated—Closed	Liquidated—No Reporting	Closed—No Reporting
Intercept	0.976	0.1237	−0.8523
Under a quarter	−0.1056	−0.081	0.0246
Within a year	0.3008	0.1808	−0.1199
Within two years	0.3137	0.5427	0.229
Alpha (Quarter)	−0.3054	−0.0704	0.235
Alpha (Year)	3.2782	0.9488	−2.3293
Age	−0.0793	0.0414	0.1207
Standard Deviation	0.0391	0.0006	−0.0385

Source: Data from Fabrice Rouah, "Competing Risks in Hedge Fund Survival," working paper, McGill University, Montreal, 2005; Foundation for Managed Derivatives Research (FMDR), Institut de Finance Mathématique de Montréal (IFM2), and Centre de Recherche en E-finance (CREF). Paper also published in the public domain of the Social Science Research Network.

TABLE 7.14 Hazard Ratios from the Cox Proportional Hazards Model under Competing Risks and with Time-Dependent Covariates, 1994–2003

Assumptions

Hazard ratios estimated for each exit type under different competing risks.

Minimum investments are assumed in $M. Avg_AUM (t) and StdDev_AUM (t) are in $100 millions.

A hazard ratio greater than 1 increases the risk of failure while a hazard ratio less than 1 decreases the risk of failure.

For each variable the p-value is from a likelihood ratio (LR) test that the covariate is identical with various exit types where the LR is obtained from only that variable included in the model. For all variables included the LR test p-value is < 0.0001.

	Liquidated	Closed	No Reporting	All Exits	LR p-value
Mean Return 1 Year	0.904	0.918	0.959	0.931	0.0007
Standard Deviation 1 Year	1.031	0.964	1.013	1.022	0.6838
High-Water Mark	1.716	1.062	1.03	1.238	0.0213
Hurdle	0.253	0.165	0.248	0.236	0.301
Incentive Fees	1.013	1.022	1.019	1.016	0.7831
Management Fees	0.863	0.976	0.857	0.881	0.0564
Time-Dependent Mean Return (t) and Time-Dependent Standard Deviation	0.939	1.035	0.946	0.977	0.1236
Avg_AUM (t)	0.634	0.587	0.994	0.91	<0.0001
StdDev_AUM (t)	1.243	1.085	1.019	1.058	0.0837

Source: Data from Fabrice Rouah, "Competing Risks in Hedge Fund Survival," working paper, McGill University, Montreal, 2005; Foundation for Managed Derivatives Research (FMDR), Institut de Finance Mathématique de Montréal (IFM2), and Centre de Recherche en E-finance (CREF). Paper also published in the public domain of the Social Science Research Network.

TABLE 7.15 Hazard Ratios from the Cox Model with Multiple Failure Types

	With Multiple Exit Types—Timing Restricted			
	Liquidated	Closed	No Reporting	LR p-value
Within a Quarter	1.285	1.672	1.349	0.0336
Within a Year	1.873	1.018	1.039	<0.0001
Within Two Years	1.669	0.849	0.565	<0.0001
Alpha (Quarter)	1.103	1.153	1.04	0.0332
Alpha (Year)	0.257	0.014	0.106	0.0003
Time	1.081	1.191	0.993	0.0135
Standard Deviation	1.068	1.045	1.074	<0.0001

	With Time-Dependent Covariates and Multiple Exit Types			
	Liquidated	Closed	No Reporting	LR p-value
Under (t)	3.809	1.405	1.4	<0.0001
Alpha (t)	0.94	0.101	0.895	<0.0001
Time	0.937	1.052	0.911	0.0135
StdDeviation (t)	1.001	1	1	0.8057

Source: Data from Fabrice Rouah, "Competing Risks in Hedge Fund Survival," working paper, McGill University, Montreal, 2005; Foundation for Managed Derivatives Research (FMDR), Institute de Finance Mathématique de Montréal (IFM2), and Centre de Recherch en E-finance (CREF). Paper also published in the public domain of the Social Science Research Network.

TABLE 7.16   Mean Survival Time of Hedge Funds by Style and Size, 1994–2003

Assumptions
Estimated mean survival time in years with +/– prorated standard error.
Large and small hedge funds are those with mean assets over the 1994–2003
  periods that are above and below the median assets of all hedge funds with
  the same style.
The log rank p-value is for the Log Rank test for equality of the survival functions
  between large and small funds.
Survival time is defined as the time until exit from the database, all exits
  aggregated.

All Exits	All Funds Mean	S.E. +/–	Large Funds Mean	S.E. +/–	Small Funds Mean	S.E. +/–
Convertible Arbitrage	5.19	0.17	5.38	0.19	4.76	0.33
Distressed Securities	4.38	0.22	5.11	0.21	3.73	0.32
Emerging Markets	5.18	0.20	5.80	0.24	4.55	0.30
Equity Hedge	6.89	0.16	7.69	0.20	5.60	0.20
Equity Market Neutral	5.46	0.26	6.40	0.32	3.36	0.19
Equity Non-Hedge	5.10	0.27	5.81	0.36	3.50	0.22
Event Driven	5.62	0.21	6.24	0.22	4.62	0.29
Fixed Income	5.91	0.23	6.52	0.29	5.44	0.38
Funds of Funds	7.10	0.13	6.82	0.10	5.97	0.21
Market Timing	4.50	0.33	4.89	0.43	3.62	0.38
Merger Arbitrage	4.85	0.23	5.11	0.28	3.65	0.23
Relative Value Arbitrage	6.18	0.38	5.39	0.27	5.55	0.52
Sector	4.79	0.19	5.43	0.25	3.88	0.23
Short Selling	3.83	0.26	4.14	0.29	2.12	0.11
All Funds	6.55	0.07	7.47	0.10	5.37	0.10

Source: Data from Fabrice Rouah, "Competing Risks in Hedge Fund Survival,"
working paper, McGill University, Montreal, 2005; Foundation for Managed Derivatives Research (FMDR), Institut de Finance Mathématique de Montréal
(IFM2), and Centre de Recherche en E-finance (CREF). Paper also published in the
public domain of the Social Science Research Network.

TABLE 7.17   Estimates of Median Survival Time from AFT Weibull Model under Given Risks and Assumptions for the Scenarios, 1994–2003

Assumptions:

Estimates of median survival time for hedge funds with the following assumptions:

Fund 1 has mean and standard deviation of returns for the last 12 months of observation of 1% and 2%, no high-water marks or hurdle rate, with incentive and management fee of 20% and 1%, minimum investment of $500K, and mean and standard deviation of assets over the last 12 months of observation of $500K each.

Fund 2 is identical to Fund 1, except that its incentive fee is 10% instead of 20%.

Fund 3 has mean and standard deviation of returns over the last 12 months of observation of 1% and 5%, a high-water mark and a hurdle rate, with incentive and management fees of 35% and 1%, minimum investment of $250K, mean and standard deviation of assets over the last 12 months of observation of $250M each.

Fund 4 is identical to Fund 3 without hurdle rate.

	All Exits	No Reporting	Liquidation	Closed
Median Survival Time for Fund 1	2.7 years	3.9 years	6.7 years	7.6 years
Median Survival Time for Fund 2	3.1 years	4.5 years	7.4 years	9.3 years
Median Survival Time for Fund 3	5.4 years	8.6 years	9.5 years	20.9 years
Median Survival Time for Fund 4	2.1 years	3.4 years	4.0 years	6.6 years

Note: To translate this table, we can assume that Fund 1 under the described assumptions would close in 7.6 years, would be in liquidation in 6.7 years, would no longer be reporting after 3.9 years, or would exit after 2.7 years.

Source: Data from Fabrice Rouah, "Competing Risks in Hedge Fund Survival," working paper, McGill University, Montreal, 2005; Foundation for Managed Derivatives Research (FMDR), Institut de Finance Mathématique de Montréal (IFM2), and Centre de Recherche en E-finance (CREF). Paper also published in the public domain of the Social Science Research Network.

TABLE 7.18 Accelerated Failure Time (AFT) from Weibull Regression Model under Competing Risks, 1994–2003

Model for survival time *T* is a function of regression coefficient. Mean return and standard deviation return are mean and standard deviation of returns expressed as a percent during the last 12 months of observations. High-water mark and hurdle rate, incentive fees, and management fees are expressed in percent; minimum investment is expressed in $100K; mean AUM and standard deviation AUM are mean and standard deviation of assets under management expressed in $millions during the last 12 months of observations.

Variable	Liquidation	Closed	No Reporting	All Exits
Intercept	2.1127	2.4588	1.9135	1.5143
Mean Return	0.0292	0.0231	−0.0038	0.0119
Standard Deviation Return	−0.0082	0.0328	0.0026	−0.0033
High-Water Mark	−0.2207	0.1497	0.0228	−0.0476
Hurdle Rate	0.8601	1.1502	0.9248	0.9235
Incentive Fee	−0.0103	−0.0202	−0.0139	−0.0131
Management Fee	−0.0413	−0.1304	0.0282	−0.034
Minimum Investment	0.0014	−0.0013	0.0021	0.0006
Mean AUM	0.0016	0.0007	0.0001	0.0006
Standard Deviation AUM	−0.0011	−0.0001	−0.0003	−0.0006
Scale Parameter	0.5819	0.59	0.5996	0.5925

Source: Data from Fabrice Rouah, "Competing Risks in Hedge Fund Survival," working paper, McGill University, Montreal, 2005; Foundation for Managed Derivatives Research (FMDR), Institut de Finance Mathématique de Montréal (IFM2), and Centre de Recherche en E-finance (CREF). Paper also published in the public domain of the Social Science Research Network.

SYSTEMIC RISK

Chan et al. (2004) investigated the relationship between hedge funds and systemic risk. Systemic risk is defined as the series of correlated defaults among financial institutions that occur over a short period of time. It is assessed that the collection of debacles comes from one event or one major sizable financial crisis such as the default of the Russian government debt in August 1998 or the failure of the large hedge fund Long-Term Capital Management. Chan et al. (2004) quantified the potential impact of hedge funds on systemic risk by developing a number of new risk measures for hedge funds and applying them to individual and aggregate hedge-fund returns data. The results led to the conclusion that the hedge fund industry is going to experience lower expected returns, and that systemic risk is increasing.

INSURANCE AND HEDGE FUNDS

Since 2005, captive insurance purposes and financial schemes have been of concern to insurance regulators very much like hedge funds have been of concern to financial industry regulators. Assuming human nature will someday change and that greed will somehow be controllable and capped, financial captives might be used in the future to enhance transparencies in reconciliation between the premium assigned for specific types of risks (Basel Accords: a revised framework 2004) and claims surging from random operational losses attached to these types of risks. In the meantime, they are used to benefit from unregulated geographies and supposedly used to isolate special risks such as technology or credit.

Financial captives exist to benefit from low regulatory environments to sample a parent company's risks into a smaller framework in order to hide inherent risks and obtain better credit ratings from supposedly independent agencies. Large insurance companies have approximately 163 financial captives, all of which are located in tax havens. There is anticipation that regulators will use insurance captives as structural vehicles to evaluate the adequate level of capital for companies. If used for rating purposes, captive insurance shell companies ought to be more appropriately structured and verified by third-party agencies. Similarly, in trends and the evolution of financial markets, regulators might use hedge funds as shells to crystallize inherent risks of larger financial structures and to evaluate transparencies and financial capital adequacies of financial institutions.

Due to the lack of regulation within the hedge fund industry, many smaller hedge funds have not been legally structured with brokers to clear and settle trades. Now, more and more hedge funds are getting brokers to perform such services and to also sustain credit risks when counterparties to hedge funds default. Brokers have generated high fees recently from hedge fund business. Yet operational risks between hedge fund operations and brokers have seldom been audited and monitored. This is mostly due to the fact that risk managers have to have more freedom to access both sides (brokers' and hedge fund managers' information) in order to audit and rate states of operations.

Hedge funds lightly started to buy insurance in 2004 and 2005 to protect traders and hedge fund managers against potential lawsuits from investors. Seldom have hedge funds purchased insurance as part of an operational risk policy to protect investors.

This type of insurance policy does not exist as of yet within the larger financial institutions as part of a larger operational risk strategy and not at all within the hedge fund world. Large financial institutions had collected information on operational risks from 2002 to 2006 in databases such as Horizon or Phoenix in order to then model off-balance-sheet or discretionary financial reserves to allocate capital for each of these operational risks. The contribution of the insurance companies in the financial markets is the application of actuarial models given claims and losses databases by industries. Banks are now globally absorbing credit exposures of all types and need such frameworks in order to model operational losses by industry. The quantification of losses given databases' results is yet to be evaluated. Each country seems to contribute in one way or another to the intellectual formation of a model to assess capital risk by industry.

TECHNOLOGY AND SYSTEM RISK

Hedge fund managers started entrepreneurial hedge fund operations in the early 1990s and have grown ever since. Elite traders from large financial corporations left the banks to start entrepreneurial endeavors—that is, trading for their own accounts. So, hedge funds began with very small operations and very little sophistication in terms of technology and systems. The originality and exoticism of the trading strategies was also difficult to model into technological infrastructures. Most traders had imported their models from Excel spreadsheets or Access from the large banks. Many hedge fund managers have internal intranets for communication, and they use Excel and Access as the main tools to calculate risks, but their operations have only started to develop on a more technologically advanced level since 2002.

A few very large hedge fund managers had advanced technologies with appropriate infrastructures during the 1990s, but they represented a minority. Risk management scenarios, value at risk, and sophisticated stress testing can be adequately and qualitatively measured only with sophisticated technological tools. Operational risk arises from failures in technologies, systems, and process risks. Hedge funds mostly outsourced risk management reports and processes with broker-dealers. Operational risk audits in hedge funds have shown that risks replicated by outsourced broker-dealers' web site reports are incomplete and lack other trading activities performed by traders in offshore locations. In some instances, the deficiencies can be revealed by differential exposures between onshore and offshore trading accounts.

FIDUCIARY RISK

A fiduciary is a person or entity that is empowered to hold the assets of another. A fiduciary relationship requires responsibility, knowledge, expertise, trust, good faith, and honesty. The fiduciary also has the obligation to act in the best interests of the client and to avoid conflicts of interest if a situation arises that has a potential benefit to the individual or entity acting as the fiduciary.

CAPACITY AND GROWTH SIZE MONITORING

Hedge funds have developed and exponentially grown in size, in trade sophistication, and in number globally. (See Figure 7.1.) The growth potential produced increases in size along with popularity. Many hedge funds' inflated returns have also been correlated to these upward trends. Subtly and gradually, regulators produced a library of hedge fund litigations and compliance cases since 2002 in order to implement required compliance registration with the SEC as of February 2006.

This correlation phenomenon between the increasing number of hedge funds in size, capacity, and returns has been also experienced with a

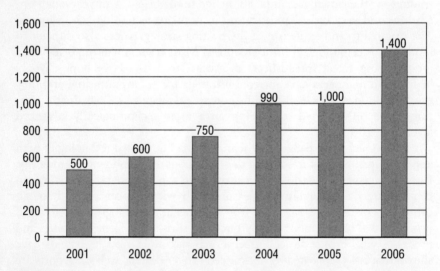

FIGURE 7.1   Hedge Fund Asset Growth from 2001 to 2006 (Estimation in USD Millions)
Source: Data from *Bloomberg Markets*, January 2006.

fundamental product: commodities. When studying commodities markets, we notice that the increase of commodity futures contracts has been directly correlated with the parallel rise in hedge funds. The prices of commodities (crude oil and gold) have also increased at an exponential rate in correlation with the exponential growth in the number of hedge funds and their respective sizes. It is at this point difficult to define how much of this growth is due to pure hedge fund growth and how much is due to the pure increase in demand from new emerging markets such as India and China. (See Figures 7.2 and 7.3.)

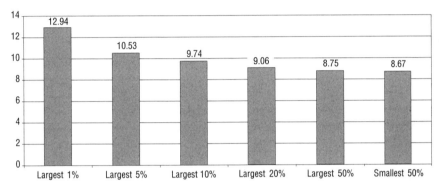

FIGURE 7.2 Hedge Fund Sizes for Equally Weighted, Live and Dead, without Historical Data Filling in Percent, as of March 2004
Source: Data from *Bloomberg Markets*, January 2006.

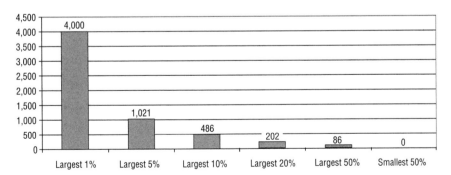

FIGURE 7.3 Assets under Management in $Millions, March 2004
Source: Data from *Bloomberg Markets*, January 2006.

TRANSPARENCY AND COMMUNICATION

Since 2002, transparency and communication in hedge funds have improved. More hedge funds include returns on asset values in their web sites, and they provide more detailed risk management information. Before trading through a hedge fund's web site, most funds require that investors sign a contractual agreement absolving the fund of all responsibility for potential losses. Most hedge funds do not provide insurance on losses and none guarantee reimbursements of fees and minimum costs.

Due to significant and large financial losses, hedge funds have been forced to become clearer and more open about risk reporting. Disclosures have been more detailed and dispatched to more parties. Levels of responsibility are better described to investors prior to their investing into hedge funds.

Prior to 2002, only a few privileged employees had access to traders' positions and prices, whereas after 2002, regulators brought many compliance cases in order to implement forward-looking laws aimed at reducing anarchy in the markets. Parts of the compliance also forced hedge fund managers to become more conservative and open to investors and third parties.

VERIFICATION OF FEES

Few hedge funds communicate their policies with regard to generation of fees. Hedge funds' fees policies are not quantified with standardized models, and they are not transparently disclosed. Very often, fees can be scalable but the scalable framework is seldom clearly described. Most of the time, fees are negotiated between the fund managers and the investors. There are discounts and breaks from the general rules in terms of lockup periods, management fees, and incoming and exit fees. Until recently, these decisions have been made based on the size of the investments, the risk levels (for illiquid markets such as real estate, funds of funds fees tend to be higher), and/or the relationships between the hedge manager and the investors.

If the hedge fund has a unique strategy and operates with innovative products in new markets, fees tend to be higher than normal. More specifically, if the investor is large and/or institutional, the investor obtains special discounts on the fee structures. Still, often the fee structure is decided randomly on a negotiation basis.

One fundamental example of improvement within the financial markets with regard to fee descriptions and disclosures is experienced by the large financial investment banks. In 2002, to respond to conflict of interest and the abnormalities of fee generation trends, they have mathematically implemented objective formulas and models to justify the calculation of

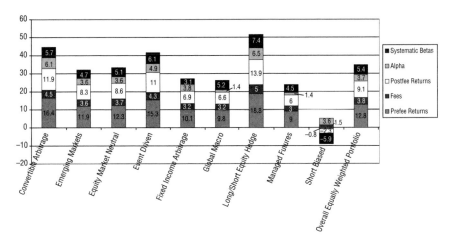

FIGURE 7.4 Hedge Funds' Sources of Risks and Returns by Trading Strategies, 1995–2004, in Percent

Source: Data from *Bloomberg Markets*, January 2006.

fees. Hedge fund fees are objectively set, but they often experience exceptions depending on the clients. (See Figure 7.4.)

TASS databases on about 2,000 funds reported fee schedules for the distribution of management fees and incentive fees from 1990 to 1997. (See Table 7.19.)

TABLE 7.19 Fee Schedules for Distribution of Hedge Fund Management Fees and Incentive Fees, 1990–1997

Management Fees	TASS Hedge Funds	TASS CTAs
NA	4%	13%
0–1%	38%	4%
1–2%	40%	53%
2–3%	10%	16%
3–4%	6%	12%
4–5%	0%	0%
5–8% (max)	2%	1%

Incentive Fees	TASS Hedge Funds	TASS CTAs
NA	17%	1%
0–5%	1%	0%
5–10%	6%	1%
10–15%	14%	10%
15–20%	51%	69%
20–25%	10%	16%
25–55% (max)	1%	3%

Source: Data from TASS Database, eLibrary, www.ssrn.com.

CONFLICT OF INTEREST AND SPECIAL NETWORKS

Hedge funds grew tremendously with the rise of the equity market in the late 1990s. They were primarily created by elite traders who had access to high-net-worth individuals who belonged to the same classes, the same school clubs, and/or same job positions. They left the large financial institutions to create their own "banking dot-com" businesses and trade the market's various products. They invented new strategies and produced phenomenal returns. With those returns, more of their acquaintances pooled together to create more capacity to trade.

Special networks are private country clubs, organizations with special membership requirements, privileged schools, and so on. These clubs build relationships in order to maintain their connections and the power surrounding them. Special forums, events, meetings, and speaking arrangements in front of groups are produced to attract similar relationships and maintain or increase social class status. The Ivy League schools in the United States or Les Grandes Ecoles in France, for example, produce events to keep alumni connected with each other and to keep them in the elite network to maintain the schools' rankings and supposed values. Yet some lesser-known schools have produced better informed individuals with harder work. The use of nepotism to protect specific classes and especially within the hedge fund world has been obvious. And thus by word of mouth, a few years ago many significant investors from these privileged networks shifted from investing in large financial institutions to hedge funds.

Employees' work history is usually kept in a database in order to track any conflict of interest with knowledgeable employees about material transactions that could interfere with the risk management of such transactions vis-à-vis third parties such as regulators. Only in the United States have regulators created a form to report such relationships in large corporations.

Another example of conflict of interest is when the same employees perform trading and pricing verifications of sizable transactions without an independent set of eyes to check accuracy and integrity. There also is conflict of interest when an employee is well connected with regulators, political contributors, and lobbyist groups who communicate proprietary information prior to placing trades.

Conflict of interest occurs when the risk manager of a large hedge fund is also the risk manager of the funds of funds it is supposed to manage or if the risk manager is personally highly invested in knowledgeable positions of its own hedge funds. Compliance officers started to enforce compliance registration with the SEC as of February 2006. Hedge fund managers are not allowed to trade positions for their personal accounts if they hold those same positions in their portfolios. They would invest in other hedge funds to avoid conflict of interest.

The risk manager is paid to disclose actual risks, not hide risks to keep his or her job. The true risk manager works for investors, not for management. This type of position description was altered in 2002 when the Financial Accounting Standards Board disclosed new policies with regard to conflict of interest (Sarbanes-Oxley 404). Family relationships and close networks are usually checked as part of clearance and background checks prior to starting a job at a hedge fund.

EXPENSES MONITORING

This report describes business expenses incurred by a hedge fund's employees, by management, and by the board of directors. This report also highlights limits of gifts to clients and investors and any kind of implicit and explicit expenses that could suggest conflict of interest. Gifts usually do not exceed $100 due to conflict of interest issues. Entertainment expenses of clients and investors are reported and signed off by the employees initiating the expenses and by management. Proofs of expenses should be attached to reports. In many hedge funds, marketers carry a business credit card to absorb the special entertainment expenses for clients. Companies' gifts to third parties are in the report, as are expenses for yearly parties. Limits of gift values are described in this type of report.

SPECIAL RESERVES FOR DISCREPANCIES AND VARIANCES

The finance department sets various types of financial reserves. Financial reserves are to help the hedge fund managers cover the risks described earlier. Most reserves are for abnormal losses and unusual types of risks in hedge funds. For example, they can be used for developing of sophisticated financial models with low market liquidity, special structured products seldom traded, or operational risks. The evolution of markets with technology, compliance, and other methodologies tends to transform traditional discretionary financial reserves into transparent modeled operational risk reserves. They are quantified as part of insurance reserves and forecasted over time horizons.

ELECTRONIC REPORTING OF POLICIES AND PROCEDURES

The hedge fund risk manager implements policies and procedures to document internal risk management practices. He or she is responsible for formulating the trading contracts to ensure that trading of transactions is performed according to regulations. Trading term sheets are also kept by risk management in order to enforce conditions met on the initial trading contracts. This documentation process is usually automated in larger financial institutions but remains very manual in hedge funds. A sophisticated high-performance risk management team sometimes creates libraries of term sheets of trades in order to maintain trades' details in records. Many companies without such libraries started to automate and scan trade documents in the late 1990s.

Risk management departments often maintain databases of trade documents to verify randomly that risk factors are appropriately replicated in the trading systems. For example, for large trades or sophisticated trades, risk management independently takes parameters of the term sheet and enters them into the trading system to verify that risks are accurately replicated and reported by the trader. Most hedge funds have established documentation policies and procedures for all trades.

As hedge funds grow larger, risk management departments have to be more prepared to obtain technological tools to perform as well and be as compliant as the competitive financial institutions. Hedge fund risk managers have to establish documentation requirements for all trading strategies and activities, including confirmation requirements and documentation of master agreements. These term sheets agreements are also entered into the databases with all trades' details relevant to collateral and credit risk information. Term sheets include signatures of traders and document trade parameters information and signatures of higher-level managers and counterparty managers as well.

For example, a hedge fund manager may seek to negotiate standardized events of default and other termination or collateral events to achieve consistency in documentation with different counterparties to the extent practicable. A hedge fund manager may also endeavor to avoid including provisions that permit counterparties to terminate or make demands for collateral solely at their discretion or based on highly subjective determinations. In case of credit downgrades, these documents are used by compliance officers as a basis to negotiate bilateral collateral agreements and actual assets valuations. Stress testing results, risk management scenarios, and pricing verification parameters can be inserted into term sheets. Usually term sheets include payoff formulas and terms of the trades but rarely mention other risks. Contractual agreements include detailed information on the rights of the counterparties. The document includes trading relationships, along with increases in margin and collateral requirements upon the occurrence of certain events, such as a sudden decrease in net asset valuations. The hedge fund risk manager ensures that trading contractual agreements are kept up to date with all third parties and that any changes in trading mandates are updated in an agreement with the involved parties and signed by management. As hedge funds continue to become more regulated, they will have to enhance their internal documentation processes and databases to keep trade information up to date.

Best practices would ideally require hedge fund managers to have internal electronic technological systems or platforms that are linked to a brokerage's database risk reports and linked to offshore administrative agents in order to reconcile all parties' reports on a daily basis and accurately define net asset values. Aside from this, it would also be ideal to have an operational risk database that historically collects all audits' issues and operational breakdowns and gaps.

Electronic documentation of policies and procedures includes the business contingency plan information. Hedge fund risk management establishes a business contingency plan as part of the company's overall policy and procedure. The business contingency plan serves as a guideline to maintain business continuity in case of catastrophic circumstances affecting the daily operations of the hedge funds. The plan is a backup strategy to maintain operations and business as usual in case of emergencies and to prevent large financial losses. It ensures that trading and middle office operations are maintained when business disruption occurs. The risk manager establishes business continuity with call tree orders to contact all the employees to ensure they are all able to function and maintain their positions to continue the hedge fund's daily operations. The most important points include contact list of all the employees and third parties.

The business contingency plan also includes technological backups to ensure and maintain daily operations. Since most of the risk management reports are generated by the outsourced prime brokers, many hedge fund managers rely on the prime brokers to maintain risk reports and basic risk management operations. The business contingency plan also ensures the backing-up or copying of essential documents and data and storing the information in hard copy or electronic format.

The business contingency plan also consists of establishing backup facilities to maintain the hedge fund's trading activities in another geographical area. Larger hedge funds rely on branches located in other countries or continents. The business contingency plan is reviewed by all the departments of the hedge fund and tested a few times a year to ensure its adequacy. Contingency planning ensures that communication to third parties and outside regulators is being performed well. Business contingency planning transfers daily tasks to backup clearing systems, credit providers, and other service and backup providers.

In conclusion, ideally risk managers ought to have the knowledge of all the risks and somehow be able to control them. However, in very few hedge funds are all those risks monitored, controlled, and enforced. The following chapter describes the minimum standards to apply a basic risk management framework to capture the largest risk exposures and gives some recommendations to limit crises.

CHAPTER 8

Basic Risk Management
Standards and Recommendations

The following standards are basic given the list of risk types the preceding chapter has reviewed. Many hedge funds have applied risk management on the surface and can use the following recommendations to implement a basic framework. As hedge funds are only starting to become regulated as of February 2006, this chapter describes the minimum practices that a hedge fund risk manager should perform in order to be in compliance with regulators. Despite the fact that hedge funds have developed so much in scope and scale within the market, risk management as prevention of losses appears late and insufficient. The topics of this section are repetitive from the previous chapter but cover specific risks in more detail.

Liquidity risk is considered to be one of the main risks and has great impact on hedge funds and funds of funds. Leverage is another risk and is linked to liquidity. Leverage is the level of indebtedness and/or borrowing from the initial capital. It can also be considered as the size of the short positions compared to the overall net long positions. This chapter describes static leverage measures—both accounting-based and risk-based leverage measures. It also includes dynamic leverage measures that can provide additional information to the hedge fund risk manager. During the 1990s, hedge funds had relied solely on brokers to assume credit risk coverage. Because hedge funds generally deal with counterparties having high credit quality, the credit risk of counterparties may be of less concern to hedge fund managers than the other sources of risk, but nonetheless it should be appropriately monitored.

Effective risk management requires that the hedge fund risk manager understands the trading strategies, the traders' behavior, and the level of risks in prices and in positions. The hedge fund risk manager is to determine the various sources of risks and assign some guidelines around these sources to improve the risk monitoring function. The risk manager is to identify and quantify the risk. Due to the fast-paced evolution of risk management since the 1990s, there are three main types of distinguished risks: market risk, credit risk, and operational risk. It is important to note that all three are highly correlated as main products in the markets. Yet their interrelationships are not as obvious as they used to be since new strategies and new innovative products have appeared. For instance, we believe that in the 1990s, the old economical models of the twentieth century were still valid and prevailed, and thus trends between interest rates and equities were logical and explainable.

It is also thought that market risk was the main risk during the equity bubble as many risks were calculated based on the mark-to-market value of the trades. Greek risk reporting (delta, gamma, vega, theta, beta, alpha) allowed explanations of main profits and losses in large financial institutions. The equity derivatives and structured products markets grew very sophisticated and ventured into other products such as corporate bonds, high-yield securities, credit derivatives, and even physical products such as commodities. With this growth, market risk merged into credit risk as many options and derivatives positions were unreconcilable and considered equivalent as debt or short positions. In many cases, it became more expensive to hedge a trade than to leave it naked. This is how suddenly, in the span of a few years, market risk became a mature form of phenomena within risk management in general and credit risk became a predominant form of risk management.

Credit risk and the shortening of positions on downgradable companies, along with external and internal company events and technological and system risks, have produced a new kind of risk: operational risk.

Operational risk remains very embryonic as it is being implemented mostly in banks and is still at the level of data collection. The magnitude of operational risk in time and scope and scale remains unknown and difficult to model. Part of the difficulty for modeling such risk is due to the fast-paced progress of risk management evolution and the lack of correlational knowledge between the different types of risks throughout risk management historical evolution.

Other industries did not go far in managing risks when market risk was at its peak in the late 1990s. Only recently have hedge fund risk managers started to become more transparent about risk descriptions and trading strategies. Hedge fund risk managers are just now recognizing that market risk incorporates elements of credit risk and liquidity risk. The correlation factors and relationships remain unclear.

Hedge fund risk managers have contented themselves with reporting top concentrated risk positions to investors in terms of Greeks. But sometimes risk managers in funds of funds have not had access to subfunds' prices and positions. They became more interested in market risk in hedge funds and started to focus more on the impact of changes in the prices of (or rates for) securities and derivatives, the volatilities of those prices, and the correlations between pairs of prices on the value of the portfolio rather than on simplistic reporting of top concentrated positions.

Part of the integration of hedge funds within the global economic and market framework consists of understanding the elements of liquidity risk and credit risk that have similar focus. The domino effect of specific risk is to be considered also between liquidity and credit risks. Changes in liquidity impact the value of a security or derivative. This element of liquidity risk is sometimes referred to as asset or market liquidity risk. Because these focus explicitly on changes in the value of an asset or a portfolio, hedge fund risk managers integrate their monitoring and management.

The hedge fund risk manager now oversees credit risk, market risks such as liquidity risk, interest rate risk, foreign exchange rate risk, equity price risk, and commodity price risk. Unlike larger financial institutions, hedge funds do not have the ability to raise capital immediately and/or to obtain credit risk limits as flexibly. Their short-term financing capabilities are also more limited as they do not have a repurchase agreement desk to maintain overnight and/or short-term positions.

Hedge funds might become more liquid in the sense that their size or capacity gives them access to special deals and/or relationships with larger financial institutions to sustain liquidity.

Leverage in hedge funds is one of the most important risks primarily due to the fact that it has never been really enforced. It is another source of risks dependent on other types of risks. The level of correlations between leverage and market risk, credit risk, or liquidity risk factors has never been assessed. Until recently each risk has been considered independent and isolated from every other. This has in larger financial institutions caused more expensive cost of capital as well. It is now believed that the higher the level of quantification and modeling of risks, the lower the cost of capital. But without human senses and perception of risks as well, it is difficult to assess the true cost of capital of a large fund. Leverage in hedge funds can also be calculated with a single leverage number, although alone it may not contain very much information. A risk-reducing transaction can increase some leverage measures while decreasing others. The liquidity or price volatility of the position being leveraged is relevant to assessing effective leverage.

The leverage employed by a fund that holds one-year Treasury bills with 10:1 leverage may be of less concern than that employed by a fund levered 2:1 with respect to the S&P 500 index. A hedge fund's capacity to absorb losses is called its funding liquidity. Leverage is measured relative to a fund's capacity to absorb losses. A fund having a higher level of accounting-based leverage is less risky than a less leveraged hedge fund with low cash positions, limited borrowing capacity, or investors who can withdraw their funds on short notice. Leverage can also be affected by volatility, liquidity, market risk variables, and correlations factors.

Credit risk in return changes the landscape of market risk. Hedge fund risk managers are also exposed to counterparty credit risk. This occurs when hedge fund traders have put on trading positions that they cannot unwind unless they take major losses due to the initial price being lowered due to the rating downgrade the company has taken. Many hedge funds have found themselves with defaulted or junk counterparties on their books because they did not unwind the trades prior to the downgrades or they had entered long-term trading agreements with the counterparties. Hedge fund risk managers have to wait for companies to restructure to regain returns from initial positions and prices. While the restructuring of many companies is currently taking place, hedge funds are also subjected to additional costs such as data entry errors, fraud, system failures, and errors in valuation or risk measurement models.

Hedge fund risk managers have established a framework to evaluate the risk of loss for a trading strategy. In order for the hedge fund risk manager to be able to manage the risks that hedge funds face, the risk management department produces procedures, policies, and tools to review risks. Hedge fund risk managers are aware of the structural limitations of the model selected and actively manage these limitations, including the impact of any model breakdown.

Hedge fund risk managers break down risks by positions and geographical time zones to better analyze strategies. In larger institutions, risks are limited by geographical areas and borrowed from one region to another if a trader wishes to take on more risks in one geographical region than another. By segregating risks geographically and at a granular positional level, hedge fund managers can also have more transparency to estimate direct or indirect relationships between strategies and they can calculate correlations. It is more challenging to reflect market risks and correlation risks for complex portfolios and structured products.

VALUE AT RISK

One of the most used market risk methodologies in the 1990s was value at risk (VaR). VaR measures the maximum change in the value of the portfolio that would be expected at a specified confidence level over a specified holding period. For example, if the 95 percent confidence level, one-day VaR for a portfolio is $1,000,000, gain or loss would be more than $1,000,000 in only 5 of every 100 trading days on average. Risk managers review trading strategies and attempt to define an adequate VaR level in order to give traders a limit on risk taking.

Value at risk can be designed by trading strategies and by geographical areas. Market risk models include specific components in order to create a risk management framework around VaR. The components of the risk management framework are: equities prices, interest rate term structure of foreign exchange level and shape, foreign exchange rates, commodities prices, credit spreads, nonlinearities, volatilities, and correlations. Risk management also includes asset liquidity, such as the potential exposure to loss attributable to changes in the liquidity of the market in which the asset is traded as an additional factor. Risk management calculates asset liquidity in various ways using the following patterns: the number of days that would be required to liquidate and/or neutralize the position in question and the value that would be lost if the asset in question were to be liquidated and/or neutralized completely within such period.

To implement VaR in a hedge fund, the risk manager must include parameters with respect to the hedge funds' internal positions and the market conditions. Value at risk can be implemented using different methodologies and, depending on the chosen methodology, it can require historical data such as prices, positions, and volatilities over a given period of time. One of the VaR calculation processes involves variance and covariance. The risk manager collects historical prices and volatilities for a given underlying asset class and the manager implements volatility or variance and correlation or covariance trends over time or a historical time frame for each position of the portfolio at a given date. The risk manager calculates the volatility estimate under the assumption that the returns for the trading strategy portfolio assume a normal distribution. This is the least process intensive and perhaps the easiest of the VaR methodologies.

Smaller hedge funds can implement such a framework in access databases, but as hedge fund capacity grows larger it is highly recommended that funds build a separate independent real-time technological VaR engine.

Another methodology is historical volatility. Under this approach a VaR portfolio generates daily profits and losses from historical data streams. The risk estimate is then set at the level consistent with the confidence interval selected for the analysis. Historical data requires large databases and appropriate infrastructures to generate VaR results. The largest hedge funds have invested in such databases but most of the smaller ones have not.

Under the Monte Carlo approach, the portfolio is repriced across large numbers of random observations that are consistent with the volatility history of the underlying instruments. Then again, the process of capturing the top 95 percent or 97 percent or 99 percent VaR consists of ranking those observations in ascending order by considering the nth loss in the distribution. The risk evaluation is then set at a level consistent with the applicable confidence interval. Historical Monte Carlo simulations are used for nonlinear correlations and trading strategies experiencing negative regressions. Monte Carlo simulations are used for more complex dynamic strategies, whereas historical simulations are used for simplistic linear methodologies and approaches. The time definition to simulate historical data is one of the most crucial factors. The time horizon or holding period should include actual market crisis events in order to be capturing meaningful and accurate statistics. Shorter time frames would not reflect reality as accurately as a longer time period.

Another important parameter is the confidence level, defined as the probability that the change in the value of the portfolio would exceed the VaR. For example, most confidence levels are 95 percent minimum, or 97 percent or 99 percent. Another significant factor is the volatility and the correlation, or the variance and covariance, respectively, of the data. The variance and covariance reflect the volatility of the underlying assets and their correlation between pairs of factors. VaR alone is not sufficient to capture risks of hedge funds, as VaR does not take into consideration correlations among products, strategies, and funds. Thus it is challenging to define a VaR limit for hedge funds given all the different strategies and products. In order to achieve such results, the hedge fund risk manager would have to have access to all risks at a granular positional level.

The time frame is the holding period necessary to capture the longest trade in the trader's book from its initiation until its maturity. Using this trade as the longest timed reference, VaR can capture all subsequent risks in connection with it. Short-term trades are more difficult to capture and they also tend to be smaller than longer-term structured trades. Normal risk management practice is to use standard holding periods of one day, three days, five days, and ten days in the base case. Depending on this timing reference, other simulated risk tests are performed consistent with this benchmark. Stress testing and scenario analysis are then adjusted according to this chosen standard. (See Figures 8.1 through 8.3.)

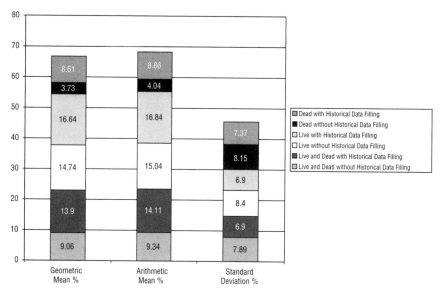

FIGURE 8.1 Equally Weighted Hedge Fund Returns, 1995–2004, in Percent
Source: Data from Yahoo! Finance.

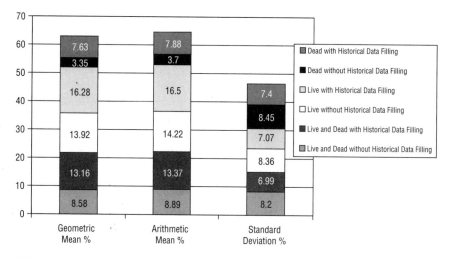

FIGURE 8.2 Equally Weighted Hedge Fund Returns with Assets under
Management, 1995–2004, in Percent
Source: Data from Yahoo! Finance.

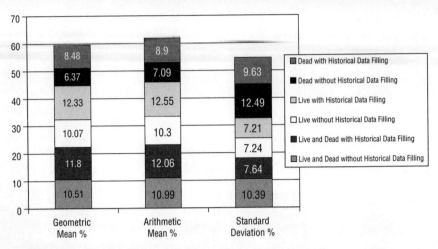

FIGURE 8.3 Value-Weighted Hedge Fund Returns, 1995–2004, in Percent
Source: Data from Yahoo! Finance.

CONFIDENCE LEVEL

Confidence level is not determined mathematically and is randomly chosen by the hedge fund manager and the risk manager. It is chosen depending on the circumstances surrounding the overall strategies of the hedge fund. It basically depends on the hedge funds. Some hedge funds use the 95 percent, 97 percent, or 99 percent level. It is rarer to use the 99 percent confidence interval. Any changes in usage of confidence level depend on the hedge fund's overall policy and procedures. But inconsistencies in confidence interval should be modified with appropriate justifications and quantitative supporting material to explain changes in policies and procedures.

With the growing importance of operational risks, hedge funds have adjusted confidence intervals in order to capture extreme event risks as well. Confidence intervals should be consistent with all calculations of VaR across asset classes, products, and strategies in order to make the overall aggregate VaR consistent with the overall calculations.

VARIANCE-COVARIANCE

Covariance data is very important as it captures linear and/or nonlinear relationships between a pair of assets' volatilities across a historical time frame. Correlation analysis is similar and assimilated to regression analysis. Many VaR models use historical correlations to define overall cost of capital. This element is also used to rate a hedge fund's credit quality. But very few hedge funds as of 2005 are rated and very few even have granular VaR levels by strategies and asset classes. Most of them have a random overall VaR.

A number of VaR models use historic correlation. However, since historic correlations are unstable, especially during periods of market stress, the hedge fund risk manager employs scenario analyses and stress testing to evaluate risk gaps and positional abnormalities with markets.

VaR alone is not sufficient to calculate overall risk management for the hedge fund. To obtain a better understanding of risk management overall, VaR is usually complemented with scenario analysis, stress testing, event risk testing, and back-testing simulations.

The risk management department of a hedge fund is responsible to implement VaR, scenario analysis, stress testing, event risk testing, and back-testing for each respective asset class (or product) and for each different trading strategy. Ideally, in funds of funds, risk management keeps a database of the positions' data and aggregates them into a centralized database in order to create new products based on the resulting risk management scenarios. Because there is low visibility of risks at a granular positional level in the funds of funds and lack of sophisticated infrastructures, it is more difficult to generate automated VaR, scenario analysis, stress testing, event risk testing, and back-testing simulations. Newly created products in the funds of funds are typically not submitted to such tests and are created based on returns of their decomposed assets.

The major downside of VaR is that it considers only one particular point of the distribution. Artzner et al. (1999) noted that VaR is not a coherent risk measure as it does not take into account the diversification effects. Conditional VaR or expected shortfall reflects this issue as it quantifies the expected loss given the fact that the loss is going to be exceeding the VaR level. Opposite from VaR, the expected shortfall is considered to be a more coherent risk measure. The estimation of VaR relies on three different variables: the target horizon, the confidence level, and the estimation model.

SKEWNESS-KURTOSIS AND COVARIANCE

Many hedge funds apply basic risk management VaR analysis of their portfolios, but a minority of them deepens quantitative risk management practices to extreme value at risk, covariance analysis, and skewness framework. Research has shown that many hedge funds exhibit significant skew and kurtosis and that a simple mean variance portfolio analysis is not adequate to measure dynamic trading strategies based on leveraged or derivatives positions. Portfolio diversification also has an impact on the outcome on skewness. Elton and Gruber (1977) and Conine and Tamarkin (1981) decomposed the mean variance methodology into a more precise mean-variance skewness-kurtosis theory to prove that the impact of portfolio or product diversification depends on each moment, co-moments, or covariance. Other researchers, such as Lai (1991), Chunhachinda et al. (1997), Sun and Yan (2003), Prakash et al. (2003), have pursued their work in integrating portfolio selection within the mean-variance-skewness framework. Consistent with Conine and Tamarkin (1981), skewness changes the entire risk picture of a hedge fund as more funds are added in the portfolio. In fact, the more added funds, the lower the skewness and the standard deviation. The hedge fund risk manager must balance the deterioration in skewness and the expected cost of managing (that is, buying or selling) an additional fund against the potential costs and benefits of reducing standard deviation and kurtosis.

Hedge fund strategies with higher market exposures such as global macro, long/short equity, and dedicated short bias exhibit higher average covariance consistent with higher correlations between funds. And hedge fund strategies with less exposures to the market such as convertible arbitrage and merger arbitrage have lower average covariance consistent with lower correlations between funds.

However, the implication of such combinations implies new types of implicit inherent risks such as systematic credit risk. This risk is lightly impacting correlation between funds. Equity market neutral funds exhibit the lowest average covariance and they have low systematic risk as market and industry exposures are netted out or neutralized via the offsetting of short and long positions.

Skewness risk exposure is reduced at a decreasing rate as the number of funds in the portfolio rises. Risk reduction from diversification within the same hedge fund strategy can be achieved by including 20 or more funds. In contrast, skewness continues to fall significantly as the number of funds in the portfolio approaches 30. So the breakeven point in gaining from both risk reduction and skewness or accepting a trade-off is important to consider in risk management of a diverse portfolio.

Strategies with negative expected skewness often also have high kurtosis or leptokurtosis, signaling high probability of extreme event variations. Merger arbitrage and distressed securities are examples of such strategies because merger arbitrage funds attempt to profit from the spread between the bid price from the acquirer and the ask price of the target after the deal is made public. If the deal fails, the fund is subject to the premium. This is similar to buying a call option and benefiting from the upside, but if not, losing only the premium cost of buying the option. Distressed securities funds can face losses if bought distressed exposures are further downgraded and thus the potential counterparty goes into bankruptcy. Agarwal and Naik (2004) named those strategies "short options"—strategies that have similar payoffs to writing an out-of-the-money put on an index.

Convertible arbitrage funds also have a short option with a known upside but an unknown downside risk. Global macro exhibits positive coskewness in consistency with the long option trading nature of the strategy. The low coskewness and high cokurtosis are fundamental characteristics of convertible arbitrage, distressed securities, and merger arbitrage funds. These funds also have in common a higher degree of collateral or credit risk.

Anson (2002) demonstrated that credit risk distributions tend to be more left-skewed and fat-tailed. Redemption risk has an effect on skewness and kurtosis risks, and so does bankruptcy or default risks. Intuitively, the higher the probability of redemptions, the greater the probability of default or bankruptcy, the lower the skewness coefficient, and the higher the kurtosis. In greater detail, Black (1976) and Christie (1982) demonstrated that there is a leverage effect explaining the economic interpretation behind the negative coskewness compounded by the positive cokurtosis. Strategies such as merger arbitrage, convertible arbitrage, and distressed situations all have higher levels of leverage. Price volatility has a greater impact on more highly leveraged funds and in effect has a second derivative affect. Chen et al. (2001) showed asymmetric volatility in stock returns. In line with this, financially distressed funds are also exposed to a higher probability of extreme value sensitivities. Information creates volatility on a large scale depending on the nature of the good or bad information.

The binomial tree theory involving either positive skewness or negative skewness, depending on the nature of the information impacting volatility upward or downward, is applied in macro funds. Macro funds can buy a put option to support the downside risk as it reduces standard deviation and kurtosis and increases skewness of the portfolio. Similarly, the same risk protection would apply by buying a put option on an equity index to protect against downward moves in equity markets and reduce negative skewness. Negative skewness can be reduced by including single strategy derivatives in equity market neutral funds as long as the magnitudes of short and long exposures are somewhat symmetrically equivalent. Thus, kurtosis in a diversified portfolio is lower than kurtosis of an individual fund. Christie-David and Chaudhry (2001) demonstrated strong evidence of positive skewness and leptokurtosis in futures markets. (See Table 8.1.)

TABLE 8.1   Risk Management Statistical Data Calculated over All 264 Funds That Survived the Period 1994–2001

	Mean	Standard Deviation	Skewness	Kurtosis	Correlation S&P	Correlation Bonds
Surviving Only	13.3788	4.232	−0.0618	5.1539	0.3575	−0.0343
Including Defunct	11.8368	4.8732	−0.1274	5.6323	0.3367	−0.0413
Survivor Bias	1.542	−0.6412	0.0656	−0.4784	0.0208	0.007

Source: Data from G. Amin and H. Kat, "Welcome to the Dark Side: Hedge Fund Attrition and Survivorship Bias over the Period 1994–2001," working paper, Case Business School, 2003; *Journal of Alternative Investments* 6, 57–73.

SCENARIO ANALYSIS

Scenario analysis attempts to replicate risks across portfolios in times when there is no particular crisis. These are the scenarios for business as usual and day-to-day operations. Event risk and stress testing capture crises, catastrophic events, and abnormal market risk situations. Value at risk is applied to the overall set of data including catastrophic data and is supposed to reflect the true cost of capital of a company in given specific defined time frames. Scenario analysis is a complementary tool to better analyze risks of catastrophic events, crises, or special situations. The hedge fund risk manager uses historical stress periods such as October 19, 1987, when the equity markets crashed; February 4, 1994, when the U.S. Federal Reserve changed direction and started increasing U.S. interest rates; December 20, 1994, when the Mexican peso was devalued; as well as hypothetical periods, designed perhaps to put the most pressure on the current portfolio.

STRESS TESTING

The hedge fund manager complements scenario analysis and VaR with the integration of stress testing by adding conditions and changing parameters of the portfolio. Stress testing allows the risk manager to obtain results by assuming effects of fictitious scenarios on the underlying assets' parameters, such as prices, volatilities, correlations, and interest rates, and adding external variables to the model such as inflation, gross domestic product (GDP), and/or other economical factors that would impact the given assets or trading strategies. Changes in market conditions are especially impacted by the following variables: changes in prices, changes in interest rate term structures, and changes in correlations between prices. Very often, the risk manager will assume nonparallel or linear shifts and/or conditions. Along the term structure of the chosen market risk variable, the risk manager will assume nonparallel moves of the yield curves and or/term structures of the interest rates to evaluate how much profits and losses would be generated if rates were to move by x amounts in the short term versus y moves in the long term. The sum of the resulting shifts is the net total assumed profits and losses on the total instruments along the term structure. Such assumptions can be generated at a granular level or at a trading strategic portfolio level or at an aggregate level.

If the portfolio contains options or instruments with options characteristics, additional changes to be considered as part of stress testing are changes in volatilities and changes in nonlinearities such as the convexity or gamma. This is defined as the second derivative of the delta. If gamma is positive, then the curve is convex up and if gamma is negative, then the curve is concave down. Delta is the first derivative assuming a 1 percent change in the underlying prices of the given asset class.

Stress testing the parameters of the liquidity factors and altering the time horizon can change the risk management landscape of the portfolio and can be used to improve the overall risk picture of the portfolio. Specific asset liquidity factors are also incorporated in the market risk model and are stressed to evaluate the impact of changes in the underlying value and/or on the total aggregate VaR. The number of days, weeks, months, and so on can be changed as well within the parameters' sections to create different risk results. By stretching the time horizon over a much longer period or time frame, the risk manager can smooth out gaps and losses from market crises. He or she can calibrate those gaps using statistical methodologies.

By analyzing hedge fund returns over long periods of time from the 1990s to now, we can assert that significant crises and or catastrophic events have been treated as such to make the overall trends reasonably smoothed. Yet not all the trends have continuously been upward since the beginning of the nineteenth century. Traditional indexes have recently leveled off into a plateau. But traditional indexes are not used as much anymore to capture hedge funds' risks and market correlations. Using stress testing and changing various parameters can consequently change correlational factors before actually performing trading.

Back-testing compares profits and losses with actual VaR limits and verifies that profits and losses do not exceed the absolute value level of the VaR limit. For larger financial institutions, regulators have put a limit on the number of times the VaR limits can be exceeded. Any excess has to be investigated and justified. It used to be that institutional traders could have profits and losses over the VaR limits three or four times per year. In hedge funds, very few risk managers apply back-testing to VaR limits because there are no regulatory requirements to perform it and because budget risks are not limited or capped as in the larger financial institutions. Budgetary limits go hand in hand with back-testing. For example, very few firms look at the number of times budgetary targets have been changed over a given period of time. Yet in some markets, such as the commodities and or the foreign exchange areas, financial budgets have been exponentially changed upward over small time frames such as a year or two.

An innovative way of assessing trading risks and aggressiveness is to analyze how many times and by how much the financial budget has been changed or increased for any given products and/or trading strategies. Back-testing captures trading aggressiveness and limits enforcements with financial capacities. Back-testing is just as important as VaR. It compares actual changes in market value of the portfolios with the VaR limits. For example, a 97 percent one-day VaR can be exceeded 3 days in every 100 days on average. Any over-the-limit situations are usually reviewed. In many cases, over-the-limit situations come from human errors, technological feeds being missed, or technological feeds being overloaded. In some cases, an over-the-limit situation comes from actual trading aggressiveness. Over-the-limit situations can be caused by a change in the portfolio's positions; a change in pricing models; a change in the underlying market, including changes in the volatility, correlation, or liquidity; and a change in the model factors.

The hedge fund risk manager can dissect profits and losses by dissecting derivatives' components and can verify how much comes from delta, from gamma, from eta, from rho or interest rates moves, and from model factors changes. The hedge fund risk manager requires its staff and the main manager and trader to be able to explain this breakdown of profits and losses' sources. By understanding the various parts of the profits and losses, the risk manager can obtain a true breakdown of the earnings and net asset valuations. This can be performed by taking a daily difference of the market values on all the portfolio's positions and by calculating the realized and unrealized profits and losses from marking to market and from sales of trades. Market factors can provide explanations for changes in profits and losses. A large change in marks or daily price on volatility can move profits and losses by significant amounts if positions are material. This daily procedure of reporting the breakdown of returns also provides detailed explanations for risk appetite and risk taking.

The Sharpe ratio is another methodology to measure trading risk–adjusted performance over a given time frame. (See Figures 8.4 through 8.7.)

The numerator of the Sharpe ratio is a measure of portfolio return during the time frame; the denominator is a measure of the risk taken to obtain profits. For the past 10 years, the Sharpe ratio for the S&P 500 has been 1 to 2. (See Figures 8.8 and 8.9.)

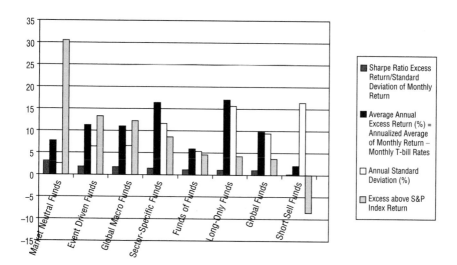

FIGURE 8.4 Ten-Year Risk Management Data for Equally Weighted Hedge Funds by Trading Strategies
Source: Data from Yahoo! Finance.

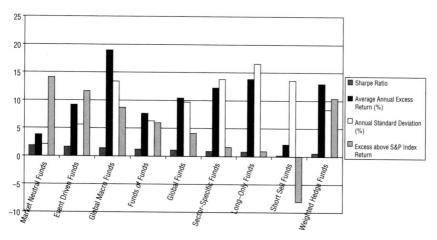

FIGURE 8.5 Ten-Year Risk Management Data for Value-Weighted Hedge Funds by Trading Strategies
Source: Data from Yahoo! Finance.

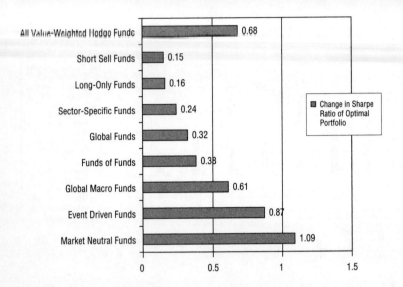

FIGURE 8.6 Change over 10 Years in Percentage in Sharpe Ratio of Value-Weighted Hedge Funds by Trading Strategies
Source: Data from Yahoo! Finance.

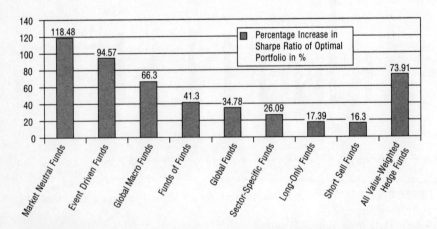

FIGURE 8.7 Ten-Year Change in Percentage in Sharpe Ratio of Optimal Portfolio for Value-Weighted Hedge Funds
Source: Data from Yahoo! Finance.

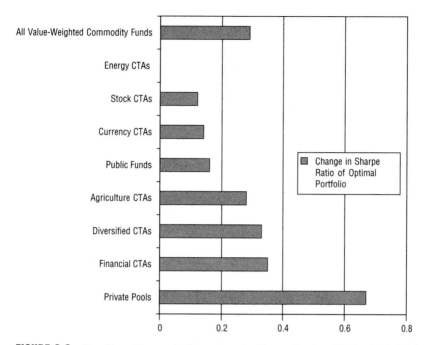

FIGURE 8.8 Ten-Year Change in Percentage in Sharpe Ratio of Value-Weighted Commodity Funds by Trading Strategies
Source: Data from Yahoo! Finance.

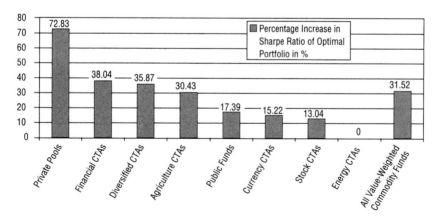

FIGURE 8.9 Ten-Year Change in Percentage in Sharpe Ratio of Optimal Portfolio for Value-Weighted Commodity Funds
Source: Data from Yahoo! Finance.

High ratios are more adequate since they mean that returns are maximized with a minimum amount of risk taking. The numerator of the Sharpe ratio is the rate of return earned on the portfolio that is above the risk-free rate of return. The denominator or the risk measurement part of the formula is measured as the standard deviation of the portfolio's daily return. So according to this methodology, the Sharpe ratio is equal to the return of the portfolio in excess of the risk-free rate over the standard deviation. (See Figures 8.10 through 8.15.)

Sharpe ratios are complementary to VaR, as VaR is a risk measurement tool and the minimum requirement of a market risk management policy. The Sharpe ratio is more informative as an accounting and financial efficiency measure of returns compared to risk taking.

There are other risk management ratios such as the capital adequacy ratios. These ratios are framed into a benchmark table with different ratings categories depending on the range the capital adequacy falls into. This is how Standard & Poor's or Moody's Investors Service set the initial rating scale of a company.

Hedge funds have not yet been rated and the actual calculations based on capital quality of hedge funds have so far been difficult to analyze, because hedge funds had not been as open as other entities to reveal their growing capacity. There is particular need now for hedge funds to improve internal controls and infrastructure quality and to get rated based on internal

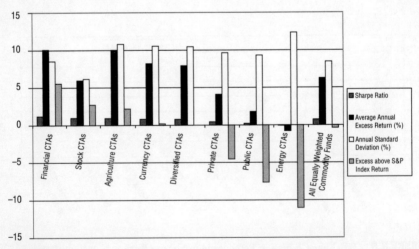

FIGURE 8.10 Ten-Year Risk Management Data for Equally Weighted Commodity Funds by Trading Strategies
Source: Data from Yahoo! Finance.

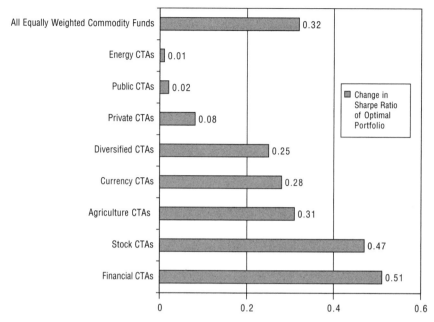

FIGURE 8.11   Change over 10 Years in Percentage in Sharpe Ratio of Equally Weighted Commodity Funds by Trading Strategies
Source: Data from Yahoo! Finance.

risk management frameworks. Hedge funds have relied on their brokers to provide them with the risk management tools they need but they remain yet insufficient to reveal more information about the details of the internal risks, the infrastructures, and the overall capital ratings.

One of the major risks of hedge funds is liquidity risk. Liquidity risk can consequently be affected by a liquidity squeeze, redemptions, and lack of short-term cash to sustain immediate operational needs. According to the Managed Funds Association, liquidity crisis has a cycle. Risk managers have to be ready to deal with market or credit risk events affecting illiquid positions such as the most leveraged ones or the short positions. Credit downgrades on counterparties can cause their share prices to drop rapidly and become more difficult or more expensive to liquidate. An initial downgrade or large loss trigger massive buying and selling on those positions and prices drop. The underlying value of the company becomes more difficult to sell. Hedge fund managers then need to liquidate positions to satisfy margin calls or redemptions called by investors. It is possible for brokers to buy back the shares of the investments from different

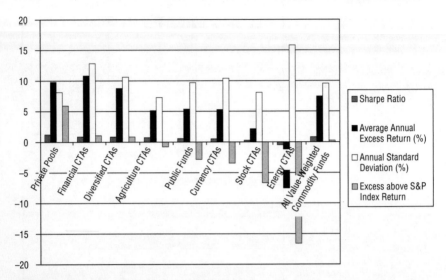

FIGURE 8.12 Ten-Year Risk Management Data for Value-Weighted Commodity Funds by Trading Strategies
Source: Data from Yahoo! Finance.

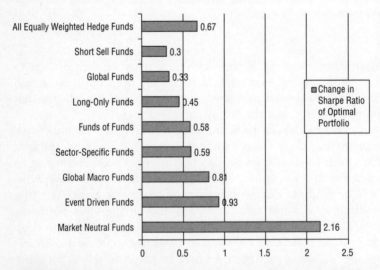

FIGURE 8.13 Ten-Year Change in Sharpe Ratio of Equally Weighted Hedge Funds by Trading Strategies
Source: Data from Yahoo! Finance.

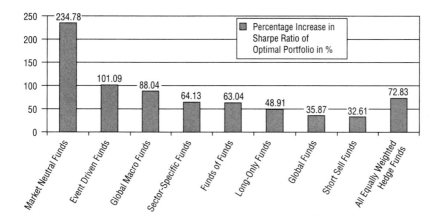

FIGURE 8.14   Ten-Year Change in Percentage in Sharpe Ratio of Optimal Portfolio for Equally Weighted Hedge Funds
Source: Data from Yahoo! Finance.

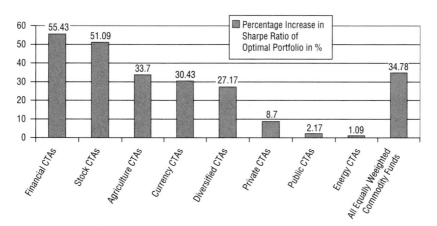

FIGURE 8.15   Ten-Year Change in Percentage in Sharpe Ratio of Optimal Portfolio for Equally Weighted Commodity Funds
Source: Data from Yahoo! Finance.

hedge funds in the markets to own larger pools, bundle the products, restructure them, and resell them for higher prices to maintain minimum value in the underlying asset. Debt restructuring is another service brokers can provide in exceptional circumstances.

The risk manager monitors redemption flows and capacity levels in order to sustain hedges and overall liquidity. The risk manager verifies cash, short-term securities issued by high-credit-quality entities, borrowing capacity, and access to borrowings under margin rules or credit lines. The risk manager relates the measures of liquidity such as cash or borrowing capacity. The larger the capacity of a fund, the larger its borrowing capacity and the larger its liquidity ability. Historical drawdown is a measure of risk and of the amount of liquidity. It is assumed that 50 percent of the value of a long position can be borrowed under current Regulation T margin requirements if underlying assets are equities. Short positions have to have a 50 percent margin requirement, allowing 50 percent of short trades to be used to fund long positions or for cash. Relative liquidity measure can be another way to monitor liquidity levels. It is calculated as VaR/(Cash + Borrowing Capacity).

LIQUIDITY OR CONCENTRATION RISK

Liquidity is mainly monitored via the daily cash report, the daily margin report, and the collateral call summary. Liquidity risk can also be assimilated with concentration risks and describes the largest positions in size or monetary terms by industry, geography, greek, strategy, and/or products.

These operational risks reports are provided by brokers, and usually they are well informed about counterparties' downgrades and problems ahead. Due to the services they provide to hedge funds, they inform hedge funds of liquidity gaps in the market. Gaps are detected using day-to-day changes on those benchmarks or key risk indicators. The risk manager also negotiates haircuts, the speed at which prime brokers can dictate an increase in margin rates and two-way collateral agreements, where appropriate, to further reduce the likelihood of running out of liquidity. Brokers are outsourcers of risks, and they give hedge fund risk managers information on liquidity with the weighted average liquidity greater than one day. Concentration reports also provide information on liquidity such as the report on market values greater than net asset values or another report on the one position margin greater than 20 percent total margin.

Brokers and hedge funds work together to improve risk management capabilities, especially when it comes to monitoring main market risks. Hedge fund risk managers and prime brokers' hedge fund risk specialists should work together and communicate mutual risks to each other. For example, the prime broker's objective is to lend cash and securities against excess good collateral, to avoid exposure to credit and reputational risk, and to manage resultant market and liquidity exposure. The risk manager's responsibility is to set reasonable collateral requirements to identify potential exposures before they become critical, and to ensure risk is commensurate with returns.

LEVERAGE

Leverage is another risk correlated with market, credit, and liquidity risks. The traditional notion of leverage is "investing borrowed funds." Basically an investor can borrow capital to increase his or her investing power to increase potential upside gains on investments. Accounting-based measures of leverage relate some measure of asset value to equity. The risk-based measure of leverage captures the risk of default, of liquidation, or of insolvency due to deteriorating market values of the portfolio. Yet the risk-based leverage measures do not bring any information on the relationship between the roles of borrowed money in the risk of insolvency.

Besides leverage, risk managers investigate the nature of the instruments within the portfolio. A hedge fund can be highly leveraged and contain risk-averse or conservative securities while another hedge fund may not be as leveraged but could contain highly sophisticated illiquid instruments. So leverage itself is not sufficient to understand the level of risks involved in the overall portfolio.

There are different accounting-based measures of leverage. There are implicit and explicit credit lines for repos (repurchase agreements), short sales, or derivatives. Credit lines in hedge funds are considered more as collateral limits with the prime broker. The risk management has been outsourced and risk limits or collateral margin plateaus have been established when entering the agreement with the broker. Any additional trading strategies or sizable added risks have to be communicated and approved by the prime brokers.

Leverage as a credit risk is an element of risk management and is solely measured as part of the risk management reports that the prime broker issues. It is seldom accounted for by the offshore administrative finance department.

The following describes the generally accepted accounting-based measures of leverage on the balance sheet: "Gross Balance Sheet Assets to Equity" are equal to on-balance-sheet assets divided by equity. This measures leverage incompletely as it does not take into account the off-balance-sheet risks—all the derivatives, the futures contracts, and the structured products of the hedge funds. It leaves out most of the actual risks and underestimates the overall risks of the portfolio. "Net Balance Sheet Assets to Equity" are equal to on-balance-sheet assets minus matched book assets divided by equity. Matched book assets are the collateralized values set aside to hedge the on-balance-sheet assets. They are usually direct hedges of the repurchase agreements' assets. This formula only considers hedges of those assets of the matched book. It underestimates risks as it does not account for the derivatives transactions and for the off-balance-sheet instruments. These accounting measures do not include financing parts of forward contracts, swaps, and other derivatives. Another accounting measure, gross accounting leverage, equals on-balance-sheet assets plus on-balance-sheet liabilities plus gross off-balance-sheet transactions, divided by equity. Unlike the other formulas, gross accounting leverage includes off-balance-sheet transactions, derivatives, and hedges.

Risk-based leverage is risk management measures (not finance-accounting measures) of leverage. Risk-based leverage is calculated as volatility in value of portfolio divided by equity. This measures risks of underlying instruments over time. The volatility also measures liquidity of the derivative instruments. Depending on liquidity of the underlying instruments, volatility can be either historical or implied. This captures assets' volatility over historical trends.

VaR divided by equity is a coefficient measure that gives a picture of the fund's capacity to absorb typical market movements. The criticism of such a measure is that it does not reflect the risk of the fund's portfolio in extreme market conditions. Scenario-derived market risk measure divided by equity is used to evaluate extreme event risk. Another method to reduce the portfolio's accounting-based leverage is to increase its cash position or the overall borrowing capacity. Thus, an increase in cash and borrowing capacity in a period following an increase in the market risk measure for the portfolio (e.g., VaR) can be the evidence of a hedge fund market risk reacting to market stress by reducing leverage.

The hedge fund risk manager is exposed to third-party transactions and therefore is directly impacted by the risks those counterparties are taking as well. These counterparties include banks, securities firms, exchanges, and other financial institutions. The risk of loss to the hedge fund as a result of risky exposures to a counterparty constitutes counterparty credit risk.

CREDIT RISK

Credit risk is more important than market risk and is the most widespread risk encountered within the global banking system. From a macroeconomical perspective, credit has been a growing concern since the burst of the equity bubble in the late 1990s. It has also been a concern in Japan as the Japanese banking system has experienced more than 16 years of deflation. During this deflationary period, interest rates have been extremely low and sometimes negative, and the buying and selling of debt has enhanced credit to become cheaper. The other forms of risks such as credit derivatives, swaps, and futures have also engendered credit creation. Collateral asset valuations on derivatives have not always been reassessed daily until recently due to technological capabilities. A downgrade in counterparties' capital value consequently produces a deterioration of collateral asset valuations and thus holding values of the third party. The credit risk agreement includes clauses about different potential defaulting counterparties. Prior to entering a transaction, the credit risk manager ensures protection of collateral asset valuations and sometimes includes scenario analysis in the contract in case of a credit crisis or loss of collateral asset values. It includes stress testing, plateaus, and agreement legal conditions with the counterparties' risk managers.

In appearance, risk management is being practiced in the majority of hedge funds, but in reality there is very little sophistication in attempts to follow the minimum standards of loss avoidance. Financial risk management has become far more quantitative in a decade but hedge funds did not prioritize and invest in hiring the appropriate resources to overcome quantitative risks. Outside of the United States, it was once believed that risk management was a service, not a corporate requirement. This way of perceiving risk management is very different from proactive risk management enforcement, and it is more or less diplomatic than truly effective. Over time, this risk management approach tends to avoid defining limits and to undermine the role and purpose of risk management itself.

Hedge funds have grown in size and in complexity and the need for a new risk management framework is required but not enforced as of yet, so very few funds attempt to invest in such improvements. To attempt to improve internal risk management in hedge funds, it is important to recognize that hedge funds are not normally distributed and that they involve more complex mathematical fit. Berenyi (2002) proposes a higher moment-based distributional risk measure, the variance-equivalent incorporating skewness and kurtosis. Stutzer (2001) proposes an alternative performance index that is a generalization of the Sharpe ratio for returns distributions showing skewness and excess kurtosis. It relies on the behavioral hypothesis of loss aversion. The index gives a preference parameter-free formula for the optimization problem that accounts for higher (positive) skewness and lower kurtosis preferences. Frameworks assuming normality of returns are not sustainable for hedge fund distributions.

One way to apply credit risk management in hedge funds is to impose a capital rating scale for the hedge fund to value internal capital adequacy and management integrity. Ratings of hedge funds are still virtually nonexistent as of 2005 and very few rating models of funds integrate integrity governance rating in the system or formula. Amin and Kat (2001) said that the distribution of returns can no longer be standardized given the levels of nonnormal skewed returns.

OMEGA

Keating and Shadwick (2002a) introduced the omega measure to better define the fitted distribution. The omega distribution includes the distributional characteristics of a returns series. The measure is a function of risk-adjusted returns that has no parametric assumption on the distribution. It is a performance measure equivalent to the returns distribution itself with all imbedded moments in it, and the omega factor takes into account the returns below and above a specific loss threshold and provides a ratio of total probability-weighted losses and gains that fully describes the risk-reward properties of the distribution. It is a unique monotone-decreasing function of the cumulative distribution of returns. It is a differentiable function and its first-order derivative is thus always negative. On its domain of definition, the omega function of a risky distribution is flatter than that of a less risky distribution. Keating and Shadwick (2002a) demonstrated that when returns are normally distributed, the omega function tends to replicate results similar to those of the Sharpe ratio. The omega function is defined such that:

$$\Omega(r) = \frac{I_2(r)}{I_1(r)}$$

where $I_1(r) = \int_{a \to r} F(x)dx$
$\qquad I_2(r) = \int_{r \to b} [1 - F(x)]dx$

F is the cumulative distribution function of the asset returns defined on the interval; $[a; b]$ and r are the return level regarded as a loss threshold. Returns below a specific loss threshold are losses, and returns above are gains. So at a given loss threshold, a higher value of omega is preferred to a low value. The omega of a risky distribution is flatter than that of a less risky distribution. The mean return of the distribution is a unique point at which the omega function takes the value 1. The probability-weighted gains are equal to the probability-weighted losses.

Using data from Hedge Fund Research and a sample of 103 data points from different strategies, Keating and Shadwick (2002a, b) found that short selling exhibits the flattest omega function and the steepest relative value. The return distribution of short selling is far riskier than that of relative value. And the researchers stated that their standard deviation confirmed this conclusion but did not standardize this into a generalization. Fund of funds and event driven strategies demonstrated that an intermediate position in terms of risk and the slope of their omega functions is similar to the general case. Using this parameter, we can say that a fund of funds strategy is riskier than event driven.

Omega's contribution consists of incorporating all the moments of the distribution and is appropriate for investment analysis when returns are not normally distributed. It provides information on investors' preferences for loss and gain. Omega is computed directly from the returns distribution and measures the total impact of the moments instead of each one of them individually. It can thus reduce the estimation error risk.

SORTINO RATIO

By definition, the Sortino ratio is a variation of the Sharpe ratio that differentiates harmful volatility from volatility in general by replacing standard deviation with downside deviation in the denominator. Thus the Sortino ratio is calculated by subtracting the risk-free rate from the return of the portfolio and then dividing by the downside deviation. The Sortino ratio measures the return to extreme volatility. This ratio allows investors to assess risk in a more appropriate manner than to simply look at excess returns to total volatility. It does not consider how often the price of the security rises as opposed to how often it falls. A large Sortino ratio indicates a low risk of large loss.

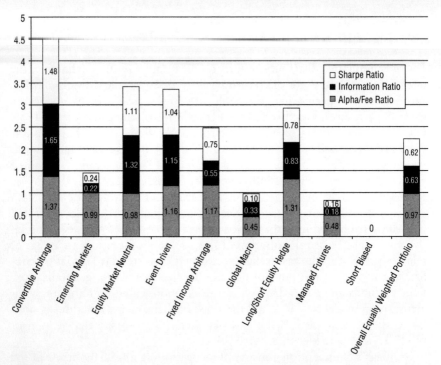

FIGURE 8.16   Comparison of Risk Ratios by Trading Strategies, 1995–2004
Source: Data from Yahoo! Finance.

SUGGESTED MINIMUM RISK MANAGEMENT FRAMEWORK FOR HEDGE FUNDS

Appendix I includes statistical information to be used for risk management purposes. It would be ideal to incorporate all these risk monitoring factors into a valid capital rating system that would measure the real quality of the hedge fund. This ideal remains highly utopian. The rating of hedge funds is still very inadequate if not nonexistent, incomplete, and highly embryonic compared to ratings of the other financial institutions. Yet hedge funds have outperformed them. As part of an operational risk strategy, it would be ideal to implement capital rating mechanisms in hedge funds and compare them with agencies' rating systems and those of the insurance companies in a three-way reconciliation process to determine a fair and adequate rating value. (See Figures 8.16 and 8.17.)

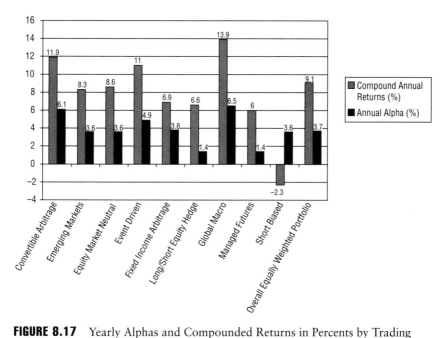

FIGURE 8.17 Yearly Alphas and Compounded Returns in Percents by Trading Strategies, 1995–2004
Source: Data from Yahoo! Finance.

CHAPTER 9

Role of Indexes in Hedge Funds

There are different uses of hedge fund indexes. An index can be used as a yardstick for investments in specific styles, instruments, or locations, or it can be used as an investment instrument. (See Table 9.1.)

Gehin and Vaissié (2004) define an index as follows:

- Unambiguous when funds are described with respect to weight in the index, style, and general partner.
- Accountable if the guidelines are submitted to an independent committee.
- Reasonable if the components of the index are compatible with the investors' risk requirements.
- Verifiable if the methodology is well described, transparent, and made available to the public.
- Representative if the index is accurately reflecting the whole universe of hedge funds or universe focused on a specific style.
- Investable if the investors are able to replicate the index when reaching and maintaining a level of tracking error. (See Table 9.2.)

Recently, hedge fund indexes and data have become publicly available; thus research and advancements in risk management knowledge are recent and current. Thanks to public domains, electronic science libraries, and data vendors such as Altvest, Hedge Fund Research, Managed Account Reports (MAR/CISDM), and TASS, data and statistics such as historical returns, times series, fund size, investment strategies, and instruments are made public. (See Table 9.3.)

Duc (2004b) compared CSFB/Tremont, HFRX, MSCI, and S&P indexes with three broad categories of alternative strategies to evaluate risk exposures. He found that risk is linked to the margin of volatility. This margin is set by a minimum and a maximum. Macro/CTA exposures ranged from 13 percent to 22 percent, long/short exposures from

TABLE 9.1 Empirical Description of Universe of Hedge Fund Indexes and Databases

	Global Hedge Fund Index	Biased with Past Historical Data Filling Information	Underlying Database Nature	Number of Funds Included in Database (Approx.)	Number of Indexes	Number of Hedge Funds in Indexes	Date of Inception	Date of First Index Return
Altvest	Yes	No	Proprietary	2,600	14	2,600	2000	1993
ABN-EurekaHedge	No	Yes	Proprietary	365	3	100	2002	2000
Barclay/GHS	Yes	No	Proprietary	2,450	18	2,450	2003	1997
Bernheim	Yes	NA	Not available	900	1	18	1995	1995
Blue X	Yes	No	Proprietary	400	1	35	2002	2002
CSFB/Tremont	Yes	No	TASS and Tremont	3,300	14	448	1999	1994
EACM	Yes	Partial	Proprietary	100	18	100	1996	1990
Feri	Yes	No	Proprietary	5,000	16	41	2001	2002
HedgeFund.net	Yes	Yes	Proprietary	2,300	37	2,300	1998	1979
Hennessee	Yes	No	Proprietary	3,500	24	690	1987	1987
HF Intelligence	Yes	Partial	Proprietary	3,200	45	2,652	2001	1998
HFR	Yes	Partial	Proprietary	2,300	37	1,400	1994	1990
LJH	Yes	NA	Proprietary	800	16	900	1992	1989
Magnum	Yes	No	Proprietary	0	16	NA	1997	NA
MAR/CISDM	Yes	No	Proprietary	2,300	19	1,600	1994	1990
MondoHedge	No	No	Proprietary	720	7	48	2003	2002
MSCI	Yes	Yes	Proprietary	1,800	191	1,500	2002	2000
S&P	Yes	No	Proprietary	3,500	10	40	2002	1998
TalentHedge	Yes	Partial	Proprietary	3,800	2	20	2003	2003
Van Hedge	Yes	No	Proprietary	5,400	16	1,300	1994	1988
Zurich Capital	No	No	Proprietary	900	5	900	2001	1998

TABLE 9.2 Overview of Major Indexes

Index Provider	Launch Date	Base Date	Number of Indexes	Strategy/Fund Weighting Methodology	Number of Funds in Database	Eligibility Population	Number of Funds in Index	Rebalancing Frequency
CSFB/Tremont	August 2003	January 2000	10 indexes + composite	Value-weighted	3,300	420	60	Semiannually
Dow Jones	November 2003	January 2002	5 indexes	Equally weighted	300	100	35	Additions and subtractions at discretion of Dow Jones management without notice
FTSE	April 2004	January 1998	11 indexes + composite	Weighted	6,000	75	40	Funds added or deleted depending on market conditions and fund events
HFRX	March 2003	January 2000	8 indexes + composite	Value-weighted	2,300	not known	Monte Carlo simulation for optimal number of funds for strategy replication	Quarterly
MSCI	July 2003	January 2000	Composite made of number of strategies using underlying managed account platform	Adj median asset weighted/equally weighted	105	not known	97	Quarterly
S&P	May 2002	January 1998	5 indexes + composite	Equally weighted	3,500	300	40	Annually at strategy level and periodically at fund level

Source: Data from EDHEC Business School (www.edhec-risk.com).

TABLE 9.3

	Barclays/GHS Hedge Fund Index	Bernheim Index	CSFB/Tremont Hedge Fund Index	EACM 100 Index	Hennessee Hedge Fund Index	Tuna Hedge Fund Aggregate Average	HFRI Fund Weighted Composite Index	Van Global Hedge Fund Index
Alrvest Hedge Fund Index	2% Jan 2001	3.6% Jan 2001	5.8% Oct 1998	3.7% Jan 2001	2.9% May 2001	2.3% Jan 2001	2.1% Aug 1998	2.2% Jan 2001
Barclay/GHS Hedge Fund Index		2.3% Apr 2000	6.7% Oct 1998	3.3% Aug 1998	2.0% Apr 2000	2.7% Aug 1998	1.4% Apr 2000	1.7% Feb 2000
Bernheim Index			2.1% Nov 1999	3.9% Dec 1999	2.3% Nov 1999	2.6% Dec 1999	2.0% Nov 1999	3.5% Mar 2000
CSFB/Tremont Hedge Fund Index				4.6% Jan 1996	5.4% Oct 1998	5.9% Oct 1998	5.8% Oct 1998	5.5% Oct 1998
EACM 100 Index					5.0% Aug 1998	2.9% Feb 2000	4.2% Aug 1998	4.5% Mar 2000
Hennessee Hedge Fund Index						4.4% Sept 1998	1.6% May 1997	1.9% Sept 1995
Tuna Hedge Fund Aggregate Average							3.6% Sept 1998	2.6% Sept 1995
HFRI Fund Weighted Composite Index								2.3% Feb 2000
Van Global Hedge Fund Index								

Note: The matrix of maximum differences between indexes reveals substantial disparities among all indexes.
The greatest difference (6.7%) occurred in October 1998 between the CSFB/Tremont Index and the Barclay/GHS Index.
Source: Data from EDHEC Business School (www.edhec-risk.com).

13 percent to 45 percent, and arbitrage/relative value from 38 percent to 67 percent. From his research, of the 159 managers covered in total by the S&P, CSFB/Tremont, and MSCI indexes in November 2003, only 14 (9 percent) were selected in more than one index, and only two were included in all three indexes. (See Figure 9.1.)

Results are directly correlated to index weightings, managers' names, and strategy implementations. The intersection between two large databases ranges between 37 percent and 59 percent. Distinctive elements are important to note:

1. The mergers and acquisitions (M&A) approach is not an active strategy index. It tends to underperform those that are more selective. Those more selective fund indexes tend to be excluded from investable indexes.
2. The aggregated underlying positions of all the hedge fund portfolios included in the Dow Jones Convertible Bond index can demonstrate reversed trades such as experiencing a short bond exposure and a long equity exposure. This never occurs to normal convertible strategies.
3. There are replacements of funds in investable indexes and these replacements are difficult to justify for a consistent approach to maintain accuracy of index measurements. This substitution is quantitatively inconsistent, and paradoxically it occurs mainly for qualitative not quantitative purposes.

Jemmco has experienced legal issues. Selective managers in indexes force investors to be more exigent and create a selective biased approach.

The maximum absolute difference between investable CSFB/HFR indexes is valued at 2 percent for long/short, 3.7 percent for macro, 1.3 percent for convertible, and 1.5 percent for market neutral. The maximum

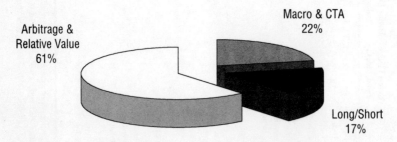

FIGURE 9.1   Strategic Exposures of CSFB/Tremont Investable Indexes
Source: Data from EDHEC Business School (www.edhec-risk.com).

absolute difference between noninvestable CSFB/HFR indexes is at 1.3 percent for long/short, 2.9 percent for macro, 0.6 percent for convertible, and 1.2 percent for market neutral. The average absolute difference between investable CSFB/HFR indexes is about 1 percent for long/short, 1.2 percent for macro, 0.7 percent for convertible, and 0.9 percent for market neutral. The average absolute difference between noninvestable CSFB/HFR indexes is a few basis points lower or 0.5 percent for long/short, 1 percent for macro, 0.4 percent for convertible, and 0.5 percent for market neutral. (See Table 9.4.)

Investable indexes and funds of funds encounter similar advantages: portfolio management is not ambiguous and cleared depending on a specific strategy. There is less heterogeneity for investable indexes than for funds of funds. Investable indexes are more lucrative and have more liquidity.

Duc questioned the weightings of the investable indexes. During the Investor Funds of Hedge Funds conference of the Transparency Council Funds of Hedge Funds in June 2004, Stephan Ewen pointed out that the equally weighted average performance of the strategy indexes was not equal to the performance of the HFRX Equally Weighted index from February to May 2004. Ewen noticed the disappearance of the HFRX Managed Futures index in early May 2004, which happened without any advance warning or explanation on the weightings. (See Figure 9.2.)

There is more heterogeneity in funds of funds partially due to the fact that single-strategy funds of funds represent more than 54 percent of the fund of funds universe. Investable indexes underperform the fund of hedge funds average when using nonsimulated returns for comparison purposes.

TABLE 9.4 Selection Principles of Noninvestable Hedge Fund Indexes

Index Providers	Minimum Size	Historical Records	Funds Closed or Defunct	Funds Closed to New Investors
Altvest	No	No	Yes	Yes
Barclay	No	No	Yes	Yes
CISDM	No	No	Yes	Yes
CSFB	$10 million	12 months	Yes	Yes
EACM	$20 million	24 months	No	No
Hennessee	$10 million	12 months	Yes	Yes
HF Net	No	No	No	Yes
HFR	No	No	Yes	Yes
MSCI	$15 million	No	Yes	Yes
Van Hedge	No	No	Yes	Yes

Source: Data from EDHEC Business School (www.edhec-risk.com).

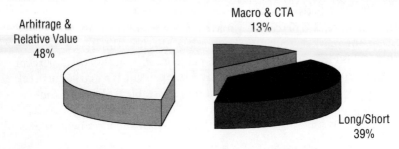

FIGURE 9.2 Strategic Exposures of HFRX Hedge Fund Indexes
Source: Data from EDHEC Business School (www.edhec-risk.com).

From 2003 to 2004, noninvestable index performance on the CSFB/Tremont Hedge Fund was 10 percent, on the HFR Hedge Fund it was 20.9 percent, and on the MSCI Hedge Fund it was 8.1 percent. (See Table 9.5.)

During the same time period, the investable index showed performance of 4.9 percent on the CSFB/Tremont Hedge Fund, 7.7 percent on the HFR Hedge Fund, and 4.3 percent on the MSCI Hedge Fund. (See Figure 9.3.)

These performance quotes reflect the actual returns compared with those of the EDHEC funds of funds; they do not include tracking fees, management fees, entrance fees, and redemption fees charged to investors, nor error-related differences. The EDHEC fund of funds index is to outperform an investable index for the various time periods corresponding to the real track record of each investable index. Note that EDHEC is considered to be the best estimator of fund of hedge funds average performance. Yet EDHEC remains as of 2004 a more quantitative way of rating hedge fund performance. Its model does not measure operational risk, management integrity, and corporate governance.

The main disadvantage of using indexes to measure risk and return adequacy is the poor data completion and quality. Hedge funds can be reasonable approximations of large databases; however, databases can be constituted by means of a biased sampling procedure and thus hedge fund indexes are not representative of the hedge funds universe. For example, databases do not reflect operational risk issues in hedge funds and therefore they do not fully describe the inherent embedded risks.

Hedge fund databases can be inaccurate, as some funds have discontinued operations due to poor returns or compliance issues. To belong to a hedge fund index is voluntary, which makes a database incomplete and nonrepresentative of the hedge fund universe. Another reason why this

TABLE 9.5 Overview of Major Noninvestable Hedge Fund Indexes

Index Provider	Launch Date	Base Date	Index Weighting Methodology	Number of Funds in Database	Number of Funds in Indexes	Rebalancing Frequency
Altvest	2000	1993	Equally weighted	2,600	2,600	Monthly
Barclay Group	2003	1997	Equally weighted	2,450	2,053	Monthly
CISDM	1994	1990	Median	2,300	1,280	Monthly
CSFB/Tremont	1999	1994	Value-weighted	3,300	431	Quarterly
EACM	1996	1996	Equally weighted	100	100	Annually
EDHEC	2003	1997	Principal component analysis	NA	NA	Quarterly
Hennessee	1987	1987	Equally weighted	3,500	690	Annually
HF Net	1998	1976–1995	Equally weighted	2,300	2,300	Continually
HFR	1994	1990	Equally weighted	2,300	1,400	Monthly
MSCI	2002	2002	Equally weighted and value-weighted	1,800	1,500	Quarterly/depends on strategy
Van Hedge	1994	1988	Equally weighted	5,400	1,300	Monthly

Source: Data from EDHEC Business School (www.edhec-risk.com).

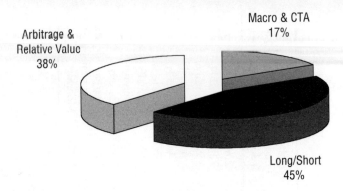

FIGURE 9.3 Strategic Exposures of MSCI Investable Indexes
Source: Data from EDHEC Business School (www.edhec-risk.com).

hedge fund universe is incomplete and unreliable is the fact that some hedge funds stop promoting their activities when they reach their capacities and capital limits.

Hedge fund databases are also unreliable in the quality of overall returns they experience because strongly performing hedge funds tend to be more willing to contribute to indexes while unsuccessful ones drop out and do not advertise themselves in indexes. Hedge fund databases are also incomplete in that they do not include Commodity Trading Advisors in the category of hedge funds.

We can deduce that indexes' heterogeneity occurs thanks to diversity of hedge fund categories, strategies, subjectivity in selection, and calculation methodologies. The inaccuracies can be characterized by the overvaluations of indexes, sometimes as high as 20 percent. In market-trend reversals, hedge fund index performances can differ significantly. From 1997 to 2000, the Tuna Hedge Fund Aggregate Average (neutral weighting) and the CSFB/Tremont Hedge Fund Index (weighted by capitalization) had performance differential of 40 percent.

The indexes' imperfections come also from the indexes' structures. For example, Duc (2004a, b) highlights that at monthly index return level, 34 percent of maximum differences measured between 10 hedge fund indexes are greater than 3 percent, and 81 percent of the monthly readings reveal maximum differences exceeding 1 percent. Again, these differences are significant in comparison to index stability. He demonstrated that 49 percent of monthly performance differences between two indexes exceed 1 percent and the maximum difference is measured at 4.2 percent. The heterogeneity of hedge fund indexes is thus not entirely assigned to differences in quantification methodologies. Duc (2004a, b) showed that heterogeneity is very high for investable indexes. EDHEC provided the information in Table 9.6 on the heterogeneity of the major composite hedge fund indexes from January 2000 through September 2004.

It is noted that hedge fund indexes are more heterogeneous than traditional indexes. In more than 15 hedge fund indexes, monthly discrepancies frequently exceed 3 percent. According to Duc, in October 1998, the Barclay and CSFB/Tremont hedge fund indexes experienced a discrepancy of 6.7 percent. Over time periods of less than three years, the differential between two hedge fund indexes totals more than 40 percent. This tendency is more obvious for strategy-specific indexes, which can have differentials of more than 20 percent and can exhibit negative correlation. Traditional indexes do not show as much of a variance. For example, the most sizable difference experienced between the Russell Value index and the Barra/S&P Value index from 1995 to 2003 is only 5 percent. (See Figure 9.4.)

Traditional indexes seemed to have leveled off toward a plateau or a limit, and they are least representative of true market movements as they do not incorporate companies' off-balance-sheet risks and derivatives markets. Hedge fund indexes are more disparate from one another mostly due to their differences in database quality and completeness but also due to the vast list of different strategies. Taken all together, hedge funds' macro

TABLE 9.6 Major Composite Hedge Fund Indexes, January 2000 through September 2004

	S&P Hedge Fund Index	CSFB/Tremont Hedge Fund Index	MSCI Hedge Fund Investable Index
Average Annual Return	7.7%	7.55%	9.75%
Minimum Monthly Return	−0.96%	−1.01%	−0.88%
Maximum Monthly Return	2.40%	2.71%	3.09%
% of Winning Months	78.95%	78.95%	75.44%
% of Losing Months	21.05%	21.05%	24.56%
Skewness	−0.01	0.47	0.27
Kurtosis	−0.46	0.06	−0.16
Annual Standard Deviation	2.64%	2.76%	3.17%
Semiannual Standard Deviation	0.80%	0.72%	0.77%
Value at Risk 95%	7.70%	7.55%	9.75%
Sharpe Ratio	2.92	2.73	3.08
Sortino Ratio 3%	9.65	10.54	12.66
Omega Ratio 3%	3.30	3.10	4.91

Source: Data from EDHEC Business School (www.edhec-risk.com).

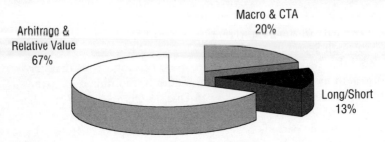

FIGURE 9.4   Strategic Exposures of S&P Hedge Funds' Indexes
Source: Data from EDHEC Business School (www.edhec-risk.com).

indexes are most representative of reality and actual market movements. Yet, analyzing random hedge fund indexes since 1998, the author noted that events and catastrophic risks have not been as representative in hedge fund indexes as in traditional indexes in terms of magnitude.

Amenc and Martellini (2003c) developed two methodologies to test the heterogeneity of returns. On the one hand, it can be measured by the maximum difference in monthly returns, and on the other hand, it can be calculated with the average and the lowest correlation between various indexes. Using the former mean, Amenc and Martellini (2003a, b) demonstrated that the maximum differences range from 1.85 percent for merger arbitrage to 22.4 percent for long/short equities from January 1998 to December 2000.

Survivorship bias depends largely on the quality of the data sources and the links to the databases. Hedge fund databases differ from each other. Fung and Hsieh (2003) noted that the number of funds common to different data vendors is relatively low. For example, in December 2000, Hedge Fund Research had about 1,150 funds, TASS 1,060 funds, and MAR 910 funds, but only 315 funds were contained in the three databases. In the same school of thought, Agarwal, Daniel, and Naik (2004) demonstrated that only 10 percent was common to TASS, Hedge Fund Research, and Zurich/MAR databases—that is, 1,776 live and 1,655 inactive funds. Duc (2004a, b) found that the percentage of common funds between two indexes varies around 50 percent as of November 2003 using providers Altvest, CISDM-MAR, Barclay, HedgeFund.net, Hedge Fund Research, and TASS. If we consider the funds that are constituents of an index, the percentage ranges between 14 percent for CISDM-MAR and 23 percent for Altvest.

According to Duc (2004a, b), the survivorship bias in hedge fund indexes is calculated at an average of 3 percent per year (Fung and Hsieh 2000) and consequently returns of global hedge fund indexes are thought to be overstated by at least the same margin. According to Ackermann, McEnally, and Ravenscraft (1999) the estimated impact of survivorship on average returns varies from a bias of 0.16 percent to 2 percent (Liang 2000; Amin and Kat 2003a, b, c) to 3 percent (Brown, Goetzmann, and Ibbotson 1999) for offshore hedge funds. Researchers on the survivorship bias topic are Brown, Goetzmann, and Ibbotson (1999), Fung and Hsieh (2000), Liang (2000, 2001), Brown, Goetzmann, and Park (2000, 2002), Gregoriou (2002), Amin and Kat (2003a, b, c), and Barès, Gibson, and Gyger (2003).

Brown, Goetzmann, and Park (2000) showed that the probability of liquidation increases with increasing risk. They found that funds in existence for at least six months tend to terminate within the next two years and less than 5 percent of all funds survive after five years. These estimates vary with time and with the survivorship bias factors. There are several factors that affect this rate. First there are those funds that have discontinued providing information on performance and returns to database and index providers because they are continuously experiencing losses. Second, some funds have performed much better than the average and have maximized their limits in terms of capacity. Others have been under investigation and no longer can provide information and contribute to databases and index producers.

Some other hedge funds are not pressured to provide information as they are not regulated in their geographical areas and operate for their own accounts without broker-dealers. Thus they do not have the incentive to participate in database surveys. Finally, there are those that have been discontinued or are inconsistent in their participation depending on their performance. The rare good story is about those funds that did well, had enough profits, and wisely decided to retire.

According to Fung and Hsieh (2002a, b) and Amin and Kat (2002), funds close out after dropping out of the databases and indexes. Duc highlights that two other researchers have different perspectives on those funds not contributing due to losses and poor performance: According to Posthuma and Van der Sluis (2003), a vast majority of bankrupted hedge funds do not repay their investors. For those particular hedge funds, there are two types of scenarios: Either the average rate of return after database exclusion is –50 percent (half of the hedge fund goes bankrupt) or this rate amounts to –100 percent (total loss). If one accounts for the constant rise in database dropouts since 1994—up to 12.3 percent in 2002 according to Amin and Kat (2002)—then the index performance is overstated somewhere between 6.2 percent and 12.3 percent.

Theories have made quantification of bias very difficult. Posthuma and Van der Sluis (2003) have also studied retroactive bias taking into account past returns of new entrants. (See Tables 9.7 through 9.10.)

TABLE 9.7 Annual Returns of Hedge Fund Indexes

	EDHEC Funds of Funds Index	Altvest Hedge Fund Index	Barclay/ GHS Hedge	Bernheim Index	CSFB/Tremont Hedge Fund Index	EACM 100 Index	Hennessee Hedge Fund Index	Tuna Hedge Fund Aggregate Average	HFRI Fund Weighted Composite Index	Van Global Hedge Fund Index	Mean Difference
1997	17%	21%	22%	NA	26%	15%	15%	22%	17%	17%	-2%
1998	4%	9%	8%	NA	0%	2%	1%	11%	3%	5%	-1%
1999	29%	36%	37%	30%	23%	24%	32%	33%	31%	37%	-3%
2000	8%	8%	12%	6%	5%	8%	8%	13%	5%	11%	-1%
2001	4%	8%	7%	2%	4%	3%	4%	8%	5%	6%	-2%
2002	1%	1%	1%	1%	3%	2%	-3%	3%	-1%	0%	0%
2003	12%	17%	18%	15%	15%	12%	21%	16%	20%	18%	-5%

Source: Data from EDHEC Business School (www.edhec-risk.com).

TABLE 9.8 Example of Performance and Risk Information over a 10-Year Period

All Indexes CSFB/Tremont Index   Start 1/31/95   End 12/31/05

Trading Strategy	Total Return	Annualized Total Return	Average Month	Best Month	Worst Month	Annualized Standard Deviation	Beta	Sharpe Ratio
Credit Suisse/Tremont Hedge Fund Index	261.01%	12.48%	1.01%	8.53%	−7.55%	7.82%	0.26	1.11
Convertible Arbitrage	195.02%	10.42%	0.84%	3.57%	−4.68%	4.64%	0.04	1.44
Dedicated Short	−32.84%	−3.58%	−0.18%	22.71%	−8.69%	17.77%	−0.88	−0.41
Emerging Markets	158.97%	9.11%	0.83%	15.34%	−23.03%	15.34%	0.52	0.35
Equity Market Neutral	215.92%	11.11%	0.89%	3.26%	−1.15%	2.81%	0.07	2.61
Event Driven	262.45%	12.52%	1%	3.58%	−11.77%	5.74%	0.21	1.53
Distressed	349.07%	14.75%	1.17%	4.10%	−12.45%	6.43%	0.22	1.71
Multi-Strategy	222.97%	11.34%	0.92%	4.66%	−11.52%	6.19%	0.21	1.22
Risk Arbitrage	128.16%	7.85%	0.64%	3.81%	−6.15%	4.33%	0.14	0.94
Fixed Income Arbitrage	106.48%	6.87%	0.56%	2.02%	−6.96%	3.77%	0	0.82
Global Macro	398.64%	15.86%	1.28%	10.60%	−11.55%	11.15%	0.17	1.08
Long/Short Equity	322.46%	14.11%	1.15%	13.01%	−11.43%	10.46%	0.41	0.99
Managed Futures	87.43%	5.92%	0.55%	9.95%	−9.35%	12.53%	−0.11	0.17
Multi-Strategy on Managed Futures	187.94%	10.17%	0.82%	3.12%	−4.76%	3.69%	0.03	1.74

Source: Data from Credit Suisse/Tremont Hedge Index (www.hedgeindex.com).

TABLE 9.9 Return and Risk Data Summary for All Investable CSFB/Tremont Indexes, 1999–2006

All Investable CSFB/Tremont Indexes Start 12/31/99   End 1/31/06

Trading Strategy	Total Return	Annualized Total Return	Average Month	Best Month	Worst Month	Annualized Standard Deviation	Beta	Sharpe Ratio
Credit Suisse/Tremont Investable Index	57.04%	7.70%	0.62%	2.71%	−1.08%	2.80%	0.03	1.78
Convertible Arbitrage	78.69%	10.01%	0.80%	3.40%	−2.36%	3.81%	0.03	1.91
Dedicated Short	−16.64%	−2.95%	−0.15%	10.88%	−13.57%	15.60%	−0.79	−0.36
Emerging Markets	195.89%	19.52%	1.53%	7.34%	−5.07%	9.06%	0.35	1.85
Equity Market Neutral	43.31%	6.09%	0.50%	2.39%	−0.48%	1.97%	0.02	1.71
Event Driven	73.97%	9.53%	0.77%	2.72%	−1.76%	3.13%	0.08	2.18
Fixed Income Arbitrage	39.23%	5.59%	0.46%	2.97%	−2.21%	3.53%	0.01	0.81
Global Macro	66.20%	8.71%	0.71%	4.36%	−1.76%	4.13%	−0.07	1.45
Long/Short Equity	23.32%	3.51%	0.33%	10.31%	−8.00%	10.16%	0.25	0.08
Managed Futures	70.65%	9.18%	0.81%	9.20%	−8.71%	13.14%	−0.25	0.49
Multi-Strategy	65.47%	8.63%	0.70%	4.87%	−1.54%	3.51%	0.08	1.69

Source: Data from Credit Suisse/Tremont Hedge Index (www.hedgeindex.com).

TABLE 9.10 Return and Risk Data Summary for All Sector CSFB/Tremont Indexes, 1999–2006

All Sector CSFB/Tremont Indexes	Start 12/31/99		End 1/31/06					
Trading Strategy	Total Return	Annualized Total Return	Average Month	Best Month	Worst Month	Annualized Standard Deviation	Beta	Sharpe Ratio
Convertible Arbitrage	66.13%	8.70%	0.70%	3.28%	−2.25%	3.67%	0.03	1.63
Dedicated Short Bias	−15.00%	−2.64%	−0.13%	9.45%	−12.54%	15.27%	−0.79	−0.35
Emerging Markets	168.23%	17.61%	1.40%	6.90%	−5.10%	9.68%	0.41	1.54
Equity Market Neutral	34.13%	4.94%	0.40%	1.45%	−0.43%	1.35%	0.02	1.65
Event Driven	75.62%	9.70%	0.78%	3.15%	−2.83%	3.87%	0.11	1.81
Fixed Income Arbitrage	45.53%	6.36%	0.52%	2.50%	−1.28%	2.73%	0.00	1.33
Global Macro	57.80%	7.79%	0.63%	4.26%	−2.12%	4.24%	−0.01	1.19
Long/Short Equity	71.16%	9.24%	0.75%	5.68%	−2.94%	5.75%	0.20	1.13
Managed Futures	75.91%	9.73%	0.85%	10.20%	−8.42%	13.00%	−0.27	0.54
Multi-Strategy	73.81%	9.51%	0.76%	4.57%	−1.43%	3.28%	0.07	2.07

Source: Data from Credit Suisse/Tremont Hedge Index (www.hedgeindex.com).

With regard to funds of funds, their representative indexes provide a more realistic approach to traditional indexes rather than to investable indexes. Funds of funds are not invested in all hedge funds and are strategy specific. A fund of funds selection exhibits underestimations for given time periods. They aim to isolate specific types of risks. (See Table 9.11.)

Also, in funds of funds, fund selection and management fees charged to investors reduce the overall average level of performance. According to Amin and Kat (2002), funds of funds' survivorship bias is approximately 0.63 percent yearly, and according to Fung and Hsieh (2002a, b) it is estimated to be at 3 percent per year for individual hedge funds and approximately 0.7 percent for funds of funds. The survivorship bias is much lower for funds of funds primarily due to these reasons:

- Funds of funds have less fluctuation in assets under management.
- Funds of funds are less subject to bankruptcy as bankruptcy of one of an FOF's constituents does not imply the bankruptcy of the fund of funds.
- Funds of funds have a greater capacity to absorb new investments.
- Per Duc (2004a, b) the due diligence process conducted in funds of funds eliminates the funds that suffer from structural problems.

The disadvantage of funds of funds is the double fee structure that makes them more expensive. (See Table 9.12.) Liew (2003) shows that actively managed funds of funds make up for this flaw.

Funds of funds' size, age, and leverage do not affect the criteria. Their assets under management are isolated from capital volatility. Their portfolio diversification can minimize the effects of low returns of some components. Funds of funds have not been as affected by risks flowing from maximal capacity. Compared with hedge fund databases, their universe is less heterogeneous.

Funds of funds' index return differentials are less significant than among hedge fund indexes. The CISDM-MAR index results from the median value of all returns and is the best estimator for hedge funds and funds of funds. From 1997 to 2003, the EDHEC index annualized mean performance amounts to 10.16 percent and its volatility to 6.41 percent. These figures are substantially different for specific isolated products. Equity's mean performance amounts to 2.54 percent and volatility to 16.45 percent while fixed income's mean performance amounts to 5.72 percent and volatility to 7.02 percent. A study of fund of funds indexes and hedge fund indexes shows that their returns do not account for catastrophic scenarios and operational risk losses.

TABLE 9.11 Intersection of Data Concentration, Amount between Various Funds of Funds and Hedge Funds Databases

Funds of Funds Information					Intersect			
	Number of Funds	Exclusivity	AA Center	Barclay	InvestHedge	HedgeFund.net	HFR	TASS
AA Center	684	17%		47%	50%	42%	41%	40%
Barclay	724	30%	44%		35%	42%	40%	34%
InvestHedge	691	23%	50%	36%		42%	40%	33%
HedgeFund.net	747	27%	39%	41%	39%		44%	32%
HFR	604	14%	46%	48%	46%	54%		42%
TASS	558	23%	49%	44%	41%	42%	46%	

Note: Intersects of funds of funds database pairs are slightly more important than among hedge fund databases.
Source: Data from EDHEC Business School (www.edhec-risk.com).

TABLE 9.12 Funds of Funds Information

	AAC Fund of Hedge Fund Benchmark	Barclay/GHS Fund of Funds Index	CISDM-MAR Fund of Funds Median	InvestHedge Composite	Tuna Fund of Funds Aggregate Average	HFRI Fund of Funds Composite Index	TASS Fund of Funds Universe Average	Van Fund of Funds Index
AAC Fund of Hedge Fund Benchmark		0.9% Dec 1999	2.8% Dec 99	1.1% Feb 00	0.1% Jan 00	2.4% Aug 98	1.8% Apr 00	1.8% Feb 98
Barclay/GHS Fund of Funds Index			3.6% Dec 98	1.5% Feb 00	0.7% Dec 99	2.4% Aug 98	1.6% Jan 98	2.1% Feb 98
CISDM-MAR Fund of Funds Median				0.7% Apr 00	3.0% Dec 99	4.4% Dec 99	3.4% Dec 99	3.5% Dec 99
InvestHedge Composite					1.7% Feb 00	2.0% Apr 00	2.2% Apr 00	2.3% Feb 00
Tuna Fund of Funds Aggregate Average						2.5% Aug 98	1.7% Jan 95	2.0% Feb 98
HFRI Fund of Funds Composite Index							1.9% Sept 98	2.7% Oct 98
TASS Fund of Funds Universe Average								2.8% Jan 86
Van Fund of Funds Index								

Note: Funds of funds index return differentials are less significant than among hedge fund indexes.
Source: Data from EDHEC Business School (www.edhec-risk.com).

Strategy-specific indexes are heterogeneous. Their monthly return variances or margins can be as high as 17 percent. For example, in 2000, the EACM long/short index showed a –1.56 percent return while the Zurich long/short index was at 20.48 percent. Seven out of 11 strategies exhibited differences of more than 7 percent between two indexes of the same strategies. Funds of funds indexes do not represent accurate estimators of strategies' returns.

CHAPTER 10

Hedge Fund Data and Attrition Rates

This chapter is related to the statistical data from different vendors such as Altvest, Hedge Fund Research (HFR), TASS, Managed Account Reports (MAR/CISDM), and Zurich Capital Markets from 1994 to 2001 highlighted in Appendix I. (See Table 10.1 and Figure 10.1.)

The TASS database of hedge funds consists of both active and defunct hedge funds with monthly returns, assets under management, and other fund-specific information for 4,781 individual funds from February 1977 to August 2004. The database is made up of live and dead funds. The database of dead funds was created in 1994, and it was then that TASS started to transfer funds from the live to the graveyard database. Hedge funds in the live database are those considered to be active at the most recent update of the database as of August 31, 2004. As of that time, the combined database of both live and dead hedge funds contained 4,781 funds with at least one monthly return observation. Out of these 4,781 funds, 2,920 funds are in the live database and 1,861 funds are in the graveyard database. Fifty of these funds were eliminated for reporting gross returns, leaving 2,893 funds in the live and 1,838 funds in the dead database. TASS also eliminated funds that reported returns on a quarterly not monthly basis. All these filters produced a final sample of 4,536 hedge funds, 2,771 of them live and 1,765 dead.

TASS adopted a transferring policy from the live into the dead database if the funds do not report returns for an 8- to 10-month period. TASS defines returns as the change in net asset value during the month, assuming any reinvestment of any distributions on the reinvestment data used by the fund, divided by the net asset value at the beginning of the month, net of management fees, incentive fees, and other fund expenses. These reported returns approximate the returns realized by investors. TASS also converts all foreign currency–denominated returns to U.S. dollar returns using the appropriate exchange rates. (See Figure 10.2.)

TABLE 10.1 Estimations of Survivorship Bias Available in Hedge Fund Research Universe

Research Reference	Database	Time Frame for Research Analysis	Fund Samples Availability	Dead Funds Sample
Ackermann et al. (1999)	HFR & MAR	1988–1995	547	146
Amin & Kat (2003a, b, c)	TASS	1994–2001	1,721	526
Anjilvel et al. (2000)	FRM	1990–2000	1,130	NA
Baquero et al. (2004)	TASS	1994–2000	1,797	612
Barès et al. (2003)	FRM	1996–1999	2,308	131
Barry (2003)	TASS	1994–2001	2,208	1,272
Brown et al. (1999)	U.S. Offshore Fund Directory	1990–1996	395	65
Capocci et al. (2004)	HFR & TASS	1994–2000	2,796	80
Darst (2000)	MAR	1995–1999	2,202	NA
Das (2003)	ZCM	1989–2000	2,467	NA
Edwards & Caglayan (2001a, b)	MAR	1990–1998	1,665	496
Edwards & Liew (1999a, b)	MAR	1982–1996	1,456	NA
Fung & Hsieh (2000)	TASS	1994–1998	1,722	602
Kazemi et al. (2002)	N/M	1998–2000	NA	NA
Liang (2000)	HFR	1993–1998	1,162	110
Liang (2000)	TASS	1993–1998	1,627	426
Liang (2003)	ZCM	1994–2001	2,357	1,193

Source: Data from EDHEC Business School (www.edhec-risk.com) and from the Social Science Research Network (www.ssrn.com).

155

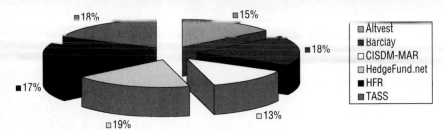

FIGURE 10.1   Number of Funds by Main Hedge Fund Databases
Source: Data from EDHEC Business School (www.edhec-risk.com) and from the
Social Science Research Network (www.ssrn.com).

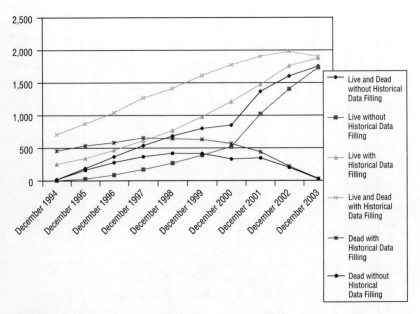

FIGURE 10.2   Number of Hedge Funds under Different Data Assumptions,
1994–2003
Source: Data from EDHEC Business School (www.edhec-risk.com) and from the
Social Science Research Network (www.ssrn.com).

By definition, a hedge fund is transferred into the graveyard database
when it no longer reports its performance or it is considered fully liquidated. It is unclear if retired funds are also considered dead funds. Many
academic papers have published broad data about live and dead hedge
funds and related statistical analysis. (See Table 10.2.)

Researchers providing such information are Mila Getmansky, Andrew
W. Lo, and Schauna X. Mei (2004) or Gaurav S. Amin and Harry Kat

TABLE 10.2 Historical Bias Available in Research

Research Reference	Database	Time Frame for Research Analysis	All Funds Sample	Defunct Funds Sample	Incubation Period in Months	Annualized Approximated Bias
Ackermann et al. (1999)	HFR & MAR	1988–1995	547	146	24	0.05
Barry (2003)	TASS	1994–2001	2,208	1,272	12	1.4
Brown et al. (1997)	TASS	1977–1996	1,230	138	27	3.6
Capocci et al. (2004)	HFR	1984–2000	2,796	801	12/24/36/60	0.96/2.76/3.48/4.20
Edwards & Caglayan (2001)	MAR	1990–1998	1,665	496	12	1.17
Fung & Hsieh (2000)	TASS	1994–1998	1,722	602	12	1.4
Posthuma & Van der Sluis (2004)	TASS	1996–2002	3,580	NA	Depends on funds	4.35
Multiperiod Sampling						
Ackermann, McEnally, & Ravenscraft (1998)	HFR & MAR	1988–1995	547	146	Depends on funds	Immaterial
Edwards & Caglayan (2001)	MAR	1990–1998	1,665	496	12/24 versus 36	0.30%
Fung & Hsieh (2000)	TASS	1994–1998	1,722	602	36	0.60%

Source: Data from EDHEC Business School (www.edhec-risk.com) and from the Social Science Research Network (www.ssrn.com).

(2002). More precisely, Getmansky, Lo, and Mei (2004) found the attrition rate to increase from 3.0 percent in 1994 to 10.7 percent in 2003 with a high of 11.4 percent in 2001. Attrition rate of funds closing to new investment have increased from 0.17 percent in 1994 to 1.47 percent in 2003. Amin and Kat (2003a, b, c) found an annual attrition rate of 2.2 percent in 1995, 5.3 percent in 1996, 4.9 percent in 1998, 15.22 percent in 1999, and 12.3 percent in 2000.

The rising rate of erosion and depletion of hedge funds comes from a number of factors. Hedge funds exhibit a higher level of attrition at an increasing rate over time. Funds of funds' attrition rates are lower due to the extra layer of hidden information but show similar trends. The factors behind attrition rates of funds are lack of capacity, size, business attitude of the manager, and performance.

Data accuracy with regard to hedge funds is highly questionable, as only 10 percent of all the live (1,776) and dead (1,655) funds are common to all three databases provided by TASS, HFR, and ZCM/MAR, per Agarwal, Daniel, and Naik (2004). Also, it is important to note that because most hedge funds are not allowed to solicit the public, the prospectuses are not included in the databases, depriving researchers of more detailed information concerning the funds' investment processes, securities, risk management framework, leverage information, hurdle rates, high-water mark levels, and other compliance and legal issues. Liquidated funds lack transparency. Ackermann, McEnally, and Ravenscraft (1999) and Brown, Goetzmann, Ibbotson, and Ross (1992) showed that the majority of hedge fund databases include data only for funds that are currently in existence, inducing a survivorship bias that affects the estimated mean and volatility of returns. (See Figures 10.3 and 10.4.)

For instance, Ackermann, McEnally, and Ravenscraft (1999) estimated that the impact of survivorship on average returns for offshore accounts varies due to a bias of 0.16 percent. Liang (2000) and Amin and Kat (2003c) approximated that the bias is about 2 percent, and Brown, Goetzmann, and Ibbotson (1999) valued it at 3 percent. Liang (2000) found that the annual hedge fund attrition rate is 8.3 percent for the 1994–1998 sample period using TASS data. Baquero, Horst, and Verbeek (2002), like Fung and Hsieh (2000, 2002b) and Liang (2000), found that surviving hedge funds outperform nonsurviving funds by about 2.1percent per year. Getmansky (2004) documented that attrition rates depended largely on past returns, asset flows, age, and assets under management capacity. Howell (2001) found that the probability of hedge funds failing in the first year is 7.4 percent and as high as 20.3

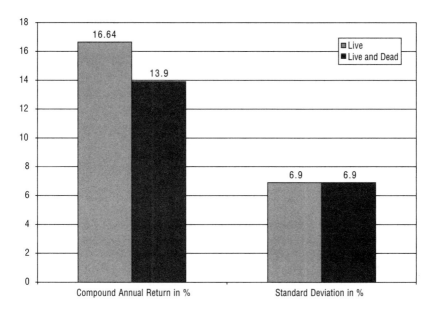

FIGURE 10.3 Survivorship Bias with Historical Data Filling in Percent, 1995–2004
Source: Data from EDHEC Business School (www.edhec-risk.com) and from the Social Science Research Network (www.ssrn.com).

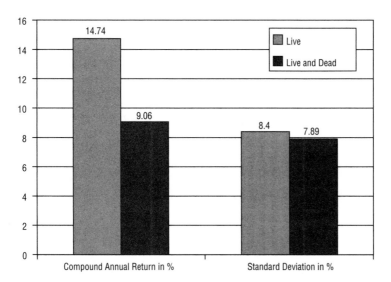

FIGURE 10.4 Survivorship Bias without Historical Data Filling in Percent, 1995–2004
Source: Data from EDHEC Business School (www.edhec-risk.com) and from the Social Science Research Network (www.ssrn.com).

percent in the second year. Underperforming younger hedge funds tend to drop out of the database faster than older ones as they tend to take more risks, according to Getmansky (2004) and Jen, Heasman, and Boyatt (2001). Brown, Goetzmann, and Park (2001a) found that the half-life of the TASS hedge funds is 30 months.

Brooks and Kat (2002) estimate that about 30 percent of new hedge funds do not survive past 36 months due to poor performance. Amin and Kat (2003c) revealed that 40 percent of them do not succeed past the fifth year. The TASS database also has the breakdown of live and dead funds among different types of investment categories. (See Table 10.3.)

Long/short equity has the highest concentration of combined funds with 1,415 hedge funds; funds of funds account for 952 funds, managed futures 511, and event driven 384. All four of these categories account for 71.9 percent of the funds in the combined database. And more precisely, 24 percent of funds of funds are live and 15 percent are in the graveyard. Managed futures funds have 7 percent live and 18 percent dead. There are 127 convertible arbitrage funds in the live database with an average return of 9.92 percent and an average standard deviation of 5.51 percent; in the graveyard database the 49 convertible arbitrage funds have an average mean return of 10.02 percent and a much higher average standard deviation of 8.14 percent. Volatility in the graveyard database is higher than in the live database.

TABLE 10.3 Number of Hedge Funds in the TASS Database

Period	Beginning	New	Dead	End	Attrition (%)
1994–1995	455	151	10	596	2.2
1995–1996	596	197	15	778	2.52
1996–1997	778	229	48	959	6.17
1997–1998	959	330	47	1,242	4.9
1998–1999	1,242	83	113	1,212	9.1
1999–2000	1,212	172	140	1,244	11.55
2000–2001	1,244	104	153	1,195	12.3

Source: G. Amin and H. Kat. "Welcome to the Dark Side: Hedge Fund Attrition and Survivorship Bias over the Period 1994–2001," working paper, Case Business School, 2003; *Journal of Alternative Investments* 6, 57–73. Parts of the data have been changed and altered by the author. Data from eLibrary, www.ssrn.com, or Social Science Research Network.

Serial correlation of returns—that is, the correlation between one month and another following one—is a determination that can be used to detect manipulation and smoothing of returns, according to Lo (2001, 2002) and Getmansky, Lo, and Makarov (2004). The six categories with highest serial correlation averages are convertible arbitrage (31.4 percent), funds of funds (19.6 percent), event driven (18.4 percent), emerging markets (16.5 percent), fixed income arbitrage (16.2 percent), and multi-strategy (14.7 percent). It would appear that smoothing is more pronounced for convertible arbitrage and fixed income arbitrage.

The median age of graveyard funds is 45 months; half of all liquidated funds never reached their fourth anniversary. The mode of the distribution is 36 months. The median assets under management for funds in the graveyard database are $6.3 million. From 1994 to 2003, the average attrition rate has been 8.8 percent. It is noticed that the rate rose in 1998 partly due to the Long-Term Capital Management near collapse and its consequences on the financial markets. The attrition rate rose to a maximum of 11.4 percent in 2001 principally due to the long/short equity category and the result of the bursting of the technology bubble. The average attrition rate for the TASS database as a whole is 8.8 percent, and the average attrition rates by categories vary drastically from 1994 to 2003. (See Tables 10.4 through 10.13 on pages 162 to 170.)

These averages highlight the different risks among investment styles. Convertible arbitrage exhibits a 5.2 percent attrition rate, the lowest average attrition rate with the second lowest average return volatility of 5.89 percent. The highest average attrition rate is 14.4 percent for managed futures with the highest average volatility of 18.55 percent. Emerging markets experienced a 16.1 percent attrition rate in 1998 principally due to the turmoil in emerging markets in 1997 and 1998 and also reflected in the −37.7 percent return in the CSFB/Tremont Emerging Markets index for 1998. (See Table 10.14 and Figure 10.5 on pages 171 and 172.)

Similarly, not too long after the equity bubble burst, from 2001 to 2003, the attrition rate of the long/short equity style rose again to 13.4 percent, 12.4 percent, and 12.3 percent, respectively, for the three years. This category represents the most important one of the industry and thus must be carefully watched. There are quantifiable models such as the Cox proportional hazards model with time-dependent predictor variables (covariates). (See Tables 10.15 and 10.16 on pages 173 and 174.)

In the model, each of the three exits is treated as a separate failure type. For each covariate, the Cox model produces a hazard ratio (HR), which represents the percent change in the hazard rate of the fund

TABLE 10.4 Survival Rate of Hedge Funds Alive in June 1994

Months	2000/2001	1999/2000	1998/1999	1997/1998	1996/1997	1995/1996	1994/1995
1	98.71	100.00	99.74	99.75	100.00	99.78	100.00
2	97.43	99.12	98.68	99.50	99.07	99.33	100.00
3	96.78	97.94	97.37	98.50	98.14	98.88	100.00
4	96.78	97.64	96.58	97.74	96.52	98.88	100.00
5	95.50	97.35	96.05	97.49	95.36	98.88	100.00
6	94.53	96.76	95.00	97.24	95.13	98.88	99.78
7	93.57	95.58	94.47	97.24	94.43	98.65	99.78
8	89.07	94.10	93.68	96.74	93.74	98.43	98.68
9	87.78	94.10	92.89	96.49	93.50	98.20	98.68
10	86.50	94.10	92.37	95.99	93.27	97.53	98.46
11	85.53	93.22	90.26	95.49	92.81	97.08	98.24
12	84.89	91.74	89.21	95.24	92.58	96.85	97.30

Note: This table shows the survival rates in % of the funds alive in June 1994 on an annually rescaled basis.

Source: G. Amin and H. Kat. "Welcome to the Dark Side: Hedge Fund Attrition and Survivorship Bias over the Period 1994–2001," working paper, Case Business School, 2003; *Journal of Alternative Investments* 6, 57–73. Parts of the data have been changed and altered by the author. Data from eLibrary, www.ssrn.com, or Social Science Research Network.

TABLE 10.5 Survivorship Bias in Mean Returns of Various Groups of Hedge Funds as Obtained over Seven Periods

Class	2000/2001	1999/2001	1998/2001	1997/2001	1996/2001	1995/2001	1994/2001
Overall	0.78	2.09	2.26	2.36	2.01	1.01	1.89
Size 1	3.39	6.38	6.31	5.39	4.40	2.31	1.77
Size 2	1.37	2.37	2.57	1.97	1.64	1.37	1.62
Size 3	0.57	1.54	1.91	1.76	2.22	1.18	1.48
Size 4	−0.43	0.07	0.24	0.45	0.12	−0.19	0.48
Age 1	1.17	3.01	4.18	1.53	3.48	0.56	3.13
Age 2	1.06	4.24	1.52	3.49	0.77	2.54	2.61
Age 3	0.91	1.22	2.64	1.39	2.48	2.63	1.05
Age 4	−0.08	1.67	0.65	2.36	2.44	1.26	0.12
Age 5	1.30	0.12	2.23	2.65	1.78	0.36	1.56
Age 6	−0.57	1.27	2.25	2.40	0.28	1.32	1.84
Age 7	0.98	1.79	1.86	1.35	1.29	1.38	1.02
Money No	0.60	2.30	2.65	2.38	2.17	1.30	1.83
Money Yes	0.93	1.95	2.00	1.98	1.90	1.53	1.89
Leverage No	0.11	1.04	1.53	1.21	0.93	0.67	1.40
Leverage Yes	1.14	2.66	2.68	2.75	2.74	2.11	2.29
Convertible Arbitrage	−0.37	−0.15	0.17	0.01	0.09	−0.28	0.34
Event Driven	0.40	1.12	1.27	0.61	0.65	0.01	0.61
Long/Short Equity	0.99	1.88	2.14	2.19	2.25	1.59	1.93
Relative Value	0.85	1.45	1.80	2.21	1.70	1.80	1.87
Emerging Markets	0.82	3.94	2.98	1.40	1.30	−0.40	1.57
Global Macro	0.89	3.23	4.05	4.13	4.12	3.65	1.40

Note: All estimates are annualized.

Source: G. Amin and H. Kat. "Welcome to the Dark Side: Hedge Fund Attrition and Survivorship Bias over the Period 1994–2001," working paper, Case Business School, 2003; *Journal of Alternative Investments* 6, 57–73. Parts of the data have been changed and altered by the author. Data from eLibrary, www.ssrn.com, or Social Science Research Network.

TABLE 10.6 Differences in Mean Returns of Surviving and Dead Funds Belonging to Various Groups of Hedge Funds

Class	2000/2001	1999/2001	1998/2001	1997/2001	1996/2001	1995/2001	1994/2001
Overall	13.12	15.02	12.84	9.63	8.03	5.13	7.30
Size 1	7.32	12.65	12.21	8.85	7.87	4.58	4.57
Size 2	11.88	10.90	7.81	5.71	2.79	2.11	5.12
Size 3	20.57	19.41	16.29	9.93	7.83	2.11	1.62
Size 4	-10.18	-0.86	1.01	2.22	-0.16	-3.42	2.38
Age 1	26.20	27.08	23.08	8.86	14.56	-2.82	12.04
Age 2	21.03	25.47	11.07	16.45	-3.06	11.01	10.41
Age 3	13.82	10.38	17.69	-2.74	12.02	11.19	6.15
Age 4	4.27	18.42	-7.12	13.13	11.86	7.24	-2.67
Age 5	29.06	-14.32	15.65	13.86	9.46	-2.63	5.88
Age 6	-33.39	11.03	16.12	12.7	-3.47	5.49	7.85
Age 7	7.34	9.95	8.78	4.8	5.94	6.38	4.57
Money No	5.90	13.56	12.89	8.39	6.64	0.59	4.88
Money Yes	16.02	15.29	12.64	9.98	8.66	7.07	8.17
Leverage No	0.70	6.52	7.36	3.67	2.36	1.27	5.03
Leverage Yes	18.05	18.32	15.51	12.59	11.91	8.86	8.92
Convertible Arbitrage	-8.08	-3.40	2.03	0.6	0.73	-1.51	2.71
Event Driven	4.55	7.66	6.91	3.57	3.37	-0.11	2.83
Long/Short Equity	21.97	18.21	15.16	11.08	10.73	7.17	11.01
Relative Value	15.23	14.92	14.3	16.28	11.65	9.50	7.51
Emerging Markets	3.30	14.19	10.23	3.32	-0.25	-4.59	2.01
Global Macro	0.63	8.48	11.00	8.62	8.08	7.58	2.85

Note: Means are estimated over seven different periods.
Source: G. Amin and H. Kat. "Welcome to the Dark Side: Hedge Fund Attrition and Survivorship Bias over the Period 1994–2001," working paper, Case Business School, 2003; *Journal of Alternative Investments* 6, 57–73. Parts of the data have been changed and altered by the author. Data from eLibrary, www.ssrn.com, or Social Science Research Network.

TABLE 10.7 Number of Funds of Funds in Database

Period	Beginning	New	Dead	End	Attrition (%)
1994–1995	104	41	1	144	0.96
1995–1996	144	21	2	163	1.39
1996–1997	163	36	1	198	0.61
1997–1998	198	62	8	252	4.04
1998–1999	252	3	12	243	4.76
1999–2000	243	22	12	253	4.94
2000–2001	253	2	32	223	12.65

Source: G. Amin and H. Kat. "Welcome to the Dark Side: Hedge Fund Attrition and Survivorship Bias over the Period 1994–2001," working paper, Case Business School, 2003; *Journal of Alternative Investments* 6, 57–73. Parts of the data have been changed and altered by the author. Data from eLibrary, www.ssrn.com, or Social Science Research Network.

brought on by a unit increase in the value of the covariate. When HR > 1 the covariate increases the hazard (decreases survival), and when HR < 1 the covariate decreases the hazard. The percent change in the hazard rate of the fund due to the covariate is given by (HR − 1) × 100%. Hazard ratios can be defined by binary covariates such as leverage or hurdle rate or continuous covariates such as returns or volatility. The Cox model does not provide estimates of survival times, but focuses only on hazard ratios and of their impact on the hazard function. To approximate hedge funds' lifetimes, an accelerated failure time (AFT) model or Weibull regression model is used. (See Tables 7.17 and 7.18 in Chapter 7.)

The following findings have been made from those models. High volatility in returns and in assets is strongly associated with liquidation, and high returns are more protective of liquidation than of other exits. The hazard ratio of 1.058 on the entire portfolio across all strategies of the funds reveals that a $100 million increase in asset volatility increases the risk of exit by 5.8 percent. Similarly, the hazard ratio of 1.243 indicates that every $100 million increase in asset volatility increases the risk of liquidation by 24.3 percent.

Asset volatility by itself increases the risk of liquidation. Rouah (2005) noted that every 1 percent increase in monthly returns decreases the hazard of all exits by 6.9 percent and decreases the hazard of liquidation by 9.6 percent. Rouah (2005) found there is no effect of leverage or redemption

TABLE 10.8 Survivorship Bias in Mean Fund of Funds Returns

Class	2000/2001	1999/2001	1998/2001	1997/2001	1996/2001	1995/2001	1994/2001
Overall	0.45	0.33	0.67	0.69	0.75	0.78	0.63
Size 1	2.43	-0.22	0.63	-0.35	0.66	0.17	-1.03
Size 2	-0.17	0.28	0.62	0.46	0.18	0.21	0.48
Size 3	0.11	0.50	0.43	0.51	0.60	0.65	0.34
Size 4	-0.04	-0.18	0.05	0.17	0.24	0.33	0.35
Age 1	0.19	0.12	1.44	0.55	1.13	1.62	0.54
Age 2	0.00	0.19	0.89	1.23	1.37	0.84	0.27
Age 3	0.65	1.53	1.08	1.01	0.89	0.21	0.67
Age 4	2.02	-0.07	0.58	0.83	0.18	0.68	0.70
Age 5	-0.65	0.59	0.37	0.36	0.82	0.12	0.92
Age 6	0.40	0.91	0.05	0.69	0.47	0.09	1.26
Age 7	0.05	-0.31	0.20	0.05	0.13	0.13	-0.06
Money No	0.15	0.13	0.53	0.47	0.70	0.38	0.13
Money Yes	0.59	0.49	0.75	0.84	0.77	1.05	1.05
Leverage No	0.50	-0.01	0.21	0.34	0.46	0.39	0.23
Leverage Yes	0.30	0.65	0.95	0.92	0.93	1.02	0.92

Note: Survivorship bias in the mean returns of various groups of funds of funds as obtained over seven different periods (annualized).

Source: G. Amin and H. Kat. "Welcome to the Dark Side: Hedge Fund Attrition and Survivorship Bias over the Period 1994–2001," working paper, Case Business School, 2003; *Journal of Alternative Investments* 6, 57–73. Parts of the data have been changed and altered by the author. Data from eLibrary, www.ssrn.com, or Social Science Research Network.

TABLE 10.9 Number of Failure Types of Dead Funds, with Mean and Standard Deviation of Returns and Assets during Their Entire History, and 12 and 6 Months of Reporting, 1994–2003

Table A: Returns in %

	Number of Funds	Entire History		Last 12 Months		Last 6 Months	
		Mean	Standard Deviation	Mean	Standard Deviation	Mean	Standard Deviation
Live	2,371	1.07	4.95	1.37	3.42	1.32	3.03
No Reporting	522	1.28	7.13	0.85	8.66	0.64	9.60
Liquidated	513	0.71	7.45	−0.06	8.30	−0.14	8.52
Closed	189	0.72	6.81	0.37	7.36	0.42	7.58

Table B: Returns in $ Millions

	Number of Funds	Entire History		Last 12 Months		Last 6 Months	
		Mean	Standard Deviation	Mean	Standard Deviation	Mean	Standard Deviation
Live	2,371	93	357	125	508	137	576
No Reporting	522	105	572	93	498	93	496
Liquidated	513	54	315	58	354	57	356
Closed	189	65	416	59	354	48	256

Assumptions: In (A) Number of live funds and exited funds for each exit type, with the mean and standard deviation of their returns. In (B) Number of live funds and exited funds for each exit type, with the mean and standard deviation of the assets under management. Returns and assets are calculated over their entire history over the last 12 months before exit and over the last 6 months before the exit.

Source: Fabrice Rouah, "Competing Risks in Hedge Fund Survival," working paper, McGill University, Montreal, 2005; Foundation for Managed Derivatives Research (FMDR), Institut de Finance Mathématique de Montréal (IFM2), and Centre de Recherche en E-finance (CREF). Paper also published in the public domain of the Social Science Research network. Data from eLibrary, www.ssrn.com, or Social Science Research Network.

TABLE 10.10 Hedge Fund Attrition Rates, 1994–2003

Year	Existing Funds	Funds Entering	Liquidated Funds	Closed Funds	Funds Not Reporting
1994	1,153	336	13	2	9
1995	1,464	474	33	2	29
1996	1,875	459	104	8	79
1997	2,314	449	92	20	103
1998	2,370	463	117	37	229
1999	2,442	536	91	39	112
2000	2,729	508	121	36	216
2001	2,852	606	101	56	134
2002	3,175	638	129	51	111
2003	3,535	519	140	52	121

Note: Number of existing funds at the beginning of each year, funds entering the database during the year, and funds experiencing each type of exit (liquidation, closed to new investment, and no longer reporting) during the year.

Source: Fabrice Rouah, "Competing Risks in Hedge Fund Survival," working paper, McGill University, Montreal, 2005; Foundation for Managed Derivatives Research (FMDR), Institut de Finance Mathématique de Montréal (IFM2), and Centre de Recherche en E-finance (CREF). Paper also published in the public domain of the Social Science Research network. Data from eLibrary, www.ssrn.com, or Social Science Research Network.

period on survival, while Gregoriou (2002) does find an effect. Rouah (2005) also mentioned that a high-water mark imposed by hedge funds increases liquidation risks. Funds with a hurdle rate tend to survive longer. Persistent volatility is a more important predictor of liquidation than short-term volatility as losing managers tend to increase volatility to improve quick profits. High returns measured by alpha lead to decreases in reporting time of funds and fund closure and have no effect on the time to liquidation of hedge funds.

EDHEC produced the information in Table 10.17 (see page 175) to provide more transparency on the due diligence operations of the indexes. This table highlights the way due diligence is conducted and how ethically the indexes and the funds making up the indexes are being produced.

The EDHEC Risk Management Centre provided information on dead and live funds in database by strategies. (See Table 10.18 on page 176.)

TABLE 10.11 Annual Mortality Rates in Percent

Year	All Exits	Liquidate	Closed	No Report	Liquidate +NoRep	Liquidate +Closed	NoRep +Closed
1994	2.08	1.13	0.17	0.78	1.91	1.30	0.95
1995	4.37	2.25	0.14	1.98	4.23	2.39	2.12
1996	10.19	5.55	0.43	4.21	9.76	5.97	4.64
1997	10.07	4.31	0.94	4.83	9.14	5.25	5.76
1998	16.16	4.94	1.56	9.66	14.60	6.50	11.22
1999	9.91	3.73	1.60	4.59	8.31	5.32	6.18
2000	13.67	4.43	1.32	7.91	12.35	5.75	9.23
2001	10.20	3.54	1.96	4.70	8.34	5.50	6.66
2002	9.17	4.06	1.61	3.50	7.56	5.67	5.10
2003	8.85	3.96	1.47	3.42	7.38	5.43	4.89

Note: Mortality rates are expressed as a proportion of hedge funds experiencing each type of exit (liquidation, of closed to new investment, and no longer reporting), experiencing liquidation or no reporting (third to last column), experiencing liquidation or closure (second to last column), and experiencing no reporting or closure (last column).

Source: Fabrice Rouah, "Competing Risks in Hedge Fund Survival," working paper, McGill University, Montreal, 2005; Foundation for Managed Derivatives Research (FMDR), Institut de Finance Mathématique de Montréal (IFM2), and Centre de Recherche en E-finance (CREF). Paper also published in the public domain of the Social Science Research network. Data from eLibrary, www.ssrn.com, or Social Science Research Network.

TABLE 10.12   Mean Monthly Returns of Live and Dead Funds and Estimates of Survivorship Bias, 1994–2003

Dead Group	Live Return	Dead Return	Bias/Month	Bias/Year
No Reporting + Liquidated + Closed	1.043	0.917	0.126%	1.510%
Liquidated + Closed	1.043	0.770	0.273%	3.280%
No Reporting + Liquidated	1.043	0.900	0.143%	1.720%
No Reporting + Closed	1.043	1.073	−0.030%	−0.360%
Liquidated	1.043	0.667	0.376%	4.510%
Closed	1.043	0.999	0.044%	0.530%
No Reporting	1.043	1.103	−0.060%	−0.720%

Note: Estimates of monthly and yearly survivorship bias are obtained by defining live funds as those alive at December 2003, and dead funds as no longer reporting, liquidated, or closed to new investment.
Source: Fabrice Rouah, "Competing Risks in Hedge Fund Survival," working paper, McGill University, Montreal, 2005; Foundation for Managed Derivatives Research (FMDR), Institut de Finance Mathématique de Montréal (IFM2), and Centre de Recherche en E-finance (CREF). Paper also published in the public domain of the Social Science Research network. Data from eLibrary, www.ssrn.com, or Social Science Research Network.

TABLE 10.13   Live Group—Alive at December 2003 + No Reporting

Dead Group	Live Return	Dead Return	Bias/Month	Bias/Year
Closed + Liquidated	1.05	0.771	0.279%	3.350%
Liquidated	1.05	0.667	0.383%	4.600%
Closed	1.05	1.000	0.050%	0.600%

Note: Estimates of monthly and yearly survivorship bias are obtained by defining live funds as those alive at December 2003 plus those no longer reporting, and dead funds as liquidated funds and funds closed to new investment. Bias/month is the difference between live returns and dead returns. Bias/year is bias/month multiplied by 12.
Source: Fabrice Rouah, "Competing Risks in Hedge Fund Survival," working paper, McGill University, Montreal, 2005; Foundation for Managed Derivatives Research (FMDR), Institut de Finance Mathématique de Montréal (IFM2), and Centre de Recherche en E-finance (CREF). Paper also published in the public domain of the Social Science Research network. Data from eLibrary, www.ssrn.com, or Social Science Research Network.

TABLE 10.14 Estimated Survival Time until Liquidation with +/– Prorated Estimated Standard Error in Prorated Years

All Exits	All Funds		Large Funds		Small Funds		Log-Rank
	Mean	S.E.	Mean	S.E.	Mean	S.E.	p-value
Convertible Arbitrage	3.54	0.06	NA	NA	3.35	0.13	NA
Distressed Securities	5.25	0.15	5.45	0.13	5.00	0.27	0.0949
Emerging Markets	6.51	0.19	6.73	0.22	6.16	0.32	0.0439
Equity Hedge	6.62	0.08	7.00	0.09	5.62	0.13	<0.0001
Equity Market Neutral	7.12	0.25	7.78	0.27	4.22	0.20	0.0003
Equity Non-Hedge	7.68	0.31	8.53	0.36	4.70	0.23	0.0015
Event Driven	4.56	0.09	4.79	0.07	3.67	0.13	0.0122
Fixed Income	7.36	0.21	7.81	0.25	4.12	0.14	0.0224
Funds of Funds	6.47	0.06	6.12	0.04	6.03	0.12	<0.0001
Market Timing	5.28	0.29	5.59	0.36	4.51	0.40	0.3415
Merger Arbitrage	4.02	0.10	3.73	0.10	4.01	0.18	0.6753
Relative Value Arbitrage	4.56	0.12	4.67	0.11	4.36	0.21	0.2464
Sector	5.52	0.14	5.47	0.14	5.16	0.24	0.0083
Short Selling	4.36	0.19	4.50	NA	1.33	NA	0.7948
All Funds	8.29	0.07	8.88	0.08	6.43	0.08	<0.0001

Note: Survival time is defined as the time until liquidation.

Source: Fabrice Rouah, "Competing Risks in Hedge Fund Survival," working paper, McGill University, Montreal, 2005; Foundation for Managed Derivatives Research (FMDR), Institut de Finance Mathématique de Montréal (IFM2), and Centre de Recherche en E-finance (CREF). Paper also published in the public domain of the Social Science Research network. Data from eLibrary, www.ssrn.com, or Social Science Research Network.

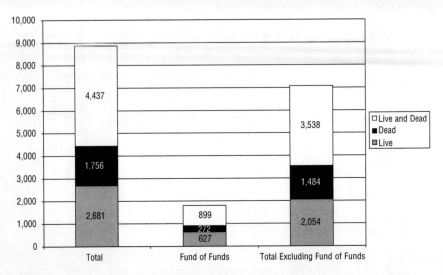

FIGURE 10.5   Number of Hedge Funds in Publicly Available Domain of CSFB
Database from January 1995 to March 2004
Source: Data from EDHEC Business School (www.edhec-risk.com) and from the
Social Science Research Network (www.ssrn.com).

CSFB/Tremont's selection criteria are:

- Member of the original index.
- Accepts new investments.
- Redemptions or initial investment greater than $100,000.
- Not a U.S.-domiciled hedge fund.
- No lockup period.
- Monthly liquidity for entry and exit.
- Advance notification of maximum one month except for event driven
  and convertible arbitrage (quarterly).
- Meets the reporting criteria of the original index.
- One of the six largest funds in the eligible funds in all 10 sectors.

(See Table 10.19 on page 177.)
   Dow Jones has the following criteria:

- Separated account.
- Assets under management greater than $50 million.
- Track record greater than two years.
- Leverage constraint depending on the strategy.

TABLE 10.15 Hazard Ratios from the Cox Proportional Hazards Model under Competing Risks and with Time-Dependent Covariates, 1994–2003

Assumptions

Hazard ratios are estimated for each exit type under different competing risks.

Minimum investments are assumed in $M. Avg_AUM (t) and Std-Dev_AUM (t) are in $100 millions.

A hazard ratio greater than 1 increases the risk of failure while a hazard ratio less than one decreases the risk of failure.

For each variable the p-value is from a likelihood ratio (LR) test that the covariate is identical with various exit types where the LR is obtained from only that variable included in the model. For all variables included the LR test p-value is <0.0001.

	Liquidated	Closed	No Reporting	All Exits	LR p-value
Mean Return 1 Year	0.904	0.918	0.959	0.931	0.0007
Standard Deviation 1 Year	1.031	0.964	1.013	1.022	0.6838
High-Water Mark	1.716	1.062	1.030	1.238	0.0213
Hurdle	0.253	0.165	0.248	0.236	0.3010
Incentive Fees	1.013	1.022	1.019	1.016	0.7831
Management Fees	0.863	0.976	0.857	0.881	0.0564
Time-Dependent Mean Return (t) and Time-Dependent Standard Deviation	0.939	1.035	0.946	0.977	0.1236
Avg_AUM (t)	0.634	0.587	0.994	0.910	<0.0001
StdDev_AUM (t)	1.243	1.085	1.019	1.058	0.0837

Note: Survival time is defined as the time until liquidation.

Source: Fabrice Rouah, "Competing Risks in Hedge Fund Survival," working paper, McGill University, Montreal, 2005; Foundation for Managed Derivatives Research (FMDR), Institut de Finance Mathématique de Montréal (IFM2), and Centre de Recherche en E-finance (CREF). Paper also published in the public domain of the Social Science Research network. Data from eLibrary, www.ssrn.com, or Social Science Research Network.

TABLE 10.16 Hazard Ratios Cox Model with Multiple Failure Types

With Multiple Exit Types—Timing Restricted			
	Liquidated	Closed	No Reporting	LR p-value
Within a quarter	1.285	1.672	1.349	0.0336
Within a year	1.873	1.018	1.039	<0.0001
Within two years	1.669	0.849	0.565	<0.0001
Alpha (Quarter)	1.103	1.153	1.04	0.0332
Alpha (Year)	0.257	0.014	0.106	0.0003
Time	1.081	1.191	0.993	0.0135
Standard Deviation	1.068	1.045	1.074	<0.0001

With Time-Dependent Covariates and Multiple Exit Types			
	Liquidated	Closed	No Reporting	LR p-value
Under (t)	3.809	1.405	1.400	<0.0001
Alpha (t)	0.940	0.101	0.895	<0.0001
Time	0.937	1.052	0.911	0.0135
Standard Deviation (t)	1.001	1.000	1.000	0.8057

Note: Survival time is defined as the time until liquidation.
Source: Fabrice Rouah, "Competing Risks in Hedge Fund Survival," working paper, McGill University, Montreal, 2005; Foundation for Managed Derivatives Research (FMDR), Institut de Finance Mathématique de Montréal (IFM2), and Centre de Recherche en E-finance (CREF). Paper also published in the public domain of the Social Science Research network. Data from eLibrary, www.ssrn.com, or Social Science Research Network.

TABLE 10.17 Index Due Diligence

Index Provider	Pricing Frequency	Initial Due Diligence	Ongoing Due Diligence
CSFB/Tremont	Monthly	Tremont	Data is compared to audited results once a year. Only data that is statistically aberrant is subject to verification during the year.
Dow Jones	Daily	Lyra Capital	Apollo Capital Management verifies trades and reconciles managed accounts valuations on a daily basis. Daily: accounts are reviewed to check leverage requirements, verify styles adequacy, and verify investments guidelines. Monthly: accounts are verified with quantitative analysis, VAR, and correlation matrices. Quarterly: correlation analysis. Annually: independent audit and background checks for each management firm.
FTSE	Daily	Harcourt	Daily risk monitoring and underlying valuation performed by prime broker and manager. The data independently valued by Derivatives Portfolio Management Limited or the administrator. MSS Capital is the platform manager to perform daily risk monitoring and management.
HFRX	Daily	Hedge Fund Research	Hedge Fund Research
MSCI	Daily	Lyxor monitors the funds' capacity and liquidity. MSCI monitors transparency, adequacy, and classification of funds.	Lyxor monitors and controls investment mandate. It verifies pricing and NAV. MSCI does full (quarterly) and partial (intraquarterly) index reviews.
S&P	Daily	Albourne Partners performs the surveys and due diligence.	Derivatives Portfolio Management Limited is the administrator and PlusFunds is the managed account platform to verify the trades and reconcile valuations and managed accounts on a daily basis.

Source: EDHEC Business School (www.edhec-risk.com) and eLibrary (www.ssrn.com).

TABLE 10.18 Number of Funds in CSFB/Tremont Live, Dead, and Combined Hedge Fund Databases, Grouped by Category

Trading Strategy	Number of CSFB/Tremont Funds in		
	Live	Dead	Combined
Convertible Arbitrage	127	49	176
Dedicated Short Selling	14	15	29
Emerging Markets	130	133	263
Equity Market Neutral	173	87	260
Event Driven	250	134	384
Fixed Income Arbitrage	104	71	175
Global Macro	118	114	232
Long/Short Equity	883	532	1,415
Managed Futures	195	316	511
Multi-Strategy	98	41	139
Fund of Funds	679	273	952
Total	2,771	1,765	4,536

Source: Data from EDHEC Business School (www.edhec-risk.com) and from the Social Science Research Network (www.ssrn.com).

FTSE Financial Times and the London Stock Exchange (UK Stock Index) has the following selection requirements:

- Unleveraged assets under management greater than two years.
- Monthly liquidity and reporting.
- Independently audited financial statements.
- Open and accepting investor subscriptions.
- Sufficient remaining capacity.
- Not part of another index product.
- Hedge funds not belonging to specialist interest strategies.

HFRX (Hedge Fund Research Index) requires:

- Open for investment.
- Daily transparency.
- Pass extensive qualitative screening and due diligence audits.

TABLE 10.19 Frequency Counts and Assets under Management of Funds in CSFB/Tremont Dead Funds Database by Category and Inclusion Code

Code	All Funds	Convertible Arbitrage	Dedicated Short Selling	Emerging Markets	Equity Market Neutral	Event Driven	Fixed Income Arbitrage	Global Macro	Long/Short Equity	Managed Futures	Multi-Strategy	Fund of Funds
					Frequency Count							
Fund liquidated	913	19	7	78	65	50	29	53	257	190	30	135
Fund no longer reporting to Tremont TASS	511	21	4	34	12	56	26	29	187	43	7	92
TASS Tremont have been unable to contact the manager for updated information	147	4	1	7	8	17	3	17	54	18	1	17
Fund closed to new investment	7	0	0	0	0	1	2	0	3	0	0	1
Fund has merged into another entity	56	2	1	5	0	6	3	6	16	9	1	7
Fund dormant	2	0	0	0	0	1	0	0	1	0	0	0
Unknown	129	3	2	9	2	3	8	9	14	56	2	21
Total	1,765	49	15	133	87	134	71	114	532	316	41	273
Code	All Funds				**Assets Under Management**							
Fund liquidated	18,754	1168	62	1677	1656	2047	1712	2615	4468	975	641	1732
Fund no longer reporting to Tremont	36,366	6420	300	848	992	7132	2245	678	10164	537	882	6167
Tremont has been unable to contact the manager for updated information	4,127	45	34	729	133	1398	50	115	931	269	2	423
Fund closed to new investment	487	0	0	0	0	100	31	0	250	0	0	106
Fund has merged into another entity	3,135	12	31	143	0	222	419	1775	473	33	3	24
Fund dormant	8	0	0	0	0	6	0	0	2	0	0	0
Unknown	3,052	42	18	222	9	159	152	32	193	1671	18	538
Total	65,931	7686	445	3620	2789	11063	4610	5215	16482	3484	1546	8991

Note: Assets under management are at the time of transfer into the dead fund database.
Source: Data from EDHEC Business School (www.edhec-risk.com) and from the Social Science Research Network (www.ssrn.com).

Morgan Stanley Capital International (MSCI) selects upon:

- Pass due diligence.
- Agree to offer frequent liquidity and sufficient capacity.
- Agree with MSCI on the classification.
- Funds should have other significant investors outside of those tracking the index.

Standard & Poor's (S&P) selection is based on:

- Separated account.
- Assets under management greater than $75 million.
- Track record greater than three years.
- Additional investment capacity greater than $100 million.

The diversification of the indexes' bases differs greatly depending on what criteria the indexes fundamentally define. Some indexes, such as the S&P, are equally weighted whereas the CSFB/Tremont is preferred value–weighted. The FTSE is investability weighted. Indexes are not standardized as to method of weighting. Also, the due diligence and the recalculation of the audits do not have the same frequency and timing. For instance, MSCI, Dow Jones, and Hedge Fund Research indexes are checked for rebalancing on a quarterly basis while rebalancing of CSFB/Tremont, FTSE, and S&P indexes is performed on a semiannual or annual basis. The audits of the indexes differ slightly depending on whether qualitative due diligence is enhanced or quantitative analysis prevails. For example, audits of Dow Jones, Hedge Fund Research, and S&P indexes are primarily based on quantitative analysis while those of CSFB/Tremont and MSCI are based on index committees' evaluations and validations. The FTSE index audit relies on results of due diligence and compliance examinations. (See Table 10.20.)

TABLE 10.20 Means and Standard Deviations of Basic Summary Statistics for Hedge Funds in the TASS and CSFB/Tremont Hedge Fund Live, Graveyard, and Combined Databases from February 1977 to August 2004

Category Description	Sample Size	Annualized Mean (%)		(%)		p₁ (%)		Annualized Sharpe Ratio		(Annualized)		Ljung-Box p-value (%)	
		Mean	Standard Deviation	Mean	Standard Deviation	Mean	Standard Deviation	Mean	Standard Deviation	Mean	Standard Deviation	Mean	Standard Deviation
Live Funds													
Convertible Arbitrage	127	9.92	5.89	5.51	4.15	33.6	19.2	2.57	4.20	1.95	2.86	19.5	27.1
Dedicated Short Selling	14	0.33	11.11	25.1	10.92	3.5	10.9	−0.11	0.70	0.12	0.46	48.0	25.7
Emerging Markets	130	17.74	13.77	21.69	14.42	18.8	13.8	1.36	2.01	1.22	1.40	35.5	31.5
Equity Market Neutral	173	6.60	5.89	7.25	5.05	4.4	22.7	1.20	1.18	1.30	1.28	41.6	32.6
Event Driven	250	12.52	8.99	8.00	7.15	19.4	20.9	1.98	1.47	1.68	1.47	31.3	34.1
Fixed Income Arbitrage	104	9.30	5.61	6.27	5.10	16.4	23.6	3.61	11.71	3.12	7.27	36.6	35.2
Global Macro	118	10.51	11.55	13.57	10.41	1.3	17.1	0.86	0.68	0.99	0.79	46.8	30.6
Long/Short Equity	883	13.05	10.56	14.98	9.30	11.3	17.9	1.03	1.01	1.01	0.95	38.1	31.8
Managed Futures	195	8.59	18.55	19.14	12.52	3.4	13.9	0.48	1.10	0.73	0.63	52.3	30.8
Multi-Strategy	98	12.65	17.93	9.31	10.94	18.5	21.3	1.91	2.34	1.46	2.06	31.1	31.7
Fund of Funds	679	6.89	5.45	6.14	4.87	22.9	18.5	1.53	1.33	1.48	1.16	33.7	31.6
Dead Funds													
Convertible Arbitrage	49	10.02	6.61	8.14	6.08	25.5	19.3	1.89	1.43	1.58	1.46	27.9	34.2
Dedicated Short Selling	15	1.77	9.41	27.54	18.79	8.1	13.2	0.20	0.44	0.25	0.48	55.4	25.2
Emerging Markets	133	2.74	27.74	27.18	18.96	14.3	17.9	0.37	0.91	0.47	1.11	48.5	34.6
Equity Market Neutral	87	7.61	26.37	12.35	13.68	6.4	20.4	0.52	1.23	0.60	1.85	46.6	31.5
Event Driven	134	9.07	15.04	12.35	12.10	16.6	21.1	1.22	1.38	1.13	1.43	39.3	34.2

(Continued)

TABLE 10.20   (Continued)

Category Description	Sample Size	Annualized Mean (%)		(%)		p_1 (%)		Annualized Sharpe Ratio		(Annualized)		Ljung-Box p-value (%)	
		Mean	Standard Deviation	Mean	Standard Deviation	Mean	Standard Deviation	Mean	Standard Deviation	Mean	Standard Deviation	Mean	Standard Deviation
Dead Funds													
Fixed Income Arbitrage	71	5.51	12.93	10.78	9.97	15.9	22.0	1.10	1.77	1.03	1.99	46.0	35.7
Global Macro	114	3.74	28.83	21.02	18.94	3.2	21.5	0.33	1.05	0.37	0.90	46.2	31.0
Long/Short Equity	532	9.69	22.75	23.08	16.82	6.4	19.8	0.48	1.06	0.48	1.17	47.8	31.3
Managed Futures	316	4.78	23.17	20.88	19.35	-2.9	18.7	0.26	0.77	0.37	0.97	48.4	30.9
Multi-Strategy	41	5.32	23.46	17.55	20.90	6.1	17.4	1.10	1.55	1.58	2.06	49.4	32.2
Fund of Funds	273	4.53	10.07	13.56	10.56	11.3	21.2	0.62	1.26	0.57	1.11	40.9	31.9
Combined Funds													
Convertible Arbitrage	176	9.94	3.08	6.24	4.89	31.4	19.5	67.47	3.66	1.85	2.55	21.8	29.3
Dedicated Short Selling	29	1.08	10.11	26.36	15.28	5.9	12.2	42.34	0.59	0.19	0.46	52.0	25.2
Emerging Markets	263	10.16	23.18	24.48	17.07	16.5	16.2	55.98	1.63	0.84	1.31	42.2	33.7
Equity Market Neutral	260	6.94	15.94	8.96	9.21	5.1	21.9	75.84	1.24	1.06	1.53	43.3	32.3
Event Driven	384	11.31	11.57	9.52	9.40	18.4	21.0	72.75	1.48	1.49	1.48	34.1	34.3
Fixed Income Arbitrage	175	7.76	9.45	8.10	7.76	16.2	22.9	79.36	9.16	2.29	5.86	40.4	35.6
Global Macro	232	7.18	22.04	17.21	15.61	2.3	19.3	66.88	0.92	0.70	0.90	46.5	30.8
Long/Short Equity	1,415	11.79	16.33	18.02	13.25	9.5	18.8	65.04	1.06	0.81	1.07	41.7	31.9
Managed Futures	511	6.23	21.59	20.22	17.07	-0.6	17.4	60.14	0.91	0.50	0.88	49.8	30.9
Multi-Strategy	139	10.49	19.92	11.74	15.00	14.7	20.9	72.53	2.16	1.49	2.05	36.7	32.9
Fund of Funds	952	6.22	7.17	8.26	7.75	19.6	20.0	69.34	1.37	1.21	1.22	35.8	31.8

Note: p-Value (Q) contains means and standard deviations of p-values for the Ljung-Box Q-statistic for each fund using the first 11 autocorrelations of returns.
Source: Data from EDHEC Business School (www.edhec-risk.com) and from the Social Science Research Network (www.ssrn.com).

CHAPTER 11

Methodologies and Models to Detect Fraud in Hedge Funds

It shall be unlawful for any investment adviser . . . to employ any device, scheme, or artifice to defraud any client or prospective client . . . to engage in any act, practice, or course of business which is fraudulent, deceptive, or manipulative.
—Section 206 of the Investment Advisers Act of 1940

As of February 1, 2006, hedge fund managers are required to register as investment advisers under the 1940 Act. Despite much research being performed on the detection of frauds in hedge funds, very few agencies and hedge funds' risk management departments spent much time creating a more complete rating model that measures integrity, ethical motivations, and prevention of returns manipulation. This chapter highlights the research resulting from lack of ethics, integrity, and true enhancement of operational risk management in hedge funds.

According to Atkins and Glassman (2004), risk-based screens had not yet been developed. The model proposed in this chapter is to provide hedge fund risk managers with a quantitative approach to detect returns abnormality and frauds. It is a procedure that identifies time series patterns indicative of fraud in the monthly returns and financial statements. According to model developers Nicolas P. B. Bollen and Veronika Krepely (2005), when managers report accurately, observed returns reflect estimates of the changes in the market value of hedge fund assets. In the case of fraud, observed returns reflect changes in the portfolio value as well as the algorithm with which managers convert asset returns to reported returns. According to Bollen and Krepely (2005), returns are adjusted and enhanced based on prior historical returns and market influences. The smoothing of the returns can be demonstrated using time series analysis on return patterns. There are very few hedge funds that provide a daily report matching explanations of profits and losses and their correlations with net asset valuations calculations. Both of those reports are the key to detect any substantial discrepancies in day-to-day trading activities, in mark-to-market valuations, or in mistakes in realized and unrealized profits and losses from sales of securities.

Getmansky, Lo, and Makarov (2004) examine innocuous explanations for serial correlation in reported monthly returns, including time varying expected returns, time varying leverage, and marking illiquid assets to market using extrapolation. The authors also pointed out that serial correlation can be caused by managerial smoothing of contemporaneous and lagged asset returns in order to inflate risk-adjusted performance.

Chandar and Bricker (2002) study a similar issue in a multiperiod model of incentives for closed-end mutual fund managers. This model allows managers to overvalue illiquid instruments when the return of liquid assets falls slightly below a benchmark, and to undervalue illiquid securities when the return of liquid assets is extremely high or low. The logic behind this model's assumptions is that most hedge fund managers tend to smooth out more losses and do not smooth gains when they occur.

The Global Association of Risk Professionals (GARP) showed that hedge fund returns tended to be higher for the month of December than for any other month, given all historical data. The logic was reiterated by the Securities and Exchange Commission in 2004 when the SEC mentioned that hedge funds tended to be more aggressive in hiding and covering up losses. This natural human behavior can be proven by analyzing returns, performance records, and risk exposures and demonstrating that in case of profits or positive results the reporting magnitude is larger or wider and in case of losses or negative performance the reporting magnitude is smoothed and narrower.

Brown, Harlow, and Starks (1996) find that mutual funds with relatively poor returns over the first six months of a calendar year tend to feature increases in risk over the remainder of the year. Brown et al. demonstrate that the positive relation between new instruments in mutual funds and their lagged performances can be measured with volatility trends. Brown et al. also show that asset diversification produces more income from fees. Other researchers, such as Chevalier and Ellison (1997) and Koshi and Pontiff (1999), discovered similar findings. Busse (2001) demonstrates that returns are directly linked to index trends and statistical patterns and have very little to do with the managerial abilities of the fund managers. In the same school of thought, Agarwal et al. (2003) find that hedge funds with higher returns experience more capital inflows than those with lower returns and vice versa.

Agarwal et al. constructed an annual measure of managerial incentives with high-water marks in parallel with historical records/data of prior capital inflows. The author showed that high compounded returns are directly correlated with fund performance and capital inflows in the following year. Brown et al. (1996) did not manage to validate the frequency of such patterns and there are very few findings on the persistence of such trends. Later on Amenc and Le Sourd (2005) performed research on the returns of hedge funds and the persistence of performance. Some researchers provided grounds for returns manipulations. For example, Asness, Krail, and Liew (2001) showed that illiquid assets cause changes in net asset valuations and these changes are not in line with benchmark indexes or underlying asset prices. The illiquid assets' valuation prices basically are not synchronized with changes in benchmarks or underlying indexes. If the assets' valuation prices are stale, traditional estimates of volatility and correlation with benchmarks are found to be biased on the downside to limit losses and improve the hedge fund's performance. The bias is in quantity and magnitude and is in pricing subjectivity as well.

Asness et al. (2001), Scholes and Williams (1977), and Dimson (1979) regressed hedge fund index returns with those of traditional indexes such as S&P 500, and discovered that a lagged factor can explain abnormal returns in hedge fund indexes. These trends will also enhance the fact that historical trends and patterns of hedge fund indexes do not account for catastrophic and event risks and returns have consistently grown over time.

Asness et al. (2001) also separate observations of contemporaneous and lagged benchmark returns depending on sign. The researchers found evidence that regression coefficients on lagged negative returns are larger than coefficients on lagged positive returns, highlighting that there is more returns smoothing when benchmarks are low. They showed that manipulating losses or low returns valuations remain at the discretion of management.

Jagannathan and Korajczyk (1986) found that asymmetric factor exposures occur when asset returns are more or less like those of derivatives products.

Getmansky, Lo, and Makarov (2004) created an algorithm that transforms asset returns into reported returns. It is a moving average of contemporaneous and lagged asset returns. The researchers showed that their model can generate nonsynchronized correlations and disparate unparallel coefficients. By doing so, they intend to make a case for human subjective bias in the mark-to-market valuations of assets in order to gradually increase returns and assets' performance. This fact was experienced when I was in the pricing verification group to independently check options prices of institutional traders. As a general rule, traders tended to price their options more favorably on the upside and to be more conservative on the downside when the underlying assets were losing.

CHAPTER 12

Selection of a Quantitative Model to Detect Fraud

The following model is intended to prove disparities and asymmetries in the statistical patterns of risk exposures and correlations and to provide grounds and basic testing for fraud. The asymmetric magnitudes on the upside have consistently been higher and wider than those on the downside. The fundamental basis for this relies on the fact that hedge fund managers are more prone to smooth losses than profits.

Research by Nicolas P. B. Bollen and Veronika Krepely (2005) provides a two-part empirical analysis. In the first part, they assess the size and power of the asymmetrical findings using simulated hedge funds returns, calibrated to match the risk exposures of a large database of hedge fund data using linear factor models. Their assumptions are such that when returns are generated under the null hypothesis of symmetric smoothing it indicates that the magnitudes of the standard errors are correct. And when returns are generated under the alternative, and the underlying factors are revealed, they reject the null 80 percent of the time using 120-month histories. This result indicated that quantitative tests can be used as screens for frauds. The second part of the test consists in analyzing hedge fund returns. Approximately 4 percent of the funds feature asymmetric smoothing, consistent with the low frequency of reported fraud cases. The authors of the model then used cross-sectional analysis to evaluate whether funds' characteristics are linked with higher instances of triggering a red flag. We find that the capital at risk is best measured by the volatility of the funds' flows and was the best predictor of potential fraudulent schemes.

The proposed model is based on the findings of Getmansky, Lo, and Makarov (2004) and their framework on symmetric and asymmetric smoothing.

Let us first review the symmetric framework.

We denote R_t the return of a hedge fund's assets in period t and assume R_t satisfies the following linear single-factor model:

(I) $R_t = \mu + \beta\Lambda_t + \varepsilon_t$ with $E[\Lambda_t] = E[\varepsilon_t] = 0$ with Λ_t and ε_t being independent

and

$$\text{VaR}[R_t] = \sigma^2$$

Note that these assumptions hold valid for linear multifactor models as well. The reported return of the hedge fund is denoted by R_t^0 and a hedge fund manager reports the weighted average of the assets' returns and k lags as follows:

(II) $\qquad R_t^0 = \Sigma_{j=0 \to k}\theta_j R_{t-j}$ where $\theta_j \in [0,1]$ for $j = 0, \ldots, k$

and

$$1 = \theta_0 + \theta_1 + \ldots + \theta_k$$

If the smoothing regression coefficients from 0 to k add to 1, then the asset returns are fully matched with observed returns. Otherwise, the discrepancies show variations between actual asset returns and reported returns. The following three equations are denoted (III):

Using the Getmansky, Lo, and Makarov (2004) assumptions, the expected observed return is expressed as $E[R_t^0] = \mu$.

The variance of observed returns is expressed as $\text{VaR}[R_t^0] = \sigma^2 \Sigma_{j=0 \to k}\theta_j^2$.

And the covariance between current and lagged observed returns is such that:

$$\text{Cov}[R_t^0, R_{t-m}^0] = \sigma^2 \Sigma_{j=0 \to k-m}\theta_j\theta_{j+m} \quad \text{if } 0 \leq m < k$$
$$\text{And } 0 \text{ if } m > k$$

The variance of observed returns is lower than the variance of asset returns. For the test of intentional smoothing, the observed returns are regressed on one of the lags; as a result, the resulting slope coefficient is equal to the covariance in the above equation divided by the variance of the observed returns such that:

$$R_t^0 = a + b_m R_{t-m}^0 + \eta_t$$

(IV)
$$B_m = \frac{\sum_{j=0 \to k-m} \theta_j \theta_{j+m}}{\sum_{j=0 \to k} \theta_j^2} \text{ for } 1 = <m = <k$$

This demonstrates that smoothing asset returns generates serial correlation in observed returns.

The following equation expresses the observed return by substituting the factor model (I) into equation (II) to obtain:

(V1) $\quad R_t^0 = \theta_0(\mu + \beta \Lambda_t + \varepsilon_t) + \theta_1(\mu + \beta \Lambda_{t-1} + \varepsilon_{t-1}) + \ldots + \theta_k (\mu + \beta \Lambda_{t-k} + \varepsilon_{t-k})$

If the identity of the factor is known, and if we regress the observed returns on the contemporaneous and lagged observations, we have:

(V2) $\quad\quad\quad\quad R_t^0 = \mu + \beta_0^0 \Lambda_t + \beta_1^0 \Lambda_t + \ldots + \beta_k^0 \Lambda_{t-k} + \gamma_t$

By comparing (V1) and (V2) equations, we notice that smoothing values reduces the measured exposure and produces exposures to the lagged factors:

$$\beta_j^0 = \theta_j \beta \text{ for } 0 = <j = <k$$

The risk-adjusted returns identified in equation (II) prove that smoothing losses or subtle apparent reduction of risk exposures occurred in at least three instances that are:

1. Nonsynchronous and illogical trading in the underlying assets; that is, there is a timing lag allowing for pricing adjustments toward the gaining side.
2. Conservatism when marked to market; that is, the volatility level of the instrument is on the gaining side, not the losing side of the pricing formula. This is easy to check by using a midpoint between the bid and ask as a mark-to-market value and comparing the aggressiveness or conservatism of the hedge fund manager's pricing policy.
3. Intentional reduction of the amplitude of the observed return values to decrease risk exposures.

Second, we review the asymmetric smoothing framework.

In the symmetric smoothing framework, θ_0, the return of the asset, is reported simultaneously without timing lags. Under asymmetric smoothing, we assume that hedge fund managers are biased toward making gains bigger than if neutrally priced and making losses smaller in magnitude than if neutrally priced. This is due to the fact that hedge fund returns are directly correlated to fees, to size of the funds, and to the number of investors attracted by higher returns. The intention of generating higher returns is also directly linked to the intention of outperforming competition. This logic leads one to believe that hedge fund managers do not report large negative returns as well as if they were asked to report positive results.

Bollen and Krepely (2005) propose an algorithm based on the decision-making intuition of a hedge fund manager using a basic constant z as a reference or benchmark to compare aggressiveness or conservatism in the pricing habits of the manager. They compare the asset return of the fund R_t to a constant z. If the return falls below z, then the manager reports some fraction θ_0 of the return in the given period and reports the remainder during the next period k using a set of weights θj such that $j = 1, 2, \ldots k$. If the return is greater than z, then the manager uses another set of weights such as Ψ. By increasing the smoothing algorithm (II) to include indicator variables, the research gave the following results on asymmetry:

$$R_t^0 = \Sigma_{j=0 \to k}[\theta_j(1 - I_{t-j}) + \Psi_j I_{t-j}]R_{t-j}^0$$

such that

$$I_{t-j} = 1 \text{ if } R_{t-j} \geq z \text{ and for } j = 0, 1, \ldots, k$$

$$I_{t-j} = 0 \text{ if } R_{t-j} < z \quad \text{and for } j = 0, 1, \ldots, k$$

Both coefficients' sums Ψ and θ are assumed to be equal to 1 to ensure that asset returns are fully reflected in reported returns. If $R_t > z$, then a larger fraction of the asset return is to be reported simultaneously, implying that $\Psi_0 > \theta_0$. This is such that we assume that hedge fund managers have greater incentive to report good performance and to hide poor returns or losses. In extreme scenarios, managers could only report consistent positive returns with full growth, and that would be shown with $\Psi_0 = 1$. So this implies that a smaller fraction of a period's asset return is represented such that:

(VI) $$\Sigma_{j=1 \to k}\Psi_j < \Sigma_{j=1 \to k}\theta_j$$

The researchers demonstrated that asymmetric smoothing results in serial correlation in hedge fund returns that depends on the magnitude of the asset returns since the degree to which the current period return is linked to lagged returns is a function of whether the lagged asset returns are above or below the benchmark reference level z. They called this particularity asymmetric serial correlation. Asymmetric serial correlation is an obvious uncontroversial mean to determine intentional smoothing to generate greater returns. Other measurements are more difficult to justify and prove manipulations of risk-adjusted returns.

The researchers found that the asymmetric smoothed returns like the symmetric ones have the same unconditional expected value as the underlying asset returns and that the smoothing framework simply determines the timing of the revealed asset returns.

They performed a regression analysis of the funds' returns by assuming one lag or one timing delay and by including a variable for the delayed returns depending on the previous ones:

(VII)
$$R_t^0 = a + [b_t^-(1 - I_{t-1}) + b_1^+ I_{t-1}]R_{t-1}^0 + \eta_t$$

where $I_{t-1} = 1$ if $R_{t-1} >= z$ and $I_{t-1} = 0$ if $R_{t-1} < z$

The researchers derived the following axiom:

If asset returns are generated by $R_t = \mu + \beta\Lambda_t + \varepsilon_t$ and observed returns are constructed as $R_t^0 = [\theta_0(1 - I_t) + \Psi_0 I_t]R_t + [\theta_1(1 - I_{t-1}) + \Psi_1 I_{t-1}]R_{t-1}$ where $I_{t-1} = 1$ if $R_{t-j} >= z$ for $j = 0,1$ and zero otherwise, then observed returns will display asymmetric serial correlation if $\theta_1 <> \Psi_1$. Asymmetric serial correlation can be detected by estimating parameters of $R_t^0 = a + [b_-^1(1 - I_{t-1}) + b_1^+ I_{t-1}]R_{t-1}^0 + \eta_t$ and will result in $b_1^- <> b_1^+$.

The researchers deduced that if a hedge fund manager tended to defer reporting poor returns, then the relation between contemporaneous and lagged returns will be larger when the lagged returns are poor. Differences between b_1^- and b_1^+ demonstrate this.

They noted that if a hedge fund manager smooths asymmetrically as in equation (VI), then they observed that fund returns possess asymmetric exposures to present versus delayed values of the factor. They demonstrated this fact by introducing factor model I into equation (VI) with delay such that:

(VII)$R_t^0 = [\theta_0(1 - I_t) + \Psi_0 I_t][\mu + \beta\Lambda_t + \varepsilon_t] + [\theta_1(1 - I_{t-1}) + \Psi_1 I_{t-1}][\mu + \beta\Lambda_{t-1} + \varepsilon_{t-1}]$

(VIII)
$$R_t^0 = \mu + [\beta_0^{0-}(1 - I_t) + \beta_0^{0+}]\Lambda_t + [\beta_1^{0-}(1 - I_{t-1}) + \beta_1^{0+}]\Lambda_{t-1} + \gamma_t$$

with conditional exposures to be $\beta_j^{0-} = \theta_j \beta$ and $\beta_1^{0+} = \Psi_j \beta$ such that $j = 0, 1$.

Bollen and Krepely (2005) found that managers who smooth asymmetrically report performances with higher present exposures to the factor when asset returns are high than when they are low, although the true exposures are constant over time. Also, the exposure to the lagged factor appears to be higher when lagged returns are lower. Bollen and Krepely (2005) demonstrated the test for asymmetric smoothing in Asness et al. (2001).

The final part of Bollen and Krepely's research involves the empirical implementation of the smoothing process. This test to detect gross frauds has been empirically tested and validated to filter the most grotesque abnormal trends in 80 percent of the cases. The goal of this first-time model is to implement different tests for all the various trading strategies, given that each strategy requires its respective set of quantitative assumptions and sets of data and indexes. Bollen and Krepely (2005) tested the model with data from the Center for International Securities and Derivatives Markets (CISDM) hedge fund database. The University of Massachusetts and Managed Account Reports LLC maintain the database through December 2003. Tables 12.1 and 12.2 summarize statistics of the returns of hedge funds, CTAs, and managed futures in the December 2003 CISDM database. Live funds are in existence as of December 2003 while dead funds were liquidated in a prior month. Listed are the number of funds, equally weighted average monthly return, standard deviation of returns (σ), Sharpe ratio, skewness, and excess kurtosis.

Table 12.2 is a statistical data summary found for CISDM dead or closed hedge funds up to December 2003. (Note that 15 percent of the entire hedge fund population has closed during 2005.)

Tables 12.3 and 12.4 represent the number of funds in the 25th, 50th, and 75th percentiles of the cross-sectional distributions of history lengths, in months, for hedge funds, CTAs, and managed futures in the December 2003 CISDM database. The live funds are in existence as of that date, while dead funds were liquidated in a prior month.

Table 12.5 provides summary statistics of CISDM indexes and asset-based style factors, including statistics of the returns of hedge fund indexes and CTA indexes in the December 2003 CISDM database, and the asset-based style (ABS) factors developed by Fung and Hsieh (2004). Data are up to 2003. Statistics include the average monthly return, standard deviation of returns (σ), Sharpe ratio, skewness, and excess kurtosis.

Simulated hedge fund returns are based on the hedge funds, CTAs, and managed futures in the December 2003 CISDM database. The simulated data is calibrated to match the risk exposures of actual hedge funds. For each fund in the sample, 20 sets of simulated hedge fund returns R_t^A are generated. To simulate a series of length n, n monthly observations with replacements from the selected factor's 10-year history are drawn. This generates n standard normal variates. Then the factor return is scaled with β^0

TABLE 12.1 Summary of Statistics of Returns of Live Hedge Funds, CTAs, and Managed Futures in the CISDM Database as of December 2003

Live Hedge Fund	Number of Funds	Monthly Return	Standard Deviation of Returns	Sharpe Ratio	Skewness	Excess Kurtosis
Event Driven	134	0.85	2.53	0.30	−0.17	4.76
Global Emerging	93	1.49	6.40	0.33	0.03	5.45
Global Established	277	1.21	4.77	0.23	0.52	3.47
Global International	36	1.03	4.83	0.15	0.19	3.39
Global Macro	42	0.97	4.09	0.23	0.37	2.83
Long-Only	11	1.23	9.31	0.13	0.23	1.82
Market Neutral	327	0.94	2.60	0.40	0.02	5.13
Sector	107	1.36	5.93	0.24	0.65	4.47
Short Selling	20	0.56	6.80	0.04	−0.01	2.32
Fund of Funds	418	0.66	1.80	0.30	−0.18	5.04
CTA Agriculture	13	1.41	5.66	0.19	0.72	2.61
CTA Currency	31	1.16	4.90	0.19	1.06	4.24
CTA Diversified	135	1.39	6.54	0.16	0.68	2.78
CTA Energy	2	1.15	4.07	0.25	1.25	2.08
CTA Financial	42	1.28	5.52	0.18	0.76	3.05
Stock Index	21	1.20	5.81	0.12	0.50	6.59
Managed Futures Public Pools	156	1.08	5.29	0.16	0.55	2.92
Managed Futures Private Pools	99	1.12	6.21	0.14	0.52	3.98

Source: eLibrary or Social Science Research Network (ssrn.com).

TABLE 12.2 Statistical Data Summary for Dead or Closed Hedge Funds in the CISDM Database up to December 2003

Dead Hedge Fund	Number of Funds	Monthly Return	Standard Deviation of Returns	Sharpe Ratio	Skewness	Excess Kurtosis
Event Driven	72	0.89	4.57	0.16	-0.16	6.41
Global Emerging	34	0.30	7.99	0.04	-0.71	5.62
Global Established	213	1.18	6.92	0.15	0.14	5.64
Global International	17	1.36	5.54	0.21	0.05	6.40
Global Macro	39	0.74	5.40	0.08	0.06	4.28
Long-Only	12	0.68	8.71	0.04	-0.25	1.58
Market Neutral	157	0.77	3.37	0.15	-0.37	5.55
Sector	51	1.80	8.52	0.20	0.44	1.92
Short Selling	6	0.41	5.93	0.04	0.20	1.18
Fund of Funds	130	0.57	3.67	0.09	-0.01	3.86
CTA Agriculture	13	2.64	12.84	0.17	0.94	4.11
CTA Currency	46	0.90	4.51	-0.02	0.99	4.18
CTA Diversifed	153	1.21	7.49	0.08	0.85	4.04
CTA Energy	4	-0.12	15.73	-0.04	1.85	11.80
CTA Financial	59	0.85	5.55	0.08	0.50	2.62
Stock Index	19	1.05	7.54	0.06	-0.05	1.34
Managed Futures Public Pools	270	0.44	4.73	0.00	0.33	3.21
Managed Futures Private Pools	151	0.79	6.23	0.07	0.44	3.94

Source: eLibrary or Social Science Research Network (ssrn.com).

TABLE 12.3 Statistical Summary of Data for Live Funds by Percentiles of Cross-Sectional Distributions of History Lengths, in Months

Live Hedge Fund	Number of Funds	25th Percentile	50th Percentile	75th Percentile
Event Driven	134	48	77	108
Global Emerging	93	49	73	93
Global Established	277	40	66	96
Global International	36	62	86	115
Global Macro	42	43	79	100
Long-Only	11	69	84	92
Market Neutral	327	36	61	89
Sector	107	42	54	88
Short Selling	20	51	79	86
Fund of Funds	418	44	71	108
CTA Agriculture	13	49	65	114
CTA Currency	31	87	108	149
CTA Diversified	135	60	100	139
CTA Energy	2	36	36	52
CTA Financial	42	74	97	116
CTA Stock Index	21	51	81	116
Managed Futures Public Pools	156	58	87	126
Managed Futures Private Pools	99	71	107	149

Source: eLibrary or Social Science Research Network (ssrn.com).

TABLE 12.4 Statistical Summary of Data for Dead Funds by Percentile

Dead Hedge Fund	Number of Funds	25th Percentile	50th Percentile	75th Percentile
Event Driven	72	37	53	86
Global Emerging	34	27	41	69
Global Established	213	37	53	89
Global International	17	44	59	82
Global Macro	39	32	48	71
Long-Only	12	32	48	78
Market Neutral	157	34	55	73
Sector	51	32	47	61
Short Selling	6	34	63	86
Fund of Funds	130	38	55	76
CTA Agriculture	13	37	61	69
CTA Currency	46	37	54	75
CTA Diversified	153	40	67	103
CTA Energy	4	27	35	73
CTA Financial	59	38	66	98
CTA Stock Index	19	32	52	64
Managed Futures Public Pools	270	35	53	83
Managed Futures Private Pools	151	42	67	121

Source: eLibrary or Social Science Research Network (ssrn.com).

TABLE 12.5 Summary Statistics of CISDM Indexes and Asset-Based Style Factors

CISDM Indexes	Average Monthly Return	Standard Deviation of Returns	Sharpe Ratio	Skewness	Excess Kurtosis
Event Distressed	0.74	1.47	0.27	−2.51	14.80
Event Driven	0.67	0.95	0.34	−2.74	18.34
Event Driven Arbitrage	0.64	0.85	0.34	−2.59	14.80
Global Emerging	0.60	3.82	0.07	−2.81	18.84
Global Established	0.95	2.20	0.28	−0.02	3.94
Global Macro	0.50	1.34	0.12	0.48	5.07
Market Neutral Arbitrage	0.93	2.18	0.27	4.49	24.18
Market Neutral Long/Short	0.70	0.47	0.76	−0.10	2.43
Market Neutral	0.73	0.31	1.22	−1.16	1.40
Short Selling	0.37	4.88	0.00	0.69	2.62
CTA Indexes Currency	0.46	1.84	0.06	1.13	4.91
CTA Discretionary	0.60	1.24	0.21	0.47	0.41
CTA Diversified	0.76	2.79	0.15	0.45	0.53
CTA Financial	0.73	3.01	0.13	0.67	0.74
CTA Stock Index	0.21	2.63	−0.05	−0.55	1.86
CTA Systematic	0.55	2.49	0.08	0.45	0.79
CTA Trend	0.80	3.77	0.12	0.34	0.24
ABS Factor for S&P 500	0.98	4.57	0.14	−0.59	0.20
ABS Factor for Wilshire Size	0.04	3.50	−0.09	0.51	3.71
ABS Factors for Bond Trend	1.50	19.12	0.06	1.41	2.10
ABS Factors for Currency Trend	−0.16	19.39	−0.03	1.40	3.35
ABS Factors for Commodities Trends	−1.14	12.62	−0.12	1.59	5.16
ABS Factor for D 10-year Treasury	−0.01	0.24	−1.48	0.35	−0.39
ABS Factor for D Credit Spread	0.00	0.13	−2.62	0.90	1.84

Source: eLibrary or Social Science Research Network (ssrn.com).

and α is added to create systematic return. The normal variate scaled is added by σ_e to create R_t^A. Simulated symmetrically smoothed returns R_t^S can then be expressed as the following function:

$$R_t^S = 0.5R_t^A + 0.5R_{t-1}^A$$

By running a regression on this equation, we obtain the following asymmetrical returns equation:

$$R_t^S = a + b_1^+ R_{t-1}^S + b_1^-(1 - I_{t-1})R_{t-1}^S + \eta_t$$

where $I_{t-1} = 1$ if the systematic component of the simulated return in month $t - 1$ is greater than its mean and zero otherwise.

The factor b_1^- tests whether serial correlation in observed returns is different when lagged systematic returns are below a given level. For the previous equation, simulation is run two ways to solve the equation for I. First, the systematic components from which returns are generated are assumed to be known. Second, we assume that they are not known. They must be recreated by determining which single factor best fits the simulated return history. The statistics relevant to the size report the frequency with which the simulated returns create a significant positive b_1^- at 5 percent, two-sided level for time series of lengths 120, 60, and 36 months. Historical data run on all the given indexes show that the rejection rate is about 2 percent, indicating that the probability of falsely rejecting the null is in line with the significance level of the test.

The following analysis compares the validation of the methodology regarding asymmetric serial correlation under controlled conditions versus actual conditions. The basis of the review focuses on the frequency with which the test identifies the asymmetric smoothing that would suggest potential fraudulent activities in the hedge fund. To achieve this, two tests are performed: one under a controlled set of conditions to determine the importance of history length on power and a second under actual circumstances to show the power to be expected under normal practical conditions.

Let's first validate the methodology on asymmetric serial correlation under a controlled set of circumstances. Asset returns using a single-factor model under the size analysis assumptions as earlier produce simulated asset returns asymmetrically smoothed R_t^S such that:

$$R_t^S = [0.5(1 - I_t) + I_t]R_t^A + 0.5(1 - I_{t-1})R_{t-1}^A$$

where $I_t = 1$ when the simulated systematic return in month t is greater than its mean for the simulation and zero otherwise.

The simulation is run with known I_t and with unknown and thus deducted I_t from simulated data. Parameters of a single-factor model $R_t^0 = \alpha + \beta^0 \Lambda_t + \varepsilon_t$ are evaluated. R_t^0 is the observed hedge fund return and Λ_t is the return of the CISDM index that maximizes the adjusted R-squared of the regression. Then, simulated asset returns are such that $R_t^A = \alpha + \beta^0 \Lambda_t^E + \xi_t$. Λ_t^E is randomly chosen from the empirical return distribution of the selected index and ξ_t is a randomly generated mean-zero normal variate with standard deviation calibrated to the original single-factor model. Simulated hedge fund returns are created by smoothing simulated asset returns such that:

$$R_t^S = a + B_1^+ R_{t-1}^S + b_1^-(1 - I_{t-1})R_{t-1}^S + \eta_t$$

where R_t^S is the simulated fund return in month t and I_{t-1} equals 1 if the simulated fund's systematic return from an optimal factor model at any month $t - 1$ is greater than the mean systematic return. Table 12.6 lists number of funds and percentage of simulations with significant positive b_1^- coefficients evaluated at the two-sided 5 percent level.

Table 12.6 provides a summary of statistics for size analysis of asymmetrical serial correlation for when factors are known when calculating I_t.

Table 12.7 provides a summary of statistics for size analysis of asymmetrical serial correlation when factors are unobservable or not known and when they must be deduced given a set of data. The data in Table 12.7 results when calculating I_t and thus when the hedge fund risk manager must deduce the factors at given month t.

Another variable on which Bollen and Krepely (2005) experimented about ways hedge fund managers have smoothed their risk-adjusted returns is power. They conducted two tests: one test under a controlled set of conditions to determine the importance of history length with regard to power and the other test performed under actual normal conditions.

Under controlled conditions, Bollen and Krepely (2005) generated asset returns utilizing a single-factor model using the same procedure as described earlier for the size analysis, by simulating asymmetrically smoothed fund returns R_t^S such that:

$$R_t^S = [0.5(1 - I_t) + I_t]R_t^A + 0.5(1 - I_{t-1})R_{t-1}^A$$

where $I_t = 1$ if simulated systematic return in month t is greater than its mean for the simulation or 0 otherwise.

Similar to the methodology used for the variable size, Bollen and Krepely (2005) ran the same simulated tests. First they assumed a known I_t,

TABLE 12.6 Summary of Statistics for Size Analysis of Asymmetrical Serial Correlation for When Factors Are Known When Calculating I_t

Hedge Fund Strategy	Number of Funds	t = 120 Months	t = 60 Months	t = 36 Months
Event Driven	197	0.02	0.02	0.02
Global Emerging	127	0.04	0.05	0.04
Global Established	479	0.02	0.02	0.02
Global International	53	0.04	0.04	0.03
Global Macro	75	0.02	0.02	0.01
Long-Only	23	0.02	0.02	0.03
Market Neutral	479	0.02	0.02	0.02
Sector	158	0.02	0.01	0.02
Short Selling	25	0.02	0.02	0.02
Fund of Funds	542	0.02	0.02	0.02
CTA Agriculture	26	0.01	0.01	0.01
CTA Currency	76	0.01	0.01	0.01
CTA Diversified	287	0.01	0.01	0.01
CTA Energy	6	0.01	0.03	0.02
CTA Financial	101	0.01	0.01	0.01
CTA Stock Index	40	0.04	0.02	0.02
Managed Futures Public Pools	424	0.01	0.01	0.01
Managed Futures Private Pools	249	0.01	0.01	0.01

Source: eLibrary or Social Science Research Network (ssrn.com).

TABLE 12.7 Summary of Statistics for Size Analysis of Asymmetrical Serial Correlation When Factors Are Unobservable or Not Known

Hedge Fund Strategy	Number of Funds	$t = 120$ Months	$t = 60$ Months	$t = 36$ Months
Event Driven	197	0.02	0.02	0.02
Global Emerging	127	0.04	0.04	0.04
Global Established	479	0.03	0.02	0.02
Global International	53	0.03	0.04	0.03
Global Macro	75	0.02	0.02	0.01
Long-Only	23	0.02	0.02	0.02
Market Neutral	479	0.02	0.02	0.02
Sector	158	0.02	0.02	0.02
Short Selling	25	0.02	0.02	0.02
Fund of Funds	542	0.02	0.02	0.02
CTA Agriculture	26	0.02	0.01	0.01
CTA Currency	76	0.02	0.02	0.01
CTA Diversified	287	0.01	0.01	0.01
CTA Energy	6	0.00	0.00	0.06
CTA Financial	101	0.01	0.01	0.01
CTA Stock Index	40	0.03	0.02	0.02
Managed Futures Public Pools	424	0.02	0.01	0.01
Managed Futures Private Pools	249	0.01	0.01	0.01

Source: eLibrary or Social Science Research Network (ssrn.com).

and then they deduced I_t given the simulated data. Tables 12.8 and 12.9 give the results for time series of lengths $t - 120$, $t = 60$, and $t = 36$ months. When I_t is a known variable, the power of the test is about 80 percent for a 120-month history. For a 60-month history, the power drops down to about 50 percent. For a 36-month history, the power is down to 30 percent. When I_t is not known, the power is reported to be lower. Consequently, the tests indicate that the power is reasonable for funds with history lengths at or above median level.

For each fund, there is a parameter using single-factor model such that:

$$R_t^0 = \alpha + \beta^0 \Lambda_t + \varepsilon_t$$

where R_t^0 is the observed hedge fund return and Λ_t is the return of the CISDM index maximizing the adjusted R-squared of the regression. Then simulated asset returns are created as $R_t^A = \alpha + \beta_0 \Lambda_t^E + \xi_t$ with Λ_t^E is randomly chosen from the empirical return distribution of the selected index and ξ_t is a randomly generated mean-zero normal variate with standard deviation calibrated to the original single-factor model. Simulated hedge fund returns are generated by smoothing simulated asset returns such that:

$$R_t^S = [0.5(1 - I_t)] + I_t)R_t^A + 0.5(1 - I_{t-1})R_{t-1}^A$$

where $I_t = 1$ if $\alpha + \beta_0 \Lambda_t^E$ is greater than the mean and zero otherwise.

Three sets of simulations are conducted using lengths of 120, 60, and 36 months. Listed is the percentage of simulated hedge funds for which asymmetric smoothing is detected using $R_t^S = a + b_1^+ R_{t-1}^S + b_1^-(1 - I_{t-1})R_{t-1}^S + \eta_t$ where R_t^S is the simulated fund return in month t and I_{t-1} equals 1 if the simulated funds' symmetric return from an optimal factor model at month $t - 1$ is greater than the mean systematic return. For each fund, the tables list the number of funds and the percentage of simulations with significant positive b_1^- coefficients evaluated at the two-sided 5 percent level. Results are listed for when I_t is known and for when the factor must be deduced given a set of data.

To conduct a power analysis of asymmetric serial correlation under actual conditions, Bollin and Krepely (2005) use a multifactor model to generate asset returns. They use the actual history lengths of the funds by regressing observed returns and comparing them with those of the CISDM, CTA, and managed futures data. From observations, the study consists of determining what subset of potential proxies for the factors Λ can best capture the time variation in the fund's returns.

TABLE 12.8 Power Analysis of Asymmetric Serial Correlation under Controlled Conditions When Factor Is Known

Hedge Fund Strategy	Number of Funds	t = 120 Months	t = 60 Months	t = 36 Months
Event Driven	197	0.82	0.53	0.35
Global Emerging	127	0.85	0.56	0.36
Global Established	479	0.80	0.50	0.32
Global International	53	0.80	0.51	0.30
Global Macro	75	0.84	0.55	0.36
Long-Only	23	0.81	0.46	0.28
Market Neutral	479	0.85	0.57	0.37
Sector	158	0.80	0.49	0.31
Short Selling	25	0.76	0.44	0.32
Fund of Funds	542	0.78	0.49	0.31
CTA Agriculture	26	0.90	0.57	0.35
CTA Currency	76	0.84	0.54	0.35
CTA Diversified	287	0.78	0.48	0.30
CTA Energy	6	0.91	0.56	0.33
CTA Financial	101	0.83	0.52	0.32
CTA Stock Index	40	0.86	0.56	0.34
Managed Futures Public Pools	424	0.75	0.47	0.29
Managed Futures Private Pools	249	0.77	0.48	0.30

Source: eLibrary or Social Science Research Network (ssrn.com).

TABLE 12.9 Power Analysis of Asymmetric Serial Correlation When Factor Is Unknown or Unobservable

Hedge Fund Strategy	Number of Funds	$t = 120$ Months	$t = 60$ Months	$t = 36$ Months
Event Driven	197	0.76	0.44	0.25
Global Emerging	127	0.77	0.46	0.26
Global Established	479	0.76	0.43	0.24
Global International	53	0.75	0.42	0.23
Global Macro	75	0.76	0.42	0.24
Long-Only	23	0.77	0.41	0.22
Market Neutral	479	0.76	0.44	0.26
Sector	158	0.76	0.42	0.24
Short Selling	25	0.74	0.40	0.25
Fund of Funds	542	0.75	0.44	0.26
CTA Agriculture	26	0.65	0.36	0.16
CTA Currency	76	0.75	0.41	0.23
CTA Diversified	287	0.71	0.39	0.21
CTA Energy	6	0.54	0.26	0.16
CTA Financial	101	0.74	0.41	0.23
CTA Stock Index	40	0.74	0.40	0.21
Managed Futures Public Pools	424	0.69	0.39	0.22
Managed Futures Private Pools	249	0.70	0.39	0.21

Source: eLibrary or Social Science Research Network (ssrn.com).

For each fund in the sample, 20 sets of simulated hedge fund returns are generated. Simulated asset returns R_t^A are created by reordering the residuals from a regression of actual fund returns on the subset of CISDM hedge fund and CTA indexes and their lags that maximizes the regression's adjusted R-squared. Then, simulated hedge fund returns are generated by smoothing the simulated asset returns such that:

$$R_t^S = [0.5(1 - I_t) + I_t]R_t^A + 0.5(1 - I_t)R_{t-1}^A$$

where $I_t = 1$ if the month t systematic return from the optimal factor model is greater than its mean and zero otherwise. Detailed data of simulated hedge fund returns on their lag:

$$R_t^S = a + b_1^+ R_{t-1}^S + b_1^-(1 - I_{t-1})R_{t-1}^S + \eta_t$$

where R_t^S is the simulated fund return in month t and $I_{t-1} = 1$ if the simulated fund's systematic return at month $t - 1$ is estimated to be greater than the mean systematic return.

Table 12.10 provides the number of funds, the average regression-

TABLE 12.10 Power Analysis of Asymmetric Serial Correction

Hedge Fund Strategy	Number of Hedge Funds	Power
Event Driven	197	0.35
Global Emerging	127	0.36
Global Established	479	0.28
Global International	53	0.35
Global Macro	75	0.28
Long-Only	23	0.33
Market Neutral	479	0.29
Sector	158	0.26
Short Selling	25	0.35
Fund of Funds	542	0.32
CTA Agriculture	26	0.28
CTA Currency	76	0.34
CTA Diversified	287	0.35
CTA Energy	6	0.17
CTA Financial	101	0.32
CTA Stock Index	40	0.26
Managed Futures Public Pools	424	0.31
Managed Futures Private Pools	249	0.32

Source: eLibrary or Social Science Research Network (ssrn.com).

adjusted R-squared, and the percentage of simulations with significant positive b_1^+ and b_1^- coefficients evaluated at the two-sided 5 percent level.

From this analysis, Bollen and Krepely (2005) noted that the percentage of simulations with significant positive b_1^- coefficients is between 30 and 35 percent. The researchers reveal the following findings:

The factor model regression provides the 25th, 50th, and 75th percentile of the cross-sectional distribution of adjusted R-squared when the regressions are limited to one contemporaneous factor, two actual factors, and an unlimited number of actual and lagged factors. For the three funds the distribution of the adjusted R-squared shifts to the right as the number of factors rises. When the number of factors is unconstrained, the median adjusted R-squared is 45 percent for hedge funds and 27 percent for CTAs, showing that a material part of hedge funds is missing. The hedge funds on average have 3.38 contemporaneous factors and about one lagged factor compared to 2.32 and 0.20 respectively for CTAs and 2.54 and 0.27 respectively for managed futures. For each fund, a subset of available factors is selected to maximize the adjusted R-squared of the regression, subject to the criterion that simpler regressions are favored if additional factors do not significantly improve the fit statistically. The following data relating to CISDM indexes shows the results when factors are known or observable. Given are the 25th, 50th, and 75th percentiles of the cross-sectional distributions of the adjusted R-squared when the number of factors is one, two, or unconstrained.

For the one-factor model, we obtain the percentiles in Table 12.11.

For the two-factor model, CISDM indexes' sectional regression distribution gives the result in Table 12.12.

The same regression is being performed on asset-based style (ABS) factors instead of CISDM indexes. The results of the experimentations show that the asset-based style factors represent a constant exposure to the underlying variables, whereas the CISDM indexes reflect the time-varying strategy or set of strategies. The funds' returns are going to be expressed differently in the regression analysis depending on whether the hedge fund manager is performing symmetrical or asymmetrical smoothing on the

TABLE 12.11 One-Factor Model

	Number of Funds	25th Percentile	50th Percentile	75th Percentile
Hedge Funds	2,158	0.15	0.30	0.47
CTAs	536	0.06	0.20	0.45
Managed Futures	673	0.12	0.35	0.60

Source: eLibrary or Social Science Research Network (ssrn.com).

TABLE 12.12 Two-Factor Model

	Number of Funds	25th Percentile	50th Percentile	75th Percentile
Hedge Funds	2,158	0.21	0.36	0.52
CTAs	536	0.09	0.25	0.49
Managed Futures	673	0.17	0.40	0.64

Source: eLibrary or Social Science Research Network (ssrn.com).

risk-adjusted returns. If the hedge fund manager is performing symmetrical smoothing, then the factor equals the sum of the exposures of the observed returns on contemporaneous and lagged factors such that:

$$\beta = \Sigma_{j=0 \rightarrow k} \beta_j^0$$

And if the hedge fund manager is performing asymmetrical smoothing on the risk-adjusted returns (that is, advantaging the upside more than the downside), then the observed factor loading β^0 is an average of the conditional factor loadings. Using the constrained factor model, CISDM indexes' sectional regression distribution gives the results in Table 12.13.

Similar tables are provided for asset-based style factors.

Table 12.14 gives the percentiles of the sectional distributions of the adjusted R-squared when the factor number is one.

The data in Table 12.15 represents the results considering the factor number as two.

The data in Table 12.16 represents the results with unconstrained factor (see page 206).

In the final part of the analysis to determine how many actual funds exhibit asymmetrical serial correlation, we run the following asymmetric regression.

The data below is the result of the regression of individual fund returns on their lag using hedge funds, CTAs, and managed futures as of December 2003 from the CISDM database. Regressions take the following equations:

$$R_t^0 = a + b_1^+ R_{t-1}^0 + b_1^-(1 - I_{t-1})R_{t-1}^0 + \eta_t$$

where R_t^0 is the observed fund return in month t and I_{t-1} equals 1 if the fund's systematic return from an optimal factor model at month $t - 1$ is greater than the mean systematic return. For each fund type the number of funds

TABLE 12.13 Conditional Factor Loadings

	Number of Funds	25th Percentile	50th Percentile	75th Percentile	Average Adjusted R-squared	Average Number Contemporaneous Factors	Average Number of Lagged Factors
Hedge Funds	2,158	0.28	0.45	0.61	0.44	3.38	1.06
CTAs	536	0.11	0.27	0.51	0.32	2.32	0.20
Managed Futures	673	0.18	0.44	0.66	0.43	2.54	0.27

Source: eLibrary or Social Science Research Network (ssrn.com).

TABLE 12.14 One-Factor Model Results

	Number of Funds	25th Percentile	50th Percentile	75th Percentile
Hedge Funds	2,158	0.07	0.15	0.27
CTAs	536	0.05	0.11	0.19
Managed Futures	673	0.07	0.13	0.21

Source: eLibrary or Social Science Research Network (ssrn.com).

TABLE 12.15 Two-Factor Model Results

	Number of Funds	25th Percentile	50th Percentile	75th Percentile
Hedge Funds	2,158	0.10	0.22	0.37
CTAs	536	0.08	0.16	0.26
Managed Futures	673	0.10	0.20	0.29

Source: eLibrary or Social Science Research Network (ssrn.com).

and the number of funds with significant positive factors b_1^- coefficients are evaluated at the two-sided 5 percent level. Table 12.17 lists results for when CISDM indexes and the asset-based style (ABS) factors developed by Fung and Hsieh (2004) are used as factors in determining I_{t-1} (see page 207). Thus, the frequency of asymmetric serial correlation is revealed in the table.

The number of funds that trigger a red flag is quite low, 157 out of 3,367 for the CISDM factors and 128 out of 3,367 for the ABS factors, or 4.66 percent and 3.80 percent, respectively. This low percentage is consistent with the low number of reported fraud cases. Bollen and Krepely (2005) noted that there is a significant coefficient across the categories, indicating that properties of specific asset classes cannot be the sole explanation for asymmetrical smoothing.

Both researchers analyzed the cross-sectional properties of the red-flagged funds and used regressions where the dependent variable takes the value of one when a given fund is red-flagged or zero otherwise. This is to evaluate whether hedge fund managers systematically perform asymmetrical smoothing in most cases.

The test to determine red flags includes different regressors such as fund age, fund size, fee structure, actual audits, lockup periods, and dead or live funds. The second set of regressors used is derived from reported returns measurements such as mean, standard deviation, and Sharpe ratio. The last set of regressors includes means and standard deviation of investor

TABLE 12.16 Unconstrained Factor Results

	Number of Funds	25th Percentile	50th Percentile	75th Percentile	Average Adjusted R-squared	Average Number Contemporaneous Factors	Average Number of Lagged Factors
Hedge Funds	2,158	0.12	0.26	0.42	0.28	2.13	0.49
CTAs	536	0.08	0.17	0.30	0.20	2.08	0.23
Managed Futures	673	0.11	0.23	0.35	0.25	2.41	0.38

Source: eLibrary or Social Science Research Network (ssrn.com).

TABLE 12.17 Frequency of Asymmetrical Serial Correlation

Hedge Fund Strategy	Number of Funds	CISDM	ABS
Event Driven	197	14	10
Global Emerging	127	6	3
Global Established	479	23	14
Global International	53	3	3
Global Macro	75	4	4
Long-Only	23	3	3
Market Neutral	479	19	21
Sector	158	14	10
Short Selling	25	0	0
Fund of Funds	542	25	17
CTA Agriculture	26	2	7
CTA Currency	76	6	2
CTA Diversified	287	12	9
CTA Energy	6	0	0
CTA Financial	101	4	4
CTA Stock Index	40	0	0
Managed Futures Public Pool	424	10	10
Managed Futures Private Pool	249	12	11
Total	3,367	157 or 4.66%	128 or 3.80%

Source: eLibrary or Social Science Research Network (ssrn.com).

fund flows. Fund flow is deducted from the time series of a fund's returns and assets under management reported in the database. So assuming $\text{TNA}_{i,t}$ is the total net assets of a hedge fund at time t and let $R_{i,t}$ be the holding period return for a hedge fund investor in fund between times t and $t - 1$, the fund flow is such that:

$$\text{DF}_{i,t} = \text{TNA}_{i,t} - \text{TNA}_{i,j-1}(1 + R_{i,t})$$

where $\text{DF}_{i,t}$ denotes dollar flow. DF is standardized by dividing it by the number of months over which it is computed. Bollen and Krepely (2005) noticed that fund size, fund age, fees, and the volatility of cash flows are highly skewed. As a result, 36 funds are dropped from the analysis for lack of sufficient data to compute the cash flow variables. Of the 3,331 funds, 126 feature asymmetric smoothing. Both cash flow variables are significant, suggesting that the probability of finding asymmetric serial correlation is higher when cash flow volatility is higher and when cash flows on average are low. Instinctively, the higher are the risks, the higher is the likelihood of smoothing and returns manipulations. From Table 12.18, a hedge fund's cash

TABLE 12.18 Cross-Sectional Analysis of Red-Flagged Hedge Funds

	Model I			Model II		
	Coefficient	Standard Error	p-Value	Coefficient	Standard Error	p-Value
Constant	-2.5768	0.2694	0.0000	-0.8033	1.4170	0.5708
ln(Cfvol)	0.2847	0.1184	0.0161	0.4512	0.1707	0.0082
Cfmu	-3.0503	1.5496	0.0493	-4.4086	2.6912	0.1014
E[r]				9.6020	14.2263	0.4997
Fee				-0.2415	0.2106	0.2514
Incentive				0.0056	0.0159	0.7260
Live				-0.1769	0.2758	0.5211
Ln (Size)				-0.0041	0.0818	0.9605
Audit				-0.7175	0.3496	0.0401
Age				0.0041	0.0027	0.1210
Ln (weight)				-0.2335	0.1210	0.5370
LR Statistic		5.2351			14.4033	
Probability (LRstat)		0.0730			0.1554	
McFadden R-squared		0.0049			0.0239	
Number of Observations		3,331			1,852	
Number of Observations Red-Flagged		126			71	
Frequency		3.78%			3.83%	

Source: eLibrary or Social Science Research Network (ssrn.com).

flow patterns and audits are the two variables distinctive of others that suggest potential frauds or red flags. The cross-sectional analysis of red-flagged hedge funds are as shown for factor models based on the asset-based style (ABS) factors developed by Fund and Hsieh (2004).

Other variables are keys to detect frauds. Liang (2000) reinforced the fact that audits have a significant impact on risk-adjusted returns. (See Figure 12.1.)

Liang mentioned other variables such as transparency, manager efforts, and the ease of calculating returns being high marks for fraud reduction. Transparent funds tend to have better data quality than other funds. Transparency can be measured by variables such as being listed on exchanges and open to the public. Managers of funds of funds do not engage in daily trading activities so they may have more time to verify return accuracy than hedge fund managers have. Funds with managers' personal investments may have better data quality because these managers may try harder to make sure the returns are correct for their own sakes. Returns of unlevered funds are easier to calculate than those of levered funds since leverage may complicate portfolio positions and daily settlement. Funds investing in a single industrial sector will have simpler returns than those that invest in multiple sectors, especially if these sectors contain less liquid assets.

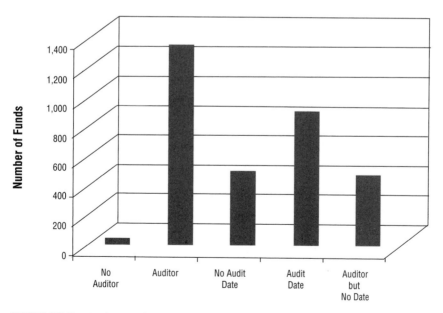

FIGURE 12.1 Auditor and Audit Date (1999 TASS Data)

CHAPTER **13**

Funds of Funds
Rating Methodology

The lack of regulatory framework for hedge funds within the financial markets has not forced hedge funds to be sophisticated in risk management and thus in capital adequacy requirements and ratings. Many hedge fund risk managers have relied on value at risk, stress testing, and scenario analysis to produce risk reports, but due to the sophistication of the strategies and the usage of complicated structures, hedge funds' risk management should have integrated variance, covariance, skewness, and extreme value theory models.

This statement is even more relevant for hedge funds using indexes to benchmark products' risks and performance. Many of the hedge fund indexes do not capture market risks that traditional indexes such as the Dow Jones or the Standard & Poor's do. Thus, with increased scrutiny of risk management in hedge funds, rising regulatory registrations to examine hedge funds, and market pressures, hedge funds will be more likely to be influenced to improve transparency and internal operations.

Rating hedge funds' capital is a way to enhance capital quality. The following rating theories summarize the inefficiencies and inadequacies in the various ways broad rating methodologies have failed. The review is aimed at giving a complete set of the various rating methodologies and by applying a few of them create a more reasonable, fair, and consistent rating methodology. Noel Amenc and Veronique Le Sourd (2005) provide a detailed analysis of the various rating models, and this is what they found.

They found inconsistencies when comparing investment vehicles trading totally different risks. For instance, the equities' averages are not accurately representative, as the mean dispersion or standard deviation of the weights is greater than their average. The performance-related ranking methods based on the information ratio (Lipper and Standard & Poor's) reinforced ratings weaknesses.

210

Also, ratings do not take into account the performances and risks of the different styles. For example, international rating agencies do not differentiate between European value and growth funds. Amenc and Le Sourd (2005) have demonstrated that almost 70 percent of the funds ranked as large cap actually have a majority exposure to the small cap style. Furthermore, most of the funds' rankings have been assigned based on their returns and performance, not on their alpha. The study has proved that most of the ratings have been based on following styles' returns over time, skills, and luck except for Aptinum.

Most of the agencies' ratings methodologies do not use extreme value at risk (EVAR) and limit analysis on structured products to the first derivatives. They rarely calculate covariance, skewness, and kurtosis, and the impact of portfolio diversification on the overall mean variance framework. Morningstar, S&P, and Aptinum do not include performance consistencies or persistence in the rating calculations, and Lipper does not include them in its model. As a result of these deficiencies, EuroPerformance and EDHEC Research Centre implemented a funds rating methodology based on alpha, value at risk, and performance, and we describe it in the next chapter. (See Table 13.1.)

Ratings are highly correlated with the amount of subscriptions. If ratings are lowered, subscriptions flow to other funds. Del Guercia and Tkac (2002) discovered that an initial Morningstar five-star rating results, on average, in six months of abnormal flows or 53 percent in excess of the normal expected flow. Their research showed that inflows of subscriptions have a direct correlation with positive rating upgrades and outflows of subscriptions with negative rating downgrades. Adkisson and Fraser (2003a) also found that investors withdrew from downgraded mutual funds and did not invest more in those upgraded funds.

Khoran and Nelling (1998) showed consistency between ratings and performance. Positively rated funds consistently gain from continuing positive returns and poorly rated funds consistently lose from continuing negative returns. However, Blake and Morey (2000) found that ratings are not a better predictor of performance than the funds' past average monthly returns. Moreover, Morey (2003) demonstrated that performance tends to fall off three years after a fund is awarded a five-star rating.

Let's first review all the various quantitative methodologies to rate funds.

S&P's model uses Markowitz's model to rate funds. S&P rates 90,000 funds in 52 countries with 54,000 in Europe and 10,000 international indexes. Geographically, S&P monitors 9,000 funds in France with half of them governed by foreign law. These 9,000 funds are categorized in 160 groups. S&P uses a minimum of three years' ($t = 36$ months) worth of

TABLE 13.1 Overview of Rating Methodologies

Provider	S&P	Morningstar	Lipper	Aptinum	EuroPerformance and EDHEC
Measure of Risk Actually Taken	Poor	Average	Poor	Very Good	Very Good
Measure of Extreme Risks	No	No	Average	No	Good
Measure of Performance Persistence	No	No	Very Good	Good	Very Good
Robustness and Confidence	Poor	Poor	Poor	Good	Very Good
Transparency and Comprehensibility	Very Good	Very Good	Good	Poor	Very Good

Source: www.edhec-risk.com.

financial data to produce ratings. Half of these funds get an official star rating. The average return R of the fund is simply written such that:

$$R_{st} = (1/N)\Sigma R_{it}$$

where N is the number of funds in strategy s such that $N > 1$, $i = 1$, and $t > 1$.

Thus the relative monthly return of each fund is computed as the difference between the fund's monthly return and the monthly mean average return such that $R_{it} - R_{st}$, and the volatility or variance of the fund is:

$$\sigma(R_i - R_S) = \sqrt{1/36\Sigma_{t=1\to36}[(R_{it} - R_{st}) - (R_i - R_s)]^2}$$

where $R_i = 1/36\Sigma_{t=1\to36}R_{it}$
$R_s = 1/36\Sigma_{t=1\to36}R_{st}$ or $R_s = 1/N\Sigma_{t=1\to N}R_{st}$

Volatility is the variance or standard deviation from the mean/average S&P risk-adjusted ratio in an information ratio (IR) or a Sharpe ratio where the riskless asset has been replaced by the return of a benchmark. The S&P risk-adjusted ratio is described as follows:

$$IR = \frac{\Sigma_{t=1\to36}(R_{it} - R_{st})}{\sigma(R_i - R_s)}$$

The benchmark is the average return of a sector, and a fund is rated depending on its consistent IR result compared to its competitors. The higher its IR, the more chances the fund has to be given stars. The reference for stars is:

Ratios in the top 10 percent are given five stars such that IR $> = 90\%$.

Ratios in the next 20 percent are given four stars with $70\% = <$ IR $< 90\%$.

Ratios in the following 20 percent are given three stars with $50\% = <$ IR $< 70\%$.

Ratios in the following 25 percent are given two stars with $25\% = <$ IR $< 50\%$.

Ratios in the bottom 25 percent are given one star such that IR $< 25\%$.

This ratio's biggest flaw is that it does not account for absolute risk.

The Morningstar rating was founded in 1985 and is also based on risk-adjusted return for different categories such as:

- Equity funds with introduction of style in European model.
- Bond and interest rate products funds.
- Balanced funds.

The fund's return is such that:

$$R = \left[\left(\frac{P_e}{P_b\Pi_{i=1/n\to\infty}}\right)\left(\frac{1+D_i}{P_i}\right)\right] - 1 \text{ such that } i = 1 \text{ and } n > 0$$

where P_e = net asset value per share at end of month
P_b = net asset value per share at beginning of month
D_i = distribution per share at time i
P_i = net asset value reinvested per share at time i
n = number of distributions during month

If there were no loads or redemption fees, the cumulative value of one Euro over a period of T months is:

$$V_u = \Pi_{t=1\to T}(1 + R_t) - 1$$

If there are loads or redemption fees, the cumulative value adjusted for loads and redemption fees is such that:

$$V = (1 - F)(1 - R)\, V_u - D(1 - F)\{\min(P_o, P_t)/P_o\}$$

where F = front load
D = deferred load
R = redemption fee
P_o = net asset value per share at beginning of period
P_t = net asset value per share at end of period

The Morningstar risk-adjusted return (MRAR) is represented as a mathematical expectation of a function or utility function of the ending value of each portfolio. This isoelastic or power function is such that:

$$u(W) = \{-W^{-y}/y\} \text{ such that } y > -1 \text{ and } y < > 0$$
$$u(W) = \{\ln(W)\} \text{ such that } y = 0$$

where W is the ending value of the portfolio and y is the parameter describing the risk.

$$u'(W) >= 0$$

If $u''(W) < 0$, then $u\,[E(W)] > E[u(W)]$.

The degree of risk aversion of investors is such that:

$$\text{RAR}(W) = -\frac{W''(W)}{u'(W)}$$

where RAR = risk-adjusted return.

The ending return on a portfolio starting with investment W_0 is such that:

$$W = W_0(1 + R)$$

where R = return:

$$u(W) = -\,(W_0^{-y}/y)(1 + R)^{-y}/y > -1$$
$$\ln[W_0(1 + R)]y = 0$$

Then:

$$W_0 = \frac{1}{1 + R_f}$$

where R_f = risk-free return:

$$(-1/y)[(1 + R)/(1 + R_F)]^{-y} \qquad y > -1 \text{ and } y <> 0$$

$$u[W_0(1 + R)] = \ln[(1 + R)/(1 + R_F) \qquad y = 0$$

And the geometric excess return is defined such that:

$$r_G = \left(\frac{1 + R}{1 + R_F}\right) - 1$$

Also,

$$u(1+r_G) = -\left[\frac{1+r_G}{y}\right]^{-y} \quad \text{with } y > -1 \text{ and } y \neq 0$$

$$\ln(1 + r_G)y = 0$$

According to Amenc and Le Sourd (2005),

The certainty equivalent geometric excess return of a risky invest-ment is the guaranteed geometric excess return that the investor would accept as a substitute for the uncertain geometric excess re-turn of that investment.

Letting $r_G^{ce}(y)$ denote the certainty equivalent geometric excess return for a given value of y",

$$u[1 + r_G^{ce}(y)] = E[u(1 + r_G)]$$

Thus:

$$\{[1 + r_G^{ce}(y)]^{-y} = E[(1 + r_G)^{-y}]$$

$$E[(1 + r_G)^{-y}]^{-1/y} - 1 \text{ such that } y > = -1 \text{ and } y < > 0$$
$$r_G^{ce}(y) \qquad e^{E[\ln(1+rG)]} - 1 \qquad y = 0$$

MRAR(y) is the annualized value of r_G^{ce} and the time series is such that:

$$\text{MRAR}(y) = [1/T\Sigma_{t=1\rightarrow T}(1 + r_{Gt})^{-y}]^{-12/y} - 1$$

where $r_{Gt} = [(1 + R_t)/(1 + R_{Ft})] - 1$ is the geometric excess return in month t. If $y < > 0$ and $y = 1$, MRAR is the annualized geometric mean of r_{Gt}.

$$\text{MRAR}(0) = [\Pi_{t=1\rightarrow T}(1 + r_{Gt})]^{-12/T} - 1$$

With loads and redemption fees, the adjustment factor is:

$$a = (V/V_u)^{1/T}$$

where V is the cumulative value adjusted for loads and redemption fees and V_u is the cumulative value not adjusted for loads and redemption fees.

The adjusted total return for month $tAR_t = a(1 + R_t) - 1$ with R_t is the total return for month t. Loads and fees can then be incorporated into the calculation of MRAR by replacing R_t with AR_t.

Morningstar computes the load-adjusted MRAR (2) of total return for three years. MRAR (2) for all funds is sorted in descending order. A number of stars is then given according to the schedule such that the top 10 percent of funds get 5 stars, the following 22.5 percent four stars, the next 35 percent three stars, the next 22.5 percent two stars, and the bottom 10 percent one star.

The United States uses a weighted average over longer periods of time: 0.6 for the five-year rating and 0.4 for the three-year rating if less than 10 years of historical data, and 0.5 for the 10-year rating, 0.3 for the five-year rating, and 0.2 for the three-year rating for more than 10 years of historical data. Chiang, Kozhevinkov, and Wisen (2003) compared this theory with the old methods and discovered that risk-adjusted returns (RAR) and excess returns from the capital asset pricing model regression have correlated star ratings.

The arbitrage pricing theory (APT) was developed by Stephen Ross in 1976 and assumed an efficient market. It defines the returns as follows:

$$R_{it} = \alpha_{it} + \sum_{k=1 \to K} \beta_{ik} \times F_{kt} + \varepsilon_{it}$$

where α_{it} = the expected mean return of asset I
β_{ik} = the sensitivity (or exposure) of asset I to factor k
F_{kt} = the return of factor k with $E(F_k) = 0$
ε_{it} = the residual return of asset i; the share of the return unexplained $E(\varepsilon_{it}) = 0$

This methodology started to reveal rankings publicly in 1999 in newspapers such as *Le Monde, El Pais, Suddeutsche Zeitung, La Stampa, Tageblatt,* and *Le Jeudi.* The ranking methodology has been simplified as of 2004 to be more understandable by the general public. This model is more complete than the capital asset pricing model as the CAPM is a one-factor model. It is a factor model analyzing asset returns to define unobservable factors.

The APT model groups assets into homogeneous classes according to behavioral distribution of returns observations. The model uses two years' worth of data. This model has about 200 groups such as equity emerging markets and equity technology. It is a multifactor model comprehensive of the different groups such as assets, styles, strategies, and geographies. The various funds or groups have each been given a coefficient reflective of the corresponding risk exposures. Each group's risk exposures are in correlation with its corresponding market beta (β). Thus, the overall beta captures all the funds' systematic risk factors such as inflation, currencies, commodities, and interest rates. A beta close to 1 reflects high correlation with overall market risks. The overall systematic risk of a fund can be expressed as the square root of the sum of the beta squared for each fund k; that is:

$$\beta_{ik} = \sqrt{\beta_{i1}^2 + \beta_{i2}^2 + \ldots + \beta_{ik}^2}$$

From this the APT risk-adjusted performance measurement is derived by dividing a one-year historical performance by the APT beta of the fund. Using this methodology, Table 13.2 lists ratings for three-year moving averages data.

Funds have not yet been fully rated due to lack of data. As of 2006, ratings of funds will become more and more prevalent. As a result of delays in regulations and increased scrutiny of due diligence in hedge funds and funds of funds, as of the beginning of 2004 less than 4 percent of the rated funds had five stars, while 12 percent received five or four stars. At least 51 percent had one star or no stars. This methodology has proved that the gap between the highest-rated ones and the lowest rated ones has widened. This also shows that the greater the arbitrage opportunities in the market, the greater the gap between qualitative and quantitative ratings of the funds.

The Lipper methodology uses consistency in performance, capital preservation, expense ratios, and total return. In Lipper's American model, tax efficiency is in the model as well. The model uses scorecards like in operational risk management to rate funds and finds the most ap-

TABLE 13.2 APT Risk-Adjusted Performance Measurement Ratings

Three-Year Moving Average	Ratings
Top 25%	5 Stars
Top 25% to 35%	4 Stars
Top 35% to 45%	3 Stars
Top 45% to 55%	2 Stars
Top 55% to 65%	1 Star
Top 65% to 75%	0 Stars
Bottom 25%	No Rating

Source: www.edhec-risk.com.

propriate ones to meet investors' needs. Lipper has a library of about 80,000 funds, 12,549 of them in France. Scores are assigned for total return, consistent return, expense, and tax efficiency and are classified in at least five categories while scores for preservation have been categorized into three asset classes: equity funds, mixed equity funds, and bond funds. The scorecards for total return takes returns into consideration without accounting for risks. Instead it can include capital preservation, performance, and consistency.

Lipper scores include consistency of returns, which is measured with two mathematical tools: the Hurst (H) exponent and the effective return. The H exponent captures the variations of prices' statistical series. Funds with high H exponents tend to be less volatile than those with low H exponents. Lipper categorized three types of variations: funds with high H values > 0.55 and least volatile, funds with 0.45 < H ≤ 0.55, and power H ≤ 0.45 with highest volatility. The effective return is equal to the excess fund return of the Lipper Global sector index over the fund's return.

Lipper employs the H exponent and effective return to implement ranking methodology such that funds are sorted in decreasing order based on their H exponent. Funds are then segregated into three groups according to:

$$H > 0.55$$
$$0.45 < H \leq 0.55$$
$$H \leq 0.45$$

Each group is then resorted in decreasing order of H. The negative returns with high H (H > 0.55) are removed and placed after those with H ≤ 0.45. The resulting group is then in the methodologically accurate order.

The Lipper score for its preservation model is the sum of negative monthly returns over three, five, and ten years such that:

$$\Sigma_{t=1 \to n} \text{Min}(0, \tau_t)$$

where n is 36, 60, or 120 months and τ_t is the return in month t.

This model is what most investors research (that is, capital preservation over greater returns), with 51 percent of mutual fund investors complying with this school of thought.

The Lipper score for expense is usually complementary to the other scores. According to William Sharpe (1997), the Sharpe ratio for funds with lower expense ratios was 75 percent higher than for those funds with higher expense ratios.

The Lipper score for tax efficiency calculates relative wealth (RW) over three , five , and ten-year periods and is such that:

$$RW = \left(\frac{1 + R_{at}}{1 + R_{bt}} \right) \times 100$$

where R_{at} is the preliquidation standard after tax return and R_{bt} is the SEC return before taxes. Relative wealth calculations explain how much value as a percentage of change is lost due to taxes.

The Lipper funds are finally sorted based on the ranking results found for each category—total return, consistent return, preservation, expense, and tax efficiency—and they are all classified into five groups, each of which is equally broken every 20 percent. The highest 20 percent of the funds are the Lipper leaders. The next 20 percent have a rank or overall score of 2, and the lowest 20 percent have a score of 5. This analysis is based on three years, five years, and ten years overall.

In conclusion, primarily due to the lack of continuity of regulations and reforms in the hedge fund industry, Amenc and Le Sourd (2005) provided research to highlight the weaknesses and unreliability of ratings systems depending on what model or theory to apply. Growth and value categories are seldom accurate as they do not account for external microeconomic forces and data, yet their performance used to be highly correlated with and depend on micro- and macroeconomic statistical data.

Now the averages of all hedge fund indexes over time taken with traditional indexes such as the S&P or the Dow Jones would be more complete, representative, or closer to real market moves and inefficiencies. Unlike traditional indexes that no longer capture market inefficiencies, some hedge fund indexes do not calibrate for extreme or catastrophic events over time and show continuous smooth upward returns trends. Both traditional indexes and hedge fund indexes should be more complementary and together should account for most market movements and efficiencies.

Bienstock and Sorensen (1992) showed that 20 percent of the stocks from a sample of 3,000 can be categorized as value or growth. Haslem and Schegara (2001) also showed that the Morningstar style groups for funds in the "large" description category and were not consistent with a clustering type statistical approach grouping funds according to shapes of the their rough returns.

Another flaw to ratings systems is that the stated strategy is not always the actual strategy being used. This is due to the fact that dynamic trading strategies are not monitored by regulators and that these changes in trading strategies have not been taken into account in regulatory filings, requests, and funds' internal databases. Thus, DiBartolomeo and Witkowski (1997) showed that there are structural shifts in trading, styles, and strategies categories and that they have an impact on funds' ratings. They found that about 40 percent of 748 funds were in an inaccurate or erroneous fund category.

In the same school of thought, Kim, Shukla, and Thomas (2000) revealed that only 46 percent of the 1,043 funds were consistent with their respective classifications and that 54 percent were misclassified into the wrong strategic groups.

This is also due to inaccuracies and variations of definitions of hedge fund styles or classes, depending on what sources are being used. More than 33 percent of strategies were misrepresented and 57 percent of the surviving funds changed their investment style at some point from 1993 to 1996. Only 27 percent kept their categories' attributes. About 33 percent were less risky than stated while 31 percent were riskier than stated.

Again in the same school of thought but in a different market, Jin and Yang (2004) showed that 50 percent of the Chinese mutual funds are not consistent with their objective groups. Very much as market news feeds markets, fund ratings feed investors' decisions, and hence these impact funds' measurements, which consequently affect funds' ratings, and so on.

Other kinds of risks that are not yet incorporated into any fund ratings are operational, process, technological infrastructure quality, and above all management integrity or compliance risks. As of yet, investors are still very much left in the dark when it comes to access to such knowledge in their investment decisions or in their effort to integrate such variables into a more accurate independent objective and complete rating system. Not until investors obtain such a system to rate funds can they qualitatively research market information to complement these quantitative systems. Table 13.3 provides some information on the 15 best funds according to Sharpe ratio as of July 30, 2004, on the French market.

Amenc and Le Sourd's (2005) research on fund ratings is summarized in Table 13.4.

TABLE 13.3 Top 15 French Funds by Sharpe Ratio

Fund Name	Value at Risk	Rank	Sharpe Ratio	Rank
Templeton Eastern Europe Fund A Euro Cap	7.23%	720	1.26203	1
Westam Compass Fund European Convergence A	8.465%	1,627	1.14898	2
Templeton Eastern Europe Fund BX Euro Cap	7.176%	675	1.14097	3
ABN Amro Funds Eastern Europe Equity Fund A Eur	8.614%	1,722	0.96509	4
State Street Emerging Europe	8.668%	1,763	0.88733	5
MMA Asie	6.465%	321	0.88301	6
Tocqueville Dividende (C)	5.163%	61	0.8241	7
USB Lux Equity Fund Central Europe B	8.154%	1,421	0.75731	8
JP Morgan Fleming Funds Europe Convergence Equity Aeur	7.825%	1,207	0.73189	9
Axa Rosenberg Equity Alpha Pacific Ex-Japan Small Cap Alpha A USD Cap	7.324%	778	0.68245	10
Off ming	7.408%	850	0.66121	11
Morgan Stanley Emerging Europe and Middle East Equity B	8.307%	1,517	0.65474	12
New Asia	6.196%	230	0.63718	13
Magellan	9.098%	2,104	0.63556	14
SocGen International A Capitalization A	4.517%	16	0.63137	15

Source: Social Science Research Network (www.ssrn.com).

TABLE 13.4 Fund Rating Criteria

Criterion	S&P	Morningstar	Lipper	Aptinum	EuroPerformance
Launching Year	1998	2001	2002	1998	2004
Media	Internet Press	Internet CD-ROM	Internet	Press Le Monde	Internet
Symbol	Star	Star	—	Star	⊕
Number of Funds in Europe	4,500	17,000	7,000	4,500	3,500
Number of Funds Studied	9,000	26,000	14,853	13,000	25,000
Number of Categories	56	83	155	200	16
Rating Methodology	Information Ratio (IR)	Risk-Adjusted Performance	Consistent Return, IR, Capital Preservation, Total Return, Expense Ratio	Arbitrage Pricing Theory (APT)	Risk-Adjusted Performance Based on Style Analysis; Extreme Loss; VaR; Performance Consistencies
Frequency of Calculation	Monthly	Monthly	Monthly	Monthly	Monthly
Data Historical Records	3 Years	3 Years	3 Years	4 Years	3 Years
Measure of EVAR	No	No	Average	No	Good
Measure of Performance Persistence	No	No	Very High	High	Very High
Robustness and Confidence	Low	Low	Low	High	Very High
Transparency and Completeness	Very High	Very High	High	Low	Very High

Source: Social Science Research Network (www.ssrn.com).

CHAPTER **14**

Hedge Funds Rating Methodology

As hedge funds are regulated under the Securities and Exchange Commission as of February 2006 and their registration is becoming more mandatory, hedge funds' rating of capital might become part of their requirement for better integration in the markets. With larger banks required to maintain capital adequacy levels and also getting into the hedge fund business for greater returns and more competitiveness, it is also fair and prudent to rate hedge funds' capital quality.

Ratings have a big impact in the sale of products in the North American markets as 70 percent of subscriptions involve four- and five-star funds. In Europe, as risk management is still far from being mature, ratings have not yet become important. The ratings' eligibility criteria are genuine integration of risk in performance, measures, robustness, reliability, transparency and legibility of ratings, performance consistency, rating objectivity and independence, rating disclosure, and rating credibility.

Three main criteria are used to measure ratings: risk-adjusted performance of the portfolio (alpha), extreme value at risk (EVAR), and performance (returns). Alpha is defined as the difference between the fund's returns and the normal returns based on all risk taking to achieve such performance. William Sharpe won the Nobel Prize for the multifactor theory model in 1992. Extreme value at risk (EVAR) provides an estimate for potential maximum losses in normal risk environments or situations. Returns and performance consistency theory is measured with two theoretical tools: One is the capacity to calculate the frequency of a portfolio's alpha over the period or gain frequency, and the second is the regularity of the outperformance according to the Hurst exponent or H factor. In order to define a rating process, alfa is measured using different methodologies. According to William Sharpe (1988, 1992) a return-based style analysis can be used to define alpha by trading style or strategies:

$$R_{it} = w_{i1} \times F_{1t} + w_{i2} \times F_{2t} + \ldots + w_{ik} \times F_{kt} + e_{it}$$

where R_i = the excess return net of fees of a given portfolio or fund
F_k = the excess return compared to index j for period t
w_{ik} = the weight of style or sum of weights being equal to 1 or 100 percent
e_{it} = residual error term

This methodology performs the regression analysis for all funds and tests the regression coefficients (variations) for each style against the Lobosco and DiBartolomeo test, and those coefficients are tested on a three-year rolling smoothing average.

The linear component is perceived to be the actual representation of risk for each given trading strategy whereas the residual e_{it} represents the noise of the model, the trading psychology, fund selection and timing, correlation factors between different strategies, other market inefficiencies. The other methodological tool used is the multi-index model or factor models. There exist five types of models:

1. General factor model.
2. Implicit factor model.
3. Explicit macroeconomic factor model.
4. Explicit microeconomic factor model.
5. Market indexes factor model.

The general factor model takes into account all factor models. The implicit factor model considers only return statistical series. The explicit macroeconomic factor model accounts for economical variables or components to create a ratings methodology. For instance, Chen, Roll, and Ross (1986) used the inflation rate, the growth of industrial output difference between long-term and short-term interest rates, and the difference in ratings between bonds. The explicit microeconomic factor model involves measurement of labor laws, capital variable calculations, and supply and demand parameters. The Barra model is an example of such theory.

The market indexes factor model uses market indexes as factors. CAPM by Sharpe (1964) is an example of such theory and bases returns on correlation of linear and nonlinear returns between strategies' or styles' returns. Another example of such theory is the replicating portfolios as approximations of the true factor, unknown and also found in Fama and French (1992). This multifactor index takes the sum of the different return strategies in excess of the risk-free rate equivalent to the return of a three-month government Treasury traded security. This is another way of measuring alpha:

$$R_{it} - r_f = \alpha_i + \beta_{i1}(F_{it} - r_f) + \beta_{i2}(F_{2t} - r_f) + \ldots + \beta_{ik}(F_{kt} - r_f) + e_{it}$$

where α_i = the abnormal fund performance
        R_{it} = the return net of fees of a portfolio
        r_f = the risk-free rate
        β_{ik} = the sensitivity of fund factor k
        F_k = the return of factor k for period t

In order to create a methodology for rating, various tools are used to segregate portfolio strategies by geographical zones and or categories.

The fund universe can be divided into 16 categories: nine for equities, five for bonds, and two for diversified funds. To measure performance and returns consistencies among all fund portfolios, this methodology monitors the returns' frequency. The Hurst exponent uses funds' excess returns at time t and compares them with returns at time $t + 1$ to demonstrate correlation. In some instances, returns at time t show strong a directional relationship with returns at time $t + 1$; then it is assumed and suggested that there is persistence and consistency in the process. If no relationship exists in the assumptions, then we can assume that a high return at time t is followed by a low return at $t + 1$ with a probability of occurrence of one-half.

According to the Hurst model, the H exponent is a measure of deviation corresponding to the basic case of an exponent equal to one-half. If H is greater than one-half, then the model proves positive consistency or persistence in performance statistical series. Or else, if the model produces an H exponent lower than one-half, then the series of returns is said to have nonlinear, noncorrelated, inconsistent persistent series of returns. To calculate the Hurst exponent, the model takes a normalized series of returns and subtracts performance averages to each component:

$$E_{rt} = R_t - \beta_t$$

where R_t = fund's returns
       β_t = benchmark's returns

$$Z(t) = E_{rt} - m$$

$$m = 1/T \Sigma_{t=1 \to T}$$

R_t represents the average of the returns in a sample.

$$Y(t) = 1/T\Sigma_{t=1\to t}$$

R_t is the average of returns in the sample.

We define $Y(t) = \Sigma_{s=0\to t} Z(s)$

$Y_1 = Z_1$

$Y_2 = Z_1 + Z_2$

$Y_3 = Z_2 + Z_3$

$Y_4 = Z_3 + Z_4$

$Y_T = Z_1 + Z_2 + Z_T$

$Y_1 = \max Y(t)$ such that $0 < t < T$

$Y_2 = \min Y(t)$ such that $0 < r < T$

The Hurst component is equal to $H = 1/\ln(T) \times \ln[(Y_1 - Y_2)/\sigma]$ such that:

$$\sigma = \sqrt{\{[1/(T-1)] \times \Sigma_{t=1\to T}(R_t - m)^2\}}$$

is the correlation factor of the returns' patterns and trends, consistencies, persistency, and so on.

If $\sigma > \frac{1}{2} \Rightarrow H > 0$ positive consistencies.

If $\sigma = \frac{1}{2}$ then funds have a random process.

If $\sigma < \frac{1}{2} \Rightarrow H < 0$ negative correlation.

The gain frequency and Hurst exponent are calculated for the previous 156 weeks. There are two types of gain frequency such that:

Gain frequency $> \frac{1}{2}$ implies alpha's consistencies or correlation.

Gain frequency $< \frac{1}{2}$ implies that alpha shows noncorrelation.

In order to capture appropriate rating methodology completion, measurement of extreme value at risk (VaR) as a function of volatility is necessary. Value at risk uses three methods to calculate a portfolio's value at risk: for example, the parametric method uses normal return assumptions. The following describes different types of value at risk methodologies.

The Cornish-Fisher type value at risk is based on an intermediary approach that provides a balance between the advantages of the historical value at risk approach (no model) and the parametric approach (sampled limitation). This is a semiparametric value at risk in an extreme value environment. This method to obtain a maximum possible loss calculates value at risk using a normal distribution formula and adjusting with Cornish-Fisher factors to include skewness and kurtosis (third and fourth moments of the equation). Using the Gaussian method, value at risk is such that:

$$P(dW =< -\text{VaR}) = 1 - \alpha$$

$$\text{VaR} = n\sigma W dt^{1/2} \text{ or } \text{VaR} = \frac{n\sigma W}{d_t}$$

where n = the number of standard deviation at $1 - \alpha$
 σ = the annual standard deviation
 W = portfolio's net asset values
 d_t = the yearly fraction or as time element of equation

Cornish-Fisher (1937) indexes the following mathematical development such that:

$$z = Z_c + \tfrac{1}{6}(Z_c^2 - 1)S + \tfrac{1}{24}(Z_c^3 - 3Z_c)K - \tfrac{1}{36}(2Z_c^3 - 5Z_c)S^2$$

where Z_c = the critical value of the probability $(1 - \alpha)$
 S = the skewness
 K = the excess kurtosis

Thus value at risk = VaR = $W(\mu - z\sigma)$.

In the rating's methodology, Cornish-Fisher's VaR is used with the following assumptions:

Alpha's average is about 28 days.

Gain's frequency lasts 156 weeks.

Hurst exponent is over 156 weekly returns.

The resulting table parameters to attribute ratings and stars are given in Table 14.1.

No stars are attributed for R^2 too low (R) as it implies that alpha must be greater than 70 percent for domestic or nondiversified categories and 60 percent for the international or diversified categories. Funds with too high value at risk are not given any stars, either.

TABLE 14.1 Parameters to Attribute Ratings and Stars

Rating	Population	Diminishing Alpha	Gain Frequency	Hurst Exponent	VaR Class	Regression Coefficient (R^2)
5 H (6)		>= 0	>= $\frac{1}{2}$	>= $\frac{1}{2}$	>= $-2\ \sigma$	>= 0.7
5 H (5)		>= 0	>= $\frac{1}{2}$		>= $-2\ \sigma$	>= 0.7
4 H (4)		>= 0	>= $\frac{1}{2}$		>= $-2\ \sigma$	>= 0.7
3 H (3)		>= −averg(mgt fee)			>= $-2\ \sigma$	>= 0.7
2 H (2)	50% +	>= −averg(mgt fee)			>= $-2\ \sigma$	>= 0.7
1 H (1)	50% −	>= −averg(mgt fee)			>= $-2\ \sigma$	>= 0.7

Source: Data from EDHEC Business School (www.edhec-risk.com) and Social Science Research Network (www.ssrn.com).

No rating is given if VaR $> -2\sigma$ and if $R^2 < 70\%$.

- *Rating of 1 or 1 star; 2 or 2 stars:* Population of funds with alpha < 0. The stronger 50 percent have a rating of 2 and the others have a rating of 1.
- *Rating of 3 or 3 stars:* Funds close to management objectives include leverage management fees.
- *Rating of 4 or 4 stars:* Exclusively positive alpha but not passing the gain frequency and Hurst coefficient tests so not consistent or persistent.
- *Rating of 5 or 5 stars:* Funds with strictly positive alpha and a gain frequency greater than or equal to 50%.
- *Rating of 5 or 6 stars:* Fund of the rating of 5 with Hurst exponent coefficient greater than $\frac{1}{2}$.

This rating methodology has been created and initiated by rating agencies EuroPerformance and EDHEC. It is recalculated every fourth Friday of each month. This rating methodology is incomplete as it does not include Treasury funds, guaranteed funds, gold and raw material funds, real estate funds, emerging markets funds such as emerging markets equities, emerging European equities, Latin American equities, and Asian equities.

It is important to acknowledge that there does not exist any rating methodology that measures the hedge fund manager's integrity and that also integrates in the rating methodology a grade derived from due diligence or operational risk management audit. However, in any rating methodology of publicly traded companies, there exists such an ideal variable. Let us now evaluate the impact of due diligence or operational risk management audits on hedge funds.

CHAPTER 15

Operational Risk, Audits, Compliance, and Due Diligence

This chapter summarizes broad ways hedge funds have used sophisticated instruments and financial engineering to generate lucrative profits and get around the principal regulatory laws. The old regulations have become inadequate in the current market conditions as they limit hedge funds with regard to size, number of investors, and types of institutions funds can deal with. The principal weakness is loopholes companies and hedge funds have found to avoid having to deal with regulations simply by applying rules that are outside the legislation and by using instruments that are not restricted such as financial engineering tools or so-called derivatives.

The second component of the problem is based on human psychology and people's tendencies to gravitate to greed and vices over time rather than to restrictive laws based on needs rather than wants. There is now evidence regarding investor behavior being directly linked to the likelihood of hedge fund managers manipulating reported returns, according to Bollen and Krepely (2005). They mention that investors in newly created funds with limited historical returns and little information on past performances are more sensitive to data accuracy than other investors who have knowledge of historical data with regard to a fund.

Shleifer and Vishny (1997) and Liu and Longstaff (2004) showed that investors with short, unpredictable investment horizons are not as misled as they do not have credibility and track records on abilities to exploit arbitrage opportunities and trading successes.

Getmansky (2004) demonstrated that funds that are open to new investors feature on average more smoothing than funds that are closed. Aragon (2004) showed that restrictions on investors' activity are more apt to occur in newly created hedge funds and are positively related to the level of smoothing. These funds have been found to be more deficient in transparency and shareholding protection activities and more aggressive in the smoothing of capital performances. There also is a strong correlation between the degree of happiness of investors getting higher returns in return for a no-questions-asked kind of risk management. Yet, according to Berk and Green (2004), there is a rationality factor involved in investors who have more experience with risk management and financial markets risks responding more quickly to hedge fund performance.

Only in recent years has the research linked to operational risk management and compliance grown enough to make future cases stronger. There are a number of legal cases with regard to hedge funds' liquidations: Long-Term Capital Management (LTCM) has been the subject of a great deal of literature, including Greenspan (1998), McDonough (1998), Pérold (1999), the President's Working Group on Financial Markets (1999–2003), and MacKenzie (2003). Furthermore, Ineichen (2001) developed a database of hedge funds and provided detailed reasons for their liquidations. Kramer (2001) focused on fraud and reviewed six of the worse cases involving the hedge fund community.

Feffer and Kundro (2003) concluded that half of the hedge funds' failures were due to operational risk management exclusively. Fraud is an element of operational risk management. They added that the most recurrent issues included misrepresentation of fund investments, misappropriation of investor funds, unauthorized trading, and inadequate resources. They reported that 6 percent of the hedge funds' operational risk failures were due to inadequate resources either in qualifications or in quantifications, 41 percent of the failures came from the misappropriation of investments, 30 percent were due to misappropriation of funds, and 14 percent were from unauthorized trading schemes.

Some new types of operational risks that have remained unquantified and unable to be accounted for involve hedge funds and large financial buyout operations. When hedge funds are bought out by a larger financial institution there are two other areas of opacity: The first area, when there is potential lack of controls, is the remuneration of the hedge fund officers and managers who are getting compensated for selling their hedge fund to a larger bank. The second area of potential abuses or lack of controls comes from operational risk consequences when integrating a hedge fund's business into a bank or a large financial structure. In this area, one controversial issue emerges from the lack of regulatory mandates to protect large business operations from being contaminated by the mingling of unaudited operations such as those of the hedge funds. Hedge fund individuals have had great amounts of influence in megamergers and acquisitions due to their large financial stakes in strategies such as event driven. And thus, they have gained more control over the actual large transactions than the laws and regulations have evolved to prevent such transactions.

The first area involves compensation packages of hedge fund managers who are lucratively paid to get involved in mergers, acquisitions, and buyouts of hedge funds in order for the buyer to benefit from new types of financial instruments. There are no industry guidelines to such salary incentives and remuneration packages to make such deals as objective and transparent as possible. In effect, due to the losses incurred in more traditional financial indexes and instruments, many larger banks and financial institutions have bought hedge fund businesses in order to benefit more quickly from hedge funds' more attractive returns to compensate from the losses in the traditional markets and instruments.

For example, the *Financial Times* reported on December 21, 2005, that the Bank of Ireland (BOI) purchased 71 percent of Guggenheim Alternative Asset Management with a stake of USD 183 million. The two hedge fund managers of Guggenheim Alternative Asset Management, Loren Katzovitz and Patrick Hughes, are expected to receive more than $1 million each as compensation for selling their hedge funds' stake to Bank of Ireland. BOI expects to make higher returns and to serve sophisticated high-net-worth types of clientele. Guggenheim Alternative Asset Management executives retain 11 percent and Guggenheim Partners 17.5 percent of the total $2.8 billion of assets under management.

The second area of compliance risk is the lack of audit prior to involving hedge funds in large sales, mergers and acquisitions, or takeovers. This is called operational due diligence risk management. There are very few consulting firms specializing in this area. Rare are the elite universities offering degrees in corporate governance. They offer corporate law degrees but very few specialize in the lawful risk management of corporations. For example, Harvard University has an embryonic corporate governance program but it does not offer degrees for specialization in corporate governance, and it does not give a certificate or a degree in corporate governance. This educational branch is part of the law school at elite institutions providing such programs, and very few or none offer any degrees specializing in corporate governance, due diligence, or operational risk management. The lack of operational risk due diligence in hedge funds is due to the lack of general education in the core business and law schools.

Operational risk due diligence and compliance risk management consist of performing an audit of internal operations to acknowledge of their status vis-à-vis the investors and shareholders or to ensure proper sale of a business to a larger bank or financial institution in order to accurately price the sale and to limit losses or strategic mistakes in the buyout.

According to Xagua Consulting, there are several levels of due diligence investors and outsiders should perform prior to joining a hedge fund. The first level is done by a "follow the herd" type of hedge fund investor.

This level is superficial and does not involve any kind of internal analysis or review of the hedge fund. Level two is the "send a questionnaire" type of investor. This level of due diligence requires the outside party to meet a number of managers and perform an analytical review of the managers' strategy and returns. In this level of audit, data such as historical returns is collected, a 30-page questionnaire is filled out, and interviews with the managers are conducted. At this level, although there is more information than at level one, the major concern is the lack of validation of the information being collected. There is no verification of the data, which is taken at face value. Most investors fall into this category.

Level three consists of reviewing the funds but not questioning too much some of the infrastructures. These types of investors attempt to deepen their knowledge of the internal operational risks of the fund such as pricing, responsibilities, management integrity, corporate culture, cash control, reconciliation of onshore and offshore account transactions, equity valuation changes from day-to-day operations, reporting details, and breakdown of commissions, fees, and expenses. These investors or third parties will try to understand funds' custodian reports and valuation of assets. Several custodians have sophisticated reporting systems allowing managers to open prime brokerage reporting systems to investors and validate information.

The next level, level four, enables the manager or the adviser to conduct a thorough review of the asset management firm. The review of the funds is very detailed, and very few funds actually go into this level of information. One of the most common inaccuracies found at this level is the actual amount of assets being managed. Many hedge fund managers inflate the capacity of the funds and with time the total net asset values or actual capacity of the fund. Many frauds have involved such discrepancies. In order to verify accurate levels of assets under management, a complete reconciliation of accounts with the custodian, the administrator, and the brokerage firm is required. In very rare cases does one person have access to all accounts, and very rarely do hedge fund risk managers perform three-way reconciliation. On December 23, 2005, the *Wall Street Journal* reported that the HMC International LLC fund had misappropriated more than $5.2 million from about 80 investors. The SEC alleged that the Montvale, New Jersey, hedge fund manager was looting the fund's trading account and that the manager used money from new investors to pay investors who were leaving the fund and sent out false monthly statements to report bright and positive performances and false asset values.

Another operational due diligence problem involving hedge funds is the lack of transparency for fees, commissions, and expenses. A thorough operational review should highlight a clear and consistent method of payments of fees versus commission rates versus expenses. The majority of hedge funds do not have an objective formula to give to auditors to explain revenue sources. Audits rarely test commission rates and the flow of individuals involved into the collection of commissions: the marketing contractor, the broker-dealer, and the new investors coming into the funds. It is unclear how investors get into the fund and who gets compensated for the seeding assets.

Qualitative operational due diligence auditing includes tests for soft dollar usage differentiation in commissions versus expenses. The review should break down fees, commissions, and expenses as part of the net asset valuations on the financial statements. Lack of audits or inaccurate unrevised audits has been convenient to hide many gains, profits, and other useful variables. How are hedge funds audited? Are they subject to new audit laws such as Sarbanes-Oxley or are they limited to internal and external audits? What is the impact of audits in hedge funds and how seriously are they taken? Despite the new regulation requiring hedge funds to register with the SEC, hedge funds remain immune to mandatory auditing requirements. Still considered very much like private structures, they do not have to submit any kind of audit but they do have to inform investors of high-level risks and to have basic compliance and risk management. More often, they choose to be audited for professionalism or responsibility to investors.

Liang (2000) compares two major hedge fund databases and finds some inconsistencies between them. Fung and Hsieh (2000); Ackermann, McEnally, and Ravenscraft (1999); and Brown, Goetzmann, and Ibbotson (1999) all document inconsistencies and different survivorship biases for hedge funds. This is primarily due to the fact that there are no standardized official rules on the definition of a surviving fund and there are different criteria of inclusion or introduction to databases depending on what database is used.

Bollen and Krepely (2005) demonstrated that knowing or not knowing the fund's returns are being audited is a major variable in the way the hedge fund manager performs smoothing of returns. They also showed that smoothing is highly correlated to assets' cash flows or capacity levels. There is also a strong correlation in the quality of risk management and its overall ratings if the fund is being audited internally only or internally and externally.

Liang (2000) demonstrated that audited funds tend to have better data quality and show more accurate and reliable returns than those that are not audited. The researcher had done extensive research on the impact of auditing on the quality of hedge funds and also showed that despite having audits, the quality of the audits remained highly inaccurate and unreliable due to either lack of data, errors in dates, or other operational audit mistakes. Audits' purposes in the hedge fund industry remain highly misleading and quietly illusionary.

The following part of this chapter presents Liang's research and deals with findings on hedge funds' auditing inaccuracies. Despite finding that most hedge funds had internal auditors, audit dates were missing. According to the TASS Management database as of December 2000, at least 37 percent of the audited hedge funds were missing audit dates.

As of December 31, 2000, TASS Management Limited had 2,562 funds (1,668 live funds and 894 dead funds) in the database. We report live funds only since dead funds may disappear at different times, which can cause difficulty when trying to compare fund assets. (See Table 15.1.)

The lack of audits and qualitative oversight review has a significant impact on the hedge funds' returns and ratings. The integration of audits into the agencies' rating systems would force competition to be more transparent and to promote an ethical corporate culture.

Liang (2002) observed two sets of data in order to lead to conclusions on the impact of auditing on hedge fund returns: one from TASS Management Limited (hereafter TASS) and another from U.S. Offshore Fund Directory (hereafter Offshore). Liang noted that both databases are major sources of hedge fund databases and that many other researchers have used them to perform their academic work. Academicians such as Fung and Hsieh (1997a, 1997c, 2000), Liang (2000), and Brown, Goetzmann, and Park (2001a, b) use TASS data, and Brown, Goetzmann, and Ibbotson (1999) use the Offshore data.

Offshore publishes data on an annual basis. From the 1990 version to the 2000 version, Offshore data contains 1,358 offshore funds. There are three versions of TASS data available for our study: July 31, 1999 (2,016

TABLE 15.1 Auditing Standards in Hedge Funds

Variable	Number of Funds	Mean	Standard Deviation	Median
Missing Auditor	67	$ 68,078,598	$ 162,637,426	$21,658,187
Non–Big Five	346	$ 82,243,912	$ 180,155,948	$18,910,000
Big Five	929	$182,855,697	$1,340,087,155	$35,500,000
Missing Date	502	$ 64,710,656	$ 228,439,363	$17,000,000
Nonmissing	840	$202,864,110	$1,402,523,705	$41,489,000

a326 funds have missing asset information.
Source: Bing Liang, "Hedge Fund Returns: Auditing and Accuracy," *Journal of Portfolio Management*, Weatherhead School, Case Western Reserve University, 2002, 1–30.

funds in total: 1,407 live funds and 609 dead funds), December 31, 2000 (2,562 funds in total: 1,668 live funds and 894 dead funds), and March 31, 2001 (2,545 funds in total: 1,543 live funds and 1,002 dead funds). We use these different versions for purposes of comparison. Liang (2000) measures the quality of hedge fund returns in three different ways.

Liang compares two major databases for consistency: TASS and Off-shore data. The same funds ought to provide identical returns regardless of which database they are in; a data problem exists if a return discrepancy between the two databases is found. The next step consists in comparing two versions of the TASS data from two different snapshots. Historical returns ought to be the same for the same funds across two different versions. Onshore funds are then compared with their offshore twins. In conclusion, funds with the same manager and identical fund characteristics ought to give similar returns. Inaccuracy is defined when return discrepancies are detected.

To measure inaccuracy of auditing, variables such as auditor name and auditing date are chosen. As of December 31, 2000, there are 1,668 live funds in the TASS data, out of which 1,552 have nonmissing auditors while 116 (6.95 percent) have auditors missing. For the 1,552 funds with nonmissing auditors, 998 have nonmissing audit dates and 554 (35.7 percent) have missing auditing dates. Of the 116 funds with missing auditors, 95 miss auditing dates and only 21 do not miss auditing dates. Consequently, Liang deduces that a nonmissing auditor is not sufficient for measuring auditing effectiveness since the audit date can still be missing. A missing auditing date is consequently used as a mark of ineffective audit quality.

Next, Liang evaluates the actual name of the auditor performing the audit by testing the consistency of auditor's names and reputations. Liang found that for the 894 dead funds, 806 have nonmissing auditors while 89 (9.94 percent) have missing auditors. For the 806 funds with nonmissing auditors, 464 have nonmissing dates and 342 (42.4 percent) have missing audit dates. In line with intuition, Liang concludes that dead funds are less effectively audited than live funds. Hedge funds with missing auditing dates are smaller than those without missing auditing dates. Moreover, funds with the Big Five auditing firms as their auditors have larger fund assets than those with non–Big Five firms: There is a correlation between the size of the audited hedge fund assets and the size of the auditing firm. The larger the hedge funds, the bigger the auditing firms.

Liang (2002) compares the same funds that exist in two different databases: TASS and the Offshore data. Since we have combined Offshore data from the 1990 version through the 2000 version, we match it with the December 31, 2000, version of TASS data. There are 1,358 funds in the

Offshore data and 2,562 funds (including 1,668 live funds and 894 dead funds) in TASS. However, there are only 251 common funds (with exactly the same names) across both databases. It turns out that all of these 251 funds are live funds. They represent 891 annual fund return observations. Annual return numbers are calculated from compounding monthly returns in TASS, whereas annual returns are directly provided by the Offshore data.

In the Table 15.2 Liang (2002) demonstrated that the average return difference between the TASS data and the Offshore data is −0.71 percent per year for these 251 common funds. The difference is significant at the 5 percent level. The absolute return difference is as high as 5.49 percent per year and significant at the 1 percent level. Therefore, the two data vendors provide different average return information for the same 251 funds. This implies that returns for a particular fund on a particular date could be different based on different data sources. To further examine which data is more accurate, we cross-check whether the reported returns in each database match the corresponding percentage change in net asset values (NAVs). In the Offshore fund data, the average discrepancy between the reported return and the percentage change of NAV is 0.29 percent per year (based on 631 observations) whereas the average discrepancy from TASS is zero. The accuracy of the TASS data is consistent with the findings in Liang (2000) that TASS provides better data quality than Hedge Fund Research, Inc. (HFR). The 0.29 percent discrepancy can explain 41 percent of the 0.71 percent return difference between TASS and the Offshore data.

As of December 31, 2000, TASS Management Limited has 2,562 funds, including 1,668 live funds and 894 dead funds in the database. The U.S. Offshore Fund Directory (Offshore) has 1,358 funds. There are only 251 funds common to both databases; these 251 funds result in 891 annual observations. The return difference is calculated as the annual return difference between TASS and Offshore. Annual returns are calculated from compounding monthly returns in TASS while annual returns are directly provided by the U.S. Offshore Fund Directory. The 251 funds are all live funds.

From this analysis, Liang (2002) also shows that funds that are effectively audited have lower return discrepancy than those that are not. The absolute return difference between the audited and nonaudited funds is 3.91 percent (8.82% − 4.91%) on an annual basis, which is significant at the 1 percent level although the raw return difference is not significant.

With the next table (Table 15.3), Liang (2002) demonstrates the raw return discrepancy and the absolute return discrepancy between the two databases, together with fund characteristics as classifying categories. In terms of raw return discrepancy, the only significant fund category (at 10 percent level) is funds of funds/hedge funds, where funds of funds have an average zero return discrepancy while hedge funds have a return discrepancy of

TABLE 15.2 Annual Return Difference between TASS and U.S. Offshore Fund Directory in Auditing Differences

All 251 Funds Variable	N	Mean	Std Dev	t-value	Assumption	Median	Min	Max
Difference	891	-0.71%	9.69%	-2.19	a	-0.11%	-75.89%	64.45%
Abs (Diff)	891	5.49%	8.01%	20.46	b	2.94%	0.01%	75.89%
Audit Date Not Missing								
Difference	760	-0.45%	7.87%	-1.58		-0.09%	-55.30%	44.75%
Abs (Diff)	760	4.91%	6.16%	21.97	b	2.92%	0.01%	55.30%
Audit Date Missing								
Difference	131	-2.24%	16.68%	-1.54		-0.30%	-75.89%	64.45%
Abs (Diff)	131	8.82%	14.31%	7.05	b	3.50%	0.02%	75.89%
Big Five								
Difference	809	-0.64%	9.33%	-1.95	c	-0.10%	-75.89%	64.45%
Abs (Diff)	809	5.32%	7.69%	19.68	b	2.96%	0.01%	75.89%
Non–Big Five								
Difference	72[d]	-2.26%	12.01%	-1.60		-0.42%	-48.68%	36.30%
Abs (Diff)	72	6.84%	10.10%	5.75	b	2.73%	0.03%	48.68%
Andersen								
Difference	48	-0.63%	7.57%	-0.58		-0.38%	-35.81%	16.12%
Abs (Diff)	48	4.61%	6.00%	5.32	b	2.49%	0.14%	35.81%
Big Four								
Difference	761	-0.64%	9.63%	-1.83	c	-0.10%	-75.89%	64.45%
Abs (Diff)	761	5.37%	8.02%	18.47	b	3.01%	0.01%	75.89%

[a]Significant at the 5% level.
[b]Significant at the 1% level.
[c]Significant at the 10% level.
[d]There are 10 observations with missing auditors.

t (Raw diff: audit date missing – nonmissing) = –1.21. t (Abs diff: audit date missing – nonmissing) = 3.08.
t (Raw diff: Big Five – non–Big Five) = –1.12. t (Abs diff: Big Five – non–Big Five) = –1.25.
t (Raw diff: Andersen – Big Four) = –0.01. t (Abs diff: Andersen – Big Four) = –0.83.

Source: Bing Liang, "Hedge Fund Returns: Auditing and Accuracy," *Journal of Portfolio Management*, Weatherhead School, Case Western Reserve University, 2002, 1–30.

TABLE 15.3 Annual Return Difference (between TASS and Offshore) and Fund Characteristics

Variable	Raw Return Difference			Absolute Return Difference		
Ifee Interval[a]	Missing	Annual	Nonannual	Missing	Annual	Nonannual
N	219	478	194	219	478	194
Mean	0.34	−0.98	−1.25	4.46	6.19	4.92
Std Dev	6.33	11.12	8.94	4.49	9.29	7.55
t-value[b]			0.33			1.84[c]
Audit Date	Yes	No		Yes	No	
N	760	131		760	131	
Mean	−0.45	−2.24		4.91	8.82	
Std Dev	7.87	16.68		6.16	14.31	
t-value		1.21			−3.08[e]	
Listed on Exchange	Missing	Yes	No	Missing	Yes	No
N	37	237	617	37	237	617
Mean	0.81	−0.38	−0.93	6.36	3.91	6.04
Std Dev	10.70	6.33	10.64	8.58	4.98	8.81
t-value			0.93			−4.44[e]

Fund Adviser

	Single	Multi	t-value		Single	Multi	t-value
N	647	244			647	244	
Mean	-0.96	-0.06			5.89	4.42	
Std Dev	10.68	6.29			8.96	4.47	
t-value			-1.55				3.24[e]

FOF/HF[a]

	FOF	HF	t-value		FOF	HF	t-value
N	239	652			239	652	
Mean	0.00	-0.97			4.45	5.87	
Std Dev	6.34	10.64			4.51	8.93	
t-value			1.66[c]				3.12[e]

Open to Public

	Missing	Yes	No	t-value		Missing	Yes	No	t-value
N	12	174	705			12	174	705	
Mean	2.92	-0.38	-0.86			8.73	3.81	5.84	
Std Dev	15.27	6.13	10.27			12.62	4.80	8.49	
t-value				0.79					-4.19[e]

Personal Investment

	Missing	Yes	No	t-value		Missing	Yes	No	t-value
N	34	555	302			34	555	302	
Mean	0.71	-0.71	-0.88			6.68	5.40	5.51	
Std Dev	11.14	8.86	10.90			8.87	7.06	9.45	
t-value				0.23					-0.18

(Continued)

TABLE 15.3 (Continued)

Variable	Raw Return Difference			Absolute Return Difference		
Industry Sector	Missing	Multi	Single	Missing	Multi	Single
N	37	492	362	37	492	362
Mean	0.81	−0.79	−0.76	6.36	5.90	4.84
Std Dev	10.71	10.42	8.48	8.58	8.62	7.01
t-value			−0.05			1.98[f]
Leverage		Yes	No		Yes	No
N		631	260		631	260
Mean		−0.83	−0.43		5.89	4.50
Std Dev		10.59	7.03		8.84	5.41
t-value			−0.66			2.86[e]

[a]FOF is classified using the Offshore fund data. So are the other two variables.
[b]t-value for the difference between annual and nonannual fee intervals.
[c]Significant at the 10% level.
[d]Audit = "No" if audit date = missing.
[e]Significant at the 1% level.
[f]Significant at the 5% level.

Source: Bing Liang, "Hedge Fund Returns: Auditing and Accuracy," Journal of Portfolio Management, Weatherhead School, Case Western Reserve University, 2002, 1–30.

–0.97 percent per year. Funds of funds report returns more accurately than hedge funds because managers of funds of funds do not have to engage in daily trading activities and therefore can spend more time concentrating on bookkeeping, verifying return accuracy, and providing investors with accurate performance information on a timely basis.

As of December 31, 2000, TASS Management Limited (TASS) has 1,668 funds in the database while the U.S. Offshore Fund Directory (Offshore) has 1,358 funds. There are only 251 funds common to both databases; these 251 funds result in 891 annual observations. The return difference is calculated as the annual return difference between TASS and Offshore. Annual returns are calculated from compounding monthly returns in TASS while annual returns are directly provided by the U.S. Offshore Fund Directory. The 251 funds are all live funds.

Regarding the absolute return discrepancy between the two databases, significant fund categories are frequency of paying incentive fees, audit date, funds listed on exchanges, funds of funds/hedge funds, funds open to the public, single/multi-industrial sectors, and fund leverage. Generally, audited funds, funds listed on exchanges, funds of funds, funds open to both U.S. and non-U.S. investors, funds open to the public, funds invested in a single sector, and unlevered funds have lower return discrepancy than the other funds. In the fund categories, return differences are significant at either a 99 percent or a 95 percent confidence level. In addition, for the frequency of paying incentive fees category, the return difference is significant at the 10 percent level between different fee payment intervals. This means that funds paying incentive fees on an annual basis have a larger return discrepancy than those paying more frequently than on an annual basis. When funds pay incentive fees more frequently than annually, they have a better opportunity to verify return accuracy.

In Table 15.4 Liang (2002) reports the regression results of the absolute return difference on fund assets and other fund characteristics. Consistent with the univariate test in Table 15.3, significant variables are fund assets, audit date, personal investment, single/multi-industrial sectors, and leverage. In general, large funds, funds with nonmissing audit dates, funds of funds, funds with managers' personal investments, funds open to the public, funds investing in a single industrial sector, unlevered funds, and funds paying incentive fees not on an annual basis have low return discrepancies. Note that the variable audit date has the highest *t*-statistic among all explanatory variables.

After Liang (2002) compares two different databases, we turn to the same data set from a single data vendor. TASS updates its data on a monthly basis, with recent information overwriting the previous data. In this section, we use two different versions of TASS data: one from July 31, 1999, and the other from March 31, 2001. The purpose of using two different versions is

TABLE 15.4   Regression Results of Absolute Difference on Fund Variables

Variable	Estimate	Standard	t-value
Intercept	0.1611	0.0359	4.48[a]
Log (asset)	−0.0052	0.0020	−2.63[a]
Audit date	−0.0324	0.0096	−3.37[a]
Single/multimanager	0.0222	0.0100	2.23[b]
Personal investment	−0.0147	0.0072	−2.03[b]
Listed on exchange	−0.0041	0.0101	−0.41
Open to public	−0.0221	0.0113	−1.96[b]
Single/multisector	−0.0173	0.0068	−2.53[a]
Leverage	0.0131	0.0077	1.71[c]
Fee interval	0.0153	0.0073	2.09[a]
Observation	661		
R^2	8.30		
Adj. R^2	7.04		

[a]1% level.
[b]5% level.
[c]10% level.
Note: The dependent variable is the absolute annual return difference between TASS and the U.S. Offshore fund directory. All independent variables are dummy variables except for Log (asset). Audit date = 1 if date is not missing and 0 if missing. Single/multimanager = 1 if single manager and 0 if multiple managers. Personal invest = 1 if yes and 0 if no. List on exchange = 1 if yes and 0 if no. Open to public = 1 if yes and 0 if no. Single/multi sector = 1 if single and 0 if multiple. Leverage = 1 if yes and 0 if no. Fee intervals = 1 if annual interval and 0 otherwise. Investor = 1 if funds are open to U.S. investors and 0 otherwise.

to examine whether there are any inconsistencies for the same fund returns over the same time horizons across two versions. Fund managers may change fund returns later to correct errors, for inflating performance, or for some other unknown reasons. Our hypothesis is that data inconsistencies may occur especially when funds are not audited.

As a matter of fact, across the two databases, there are 3,638 monthly return observations that are different for the same funds over the same time horizons. These 3,638 observations are from 461 hedge funds. If data were perfectly accurate, there would be no inconsistencies at all.

In the next table on monthly return discrepancies (Table 15.5), Liang (2002) reports the distribution for return discrepancies between the two data versions. Although the majority (98 percent) have a return discrepancy between −1.0 percent and 1.0 percent, these differences can be as high

TABLE 15.5 Monthly Return Discrepancies between 1999 and 2001 TASS Databases

Difference (%)	Frequency	Percentage (%)	Cumulative Frequency	Cumulative %
−22.85	2	0.05	2	0.05
−17.75	1	0.03	3	0.08
−5.00	1	0.03	39	1.07
−1.00	1	0.03	234	6.43
−0.50	3	0.08	390	10.72
0.00	3	0.08	1,928	53.00
0.50	5	0.14	3,294	90.54
1.00	3	0.08	3,437	94.47
5.00	1	0.03	3,605	99.09
23.10	2	0.05	3,637	99.97
26.90	1	0.03	3,638	100.00

Note: There are 16,699 monthly return observations (563 funds) that are missing in 1999 data but exist in 2001 data (up to 1999.07). Out of these 563 funds, only 80 (14.2%) have nonmissing audit dates. There are 15,700 monthly return observations (429 funds) that are missing in 1999 data but exist in 2001 data (up to 1999.05), allowing a two-month window. Out of these 429 funds, only 40 (9.32%) have nonmissing audit dates. There are 92,374 return observations (from 1,830 funds) that are identical on the same date for the same funds. Out of these 1,830 funds, there are 639 (34.9%) audited funds and 1,191 (65.1%) nonaudited funds.
Source: eLibrary or Social Science Research Network (ssrn.com).

as −23 percent and 27 percent per month for the exact same funds appearing in two different data versions. The return difference is defined as 2001 minus 1999. To save space, the table does not report all differences.

In Table 15.6, showing monthly return differences with funds' characteristics, Liang (2002) showed that raw (absolute) return difference between 2001 and 1999 is 37 percent (0.53 percent) per month. We can also see that the raw return (absolute) difference between the 2001 and 1999 data is only 0.01 percent (0.46 percent) per month if funds are audited compared to −0.15 percent (0.69 percent) per month if funds are not audited. The 0.15 percent monthly difference is equivalent to an annual return difference of 1.81 percent. The difference is significant at the 5 percent level; the absolute return difference between the audited and nonaudited funds is 0.22 percent (0.6866% − 0.4623%) a year, which is significant at the 1 percent level. These all indicate that nonaudited funds indeed have large errors and low data quality. In addition, the absolute return difference is 0.36% (0.7574% − 0.4006%) between Big Five auditors and non–Big Five auditors. The

TABLE 15.6 Monthly Return Difference (between 2001 and 1999) and Fund Characteristics

Variable	Raw Return Difference		Absolute Return Difference	
461 Funds				
N	3,638		3,638	
Mean	−0.0370		0.5289	
Std Dev	1.6557		1.5694	
t-value		−1.35		20.33[a]
Nonmissing Date				
N	2,558		2,558	
Mean	0.0120		0.4623	
Std Dev	1.4533		1.3779	
t-value		0.42		16.97[a]
Missing Date				
N	1,080		1,080	
Mean	−0.1532		0.6866	
Std Dev	2.0533		1.9410	
t-value		−2.45[b]		11.62a
Big Five				
N	2,611		2,611	
Mean	−0.0206		0.4006	
Std Dev	1.0899		1.0138	
t-value		−0.97		20.19[a]
Non–Big Five				
N	612[c]		612	
Mean	−0.0169		0.7574	
Std Dev	2.4231		2.3016	
t-value		−0.17		8.14[a]
Andersen				
N	174		174	
Mean	0.0971		0.2587	
Std Dev	0.7276		0.6867	
t-value		1.76[d]		4.97[a]

TABLE 15.6 *(Continued)*

Variable	Raw Return Difference	Absolute Return Difference
Big Four		
N	3049	3049
Mean	–0.0265	0.4803
Std Dev	1.4708	1.3904
t-value	–0.99	19.07[a]

t-(Raw diff: audited – nonaudited) = 2.41. *t* – (Abs diff: audited – nonaudited) = –3.45.

t-(Raw diff: Big Five – non–Big Five) = –0.04. *t* – (Abs diff: Big Five – non–Big Five) = –3.75.

t-(Raw diff: Andersen – Big Four) = 2.02. *t* – (Abs diff: Andersen – Big Four) = –3.84.

[a]1% level.
[b]5% level.
[c]There are 415 cases where auditors are missing.
[d]10% level.

Data is from TASS Management Limited. There are two versions: July 31, 1999, and March 31, 2001. In the 2001 data, there are 2,545 funds (1,543 live funds and 1,002 dead funds). In the 1999 data, there are 2,016 funds (1,407 live funds and 609 dead funds). There are 3,638 monthly return observations that are different for the same 461 funds across the two versions. The return difference is defined as 2001 – 1999. Audit = "No" if audit date = missing.

Source: Bing Liang, "Hedge Fund Returns: Auditing and Accuracy," *Journal of Portfolio Management*, Weatherhead School Case Western Reserve University, 2002, 1–30.

difference is significant at the 5 percent level. This may suggest that Big Five firms provide better auditing service than the non–Big Five firms. Although Arthur Andersen funds had larger errors than the other Big Five funds when raw return difference was used, the absolute return differences for the other funds are higher than that for Arthur Andersen funds.

In the next data display (Table 15.7), Liang (2002) shows the average return differences across the two versions and fund characteristics as classifying categories. The researcher reports not only raw return differences but also absolute return differences. In this table, audit date is the only significant variable in determining the raw return difference; other variables are not significant in explaining the return difference across the two data versions. Absolute return differences are significantly related to variables such

TABLE 15.7 Monthly Return Difference (between 2001 and 1999) and Fund Characteristics

Variable	Raw Return Difference			Absolute Return Difference		
Audit Date	Yes	No	t-value	Yes	No	t-value
N	2,558	1,080		2,558	1,080	
Mean	0.012	−0.1532	2.40[a]	0.4623	0.6866	−3.45[b]
Std Dev	1.4533	2.0533		1.3779	1.941	
Fund Adviser	Missing	Single	Multi	t-value	Missing	Single	Multi	t-value

Fund Adviser	Raw Return Difference				Absolute Return Difference			
	Missing	Single	Multi	t-value	Missing	Single	Multi	t-value
N	411	2,469	758		411[c]	2,469	758	
Mean	−0.1723	−0.0201	−0.0189	−0.03	1.0076	0.5199	0.2985	5.64[b]
Std Dev	2.8257	1.5931	0.7488		2.6452	1.5060	0.6869	

FOF/HF	Raw Return Difference				Absolute Return Difference			
	Missing	FOF	HF	t-value	Missing	FOF	HF	t-value
N	24	835	2,779		24	835	2,779	
Mean	−0.2138	−0.0212	−0.0403	0.42	0.6946	0.3145	0.5918	−6.48[b]
Std Dev	1.2362	0.8490	1.8329		1.0355	0.7888	1.7352	

Personal Investment

	Missing	Yes	No		Missing	Yes	No	
N	411	2,556	671		411	2,556	671	
Mean	-0.1723	-0.0114	-0.0520	0.71	1.0076	0.4462	0.5505	-2.00[a]
Std Dev	2.8257	1.4827	1.2641		2.6452	1.4139	1.1389	

Industry Sector

	Missing	Multi	Single		Missing	Multi	Single	
N	411	2,006	1,221		411	2,006	1,221	
Mean	-0.1723	-0.0153	-0.0273	0.21	1.0076	0.3391	0.6796	-6.39[b]
Std Dev	2.8257	1.1966	1.7688		2.6452	1.1476	1.6332	

Leverage

	Missing	Yes	No		Missing	Yes	No	
N	411	2,449	778		411	2,449	778	
Mean	-0.1723	-0.0182	-0.0250	0.11	1.0076	0.4814	0.4254	0.96
Std Dev	2.8257	1.4172	1.5098		2.6452	1.3330	1.4488	

Data is from TASS Management Limited (TASS). There are two versions: July 31, 1999, and March 31, 2001. In the 2001 data, there are 2,545 funds (1,543 live funds and 1,002 dead funds). In the 1999 data, there are 2,016 funds (1,407 live funds and 609 dead funds). There are 3,638 monthly return observations that are different for the same 461 funds across the two versions. The return difference is defined as 2001 − 1999. Audit = "No" if audit date = missing.
[a]Significant at the 5% level.
[b]Significant at the 1% level.
[c]411 observations are from 362 funds.

as auditing, funds of funds or hedge funds, manager's personal investment, or single/multi-industrial sectors. Generally, audited funds, funds of funds, and funds with manager's personal investment have fewer absolute return errors. For example, audited funds have an absolute return difference of 0.46 percent per month whereas nonaudited funds have an error rate of 0.69 percent. The difference between 0.46 percent and 0.69 percent is significant at the 1 percent level. Note that 411 observations from 362 funds with missing information on single/multi-fund managers, manager's personal investment, single/multi-industrial sectors, and leverage ratio result in the largest error regardless of raw return or absolute return measures.

Table 15.8 reports the audit date distribution according to the 2001 data. To consider the common time horizon, Liang (2002) focuses on July 1999. Out of 461 funds having inconsistent returns in our sample, 201 (43.6 percent) are not effectively audited and 206 (44.69 percent) are audited. Auditing dates are clustered in a few Decembers, with December 1998 capturing the largest amount of audited funds in any given month. However, there is no increasing trend observable for fund auditing: In December 1999 we have 44 audited funds, whereas in December 2000 there are only two.

Data is from TASS Management Limited (TASS). There are two versions: July 31, 1999, and March 31, 2001. There are 3,638 monthly return observations that are different for the same 461 funds across the two databases. Audit dates are from the 2001 data.

Finally, Liang (2002) examines onshore funds with their offshore equivalents and expects that these pairs offer similar returns if they belong to the same fund family, have the same fund manager, use the same investment strategy and same leverage, and charge the same fees. The only difference between the two vehicles is the fund location, which should not be critical for determining fund returns. In the 1999 version of TASS data, there are 1,407 live funds. We find 37 pairs of onshore funds with their equivalent offshore vehicles. Deleting one pair that has abnormally high return differences in two months out of the 12-month history, we have 36 pairs left in our final sample.

In Table 15.9, 16 audited pairs and 20 nonaudited pairs are audited. The average monthly return difference between the onshore funds and offshore funds is 0.12 percent per month for the audited pairs and 0.24 percent for the nonaudited pairs. Although the latter doubles the former, the difference is not statistically significant. The average absolute return difference is 0.17 percent for the audited pairs and 0.33 percent for the nonaudited pairs. The difference between 0.17 percent and 0.33 percent is significant at the 5 percent level. Therefore, audited pairs have less return discrepancy than the nonaudited pairs. Remember that error may occur either way, so we use not only the raw return difference but also the absolute return difference.

TABLE 15.8　Audit Date Distribution

Audit Date	461 Funds				All Funds			
	Frequency	Cumulative Frequency	%	Cumulative %	Frequency	Cumulative Frequency	%	Cumulative %
9312	6	6	1.30	1.30	18	18	1.08	1.08
9402	1	7	0.22	1.52	1	19	0.06	1.14
9403					2	21	0.12	1.26
9404	1	8	0.22	1.74	1	22	0.06	1.32
9405					1	23	0.06	1.38
9406	1	9	0.22	1.95	4	27	0.24	1.62
9409					3	30	0.18	1.80
9410	1	10	0.22	2.17	1	31	0.06	1.86
9412	1	11	0.22	2.39	7	38	0.42	2.28
9512	2	13	0.43	2.82	10	48	0.60	2.88
9606	1	14	0.22	3.04	9	57	0.54	3.42
9612	2	16	0.43	3.47	23	80	1.38	4.80
9703	7	23	1.52	4.99	12	92	0.72	5.52
9704					1	93	0.06	5.58
9706	1	24	0.22	5.21	5	98	0.30	5.88
9709					1	99	0.06	5.94
9711					2	101	0.12	6.06
9712	51	75	11.06	16.27	131	232	7.85	13.91
9801	1	76	0.22	16.49	9	241	0.54	14.45
9802	1	77	0.22	16.70	1	242	0.06	14.51
9803	4	81	0.87	17.57	7	249	0.42	14.93
9804	2	83	0.43	18.00	7	256	0.42	15.35
9805					1	257	0.06	15.41
9806	3	86	0.65	18.66	17	274	1.02	16.43
9807					3	277	0.18	16.61
9808	1	87	0.22	18.87	3	280	0.18	16.79
9809	1	88	0.22	19.09	21	301	1.26	18.05
9810	2	90	0.43	19.52	4	305	0.24	18.29
9811					2	307	0.12	18.41
9812	106	196	22.99	42.52	356	663	21.34	39.75
9903	4	200	0.87	43.38	10	673	0.60	40.35
9904					2	675	0.12	40.47
9905					1	676	0.06	40.53
9906	5	205	1.08	44.47	20	696	1.20	41.73
9907	1	206	0.22	44.69	1	697	0.06	41.79
9908	1	207	0.22	44.90	4	701	0.24	42.03
9909	4	211	0.87	45.77	9	710	0.54	42.57
9910	1	212	0.22	45.99	4	714	0.24	42.81
9911					1	715	0.06	42.87
9912	44	256	9.54	55.53	288	1,003	17.27	60.13
0001					1	1,004	0.06	60.19
0003	1	257	0.22	55.75	7	1,011	0.42	60.61
0006	1	258	0.22	55.97	4	1,015	0.24	60.85
0011					1	1,016	0.06	60.91
0012	2	260	0.43	56.40	3	1,019	0.18	61.09
Missing	201	461	43.60	100.00	649	1,668	38.91	100.00

TABLE 15.9　Monthly Return Discrepancy between Onshore Funds and Offshore Funds

Category	N	Raw Return Difference	Standard Deviation	Absolute Return Difference	Standard Deviation
Audited	16	0.1153%	0.1719%	0.1665%	0.1190%
Not Audited	20	0.2427%	0.3664%	0.3282%	0.2879%

t-retdiff = 1.377.
t-absdiff = 2.279.

In Table 15.10, "Fund Characteristics for 36 Matched Onshore Funds with Their Offshore Equivalents," Liang (2002) lists the average assets and ages for these 36 pairs. The average onshore fund has a total asset valuation under management of $58 million, compared with $33 million for the offshore funds. The average fund age for the onshore funds is 58 months, whereas it is only 39 months for the offshore vehicles. The 19-month difference is significant at the 5 percent level. Therefore, onshore funds are larger and older than their offshore equivalents. It seems that fund managers establish onshore funds first, and then start an offshore equivalent at a later stage when they gain some expertise in fund management and want to attract investors from different countries. The average time lag is about one and a half years.

Data in Table 15.10 is from TASS as of July 31, 1999. Pairs are matched for onshore funds with their offshore equivalents. Using 1,407 live funds only and imposing restrictions on the same fund name, same fund manager, same leverage, same strategy, and same fees across the two vehicles, we find that there are 36 matched pairs usable for analysis.

Liang (2002) finds that there is a positive correlation between the audit dummy variable (defined as 1 if one or both of the audit dates is nonmissing and zero if both audit dates are missing for the pair) and the fund assets. The correlation coefficient between the logarithm of onshore assets and the audit dummy is 0.55 with a p-value of 0.0006, while the correlation coefficient between the logarithm of offshore assets and the audit dummy is 0.31 with a p-value of 0.0627. Therefore, large funds tend to be audited whereas small funds tend not to be audited. Large funds are more likely to have auditors than their smaller counterparts because their large assets and more complicated positions may also require more scrutiny than smaller funds.

TABLE 15.10 Fund Characteristics for 36 Matched Onshore Funds with Their Offshore Equivalents

Variable	U.S. Return	Offshore Return	U.S. Assets	Offshore Assets	United States Management Fee	Offshore Management Fee	U.S. IFee	Offshore IFee	U.S. Age	Offshore Age
Mean	1.2551	1.0690	$57,793,624	$32,515,738	1.2153	1.2100	20.3472	20.3472	57.5833	38.9444
Standard Deviation	0.9628	1.0731	$73,546,712	$41,757,433	0.5041	0.5000	2.5462	2.5462	44.2315	25.5689
N	36	36	35	36	36	36	36	36	36	36

Source: Bing Liang, "Hedge Fund Returns: Auditing and Accuracy," *Journal of Portfolio Management,* Weatherhead School, Case Western Reserve University, 2002, 1–30.

To sum up, Liang (2002) entirely conducted this research to investigate data accuracy for hedge funds and explore reasons why discrepancy in fund returns exists across different data sources. Liang (2002) compares the same funds that appear in two different databases for return discrepancy, analyzes fund returns in the same database but from two different versions (a previous version and an updated version), and compares onshore funds with their equivalent offshore products to see whether return discrepancy between the two occurs.

The findings are: First, audited funds have a much lower return discrepancy than nonaudited funds. Auditing makes a clear difference in data quality. Unfortunately, over 40 percent of hedge funds in the sample are not effectively audited (i.e., they don't have a clear auditing date). In addition, there is no increasing trend for fund auditing based on auditing dates. Given the strong correlation between auditing and data accuracy, we strongly recommend that hedge funds should be audited and investors should look for audited funds instead of nonaudited ones.

Second, dead funds are less effectively audited than live funds. This may be caused by bad data quality of these funds with missing information or poor administration of the funds.

Third, there is a significantly positive correlation between the auditing dummy variable and fund size. Large funds tend to be audited whereas small funds tend not to be. This is probably because large funds can afford to have an auditor and there is more need for auditing their large money pools or complicated portfolio positions. Since large funds are more likely to be audited, they provide better data quality than their smaller counterparts.

Fourth, funds listed on exchanges, funds of funds (compared with hedge funds), funds with both U.S. and non-U.S. investors, funds open to the public, funds invested in a single sector (compared with multiple sectors), and unlevered funds have better data quality than the other funds. It is understandable that these fund managers have done due diligence to better keep their books and to report return information more accurately since these funds are funds of funds, listed on exchanges, and open to the public. Their returns also may be easily calculated since they do not use leverage and invest only in a single industrial sector.

Finally, Liang (2002) found that, on average, onshore funds are about 80 percent larger and one and a half years older than their equivalent offshore products. The researcher compared matched pairs between onshore and offshore funds with the same fund family, manager, and leverage, style, and fee structure and found that hedge fund managers normally first establish an onshore vehicle in the United States. Once managers have gained experience and a fund has become sizable, they start an offshore equivalent for the tax advantages and to attract foreign investors. This also enhances our findings about positions in onshore accounts not accurately mirroring those in offshore accounts and the very fact that there are very few reconciliations performed between both operational infrastructures. Some very basic recommendations can be offered in order to remedy operational and compliance risks. Those minimum risk management standards are seldom applied. The recommendations are:

The hedge fund manager needs to follow trading mandates consistently over time. All changes in products and trading strategies need to be communicated to internal parties, investors, and local regulators. Hedge fund managers determine initial products, trading strategies, and markets in which to operate. Risk managers follow the initial business plan and use it as a reference to set capital limits over time. Any substantial changes in mandates, risks, and budgetary limits get evaluated and reviewed.

The market risk implementation follows from the initial business plan. Market risk limits are decided on depending on the capacity or size of the hedge fund. Capacity is one of the main risks. Very few hedge funds have considered putting a limit on capacity. If they have, they have created other funds attached to the initial one to replicate the same capacity but under a different name, under a different legal structure, or in another geographical market. In some of those hedge funds, one of the risks that had occurred is conflict of interest between investors and management that oversees several funds with different names.

The market risk limits are determined depending on the types of products being traded and the geographical market in which the hedge fund manager wants to trade. Limits can be set in various forms such as value at risk by strategies, limits on concentrated positions, limits on number of trades, limits on stress testing of the portfolio, limits on Greeks (delta, gamma, vega, rho, beta), and minimum liquidity. Managers decide the initial types of risk limits they are to monitor over time in order to collect historical information on positions compared with initial set limits. Any changes of limits over time are usually also documented properly with corresponding justifications.

The hedge fund manager implements a core risk management department that oversees the risk monitoring function. Risk managers are to collect agreed positions, trade prices, and risk information. They collect this information from the brokers' reports or downloads published on the brokers' web sites. Then, risk managers monitor the funds' positions and prices with the set limits. Any abnormalities are collected, analyzed, documented, and reported to upper management. Very few hedge funds have daily risk calls to explain abnormalities in the traders' books. Until recently most meetings in hedge funds have been to evaluate fund strategies to be selected for the overall portfolio. But note that granular risk management at a position-detailed level has not occurred until very recently.

The hedge fund asset manager and the risk manager monitor over time the evolution of the returns with risk limits. They verify accuracy of profits and losses with the trade pricing verification function and market evolution. Any major changes in capacities impact internal limits and are explained accordingly.

The hedge fund manager and the risk manager agree on an initial market risk limit to be accountable for and they implement together how they are going to monitor the limit over time by implementing policies and procedures on the trading and risk managing activities. Any changes in initial strategic or trading policies typically are reported to the risk manager and to upper management. Seldom do hedge funds request permission from regulators to trade specific strategies and instruments and even less often do they request from regulators permission for changes of trading strategies, instruments, and capacity. This liberty of hedge funds has in retrospect changed the landscape of the financial markets and the way regulators operate to implement compliance in new fields.

CHAPTER 16

Derivative Structured Products and Corporate Laws to Hide Risks

Due diligence and compliance risk management also consist of dissecting complicated transactions involving derivatives and analyzing market inefficiencies arising from using derivatives outside the law and what could create unfair treatment in markets.

One loophole to get around the law of registering with regulators is to define the hedge fund as a private equity fund. The shell of holding private equity stakes in hedge funds prevents regulators from applying any legislation attached to hedge funds while still gaining the benefits from the investments in the funds. Valuation models do not have to be transparent, and managers are not liable for not adhering to the compliance law of 2006. This is why magazines and journals started to report hedge fund performance along with that of mutual funds and equity funds. They mingle with each other without any clear distinction when it comes to risk management and compliance rules.

The fundamental usage of derivatives was aimed at lowering market risk exposures but not credit risks and monitoring collateral asset valuations that those instruments implicitly alter. Very often, this practice is performed by dissecting all the components of the trades and the term sheet contracts with counterparties. Few brokerage operations have a due diligence department checking the accuracy of trades' legal contracts and actual signatures. Marcel Kahan and Edward B. Rock (November 2005) in their paper on "Hedge Funds in Corporate Governance and Corporate Control" have taken a two-sided view with regard to the overall compliance issues revolving around complicated instruments.

They analyzed regulatory implications, conflicts of interest, and other inherent risks. Hedge funds generate high revenues as multiplying factors are directly linked to fees—management fees, incentive fees, and performance fees. Statistics in Appendix I show that fees do impact on the survival chances of the funds. Very much like mutual funds, pension funds, or insurance companies, hedge funds act in the interest of fee production primarily—not in the interest of the shareholder or of the investors, but rather in the interest of the officers of the hedge funds and of the fund manager.

Another way hedge funds impact the markets is by using voting rights. Martin and Partnoy and Black and Hu (2005) have released findings on how empty voting rights affect hedge funds' strategies. The topic of empty voting was also reviewed by Kahan and Rock (2005), and here is the evidence they describe:

> *Mylan Laboratories and King Pharmaceutical entered a merger agreement and Mylan acquired King for a given number of shares while Perry Corporation, a 7 million shareholder of King and hedge fund, agreed on the merger. Perry owned 9.9 percent of Mylan while also hedging economical risk with Bear Stearns and Goldman Sachs with equity derivative swaps. By doing so, Perry's shareholders or investors' votes had no economical impact. The votes occurred solely based as a shareholder of King as it has no financial interest in Mylan. Perry's takeover of Mylan's share is an example of empty voting as its shares are fully hedged with Goldman Sachs and Bear Stearns and thus does not profit or bring shareholders' interests.*

Kahan and Rock used another example of Black and Hu's empty voting. Company A acquires part of company B while entering an equity derivative swap so A does not bear economical risk with B and can vote the shares to approve the merger since it owns the shares. The equity derivatives swap cancels risks, and gains and losses cancel each other out. Bettis, Bizjak, and Lemmon (2001) demonstrate equity derivative usage for insider trading and economical risk returns manipulation. After the vote is passed, A can sell its shares and cancel the swap.

Another similar empty voting situation is as follows: Company A acquires part of company B before the record date and enters a zero cost collar by shorting a call option on B's shares and buying a put option on the shares. Profits from the call then hedge the premium cost of the put and thus flatten economical risk of A. Similarly, A acquires part of B before the record date while shorting the same number of B shares to a third party in order to flatten net total exposure. Company A votes B shares while delivering B shares to the third party.

Empty voting can also occur before the record date of acquisition if company A acquires company B and sells out B shares after the record date while voting as well. Christofferssen, Geczy, Musto, and Reed (2002) also demonstrated in "The Market for Record Date Ownership" that buying shares before the record date and selling them after the record date fits an arbitrage strategy that generates profits by leveraging or arbitraging between different tax treatments of dividends. Whoever owns the shares on or at the record date defines who is entitled to vote and benefits from dividends. In all of these transactions, although net economical risk between A and B is flat, A and B show opposite economical incentives while also providing A the advantage of voting rights. Kahan and Rock (2005) explain that A's and B's interests diverge as A enters into a merger deal and pays a high price for B. Company A shareholders benefit from A's approval.

Compliance and regulatory laws do not have rules and requirements surrounding structured products loopholes and insiders' manipulation for their own benefit primarily due to the complexities of the deals and the lack of skilled, knowledgeable lawyers who can evaluate the fairness of such transactions. The challenge also remains in catching up with the gargantuan numbers of unverified transactions and inappropriate use of these transactions. No parties in the financial markets have taken the initiative on implementing regulatory framework around these structured instruments. The regulations remain primarily in the filing and registering of funds and in preventing massive frauds from occurring.

Complications also arise from the impact of structured products on other types of risks. Christofferssen, Geczy, Musto, and Reed (2002) found that another fundamental problem in such transactions relies on the generation of credit risk. Evidently all the empty voting situations net out financial and economical risks while giving one company the exclusive voting rights. But these transactions require minimum credit lending or capital set aside or collateral in case the company's rating quality is downgraded during ownership of the shares. If A shorts stock B by borrowing shares in order to sell them, brokerage companies will find a short seller to borrow from the custodian bank holding shares or certificates for custodial clients: mutual funds, pension funds, and insurance companies. The short seller provides credit collateral or cash valued at 102 percent of the shares' value. The cost of borrowing shares equals the difference between the overnight interest market rate and the rebated amount.

There are other ways sophisticated instruments have been lucrative when there is absence of compliance and legislation around those instruments. For instance, private investments in public equity (PIPEs) have been used for lucrative and profitable purposes but their manipulations remain highly controversial. A structured product that has been less successful than others on the market, a PIPE is a security involving an illiquid private placement with a commitment by the issuer to file a registration statement within a short period of time. They involve a floating conversion rate such that conversion into common stock is at a discount to the price of the stock at the time the PIPE was issued but also at a discount to the price of the common stock when PIPE was registered. This later reset of the conversion rate at registration makes PIPEs holders short the stock to decrease market price until the reset date to raise the number of convertible shares obtained.

Angelo Gordon and Co. and Citadel took advantage of this strategy. They are hedge funds that heavily shorted eToys' shares in order to decrease its market price until the reset date to cash in on a larger number of eToys' shares. This practice has slowly vanished from the market after numerous lawsuits. This is another example of an arbitrage opportunity that impacted overall securities market structures. Other cases involving similar problems are: *Log on America, Inc. v. Promethean Asset Management LLC*, HFTP Investment LLC, Fisher Capital Ltd., Wingate Capital Ltd., Citadel Limited Partnership, and Marshall Capital Management Inc. In the same school of thought, Whittier and Leib M. Lerner released a book entitled *Disclosing Toxic PIPEs: Why the SEC Can and Should Expand Reporting Requirements Surrounding Private Investment in Public Equity*. Zacchari T. Knepper also described those securities as highly damaging to the market in *Future Priced Convertible Securities and the Outlook for Death Spiral Securities Fraud Litigation*.

In a disagreement between parties, buying out the disinterested party to make the deal happen is another controversial compliant form of conducting business. It is a subtle or implicit form of bribery. Buying a hedge fund's interest occurs in the following scenario: Company A owns a stock interest in company B. B and C have opted to merge but A does not agree with the merger deal. Then B and C enter into an agreement with A to give A an interest or a premium above the merger consideration in order to buy A's shareholders' interest and close the merger deal.

Market timing is illegal, and it involves the buying and selling of mutual fund shares at closing prices of net asset values. Yet, hedge funds and mutual funds have been involved in numerous lawsuits when trading of shares occurred after local closing market prices. Late trading is also illegal and involves investors placing buy and sell orders in mutual funds after closing of the U.S. markets. Different from late trading, market timing gives investors tradable timing arbitrage opportunities due to international time zone differences. Investors trade on the fact that closing prices of actively traded stocks change after Asian and European closings but before U.S. closings. A way to remedy such unfair trading practices and obvious geographical advantage is to consider fair asset values rather than closing trading prices.

Hedge funds have been actively engaged in these questionable market practices. New York Attorney General Eliot Spitzer had uncovered cases with Canary Capital Partners, Alliance Capital, Bank of America, Bank One, Canadian Imperial Bank of Commerce, Conseco, Pilgrim Baxter, and Pimco.

Pumping and dumping is another illegitimate activity many hedge funds have exhibited. This is when a high-profile, highly reputable hedge fund investor buys a company to change its management structure and boost its pricing valuation shares solely based on reputation and speculation by the network of that individual. Then, at peak price, the large well-known investor sells the company to make share prices drop shortly thereafter. In the beginning of 2005, Carl Icahn, a large investor, obtained antitrust clearance to acquire up to $1 billion or 24 percent of the stock of Timple Inland Company in Austin, Texas. The stock price went from $64 per share to $84 per share within a month due to his reputation and high-interest stake in the company. After March 24, Icahn withdrew his intent of buying interest and prices fell 9 percent. It was not reported what Icahn gained from his bid.

Hedge funds can also act as short-term investors due to the speculative nature of the investments and strategies. They trade high volume and use mostly derivatives, and this highlights a major discrepancy between the high-risk, high-return, short-term tendencies of hedge funds and their shareholders, who tend to be more long-term, buy-and-hold, conservative, risk-averse individuals. Long-term investors are mainly interested in long-term horizons. For example, when the Deutsche Boerse intended to acquire the London Stock Exchange, hedge funds opposed the deal as they owned large stakes in Deutsche Boerse, having taken positions in event risk strategies. Shareholders have not benefited from potential larger share values from merging London Stock Exchange with Deutsche Boerse, but they could have lost a lot as well if the deal valuations had failed.

Another case where the role of hedge funds is highly debatable relates to Lampert, Kmart, and Sears. As Lampert acquired parts of Kmart, its stock was shorted and its worth went from $15 to $108 a share. Had hedge funds attempted to block the acquisition, shareholder values would not have risen. Hedge funds try to buy at the lowest possible price, as their interests diverge from those of shareholders.

Kahan and Rock (2005) also mentioned the implication of Delaware law on "vote buying" involvement in hedge fund strategies. It is an agreement of a shareholder or bondholder to vote shares in a particular way in exchange for payment. The basis of the Delaware law highlights that investors should not be able to value any particular views with regard to ownership positions and that they should be separate and independent from offsetting short positions. For example, in *In re Digex*, Elliott Associates, a large hedge fund, entered a settlement of $165 million to reward beneficiary and records owners of Digex Class A common stock. Under this case, it was argued that short sellers are also new "inherent" owners of shares. Another case, involving Deephaven Risk Arbitrage Trading and United Global Com, raised the question of whether a net short shareholder would be able to require inspections of books and records under the Delaware law. The paper suggests there is little likelihood that Delaware law would impact empty voting rights of shareholders.

Some other constraints have made hedge funds more accessible than mutual funds. This had made hedge funds more likely to be one of the last resorts for creation of products that are almost completely free of regulatory and tax burdens for high-net-worth individuals. The trend is for countries that have been relatively free of regulations up to now to enact government restrictions, depending on their geographical areas: Sarbanes-Oxley (SOX) 404 and SEC for the United States, Euro Savings Directive for Europe, and Basel Accords globally.

Hedge funds have been popular as they have not been subject to the same levels of bureaucratic disclosure to shareholders such as a semiannual list of their holdings and net asset values. Now they must disclose how they voted shares of the portfolio's companies in order to discourage them from taking sizable positions in portfolio companies. They are also now liable for the marketing materials they disseminate and/or any misleading information they communicate.

Mutual funds must also comply with some minimum standard diversification requirements in line with subchapter M of the Internal Revenue Code. Fifty percent of the assets of a mutual fund are subject to the limitation that the fund may own no more than 10 percent of the outstanding securities of the portfolio. Stock cannot represent more than 5 percent of the asset value of the fund. Due to their diversification requirements, funds must also comply with the Investment Company Act. And thus, 75 percent of the assets of a mutual fund are subject to the limitation that a fund can own no more than 10 percent and the stock of any company can be no more than 5 percent of the asset value in the fund. Therefore, large positions are not an option in mutual funds, and this has made higher-positioned speculators of hedge funds.

Another flaw with hedge funds being highly unregulated and growing very large is due to their size and power. They have managed to acquire as much influence as institutional investors, and by doing so, they have created conflicts of interest with pension funds, insurance companies, mutual funds, university endowment funds, other institutions, and high-net-worth entities more for the direct interest of fund managers than the interests of the shareholders. Managers of public pension funds are typically government officials who are accountable to high-profile politicians who pursue political motivations. Union representatives are also politically motivated and restrict the maximization of investment returns. For instance, CalPERS, the largest and traditionally most active public pension fund, had been the subject of poor publicity due to the union's active role. New York State Common Retirement Funds, worth $115 million, had questionably benefited by local law firms' large contributions in favor of local politicians' campaign interests and assigning them a questionable monopoly on internal management decisions of the funds.

Most managers charge incentive fees to allocate resources to manage portfolios. Those who do not have incentive fees tend to be short of back office and risk management resources. Index fund managers usually charge incentive fees but tend not to spend in infrastructural, back office, and risk management resources in order to keep profits high.

Not to complicate the overall regulatory system even more, basic credit rules recommended by the Basel Committee on Banking Supervision could be applicable. Some reforms or regulatory solutions can be provided to fix these inefficiencies. In the example of empty voting, regulation is difficult to provide because shareholders would have an interest in the outcome of the votes. Empty voting with derivatives' hedges (with zero collar or equity derivatives swaps) flattens out economical interests; however, derivatives increase credit risks and assets' hidden collateral values. This part could be handled with the same rules as those used by financial institutions and/or commercial banks.

With regard to empty voting concepts, Christofferssen, Geczy, and Reed (2005) issued a working paper on "Vote Trading and Information Aggregation" in the interest of shareholders to debate in favor of allowing vote trading. Roberta Karmel (2004), in "Should a Duty to the Corporation Be Imposed on Institutional Shareholders," suggested the implementation of a fiduciary duty on shareholders that could be created within the Delaware mergers and acquisitions (M&A) jurisprudence framework. The Committee on Operations (1991) proposed suggestions on "short-selling activity in the stock market: market effects and the need for regulations," according to the Report of the Committee on Government Operations, House of Representatives (1991).

Awareness about short positions was already a topic of discussion in the early 1990s. Limiting shareholders to voting net long positions by charter provisions would require a proposed solution to empty voting along with a mandatory rule record date holder of the sold shares. The SEC released in 1991 public disclosure of material short security positions according to the Securities Exchange Act of 1934. It argued that it had broad authority to adopt rules that define or provide a means reasonably designed to prevent fraudulent manipulative or deceptive conduct.

Few firms have a system allowing shareholders to vote net long instead of gross positions partially due to null reforms on such ideas. According to Kahan and Rock (2005), only Merrill Lynch has a sound and reasonable objective proxy voting system: DTC. DTC basically executes an omnibus proxy granting its members such as Merrill to vote the shares that DTC holds for them. ADP is a service provider that sends confidential voting information and materials (e.g., 13D reports) to DTC members' shareholders. Newer shareholders do not yet get as many votes per share as the oldest shareholders under the Tenure Voting Statute. Under the *Providence and Worcester v. Baker* case, each holder of common stock has one vote per share for the first 50 shares and only one vote per 20 shares for all shares above 50. In hedge funds, limiting shareholders to voting net long positions seems reasonable. Most hedge funds would opt for it except those reluctant to have administrative burdens despite any rules. In Perry's strategy in the Mylan-King case, it had short positions netting out King shares. Derivatives (zero collar, equity derivatives swaps, futures contracts hedging, stock shorting) could be structured so that Perry holds risk if King stock dropped at set lock levels or plateaus such as 3 percent, 5 percent, or 7 percent.

Another obstacle difficult to manage and reform is corporate governance politics within a hedge fund's relationships that can also contribute to weakening the overall hedge fund's genuine interest of managing its portfolio and risks. There are human conflicts and personal interest in power and greed. (And this is not only in hedge funds!) For example, Third Point LLC, a $2.5 billion hedge fund, targeted Star Gas Partners LP, a heating oil distributor, after acquiring approximately 6 percent of Star Gas' units. Third Point demanded that Star Gas CEO Irik Sevin resign, according to www.prnewswise.com of February 14, 2005. Another example of such internal influence altering shareholders' stakes is Barrington in 2003 convincing Institutional Shareholder Services, a proxy voting advisory service, to recommend that its client vote for two Barrington directors' nominees. In July 2003, Barrington's strategy succeeded: VF Corporation acquired Nautica for $587 million and Barrington withdrew its proxy fight. A year later, Steven Madden, Ltd. and Barrington reached an agreement to spend $2.5 million to pay dividends to shareholders.

Another hedge fund, The Children's Investment Fund Management (TCI), interfered in the merger of Deutsche Boerse and the London Stock Exchange fearing it would deplete value if unsuccessful. In this instance shareholders gain and are protected by the hedge fund management values and corporate practices, as half of the TCI management fee of 1 percent is donated to The Children's Investment Fund Foundation.

Another example of hedge funds' corporate governance influencing shareholders' stakes is the MONY-AXA case. Hedge funds Highfields, Southeastern Asset Management (with 4.9 percent ownership), Third Avenue Management, and Angelo Gordon and Co. (owning 13.6 percent of MONY Star) stopped the merger using different means.

Hedge funds affect shareholders' values by influencing portfolio companies to be acquired by others and also have tried to acquire companies. They bid to alter corporate governance and change capital framework. They add a third party target in a deal that they acquired. For example, Circuit City rejected a takeover bid by the Highfields hedge fund. Another example of hedge funds influencing deal structures and shareholder interests involves investors Gabelli, Steel Partners, and Pirate Capital. Steel Partners and GenCorp had intended to merge, but the GenCorp board rejected Steel Partners' bid. The latter counteroffered with a proxy contest. The board agreed that Steel Partners should withdraw its shareholder proposal and succeeded at implementing the corporate governance changes that it had initially proposed.

Another example of hedge funds influencing shareholding status and overall corporate governance was experienced with Beverly Enterprises. Hedge funds Formation Capital, Appaloosa Management, Franklin Mutual Advisers, and Northbrook NBV bid to acquire Beverly Enterprises by entering a proxy battle and electing a new management structure made up of the hedge funds' directors. Beverly's shareholding corporate governance structure had radically changed. Beverly ended up being auctioned and sold.

Finally, hedge funds can have the object of becoming controlling shareholders as a bulk of larger industrial corporations. A corporate governance example involves Kmart. It filed for bankruptcy in February 2002 and emerged a year later from Chapter 11. Its hedge fund ESL, managed by Edward Lampert, had a 50 percent stake in Kmart and had acquired $2 billion in financial claims converted into stock during restructuring. Beckey Yerak lifted Kmart's stock into the blue yonder as of July 2004. In November 2004, the *New York Times* reported that Kmart was acquired by Sears for $11 billion. The ESL hedge fund also owned a large stake in Sears and its part increased by 15 percent at the time of the merger. Kmart stock rose to $109 a share by November 2004 from $15 a share in May 2003 with Sears' shares rising simultaneously. ESL's significant stake obviously in parallel influenced the deal to merge and also profited from shareholdings in both companies.

The lack of regulations and compliance over many years has had a serious impact on the way financial markets are being shaped now. Amanda Cantrell reported on November 15, 2005, that "hedge funds, investors, and managers worry that hedge funds are making ever bigger, unhedged bets on stocks."

According to Cantrell (2005), traditional stock hedge funds are behaving very much like plain old stock funds as they are buying more stocks outright rather than hedging positions with options costing a premium. The reporter mentioned that hedge funds were originally designed to produce positive results in up or down markets mainly by using investments to offset risk or hedge against market declines. Initially and in their original theoretical strategic plans, when stock rose, absolute return funds would rise, but when stocks fell funds would fall less. Yet recently, primarily from the lack of due diligence, corporate governance, and consistent risk management monitoring, industry analysts are starting to recognize several factors that have diverted hedge fund managers away from their original trading mandates. Hedge funds have initiated forays into risky speculative and large trading strategies and instruments.

CHAPTER 17

The Evolution and Involvement of Regulations and Compliance

One of the greatest aspects involving hedge fund regulation is the overwhelming amount of regulatory discussion but the lack of actual drastic reforms and actions to be performed in time to deal with funds' growing trends and returns. One would have thought after the Long-Term Capital Management fiasco in 1998, which sank markets in absolute terms and forced the innovative coalition of players to rescue the market, that no hedge funds would ever be created without prior supervision and permission of global regulators. However, hedge funds have proliferated and flourished like never before.

A hedge fund risk manager and the compliance risk manager are both in charge of complying with local, national, and international regulators to make sure that the hedge funds' trading strategies and instruments are compliant with the markets in which the fund manager is established. In the United States, legislation requires funds to register with SEC as of February 2006 and hedge funds must file the appropriate forms to conduct trading of specific instruments in specific markets. The forms to file are also passed to auditors in order for internal and external auditors to be aware of internal operational issues in process. Now more and more filing is performed electronically via systems such as Horizon or Phoenix, but very few hedge funds have operational risk databases to report audit issues because hedge funds have not been as strictly regulated as other financial structures. Also, the enforcement approaches regulators have taken are aimed more at fraud prevention than actual bureaucratic filing and regulations as in the old days. So, this practical application of regulation has been scattered, on a case-by-case basis, and quite random. It would appear that a lot of hedge funds have escaped such processes.

As described by the SEC in 2003, most hedge funds have managed to get around various Acts, such as the 1933 Securities Act, the 1940 Investment

Act, and the 1940 Investment Advisers Act. These exemptions have allowed hedge fund managers to avoid disclosures of all derivatives, structured products, and other off-balance-sheet instruments and strategies. This lack of disclosure and the illiquidity associated with the market conditions of the late 1990s and the traded instruments have given managers a vast amount of freedom in managerial and financial statements reporting. The SEC in 2004 described 46 enforcement actions involving hedge fund frauds since 1999 questioning the valuation of hedge fund assets as well as the fairness of prices at which investors buy and sell fund shares. Now there have been more than 50 SEC actions. Consequently, the SEC changed the Investment Advisers Act on October 26, 2004. As of 2006, hedge fund managers are forced to invest in tighter risk management operations and infrastructures and register with the SEC. Hedge funds are submitted to tighter controls, risk management, and technologies. It is perceived that fund managers who have grown in capacity and have also invested in risk management and systems will survive while the smaller hedge fund traders will not integrate into the global financial system framework.

Hedge funds will also tend to be under more scrutiny on their risk management performances and returns. It is thought that the hedge fund industry has doubled since 2001 without progress in reforms and regulations. Nowadays, virtually everyone is invested in hedge funds either through direct investments or through pension funds or universities' endowments. From 2003 to 2005, funds appear to have less hedging to double net long exposures according to an article in *CNN Money* reporting on Markov Processes, the New York–based financial services consulting firm. Markov Consulting Company analyzed returns for long and short hedge funds using the CSFB/Tremont index and Hedge Fund Research index and compared outcomes with the Standard & Poor's 500 index. The Markov study shows that the levels are similar to those from before 2001. They concluded that it took two years of hedge fund gains to attract new hedge fund managers and speculators. Managers who deviate from their trading strategies and traded instruments tend to bring more risk to the markets.

On Investorsoffshore.com, Jeremy Hetherington-Gore reported in November 2005 that a "hedge fund downturn" could potentially be occurring, yet we have seen high returns at the beginning of 2006. It is thought that these are the last few high years of the hedge funds' lucrative returns. The month of October's results were of particular concern and also prodded regulators to become more aware of trends in hedge fund returns. Although the month of November would benefit from gains, October encountered losses due to high-profile hedge funds fraud such as experienced by Portus in Canada and Bayou in the United States, and also due to other corporate scandals such as the fall of Refco. Hedge funds held positions in Refco. The chief investment officer of global macro fund Third Wave Global Investor mentioned that "Outside Japan, most of main markets were down in October, emerging markets incurred losses, and long macro funds with downward moves produced additional losses. Atticus Capital's USD 8 billion manager was down 9 percent in October yet the funds' net of year return is up 40 percent. Third Point is another hedge fund example encountering a loss of 9 percent for the month, yet the fund's return is up 11 percent for the year."

The Financial Services Authority (FSA) requested hedge funds and financial institutions involved with hedge funds to take more preventive steps in risk management. The Financial Services Authority intends to implement a regulatory plan similar to that of the Securities and Exchange Commission. The FSA plan requires a more transparent framework for hedge funds. For example, on November 7, 2005, the FSA introduced new rules based on takeover code requiring hedge funds to report their exposure to shares in takeover, acquisition, or merger situations via hedging derivatives contracts. The FSA is requiring more transparency with regard to takeover situations.

The Alternative Investment Management Association (AIMA) proposed to work with the FSA to create a new center of hedge fund expertise aimed at monitoring hedge fund activities. The AIMA also suggested standardization of rules among hedge funds and created Sound Practices Guidelines.

The Banking Supervision Committee of the European Central Bank (ECB) chairman, Edgar Meister, observed that "hedge funds' recurring losses and crises could destabilize the financial markets." He also mentioned that large corporate European banks and broker-dealers encounter challenges in monitoring aggregate hedge fund exposures due to lack of transparency.

In addition to the FSA, SEC, and ECB, the International Organization of Securities Commissions (IOSCO), the global securities markets regulator, is in the process of drafting new rules to tighten and control hedge funds' derivatives deals. Jochen Sanio, the head of BaFin, the German financial regulator, reported that hedge funds "pose a big threat to the financial industry." Most regulators are getting ready to agree on regulating hedge funds globally.

As of February 2006, hedge fund managers with more than $30 million in assets are to register with the SEC as investment advisers. The main challenge of this law is its geographical restriction: In order to get around this law, a vast majority of hedge funds had offshored main accounts in low-regulatory areas, so the law's effectiveness outside of the United States remains controversial. The SEC is also facing the challenge of not having the resources or the expertise to sustain due diligence in all hedge funds in offshore areas.

The hedge fund industry has taken attention, resources, and time away from the mutual fund industry's problems. The SEC's budget was cut and it had to make selective decisions on targeted investigative areas. According to the Alternative Investment Management Association, doubling the budgetary threshold (assets under management) to $50 million would exclude 1,000 hedge funds from registration rules checking. Hedge funds and mutual funds have different legal frameworks and also have different trading activities. Implementing regulations and rules for hedge funds implies understanding in great detail derivatives contracts and the sophisticated trading strategies hedge fund managers practice. According to Fung and Hsieh (1999a, b), the difference in returns between hedge funds and mutual funds is due to the variety of trading strategies. Hedge funds use dynamic trading while mutual funds have static long-term buy-and-hold strategies. Hedge funds also use leverage.

The United States uses three sets of regulators to monitor financial markets' stability. The Securities and Exchange Commission (SEC) oversees publicly traded securities while the Commodity Futures Trading Commission (CFTC) oversees the futures. The Federal Reserve, the Office of the Comptroller of the Currency, and the Office of Thrift Supervision monitor the commercial and thrift industries.

Until 2006, hedge funds have been excluded from these three institutions and have lacked regulatory supervision. Under the SEC and its Securities Act of 1933, firms are required to file disclosure reports. Under Regulation D (Rule 506), a hedge fund can claim the status of a private placement and by doing so is exempt from registrations and disclosure requirements. In order to apply for this designation, hedge funds cannot have more than $1 million in financial wealth or earn more than $200,000 in the previous two years.

Under the Securities Exchange Act of 1934, brokerage firms face conflict of interest to execute customer orders while trading their own accounts. Hedge funds have been exempted from registration as broker-dealers and the costly reporting requirements if they trade for their own accounts. For these cases, risks are greater as there is less third-party verification of the hedge funds' internal trading activities. In fact, fraudulent cases have been found in many such funds. In some cases, the largest hedge funds have also started their own broker-dealer operations in order to provide a new service to smaller hedge funds. For instance, WYP Asset Management and Twin WYP Fund use Man Financial as their prime broker to launch new operations as of late 2004 and trade long/short futures contracts hedging strategies.

Furthermore, hedge fund managers are exempt from registering under the Investment Advisers Act of 1940 if a hedge fund has fewer than 15 clients and if it does not solicit business from the general public. Now, note that some hedge funds have advertised their products in widely sold newspapers. Some high-profile financial newspapers have carried advertisements of hedge funds that solicit business from individuals. A collection of hedge funds have also claimed that information regarding their clients is private and confidential so hedge funds escape effective application of such laws. Such laws also constitute a market risk on their own as the concentration risk of sudden redemptions occurring could quickly limit liquidity of a fund consisting of fewer than 15 very high-net-worth clients if they redeem substantial shares simultaneously.

The 1940 Act regulates the mutual fund industry as mutual funds are considered to be investment companies. Hedge funds are not considered to be investment companies and thus are exempt from this legislation and its disclosure requirement and leverage restrictions affecting investment companies. The latest laws related to this Act increased exemptions from 99 to 499 investors provided each brings more than $5 million in assets.

There are no regulations with regard to hedge fund fee structures. Thus hedge funds' fees have been randomly higher than those of other financial vehicles, and some of their compounding effects (high-water marks) have played a detrimental role in the liquidity of the funds. In theory hedge funds trading derivatives futures contracts should register under the Commodity Exchange Act of 1974, which regulates the futures markets and aims to protect market participants against manipulation, abusive trade practices, and fraud.

Hedge funds should register with the National Futures Association (NFA) and also be approved by the Commodity Futures Trading Commission (CFTC). We notice that many hedge funds are not registered with the NFA and the CFTC. Finally, we note that the Federal Reserve and the attached agencies regulate banks, not hedge funds. The U.S. Treasury requires traders to report substantial positions in foreign exchange and U.S. Treasury securities. The SEC compels traders to report positions exceeding 5 percent of shares of a publicly traded firm. The Federal Reserve requires a limit on margin for stock purchases applying to all traders. And finally, the CFTC requires all traders to report large daily futures positions, margin, and limits on futures contracts. There are no centralized records of regulatory exams in hedge funds. Hedge funds do have an operational risk database to respond to all compliance and risk management issues as hedge funds were not required to practice operational risk management until February 2006.

Another fine advantage of using hedge funds as limited partnerships or limited liability corporations is the avoidance of double taxation. But hedge funds have been considered more as private limited partnerships to minimize high-net-worth investors' taxes. Hedge funds have purposely been created for non-U.S. individuals to register them in tax-free jurisdictions. That is why most hedge funds have a mirror structure including a limited partnership and a limited liability corporation. Tax filing is then up to the personal investor's unique situation. Offshore and U.S. investors also lucratively cooperate to report similar trading patterns in parallel. Financial statements of both entities are separately filed but could be footed with others' notes and disclosures. It would appear that many hedge funds have been used by university endowments, pension funds, wealthy family portfolios, and proprietary trading desks.

According to Fung and Hsieg (1999a, b), as of 1997, the Harvard University endowment fund was valued at $11.9 billion with $29 billion of long positions and approximately $17 billion of short positions. According to Watson Wyatt Worldwide, as of December 2004, hedge funds represented 25 percent of the total investment in alternative assets by institutions. Hedge funds' unregulated alternative investment strategies accounted for 33 percent of the insurance companies, and they accounted for 76 percent of all other institutions. They amounted to 35 percent of the total global mutual funds industry and 82 percent of the high-net-worth industry. This integration and concentration growth in various parts of the markets was also parallel with unprecedented returns. For example, Gottex Fund Management had 253.08 percent profit as of end of December 2004. Paamco reported 127.08 percent profit, Russell Investment Group gained 97.37 percent, and Credit Suisse First Boston's returns were 73 percent. Hedge funds' regulatory structures have also evolved into more or less funds of funds and private equity structures in order to avoid disclosure of internal valuations models and to reject responsibility for losses of investors and shareholders. The equity ownership is designed so that the largest concentrated fund managers of funds never own more than 50 percent in order to avoid liability for losses by investors.

Table 17.1 summarizes the evolution of hedge funds and CTA funds in number and as well as their assets sizes. The source is TASS. TASS Hedge Funds Database lists in excess of 2,000 funds and managers and serves as the foundation for the CSFB/Tremont Hedge Fund index. It contains several key features such as investment strategy and style, assets, instruments, leverage, monthly performance, and market indexes.

The Securities and Exchange Commission enforcement actions during 1997 and 2002 involving hedge funds totaled 3,076 and the Commodity Futures Trading Commission (CFTC) enforcement actions during the same period totaled 263. From the CFTC's perspective, the vast majority of the

TABLE 17.1 Evolution of Hedge Funds and CTAs

	1985	1990	1991	1992	1993	1994	1995	1996	1997
Hedge Funds	37	231	310	442	644	856	1027	1076	987
CTAs	114	404	468	557	577	558	488	363	291
Hedge Fund Assets	NA	6.5	10.1	17.9	35.8	41.3	50.4	59.4	64.6
CTA Assets	5.9	34.3	36.6	41.3	49.9	41.8	22.6	12.8	17.1

Source: Data from TASS.

54 cases involving commodity pools/CPOs were unregistered pool cases or 78 percent. Most involved outright misappropriation of investor funds. These funds had been wrongly allocated or hedged, sometimes without any futures trading.

Sometimes the limit of the number of participants was not respected, such as 250 instead of 50, or the limit on funds invested was $140 million instead of $10 million. The CFTC/NFA enforcement cases involving pools and CPOs totaled 677 cases during 1993 and 2002. About 77 of them or 11 percent were unregistered pool cases, and 48 of them or 7 percent were pool cases against registrants. The rest, 552 cases or 82 percent were non-pool or commodity pool operator (CPO) class; they represented fraud cases involving foreign exchange, precious metals, seasonality, CTA trading system, trade allocation, and investment banking fraud.

There are controversial similarities about the trends of the equity market bubbles and the one of commodities prices. And there are some remarkable correlations between the growing number of hedge funds since the mid-1990s and the number of futures contracts traded on commodities. There is an obvious relationship between the growth in hedge funds trading commodities and the growth in commodity futures contracts and also the inflation of commodity prices since then. It is unclear whether the rise in commodities prices is mainly due to hedge funds' appearance or due to the appearance of new middle classes in emerging democracies needing more natural resources. Hedge funds increasingly began to trade commodity futures contracts simultaneously when petroleum prices started to rise in parallel. It is difficult to quantify how much of the inflation of oil prices comes from hedge funds trading on inefficiencies and smoothing returns and how much comes from actual growing demand of emerging markets.

Now numerous hedge funds propose industry-specific indexes by strategies to measure isolated specific risk exposures.

Compliance has improved in hedge funds as the Global Association of Risk Professionals (GARP) risk center reported on February 3, 2006. According to Greenwich Associates, compliance costs in hedge funds occurred mostly during the year 2005 and the expenses are solely reserved for the registration of hedge funds in the United States. The expectation is that costs will rise again due to the new era of regulation involving hedge funds. Costs occurring due to registration are expected to be considerably below those of actually practicing risk management and compliance in the funds. The compliance costs incurred so far primarily relate to:

- Creating effective record keeping systems and practices especially for e-mail retention.

- Monitoring and enforcing rules regarding personal trading by fund employees.
- Getting support from senior management for compliance-related efforts.

According to Greewich Associates' survey, 90 percent of funds said their compliance staffing levels rose last year, with most funds experiencing increases on the order of 10 to 25 percent. Other significant drivers of increased compliance costs were information technology (IT) expenditures and business costs such as fees paid to outside consultants and the expense of preparing registration documentation and planning for registration.

These trends are leading us to believe that there are hopeful changes in improving transparency, compliance, and risk management in most hedge funds, first in the United States and hopefully in other offshore geographies.

CHAPTER 18

Hedge Funds' Future

As of 2005, returns in hedge funds have appeared disparate and uneven. According to Atkins and Hays (2004), one-fifth of all funds failed, and before starting to be implemented in Europe, the failure rate for European hedge funds increased from 7 percent to 10 percent per annum. Now more and more indexes are getting built without any major standardized frameworks on their methodology as they are initiated by private companies. This is positive as it fosters competition, but the new frameworks resemble themselves and there is a lack of completeness and failure to include all risks. And more and more indexes are becoming strategy- and industry-specific, which complicates the level of monitoring an industry as a whole.

Whereas the industry is evolving greatly in index formation or in instruments and strategy innovations, general trends and increased frauds and scandals have proved a lack of operational risk management, compliance, and due diligence in hedge funds and funds of funds. In the *Wall Street Journal* of December 23–26, 2005, Henny Sender reported hedge fund flows becoming more fickle. According to him, Severn River Capital Management is the prototype that indicates hedge funds are undergoing a critical phase. The Greenwich, Connecticut, fund had hired many staffers and boosted operations with an initial amount of $750 million in capital. Yet the fund never reported profits and is down 7.5 percent since its inception in 2004. Due to poor initial performance, the fund's capacity has been suffering from redemptions and consequential lack of liquidity. According to Sender, capital flows in hedge funds have been diminishing to half the level of last year and most of the capital is allocated into pools of investment vehicles for a fee to make up funds of funds to account for at least 40 percent of all inflows.

The consulting firm Mercer Oliver Wyman has reported that funds of funds and hedge funds are experiencing some withdrawals of capital. This withdrawal of capital is primarily due to the lack of performance during 2005. Another consulting firm, Lyster Watson, reported that 15 percent of its total approximated funds universe or 1,300 funds stopped reporting results on performance. This is the highest failing rate of funds in a decade. Many of them are suspected to have closed down.

However, the research study also shows that the disparate gains have been growing at incredible rates for those funds that stayed. So while some 15 percent of the entire hedge funds universe disappeared in 2005, it would appear that they have been "eaten" by bigger sharks in the markets, those that have shown incredible returns difficult to even justify from a legitimate perspective and from a consistent trading strategy. An example of such aberration is the TPG Axon fund run by an ex–Goldman Sachs head trader, Dinakar Singh, who has raised 10 percent more funds in his $5.5 billion fund, which returned 13.5 percent in the onshore and 12.6 percent in the offshore accounts.

A few problems are starting to appear with the hedge funds industry. For example, the purchase of convertible bonds is a lucrative business if the underlying company's stock drops in times of distress. But hedge funds multiplied and grew and while they all simultaneously bet on distressed companies' prices to come down, lots of those hedge funds found pricing discrepancies on the downside to tighten or narrow to ultimately create a smaller pricing spread and to defeat the initial purpose of the strategy. This is what happens when the pricing gap closes as more traders bid on the underlying security prices.

Henny Sender also mentioned another problem that arose within the funds of funds world. Funds of funds' flows are unreliable beyond the 90-day period. "These funds eschew commitments to keep their money in any one fund for more than 90 days." We may conclude that hedge funds' growth in size, in influence, and in simultaneous strategies have also caused each others' issues in the markets.

The Global Association of Risk Professionals reported as of January 2006 that the hedge fund industry was continuing to grow but at a decreasing rate; that is, we may think that the hedge fund industry is reaching a ceiling as investors are now more familiar with them and continue to use hedge funds to diversify their portfolios in more common ways.

The growth rate of net inflows has slowed from 19 percent in 2004 to 4 percent in 2005 after a peak of 34 percent in 2001. Hennessee Group estimated that the hedge fund industry's assets increased by $121 billion in 2005 to $1.12 trillion. The increase in assets accounts for 12 percent of the growth over industry assets since the beginning of 2005. This 12 percent is made up of an initial inflow of $40 billion or 4 percent, and the remaining $81 billion or 8 percent is the result of positive performance. Effectively, the Hennessee Hedge Fund index advanced 8.03 percent during 2005.

The registration of hedge funds with regulators has conveniently come late. What are the next innovative and original products and next market patterns to avoid abnormalities from traditional market returns and risk management practices?

Conclusion

The conclusion starts with the inclusion of some quotes to highlight and summarize the author's state of mind with regard to risk management in general.

"*Risk management and technological advancements balance global markets, and they create a wonderful world of illusions and dreams where everything is fake and made up and everyone is acting.*"

"*I have been a lost soul in the world of the living dead, and I am not so sure I can recover.*"

"*It takes a second to break trust; it takes years, possibly decades, to restore it and to maintain it.*"

"*Give her a book to keep her busy until then, even if she can't read, write, or speak.*"

"*We do not have the time to forget, nor can we afford to.*"

"*I can't hear you or understand you, I am conveniently deaf and stubborn in the memory of those who have left us.*"

"*Wisdom is an excuse for cowardice, hypocrisy, and an easy proof of lower intelligence; courage and rebellion are marks of honesty and sincerity of true intelligible actions.*"

"*I won't be there to see it either, but some of us already may and certainly will.*"

"*To our children and grandchildren and to those who will never understand, as too much time has gone by.*"

On the one hand, as we advanced into current times, we may argue that the lack of regulations and compliance benefited the market as it gave opportunities to renew itself with new products, concepts, trading strategies, and technologies. On the other hand, we may debate that permanently creating new products and trading strategies to privilege specific classes has also enhanced the gap between the lowest and highest social classes and has slowly eroded the middle classes' purchasing power at the cost of the new generations regardless of the classes to which they belong.

Changes in the market also changed the true way of assessing inflation on our day-to-day lives. Effectively, markets' infrastructural problems inhibit larger consequences that even higher classes can no longer sustain throughout the process of globalization. Hedge funds have basically created a new market by leveraging economical and trading inefficiencies and imperfections. By doing so, they are somewhat complementary of those other more regulated financial entities or structures. They have created a basis for new reforms and new skill sets in the financial industries and within corporate governance.

Part of the problem with the complexities of hedge fund products and lack of regulation is that hedge fund participants involve private investors and individuals who learn and network together more quickly than those involved in the bureaucratic process of implementing regulations. It is almost as if the involvement of government in the markets had become a burden in itself because of the way it has functioned for two centuries. Thus old regulatory solutions may no longer be adequate recipes for hedge funds.

During the past decade, some of the most sizable corporate mergers and acquisitions have occurred against some fundamental market laws and regulations. Why so much illegal laissez-faire in a decade?

Hedge funds have had more lucrative returns than any other financial structures and thus have had more weight and influence to change corporate governance structures in large mergers and acquisitions. Due to the sizable speculative positions they take and/or hold in events involving financial markets, their management and networking both have grown to help them become as powerful as the largest corporate entities. Yet the consequences of their last few years' stakes are left to be seen from an internal infrastructural risk management perspective and from an external compliance and regulatory reforming evolution. As they metamorphose and mutate with other financial entities, some of them may keep their hedge funds identity and structures and some of them may disappear in the mingling under the corporate governance umbrella.

As hedge funds have drastically changed the landscape of financial markets, they are overdue to be subject of gradual reforms and balanced regulatory improvements as a remedy to prevent market instability or crisis. They are to be made more regulated cautiously and carefully. Too much activism and excessive regulation could undermine hedge funds' real benefits to the innovative and efficient advancements and processes of the financial markets. Let us acknowledge that old regulations can no longer sustain new market synergies, product diversity, and technologies.

The new intelligent market regulations have to become an integral part of the markets with responsible agents working as independent regulators themselves, not as self-interested corrupt individuals. The gap between the past mentality and the hopeful mind-set is wide but certainly possible to bridge if reforms are agreed to and applied by everyone.

Statistical Data

TABLE AP I.1 Risk Management Data of Hedge Funds in Bull and Bear Markets

Data as of 2000	Bull Markets: S&P Return Rises by > 1%					Bear Markets: S&P Return Falls by > 1%				
	Rank by Sharpe Ratio	Sharpe Ratio	Average Annual Excess Return (%)	Correlation with S&P 500	Confidence Level in %	Rank by Sharpe Ratio	Sharpe Ratio	Average Annual Excess Return (%)	Correlation with S&P 500	Confidence Level in %
Equally Weighted Hedge Funds										
Market Neutral Funds	1	3.71	14.22	0.35	5	2	0.61	6.46	0.558	5
Event Driven Funds	3	3.03	24.18	0.216	10	3	-1.43	-4.19	0.792	5
Global Macro Funds	4	2.88	23.71	0.344	5	4	-1.44	-4.52	0.317	5
Sector-Specific Funds	2	3.06	40.28	0.361	5	7	-2.28	-21.48	0.611	5
Funds of Funds	7	2.07	15.88	0.223	10	5	-1.6	-3.61	0.657	5
Long-Only Funds	6	2.24	40.02	0.419	5	6	-1.91	-25.02	0.636	5
Global Funds	5	2.56	28.88	0.466	5	8	-2.73	-20.71	0.834	5
Short Sell Funds	8	-1.46	-19.13	-0.453	5	1	3.44	61.39	-0.698	5
All Equally Weighted Hedge Funds	NA	2.9	22.06	0.406	5	NA	-2.11	-7.62	0.792	5
Value-Weighted Hedge Funds										
Market Neutral Funds	1	2.56	9.59	0.113		2	0.27	5.46	0.665	5
Event Driven Funds	4	2.46	18.66	0.058		4	-0.59	1.62	0.751	5
Global Macro Funds	7	2.05	32.28	-0.013		3	-0.33	0.44	0.302	
Funds of Funds	2	2.51	20.71	0.323	5	7	-2.17	-8.82	0.651	5
Global Funds	3	2.49	29.03	0.428	5	8	-2.49	-19.22	0.822	5
Sector-Specific Funds	5	2.19	35.04	0.273	5	6	-1.97	-22.2	0.311	
Long-Only Funds	6	2.12	39.92	0.487	5	5	-1.9	-26.48	0.608	5
Short Sell Funds	8	-0.92	-7.61	-0.375	5	1	2.65	40.79	-0.641	5
All Value-Weighted Hedge Funds	NA	2.48	25.67	0.068		NA	-1.04	-3.85	0.556	5

Equally Weighted Commodity Funds

Financial CTAs	3	1.18	14.89	0.383	5	1	1.45	17.26	-0.435	5
Stock CTAs	1	1.97	16.97	0.304	5	8	-1.17	-2.27	0.266	
Agriculture CTAs	2	1.32	19.16	-0.137		7	0.42	9.44	-0.333	
Currency CTAs	6	0.32	8.28	0.227	10	2	1.4	19.64	0.183	
Diversified CTAs	4	0.62	11.3	0.161		3	1.34	18.9	-0.438	5
Private CTAs	5	0.42	8.9	0.188		4	0.75	12.14	-0.514	5
Public CTAs	7	0.13	6.12	0.245	10	6	0.51	9.64	-0.446	5
Energy CTAs	8	-0.65	-3.16	0.173		5	0.55	11.66	-0.261	
All Equally Weighted Commodities Funds	NA	0.54	11.77	0.231	10		1.31	17.18	-0.39	10

Value-Weighted Commodity Funds

Private Pools	1	1.05	13.43	0.194		1	1.88	20.16	-0.521	5
Financial CTAs	2	0.75	14.47	0.33	5	3	1.31	21.64	-0.409	5
Diversified CTAs	3	0.62	11.41	0.18		2	1.39	19.58	-0.491	5
Agriculture CTAs	5	0.49	8.41	0.007		7	0.81	10.81	-0.067	
Public Funds	4	0.52	9.94	0.282	5	6	0.83	12.9	-0.318	
Currency CTAs	6	0.05	5.44	0.189		5	1	15.36	0.004	
Stock CTAs	7	-0.45	1.21	-0.037		4	1.3	15.42	-0.032	
Energy CTAs	8	-0.67	-5.76	0.066		8	-0.36	-0.77	0.248	
All Valued Weighted Commodities Funds	NA	0.55	10.63	0.227	5	NA	1.45	19.66	-0.443	5

Source: Data from Alexander Fabre-Bulle and Sebastien Pache, "The Omega Measure: Hedge Fund Portfolio Optimization," University of Lausanne, Ecole des HEC, 2003. Data from eLibrary, www.ssrn.com, or Social Science Research Network and altered by the author.

TABLE AP 1.2 Risk Management Data Ratios of Hedge Funds in Bull and Bear Markets

Data as of 2000	Bull Markets			Bear Markets		
	Rank by Increase in Sharpe Ratio	Change in Sharpe Ratio of Optimal Portfolio	Weight in Optimal Portfolio in %	Rank by Increase in Sharpe Ratio	Change in Sharpe Ratio of Optimal Portfolio	Weight in Optimal Portfolio in %
Equally Weighted Hedge Funds						
Market Neutral Funds	2	0.35	58	2	1.75	100
Event Driven Funds	1	0.96	55	3	1.5	100
Global Macro Funds	4	0.17	24	NA	0	0
Sector-Specific Funds	3	0.33	34	NA	0	0
Funds of Funds	5	0.16	12	1	4.7	76
Long-Only Funds	8	0.03	8	NA	0	0
Global Funds	6	0.08	18	NA	0	0
Short Sell Funds	7	0.07	22	NA	0	0
All Equally Weighted Hedge Funds	NA	0.24	43	NA	0	0
Value-Weighted Hedge Funds						
Market Neutral Funds	3	0.18	42	NA	0	0
Event Driven Funds	1	0.89	49	3	0.81	100
Global Macro Funds	2	0.48	16	2	0.86	100
Funds of Funds	4	0.15	25	NA	0	0
Global Funds	6	0.06	14	NA	0	0
Sector-Specific Funds	5	0.11	12	1	4.12	100
Long-Only Funds	NA	0	0	NA	0	0
Short Sell Funds	NA	0	0	NA	0	0
All Value-Weighted Hedge Funds	NA	0.43	25	NA	0	0

Equally Weighted Commodity Funds

Financial CTAs	NA	0	0	2	2.52	100
Stock CTAs	1	0.42	14	5	1.86	100
Agriculture CTAs	NA	0	0	3	2.42	100
Currency CTAs	NA	0	0	1	2.71	100
Diversified CTAs	2	0.11	19	8	0.21	100
Private CTAs	NA	0	0	4	1.9	100
Public CTAs	NA	0	0	6	1.67	100
Energy CTAs	NA	0	0	7	1.63	100
All Equally Weighted Commodities Funds	NA	0	0	NA	2.38	100

Value-Weighted Commodity Funds

Private Pools	2	0.01	3	1	2.95	100
Financial CTAs	1	0.04	9	6	2.2	100
Diversified CTAs	NA	0	0	3	2.48	100
Agriculture CTAs	NA	0	0	2	2.51	100
Public Funds	NA	0	0	5	2.22	100
Currency CTAs	NA	0	0	4	2.29	100
Stock CTAs	NA	0	0	7	2	100
Energy CTAs	NA	0	0	8	0.92	100
All Value-Weighted Commodities Funds	NA	0	0	NA	2.62	100

The change in the Sharpe ratio of the optimal portfolio is calculated as the difference between the Sharpe ratio of the optimal benchmark portfolio and the Sharpe ratio calculated after the equally weighted funds, the value-weighted funds, and the commodity funds are added into the optimal benchmark portfolio. The optimal benchmark portfolio in the bull markets consists of 56% S&P index, 17% intermediate-term government bonds, and 27% other securities, and has a Sharpe ratio of 5.31.

Change in the Sharpe ratio of the optimal portfolio is calculated in the same way: It is the difference between the Sharpe ratios before and after the equally weighted funds and the value-weighted funds portfolios of hedge funds and commodities funds are added into the optimal benchmark portfolio. The optimal benchmark portfolio in the bear markets consists of 100% allocated in intermediate-term government bonds. It has a Sharpe ratio of –1.21.

Source: Data from Alexander Fabre-Bulle and Sebastien Pache, "The Omega Measure: Hedge Fund Portfolio Optimization," University of Lausanne, Ecole des HEC, 2003. Data coming from www.ssrn.com or from the Social Science Research Network and altered by the author.

TABLE AP I.3 Risk Management Data Ratios of Hedge Funds

Data as of 2000	Sharpe Ratio	Ranking by Sharpe Ratio	Roy's Criteria with 10% Minimum Annual Return	Ranking by Roy's Criteria	Kataoka's Criteria with $x - 5\%$ Minimum Annual Return	Ranking by Kataoka's Criteria
Equally Weighted Hedge Funds						
Market Neutral Funds	3.06	1	1.03	1	8.44	1
Event Driven Funds	1.77	2	0.96	3	5.66	2
Global Macro Funds	1.69	3	0.9	4	5.14	3
Sector-Specific Funds	1.42	4	0.97	2	2.21	4
Funds of Funds	1.11	5	0.14	7	2.03	5
Long-Only Funds	1.09	6	0.77	5	-3.76	7
Global Funds	1.05	7	0.5	6	-0.76	6
Short Sell Funds	0.13	8	NA	NA	-20.05	8
Value-Weighted Hedge Funds						
Market Neutral Funds	1.83	1	NA	NA	5.25	1
Event Driven Funds	1.64	2	0.73	2	4.86	2
Global Macro Funds	1.42	3	1.04	1	1.91	4
Funds of Funds	1.22	4	0.41	6	2.19	3
Global Funds	1.08	5	0.55	3	-0.63	5
Sector-Specific Funds	0.89	6	0.52	5	-5.5	6
Long-Only Funds	0.84	7	0.53	4	-8.48	7
Short Sell Funds	0.16	8	NA	NA	-15.23	8

Equally Weighted Commodity Funds

	Roy		Kataoka		Omega	
Financial CTAs	1.19	1	0.58	1	0.96	1
Stock CTAs	0.97	2	0.14	2	0.74	2
Agriculture CTAs	0.93	3	0.46	3	-2.8	3
Currency CTAs	0.79	4	0.3	3	-4.18	4
Diversified CTAs	0.77	5	0.27	4	-4.35	5
Private CTAs	0.43	6	NA	NA	-6.84	6
Public CTAs	0.2	7	NA	NA	-8.6	7
Energy CTAs	-0.06	8	NA	NA	-16.13	8

Value-Weighted Commodity Funds

	Roy		Kataoka		Omega	
Private Pools	1.21	1	0.58	1	1.36	1
Financial CTAs	0.85	2	0.45	2	-5.34	4
Diversified CTAs	0.83	3	0.35	3	-3.73	3
Agriculture CTAs	0.71	4	0.01	6	-1.92	2
Public Funds	0.56	5	0.03	4	-5.67	5
Currency CTAs	0.51	6	0.02	5	-6.9	7
Stock CTAs	0.27	7	NA	NA	-6.26	6
Energy CTAs	-0.48	8	NA	NA	-28.61	8

Assumptions: Roy's criteria values are computed for a 10% annual return; that is, a 10% return is assumed to be the level of return below which the investors do not want to fall. To compute Roy's criteria, the minimum return should lie below the mean return of the portfolio. Any hedge fund portfolio that has an annual return below 10% is omitted from the analysis. Kataoka's criteria values are derived according to the predetermined probability value of $x - 5\%$.

Source: Data from Alexander Fabre-Bulle and Sebastien Pache, "The Omega Measure: Hedge Fund Portfolio Optimization," University of Lausanne, Ecole des HEC, 2003. Data coming from www.ssrn.com or from the Social Science Research Network and altered by the author.

TABLE AP I.4 Risk Management Data Ratios

Data as of 2000	Sharpe Ratio			Roy's Criteria			Kataoka's Criteria		
	Rank by Sharpe Ratio of Optimal Portfolio	Sharpe Ratio of Optimal Portfolio	Weight in Optimal Portfolio in %	Rank by Roy's Criteria of Optimal Portfolio	Roy's Criteria of Optimal Portfolio	Weight in Optimal Portfolio in %	Rank by Kataoka's Criteria of Optimal Portfolio	Kataoka's Criteria of Optimal Portfolio in %	Weight in Optimal Portfolio in %
Equally Weighted Hedge Funds									
Market Neutral Funds	1	3.08	96	1	1.03	100	1	8.45	98
Event Driven Funds	2	1.85	72	3	0.96	100	2	5.96	83
Global Macro Funds	3	1.73	74	4	0.9	100	3	5.3	78
Sector-Specific Funds	4	1.51	51	2	0.97	100	5	3.98	42
Funds of Funds	5	1.5	35	7	0.41	24	4	4.33	33
Long-Only Funds	6	1.37	36	5	0.74	88	8	2.76	23
Global Funds	7	1.25	64	NA	0.38	0	6	3.35	54
Short Sell Funds	8	1.22	45	6	0.5	90	7	2.89	33
Value-Weighted Hedge Funds									
Market Neutral Funds	1	2.01	83	NA	0.38	0	1	5.57	89
Event Driven Funds	2	1.79	73	2	0.73	92	2	5.53	78
Global Macro Funds	3	1.53	45	1	1.04	90	3	4.08	37
Funds of Funds	4	1.3	63	6	0.44	74	4	3.32	53
Global Funds	5	1.24	44	3	0.55	95	5	2.92	33
Sector-Specific Funds	6	1.16	26	NA	0.38	0	6	2.91	23
Long-Only Funds	7	1.08	28	4	0.53	75	8	1.97	17
Short Sell Funds	8	1.07	29	5	0.52	76	7	2.01	16

Equally Weighted Commodity Funds

Fund									
Financial CTAs	1	1.43	58	1	0.69	71	1	3.71	47
Stock CTAs	2	1.39	38	2	0.6	56	2	3.64	29
Agriculture CTAs	3	1.23	34	3	0.5	49	3	2.97	27
Currency CTAs	4	1.2	33	4	0.49	50	5	2.83	24
Diversified CTAs	5	1.17	50	NA	0.38	0	4	2.96	40
Private CTAs	6	1	22	NA	0.38	0	6	2.06	18
Public CTAs	7	0.94	8	NA	0.38	0	7	1.71	11
Energy CTAs	8	0.93	3	NA	0.38	0	8	1.7	7

Value-Weighted Commodity Funds

Fund									
Private Pools	1	1.59	57	1	0.74	70	1	4.61	55
Financial CTAs	2	1.27	37	4	0.39	12	2	3.49	34
Diversified CTAs	3	1.25	38	3	0.55	54	3	2.91	28
Agriculture CTAs	4	1.2	33	2	0.59	55	5	2.53	21
Public Funds	5	1.08	27	NA	0.38	0	4	2.83	25
Currency CTAs	6	1.06	24	4	0.39	11	6	2.33	19
Stock CTAs	7	1.04	25	4	0.39	16	7	2.12	18
Energy CTAs	NA	0.92	0	NA	0.38	0	NA	1.51	0

Risk Management Assumptions: The benchmark portfolio is made up of 23% S&P 500 index, 3% U.S. small stock index, 70% intermediate-term government bonds, and 4% long-term government bonds, and has a Sharpe ratio of 0.92.

Roy's criteria measure is 0.38.

Roy's criteria are computed for a 10% annual return.

To compute Roy's criteria, the minimum return should lie below the mean return of the portfolio.

The optimal benchmark portfolio consists of 3% S&P 500 index, 8% U.S. small stock index, and 89% intermediate-term government bonds.

It has Kataoka's criteria measure of 1.51. Kataoka criteria values are derived according to the predetermined probability value of $x - 5\%$.

Source: Data from Alexander Fabre-Bulle and Sebastien Pache, "The Omega Measure: Hedge Fund Portfolio Optimization," University of Lausanne, Ecole des HEC, 2003. Data coming from www.ssrn.com or from the Social Science Research Network and altered by the author.

TABLE AP I.5 Attrition Rates for All Hedge Funds in the TASS and
CSFB/Tremont Hedge Fund Database and within Each Style Category from
January 1994 to August 2004

Year	Existing Funds	New Entries	New Exits	Intrayear Entry and Exit	Total Funds	Attrition Rate (%)	Index Return (%)
All Funds							
1994	769	251	23	2	997	3	−4.4
1995	997	299	61	1	1,235	6.1	21.7
1996	1,235	332	120	9	1,447	9.7	22.2
1997	1,447	356	100	6	1,703	6.9	25.9
1998	1,703	346	162	9	1,887	9.5	−0.4
1999	1,887	403	183	7	2,107	9.7	23.4
2000	2,107	391	234	9	2,264	11.1	4.8
2001	2,264	460	257	6	2,467	11.4	4.4
2002	2,467	432	246	9	2,653	10	3
2003	2,653	325	285	12	2,693	10.7	15.5
2004	2,693	1	87	1	2,607	3.2	2.7
Equity Market Neutral							
1994	12	7	1	0	18	8.3	−2
1995	18	10	0	0	28	0	11
1996	28	10	0	0	38	0	16.6
1997	38	14	0	0	52	0	14.8
1998	52	29	2	2	79	3.8	13.3
1999	79	36	14	1	101	17.7	15.3
2000	101	17	13	0	105	12.9	15
2001	105	49	9	0	145	8.6	9.3
2002	145	41	14	2	172	9.7	7.4
2003	172	23	32	0	163	18.6	7.1
2004	163	0	5	0	158	3.1	4.7
Long/Short Equity							
1994	168	52	2	0	218	1.2	−8.1
1995	218	74	7	0	285	3.2	23
1996	285	116	21	2	380	7.4	17.1
1997	380	118	15	2	483	3.9	21.5
1998	483	117	33	2	567	6.8	47.2
1999	567	159	42	3	684	7.4	2.1
2000	684	186	55	5	815	8	−3.7
2001	815	156	109	3	862	13.4	−1.6
2002	862	137	107	5	892	12.4	17.3
2003	892	83	110	2	865	12.3	1.5
2004	865	0	27	0	838	3.1	

TABLE AP 1.5 *(Continued)*

Year	Existing Funds	New Entries	New Exits	Intrayear Entry and Exit	Total Funds	Attrition Rate (%)	Index Return (%)
Convertible Arbitrage							
1994	26	13	0	0	39	0	−8.1
1995	39	12	0	0	51	0	16.6
1996	51	14	7	0	58	13.7	17.9
1997	58	10	3	0	65	5.2	14.5
1998	65	14	5	0	74	7.7	−4.4
1999	74	10	3	0	81	4.1	16
2000	81	17	3	0	95	3.7	25.6
2001	95	25	5	0	115	5.3	14.6
2002	115	22	6	0	131	5.2	4
2003	131	11	10	0	132	7.6	12.9
2004	132	0	10	0	122	7.6	0.6
Event Driven							
1994	71	16	0	0	87	0	0.7
1995	87	27	1	0	113	1.1	18.4
1996	113	29	3	0	139	2.7	23
1997	139	31	3	0	167	2.2	20
1998	167	28	2	1	193	1.2	−4.9
1999	193	29	19	1	203	9.8	22.3
2000	203	38	15	0	226	7.4	7.2
2001	226	34	19	3	241	8.4	11.5
2002	241	40	30	2	251	12.4	0.2
2003	251	21	23	1	249	9.2	20
2004	249	0	15	0	234	6	5.7
Managed Futures							
1994	181	52	8	1	225	4.4	11.9
1995	225	41	30	0	236	13.3	−7.1
1996	236	42	49	2	229	20.8	12
1997	229	37	36	1	230	15.7	3.1
1998	230	25	37	0	218	16.1	20.7
1999	218	35	40	1	213	18.3	−4.7
2000	213	13	35	0	191	16.4	4.3
2001	191	18	19	0	190	9.9	1.9
2002	190	22	32	0	180	16.8	18.3
2003	180	23	21	2	182	11.7	14.2
2004	182	0	5	0	177	2.7	−7

(Continued)

TABLE AP I.5   *(Continued)*

Year	Existing Funds	New Entries	New Exits	Intrayear Entry and Exit	Total Funds	Attrition Rate (%)	Index Return (%)
Dedicated Short Selling							
1994	11	1	0	0	12	0	14.9
1995	12	0	1	0	11	8.3	−7.4
1996	11	3	1	0	13	9.1	−5.5
1997	13	3	1	0	15	7.7	0.4
1998	15	1	0	0	16	0	−6
1999	16	4	1	0	19	6.3	−14.2
2000	19	2	1	0	20	5.3	15.8
2001	20	1	6	0	15	30	−3.6
2002	15	1	1	0	15	6.7	18.2
2003	15	1	1	0	15	6.7	−32.6
2004	15	0	2	0	13	13.3	9.1
Fixed Income Arbitrage							
1994	22	16	3	0	35	13.6	0.3
1995	35	12	2	0	45	5.7	12.5
1996	45	16	4	0	57	8.9	15.9
1997	57	15	4	1	68	7	9.4
1998	68	16	14	0	70	20.6	−8.2
1999	70	13	8	0	75	11.4	12.1
2000	75	9	11	0	73	14.7	6.3
2001	73	20	7	0	86	9.6	8
2002	86	23	5	0	104	5.8	5.7
2003	104	12	9	0	107	8.7	8
2004	107	0	4	0	103	3.7	4.7
Multi-Strategy							
1994	17	5	3	1	19	17.6	0
1995	19	7	2	0	24	10.5	11.9
1996	24	14	1	0	37	4.2	14
1997	37	13	3	0	47	8.1	18.3
1998	47	8	5	1	50	10.6	7.7
1999	50	10	2	0	58	4	9.4
2000	58	10	2	1	66	3.4	11.2
2001	66	16	1	0	81	1.5	5.5
2002	81	14	5	0	90	6.2	6.3
2003	90	14	14	4	90	15.6	15
2004	90	0	0	0	90	0	2.8

TABLE AP I.5 *(Continued)*

Year	Existing Funds	New Entries	New Exits	Intrayear Entry and Exit	Total Funds	Attrition Rate (%)	Index Return (%)
Emerging Markets							
1994	44	25	0	0	69	0	12.5
1995	69	34	1	0	102	1.4	−16.9
1996	102	25	4	0	123	3.9	34.5
1997	123	40	8	0	155	6.5	26.6
1998	155	22	25	1	152	16.1	−37.7
1999	152	26	18	0	160	11.8	44.8
2000	160	20	25	2	155	15.6	−5.5
2001	155	5	28	0	132	18.1	5.8
2002	132	4	11	0	125	8.3	7.4
2003	125	12	13	1	124	10.4	28.7
2004	124	0	1	0	123	0.8	3.1
Global Macro							
1994	50	11	3	0	58	6	−5.7
1995	58	19	5	0	72	8.6	30.7
1996	72	16	13	4	75	18.1	25.6
1997	75	19	6	1	88	8	37.1
1998	88	20	7	2	101	8	−3.6
1999	101	12	15	1	98	14.9	5.8
2000	98	18	33	0	83	33.7	11.7
2001	83	15	9	0	89	10.8	18.4
2002	89	26	9	0	106	10.1	14.7
2003	106	15	8	1	113	7.5	18
2004	113	0	1	0	112	0.9	4.4
Fund of Funds							
1994	167	53	3	0	217	1.8	0
1995	217	63	12	1	268	5.5	0
1996	268	47	17	1	298	6.3	0
1997	298	56	21	1	333	7	0
1998	333	66	32	0	367	9.6	0
1999	367	69	21	0	415	5.7	0
2000	415	61	41	1	435	9.9	0
2001	435	121	45	0	511	10.3	0
2002	511	102	26	0	587	5.1	0
2003	587	110	44	1	653	7.5	0
2004	653	1	17	1	637	2.6	0

Index returns are annual compound returns of the CSFB/Tremont Hedge Fund indexes. *Note:* Attrition rates for 2004 are severely downward biased as there is a timing lag of 8 to 10 months before moving a nonreporting fund from the Live to the Graveyard database. Thus as of August 2004 many nonreporting funds in the Live database have not yet been moved to the Graveyard database.
Source: Data from Alexander Fabre-Bulle and Sebastien Pache, "The Omega Measure: Hedge Fund Portfolio Optimization," University of Lausanne, Ecole des HEC, 2003. Data from eLibrary, www.ssrn.com, or Social Science Research Network and altered by the author.

TABLE AP I.6 Decomposition of Attrition Rates and Returns by Category for All Hedge Funds in the TASS and CSFB/Tremont Hedge Fund Database from January 1994 to August 2004

Year	All Funds	Convertible Arbitrage	Short Biased	Dedicated Emerging Markets	Market Neutral	Equity Event Driven	Income Arbitrage	Fixed Global Macro	Short Equity	Long/Managed Futures	Multi-Strategy	Fund of Funds
Total Attrition Rates and Components by Category (in %)												
1994	3	0	0	0	0.1	0	0.4	0.4	0.3	1	0.4	0.4
1995	6.1	0	0.1	0.1	0	0.1	0.2	0.5	0.7	3	0.2	1.2
1996	9.7	0.6	0.1	0.3	0	0.2	0.3	1.1	1.7	4	0.1	1.4
1997	6.9	0.2	0.1	0.6	0.1	0.2	0.3	0.4	1	2.5	0.2	1.5
1998	9.5	0.3	0	1.5	0.7	0.1	0.8	0.4	1.9	2.2	0.3	1.9
1999	9.7	0.2	0.1	1	0.7	1	0.4	0.8	2.2	2.1	0.1	1.1
2000	11.1	0.1	0	1.2	0.6	0.7	0.5	1.6	2.6	1.7	0.1	1.9
2001	11.4	0.2	0.3	1.2	0.4	0.8	0.3	0.4	4.8	0.8	0	2
2002	10	0.2	0	0.4	0.6	1.2	0.2	0.4	4.3	1.3	0.2	1.1
2003	10.7	0.4	0	0.5	1.2	0.9	0.3	0.3	4.1	0.8	0.5	1.7
2004	3.2	0.4	0.1	0	0.2	0.6	0.1	0	1	0.2	0	0.6
Mean	8.8	0.2	0.1	0.7	0.4	0.5	0.4	0.6	2.4	1.9	0.2	1.4
Standard Deviation	2.7	0.2	0.1	0.5	0.4	0.4	0.2	0.4	1.6	1	0.2	0.5
Annual Returns of CSFB/Tremont Hedge Fund Indexes by Category (in %)												
1994	-4.4	-8.1	14.9	12.5	-2	0.7	0.3	-5.7	-8.1	11.9	0	0
1995	21.7	16.6	-7.4	-16.9	11	18.4	12.5	30.7	23	-7.1	11.9	0
1996	22.2	17.9	-5.5	34.5	16.6	23	15.9	25.6	17.1	12	14	0
1997	25.9	14.5	0.4	26.6	14.8	20	9.4	37.1	21.5	3.1	18.3	0
1998	-0.4	-4.4	-6	-37.7	13.3	-4.9	-8.2	-3.6	17.2	20.7	7.7	0
1999	23.4	16	-14.2	44.8	15.3	22.3	12.1	5.8	47.2	-4.7	9.4	0
2000	4.8	25.6	15.8	-5.5	15	7.2	6.3	11.7	2.1	4.3	11.2	0
2001	4.4	14.6	-3.6	5.8	9.3	11.5	8	18.4	-3.7	1.9	5.5	0

	3	4										
2002	15.5	12.9	18.2	7.4	7.4	0.2	5.7	14.7	-1.6	18.3	6.3	0
2003			-32.6	28.7	7.1	20	8	18	17.3	14.2	15	0
2004	2.7	0.6	9.1	3.1	4.7	5.7	4.7	4.4	1.5	-7	2.8	0
Mean	11.6	11	-2	10	10.8	11.8	7	15.3	13.2	7.5	11	0
Standard Deviation	11.3	10.5	15.5	25.2	5.6	10.4	6.8	13.9	16.5	9.4	4.3	0

Total Assets under Management (in $MM) and Percent Breakdown by Category (in %)

	Total Assets											
1994	57,684	3.8	0.7	9.3	1	9.5	3.9	20.5	20.7	5.1	7.5	18
1995	69,477	3.9	0.5	8.1	1.3	10	4.7	18.5	22.9	4	9.2	17
1996	92,513	4.2	0.4	8.7	2.3	10.1	5.9	17.9	23.4	3.2	7.8	16.1
1997	137,814	4.7	0.4	8.9	2.7	10.4	6.7	18.8	21.9	2.7	7.5	15.3
1998	142,669	5.5	0.6	4	4.4	12.5	5.7	16.8	24.4	3.3	6.8	16
1999	175,223	5.3	0.6	4.6	5.2	11.7	4.6	9.1	34.5	2.8	6.6	15.1
2000	197,120	5.4	0.5	2.5	5.5	10.6	3.3	1.9	31.1	1.9	4.4	12.7
2001	246,695	8.1	0.3	2.8	7.4	13.9	4.7	2.3	35.3	3	5.5	16.6
2002	277,695	8.5	0.3	3.1	7.2	13	6.2	3.1	30.2	3.9	6.1	18.4
2003	389,965	8.8	0.1	4.3	6	13	6.2	5.4	25.7	5	5.8	19.7
2004	403,974	8.8	0.2	4.2	5.9	13.5	7.1	6.6	26.3	5.3	6.8	15.3
Mean	178,685	5.8	0.5	5.6	4.3	11.5	5.2	11.4	27	3.5	6.7	16.5
Standard Deviation	103,484	1.9	0.2	2.8	2.4	1.5	1.1	7.8	5.3	1	1.4	2

Assumptions: There is a delay of 8 to 10 months before moving a nonreporting fund from the Live to the Graveyard database; therefore, as of August 2004, many nonreporting funds in the Live database have not yet been moved to the Graveyard. Consequently, the reported means and standard deviations in all three panels computed over 2004 is overstated.

Source: Data from Alexander Fabre-Bulle and Sebastien Pache, "The Omega Measure: Hedge Fund Portfolio Optimization," University of Lausanne, Ecole des HEC, 2003. Data from eLibrary, www.ssrn.com, or Social Science Research Network and altered by the author.

TABLE AP I.7 Means and Standard Deviations of Maximum Likelihood Estimates of MA (2) Smoothing Process R = etc. for Coefficients

	Sample Size	1 Mean	1 z-Statistic	2 Mean	2 z-Statistic	3 Mean	3 z-Statistic	Residual Coefficient Mean	Residual Coefficient z-Statistic
Live Funds									
Convertible Arbitrage	57	0.724	12.15	0.201	9.16	0.076	5.67	0.635	7.42
Dedicated Short Selling	8	0.96	1.66	0.091	8.22	-0.051	-1.73	0.944	1.12
Emerging Markets	87	0.818	14.99	0.157	17.56	0.025	2.43	0.723	14.15
Equity Market Neutral	49	0.887	3.88	0.034	1.17	0.079	3.93	0.894	1.8
Event Driven	128	0.774	19.63	0.158	16.75	0.068	8.61	0.665	18.68
Fixed Income Arbitrage	43	0.789	9.8	0.144	9.67	0.067	4.36	0.686	10.06
Global Macro	48	0.989	0.44	0.053	2.8	-0.042	-2.04	1.048	-0.86
Long/Short Equity	389	0.871	14.08	0.099	15.78	0.03	4.06	0.838	7.68
Managed Futures	104	1.09	-5.16	0.009	0.74	-0.099	-8.51	1.257	-5.99
Multi-Strategy	39	0.777	10.45	0.13	7.47	0.093	7.93	0.663	10.31
Fund of Funds	274	0.856	3.18	0.104	3.87	0.04	1.98	1.61	-0.77
All	1,226	0.865	12.04	0.106	15.34	0.029	5.15	1.011	-0.06
Dead Funds									
Convertible Arbitrage	22	0.705	10.54	0.203	10.52	0.092	4.11	0.582	11.51
Dedicated Short Selling	8	1.18	-0.74	0	0	-0.179	-1.09	2.073	-0.55
Emerging Markets	49	0.868	4.98	0.126	7.54	-0.006	0.34	0.831	2.54
Equity Market Neutral	16	0.902	1.86	0.089	2.4	0.009	0.31	0.897	1.17
Event Driven	55	0.812	8.34	0.158	11.37	0.029	1.75	0.739	6.65
Fixed Income Arbitrage	22	0.749	5.49	0.151	6.1	0.1	3.11	0.672	4.09
Global Macro	40	1.012	-0.31	0.041	1.35	-0.053	-2.15	1.14	-1.45
Long/Short Equity	143	0.905	6.6	0.072	683	0.023	2.09	0.887	3.93
Managed Futures	126	1.131	-4.58	-0.066	-3.21	-0.065	-3.84	1.479	-4.47
Multi-Strategy	8	0.944	0.8	0.031	0.47	0.026	1.17	0.96	0.28
Fund of Funds	122	0.913	3.76	0.099	7.43	-0.012	-0.81	0.958	0.74
All	611	0.94	5.47	0.065	9.12	-0.006	-0.85	1.02	-0.61

TASS Live and Graveyard databases with at least five years of returns history during the period from November 1977 to August 2004; z-statistics are asymptotically standard normal distribution.

Source: Data from Alexander Fabre-Bulle and Sebastien Pache, "The Omega Measure: Hedge Fund Portfolio Optimization," University of Lausanne, Ecole des HEC, 2003. Data from eLibrary, www.ssrn.com, or Social Science Research Network and altered by the author.

TABLE AP I.8 Overall Hedge Fund Survival Rates

This table shows what percentage of the hedge funds alive in June of each year survived for more than 1, 2, . . . 60 months.

Months	2000	1999	1998	1997	1996	1995	1994
1	100.00%	100.00%	100.00%	100.00%	100.00%	100.00%	100.00%
2	98.95%	99.17%	99.19%	99.79%	99.36%	99.50%	100.00%
3	97.99%	98.43%	97.58%	99.27%	98.84%	99.16%	100.00%
4	97.59%	97.28%	96.46%	98.75%	97.69%	99.16%	100.00%
5	96.70%	96.53%	95.65%	98.54%	96.92%	99.16%	100.00%
6	95.58%	95.71%	94.93%	98.23%	96.79%	99.16%	99.78%
7	94.29%	94.39%	94.36%	98.12%	96.40%	98.99%	99.78%
8	92.04%	92.74%	93.80%	97.18%	95.50%	98.83%	98.68%
9	91.24%	91.75%	93.48%	96.98%	95.37%	98.66%	98.68%
10	89.31%	91.34%	93.08%	96.45%	95.24%	97.99%	98.46%
11	88.42%	90.43%	91.63%	95.52%	94.47%	97.65%	98.24%
12	87.70%	88.45%	90.90%	95.10%	93.83%	97.48%	97.80%
13		87.71%	90.50%	94.79%	93.70%	97.48%	97.58%
14		86.63%	89.89%	93.85%	93.57%	96.64%	97.14%
15		85.64%	89.21%	91.76%	93.06%	95.97%	96.70%
16		85.31%	88.41%	90.62%	92.67%	94.63%	96.70%
17		84.57%	87.76%	90.20%	92.54%	93.62%	96.70%
18		83.58%	87.12%	89.26%	92.29%	93.46%	96.70%
19		82.51%	86.07%	88.74%	92.29%	92.95%	96.48%
20		80.36%	84.54%	88.22%	91.13%	92.11%	96.26%
21		79.62%	83.66%	87.80%	90.87%	91.55%	96.04%
22		78.05%	83.33%	87.28%	90.23%	91.78%	95.38%
23		77.23%	82.77%	85.51%	89.59%	90.94%	94.95%
24		76.49%	81.16%	84.78%	89.20%	90.60%	94.73%
25			80.52%	84.46%	89.07%	90.44%	94.73%
26			79.55%	83.63%	88.17%	90.27%	93.85%
27			78.66%	82.79%	86.12%	89.60%	92.97%
28			78.50%	81.86%	84.83%	89.09%	91.43%
29			77.78%	81.13%	84.45%	88.93%	90.33%
30			76.89%	80.50%	83.68%	88.59%	90.11%
31			75.03%	79.56%	83.16%	88.59%	89.45%
32			73.91%	78.31%	82.52%	88.26%	88.79%
33			73.35%	77.89%	82.13%	87.92%	88.57%
34			72.46%	77.69%	81.75%	87.42%	88.35%
35			71.66%	77.06%	79.56%	86.91%	87.91%
36			71.01%	75.50%	78.92%	86.74%	87.69%
37				74.87%	78.53%	86.58%	87.47%
38				74.04%	77.76%	85.74%	87.25%

(Continued)

TABLE AP I.8   *(Continued)*

This table shows what percentage of the hedge funds alive in June of each year survived for more than 1, 2, . . . 60 months.

Months	2000	1999	1998	1997	1996	1995	1994
39				72.99%	76.86%	83.89%	86.37%
40				72.78%	75.84%	82.72%	85.71%
41				71.85%	75.32%	82.21%	85.49%
42				71.12%	74.81%	81.54%	85.27%
43				70.28%	74.16%	81.21%	85.27%
44				67.67%	73.01%	80.54%	84.84%
45				67.05%	72.62%	80.03%	84.62%
46				66.11%	72.49%	79.70%	84.18%
47				65.17%	71.85%	77.52%	83.74%
48				64.75%	70.31%	76.85%	83.52%
49					69.67%	76.68%	83.30%
50					68.77%	76.01%	82.42%
51					67.61%	75.17%	81.32%
52					67.35%	74.50%	80.66%
53					66.32%	74.33%	80.22%
54					65.68%	73.99%	79.34%
55					64.78%	73.15%	78.90%
56					61.95%	71.98%	78.24%
57					61.31%	71.98%	77.58%
58					60.41%	71.98%	77.14%
59					59.77%	73.31%	75.38%
60					59.51%	69.97%	74.51%

Source: Data from Alexander Fabre-Bulle and Sebastien Pache, "The Omega Measure: Hedge Fund Portfolio Optimization," University of Lausanne, Ecole des HEC, 2003. Data from www.ssrn.com, or Social Science Research Network and altered by the author.
Data also available from G. Amin and H. Kat, "Welcome to the Dark Side: Hedge Fund Attrition and Survivorship Bias over the Period 1994–2001," working paper, Case Business School, 2003; *Journal of Alternative Investments* 6, 57–73.

TABLE AP I.9 Ratios of Dead and Surviving Hedge Funds over Seven Different Time Periods

Class	2000/ 2001	1999/ 2001	1998/ 2001	1997/ 2001	1996/ 2001	1995/ 2001	1994/ 2001
Overall	0.14	0.15	0.14	0.14	0.14	0.12	0.1
Size 1	0.5	0.66	0.54	0.56	0.63	0.54	0.49
Size 2	0.21	0.27	0.24	0.23	0.24	0.2	0.2
Size 3	0.11	0.12	0.12	0.13	0.14	0.13	0.12
Size 4	0.06	0.05	0.05	0.05	0.04	0.04	0.03
Age 1	0.1	0.13	0.14	0.12	0.15	0.13	0.12
Age 2	0.11	0.19	0.11	0.17	0.15	0.12	0.13
Age 3	0.15	0.13	0.17	0.16	0.13	0.14	0.09
Age 4	0.11	0.19	0.17	0.11	0.16	0.1	0.11
Age 5	0.17	0.18	0.11	0.16	0.12	0.12	0.09
Age 6	0.2	0.11	0.15	0.15	0.15	0.09	0.09
Age 7	0.16	0.15	0.13	0.11	0.09	0.08	0.06
Money No	0.12	0.16	0.15	0.15	0.16	0.14	0.13
Money Yes	0.16	0.15	0.13	0.12	0.12	0.1	0.09
Leverage No	0.13	0.11	0.1	0.11	0.11	0.1	0.08
Leverage Yes	0.15	0.18	0.16	0.16	0.16	0.13	0.12
Convertible Arbitrage	0.03	0.04	0.05	0.05	0.05	0.06	0.04
Event Driven	0.12	0.13	0.1	0.07	0.06	0.05	0.03
Long/Short Equity	0.12	0.12	0.1	0.12	0.12	0.1	0.08
Relative Value	0.11	0.16	0.17	0.19	0.21	0.19	0.22
Emerging Markets	0.28	0.23	0.24	0.21	0.2	0.14	0.12
Global Macro	0.27	0.34	0.34	0.28	0.29	0.26	0.29

All estimates are annualized, and each ratio has dead and surviving funds included. *Source:* Data from Alexander Fabre-Bulle and Sebastien Pache, "The Omega Measure: Hedge Fund Portfolio Optimization," University of Lausanne, Ecole des HEC, 2003. Data from www.ssrn.com, or Social Science Research Network and altered by the author.

TABLE AP I.10   Funds of Funds Survival Rates

This table shows what percentage of the hedge funds alive in June of each year survived for more than 1, 2, . . . 60 months.

Months	2000	1999	1998	1997	1996	1995	1994
1	100.00%	100.00%	100.00%	100.00%	100.00%	100.00%	100.00%
2	99.21%	100.00%	99.60%	100.00%	100.00%	99.31%	100.00%
3	98.42%	100.00%	99.21%	99.49%	100.00%	99.31%	100.00%
4	97.63%	100.00%	98.81%	98.48%	100.00%	99.31%	100.00%
5	95.65%	99.59%	98.02%	98.48%	100.00%	99.31%	100.00%
6	94.07%	99.59%	97.62%	98.48%	100.00%	99.31%	100.00%
7	94.07%	98.35%	97.62%	97.98%	99.39%	99.31%	100.00%
8	91.70%	97.53%	95.24%	97.47%	99.39%	99.31%	99.04%
9	90.91%	96.30%	95.24%	97.47%	99.39%	99.31%	99.04%
10	90.12%	95.88%	95.24%	97.47%	99.39%	98.61%	99.04%
11	88.14%	95.06%	95.24%	97.47%	99.39%	98.61%	99.04%
12	87.35%	95.06%	95.24%	95.96%	99.39%	98.61%	99.04%
13		94.65%	95.24%	95.45%	99.39%	98.61%	99.04%
14		93.83%	95.24%	94.95%	98.77%	98.61%	98.08%
15		93.00%	95.24%	94.44%	97.55%	98.61%	98.08%
16		92.18%	95.24%	96.94%	97.55%	98.61%	98.08%
17		90.53%	95.24%	92.93%	97.55%	98.61%	98.08%
18		88.89%	95.24%	92.42%	96.93%	98.61%	98.08%
19		88.89%	94.05%	92.42%	96.93%	98.61%	98.08%
20		86.42%	93.25%	89.39%	96.93%	98.61%	98.08%
21		85.60%	92.06%	89.39%	96.93%	98.61%	98.08%
22		85.19%	91.67%	89.39%	96.93%	98.61%	97.12%
23		83.13%	90.87%	89.39%	95.09%	98.61%	97.12%
24		82.30%	90.87%	89.39%	94.48%	98.61%	97.12%
25			90.48%	89.39%	93.87%	98.61%	97.12%
26			89.68%	89.39%	93.25%	98.61%	97.12%
27			88.89%	89.39%	92.64%	97.92%	97.12%
28			88.10%	89.39%	91.41%	96.53%	97.12%
29			86.51%	89.39%	91.41%	96.53%	97.12%
30			84.92%	89.39%	91.41%	96.53%	97.12%
31			84.92%	89.39%	88.34%	95.83%	97.12%
32			82.54%	88.38%	88.34%	95.83%	97.12%
33			81.35%	86.87%	88.34%	95.83%	97.12%
34			79.37%	86.37%	88.34%	95.83%	97.12%
35			78.57%	85.86%	88.34%	95.83%	97.12%
36			77.70%	85.86%	88.34%	94.44%	97.12%
37				85.86%	88.34%	93.75%	97.12%
38				84.85%	88.34%	93.06%	97.12%
39				83.84%	88.34%	93.36%	97.12%

TABLE AP I.10   *(Continued)*

Months	2000	1999	1998	1997	1996	1995	1994
40				82.83%	88.34%	91.67%	95.19%
41				82.83%	88.34%	90.28%	95.19%
42				80.81%	88.34%	90.28%	95.19%
43				80.81%	88.34%	90.28%	94.23%
44				79.80%	87.12%	87.50%	94.23%
45				78.79%	85.89%	87.50%	94.23%
46				78.28%	85.89%	87.50%	94.23%
47				75.76%	84.66%	87.50%	94.23%
48				74.75%	84.66%	87.50%	92.31%
49					84.66%	87.50%	92.31%
50					83.44%	87.50%	91.35%
51					82.21%	87.50%	90.38%
52					80.98%	87.50%	89.42%
53					80.98%	87.50%	88.46%
54					78.53%	87.50%	88.46%
55					78.53%	87.50%	88.46%
56					77.30%	86.81%	86.54%
57					76.69%	85.42%	86.54%
58					76.07%	85.42%	86.54%
59					74.23%	84.03%	86.54%
60					74.23%	84.03%	86.54%

Source: Data from Alexander Fabre-Bulle and Sebastien Pache, "The Omega Measure: Hedge Fund Portfolio Optimization," University of Lausanne, Ecole des HEC, 2003. Data from www.ssrn.com, or Social Science Research Network and altered by the author.

TABLE AP I.11 Historical Data Statistical Properties by Fund Strategies and by Indexes

	Historical Data Statistical Properties						Centralized Normalized Moments				
	Mean	Minimum	Maximum	Standard Deviation	Skewness	Kurtosis	5th Moment	6th Moment	7th Moment	8th Moment	Jarque-Bera Statistic
CSFB/Tremont Indexes											
Hedge Fund Index	0.89%	-7.55%	8.53%	2.63%	0.1	4.1	-0.3	25.9	-11.9	204.5	4.3
Convertible Arbitrage	0.82%	-4.68%	3.57%	1.41%	-1.6	6.9	-21.3	81.8	-294.4	1,121	103.2
Dedicated Short Bias	0.13%	-8.69%	22.71%	5.31%	0.9	5	15.2	64.9	260.4	1,101	28.7
Emerging Markets	0.55%	-23.03%	16.42%	5.48%	-0.5	5.8	-11.7	76.4	-249.8	1,281.2	34.4
Equity Market Neutral	0.89%	-1.15%	3.26%	0.93%	0.1	2.9	1.2	12.5	10.1	61.3	0.2
Event Driven	0.86%	-11.78%	3.68%	1.84%	-3.3	22.9	-151.5	1,040.1	-7,147.1	49,209	1,797.5
Fixed Income Arbitrage	0.59%	-6.96%	2.02%	1.16%	-3.5	20.6	-125.2	794.8	-5,114.7	33,181	1,472.9
Global Macro	1.18%	-11.55%	10.60%	3.76%	0	4.3	-1.8	29	-33.9	2,48.5	5.9
Long/Short Equity	1.00%	-11.44%	13.01%	3.40%	0.2	5.5	1	55.1	-1.2	651.7	24.8
Managed Futures	0.54%	-9.35%	9.95%	3.43%	0.1	4	0	23.2	-3.8	155.3	3.4
Hedge Fund Research (HFR)											
Convertible Arbitrage	0.88%	-3.19%	3.33%	1.04%	-1.3	6	-16.6	65.5	-222.8	851	61.6
Distressed Securities	0.82%	-8.50%	5.06%	1.66%	-1.8	11.8	-56.4	326	-1,796.2	10,194	363.4
Emerging Markets (Total)	0.58%	-21.02%	14.80%	4.68%	-0.7	6.6	-18.3	107.2	-422.4	2,147	60
Equity Hedge	1.26%	-7.65%	10.88%	2.89%	0.3	4.3	3.4	33.3	40.8	317.5	7
Equity Market Neutral	0.78%	-1.67%	3.59%	0.98%	0	3.2	0.5	15.6	6.6	93.6	0.1

Equity non-Hedge	1.08%	-13.34%	10.74%	4.40%	-0.4	3.3	-4.4	19.9	-44.3	164.2	3.6
Event Driven	1.03%	-8.90%	5.13%	2.01%	-1.3	8	-31.2	154.7	-731.4	3,598	131.7
Fixed Income (Total)	0.70%	-3.27%	3.28%	0.97%	-1.2	7	-21	94.3	-346.9	1,463.7	88.3
Fixed Income: Arbitrage	0.48%	-6.45%	3.04%	1.29%	-2.8	15.7	-79	419.3	-2,206.4	1,1679	793.2
Fixed Income: Convertible Bonds	0.70%	-13.06%	14.42%	4.11%	-0.5	5.3	-4.5	44.7	-38.4	437.4	24.1
Fund of Funds	0.63%	-7.47%	6.85%	1.89%	-0.2	6.2	-9.1	80.9	-215.1	1,308.9	42.1
Macro	0.83%	-6.40%	6.82%	2.27%	0	3.6	-1.3	20.9	-21.1	157	1.2
Merger Arbitrage	0.91%	-5.69%	2.47%	1.13%	-2.5	13.5	-71.1	401.9	-2,303.2	13,337	557.7
Relative Value	0.75%	-2.96%	2.01%	0.74%	-1.9	9.5	-40	188.5	-890.4	4,303.1	230.1
Short Selling	0.59%	-21.21%	22.84%	7.08%	0.2	3.9	1.4	26.3	12.7	218.7	3.3
Statistical Arbitrage	0.70%	-2.00%	3.60%	1.14%	-0.2	3	-0.9	13.2	-3.4	68.7	0.7
Traditional Indexes											
SSB WGBI	0.57%	-5.08%	7.71%	2.21%	0.2	3.7	3.2	24	39.7	199	2.1
MSCI	0.40%	-13.45%	8.91%	4.13%	-0.6	3.3	-5.4	21.2	-54.4	190.1	5.5

Source: Data from Alexander Fabre-Bulle and Sebastien Pache, "The Omega Measure: Hedge Fund Portfolio Optimization," University of Lausanne, Ecole des HEC, 2003. Data from www.ssrn.com, or Social Science Research Network and altered by the author.

TABLE AP I.12 Performance Rankings for Indexes by Strategies Measured by Sharpe Ratio, Sortino Ratio, and Omega

	Sharpe Ratio						Sortino Ratio			
	Sharpe Ratio	Ranking for Sharpe	VaR Modified Sharpe	Ranking for VaR Modified Sharpe	Adjusted VaR Modified Sharpe	Ranking for Adjusted VaR Modified Sharpe	0.00%	Ranking of 0.00%	0.10%	Ranking of 0.10%
CSFB/Tremont Indexes										
Hedge Fund Index	0.3	5	0.15	5	0.14	3	0.64	5	0.55	4
Convertible Arbitrage	0.51	2	0.29	2	0.18	2	0.92	2	0.78	2
Dedicated Short Bias	0.01	12	0	12	0	12	0.04	12	0.01	12
Emerging Markets	0.08	10	0.04	10	0.03	11	0.15	10	0.12	10
Equity Market Neutral	0.84	1	0.61	1	0.66	1	3.45	1	2.7	1
Event Driven	0.41	4	0.22	4	0.08	8	0.66	4	0.57	3
Fixed Income Arbitrage	0.42	3	0.23	3	0.11	6	0.68	3	0.55	5
Global Macro	0.29	6	0.14	6	0.12	4	0.57	6	0.51	6
Long/Short Equity	0.27	7	0.13	7	0.11	5	0.55	7	0.48	7
Managed Futures	0.13	9	0.06	9	0.06	9	0.26	9	0.21	9
SSB WGBI	0.21	8	0.1	8	0.1	7	0.46	8	0.36	8
MSCI	0.07	11	0.03	11	0.03	10	0.14	11	0.1	11
Hedge Fund Research (HFR)										
Convertible Arbitrage	0.75	2	0.5	2	0.3	3	1.65	3	1.39	3
Distressed Securities	0.43	8	0.24	8	0.11	10	0.8	9	0.68	9
Emerging Markets (Total)	0.1	16	0.05	16	0.03	16	0.18	16	0.15	16
Equity Hedge	0.4	9	0.21	9	0.2	7	0.93	7	0.83	7
Equity Market Neutral	0.69	4	0.45	4	0.45	1	2.26	1	1.8	1
Equity Non-Hedge	0.22	13	0.11	13	0.09	13	0.39	14	0.35	14
Event Driven	0.46	7	0.26	7	0.14	9	0.87	8	0.77	8
Fixed Income (Total)	0.62	5	0.38	5	0.22	5	1.35	5	1.1	6
Fixed Income Arbitrage	0.29	11	0.15	11	0.07	14	0.5	12	0.38	12
Fixed Income Convertible Bonds	0.15	15	0.07	15	0.05	15	0.25	15	0.21	15
Fund of Funds	0.28	12	0.14	12	0.1	12	0.6	11	0.48	11
Macro	0.32	10	0.16	10	0.15	8	0.71	10	0.6	10
Merger Arbitrage	0.71	3	0.47	3	0.21	6	1.31	6	1.13	4
Relative Value	0.87	1	0.66	1	0.3	2	1.93	2	1.59	2
Short Selling	0.07	18	0.03	18	0.03	17	0.13	18	0.11	17
Statistical Arbitrage	0.53	6	0.31	6	0.29	4	1.41	4	1.12	5
SSB WGBI	0.21	14	0.1	14	0.1	11	0.46	13	0.36	13
MSCI	0.07	17	0.03	17	0.03	18	0.14	17	0.1	18

Source: Data from Alexander Fabre-Bulle and Sebastien Pache, "The Omega Measure: Hedge Fund Portfolio Optimization," University of Lausanne, Ecole des HEC, 2003. Data from www.ssrn.com, or Social Science Research Network and altered by the author.

					Omega						
0.63%	Ranking of 0.63%	0.00%	Ranking for 0.00%	0.10%	Ranking for 0.10%	0.63%	Ranking for 0.63%	Synchronized LIBOR	Ranking for Synchronized LIBOR	Synchronized FOF	Ranking for Fund of Funds
0.16	5	2.32	5	2.1	5	1.22	6	1.88	5	1.69	1
0.17	4	3.68	2	3.2	2	1.33	3	2.68	2	1.21	6
−0.13	12	0.99	12	0.94	12	0.72	12	0.89	12	0.75	12
−0.02	7	1.19	1	1.13	10	0.88	7	1.08	10	0.87	8
0.5	1	10.62	1	8.05	1	1.9	1	5.7	1	1.38	5
0.16	6	3.15	4	2.77	3	1.28	4	2.38	3	1.57	2
−0.04	10	3.22	3	2.69	4	0.79	11	2.18	4	0.85	10
0.23	2	2.13	6	1.99	6	1.38	2	1.85	6	1.52	4
0.18	3	2.04	7	1.88	7	1.23	5	1.73	7	1.54	3
−0.04	8	1.43	9	1.32	9	0.87	8	1.21	9	0.86	9
−0.04	9	1.82	8	1.62	8	0.87	9	1.43	8	0.88	7
−0.07	11	1.2	10	1.13	11	0.82	10	1.06	11	0.78	11
0.34	2	6.41	3	5.38	3	1.74	2	4.24	3	1.42	4
0.15	7	3.29	8	2.84	8	1.23	7	2.4	9	1.38	5
−0.01	15	1.25	16	1.18	16	0.88	15	1.12	16	0.89	14
0.38	1	2.92	9	2.67	9	1.64	3	2.41	8	2.46	1
0.25	5	7.22	2	5.68	2	1.41	5	4.35	2	1.16	8
0.15	8	1.71	14	1.62	13	1.21	8	1.53	13	1.34	7
0.29	4	3.37	7	2.99	7	1.55	4	2.63	7	2.1	2
0.1	10	5.42	5	4.32	5	1.11	10	3.39	5	1.05	10
−0.13	18	2.47	10	2.05	11	0.6	18	1.67	11	0.74	17
0.02	12	1.46	15	1.36	15	0.96	12	1.27	15	0.95	12
0	13	2.21	12	1.92	12	0.9	14	1.65	12	NA	NA
0.14	9	2.47	11	2.19	10	1.17	9	1.93	10	1.35	6
0.32	3	5.46	4	4.67	4	1.75	1	3.89	4	1.44	3
0.21	6	9.03	1	7.12	1	1.4	6	5.1	1	1.13	9
−0.01	14	1.15	18	1.11	18	0.91	13	1.07	17	0.91	13
0.09	11	4.31	6	3.46	6	1.1	11	2.74	6	1.01	11
−0.04	16	1.82	13	1.62	14	0.87	16	1.43	14	0.88	15
−0.07	17	1.2	17	1.13	17	0.82	17	1.06	18	0.78	16

TABLE AP I.13   Risk Ordering for the CSFB/Tremont Indexes by Strategies

	Sigma and Variances								Downside	
Tremont Indexes by Strategies	Sigma	Ranking for Sigma	VaR Sigma	Ranking for VaR Sigma	Adjusted VaR Sigma	Ranking for Adjusted VaR Sigma	0.00%	Ranking for 0.00%	0.10%	Ranking for 0.10%
CSFB/Tremont Indexes										
Hedge Fund Index	2.63%	6	5.22%	6	5.68%	5	1.38%	6	1.43%	6
Convertible Arbitrage	1.41%	3	2.47%	3	4.07%	2	0.88%	3	0.92%	3
Dedicated Short Bias	5.31%	11	12.23%	12	9.76%	10	3.33%	11	3.39%	11
Emerging Markets	5.48%	12	12.18%	11	17.19%	12	3.73%	12	3.78%	12
Equity Market Neutral	0.93%	1	1.29%	1	1.20%	1	0.26%	1	0.29%	1
Event Driven	1.84%	4	3.43%	4	8.93%	9	1.31%	5	1.33%	5
Fixed Income Arbitrage	1.16%	2	2.11%	2	4.60%	3	0.86%	2	0.89%	2
Global Macro	3.76%	9	7.56%	9	8.73%	8	2.09%	9	2.13%	8
Long/Short Equity	3.40%	7	6.91%	7	8.31%	7	1.83%	7	1.87%	7
Managed Futures	3.43%	8	7.44%	8	8.01%	6	2.09%	8	2.14%	9
SSB WGBI	2.21%	5	4.58%	5	4.61%	4	1.24%	4	1.29%	4
MSCI	4.13%	10	9.19%	10	10.72%	11	2.91%	10	2.96%	10
Hedge Fund Research (HFR)										
Convertible Arbitrage	1.04%	4	1.55%	3	2.62%	4	0.53%	5	0.56%	5
Distressed Securities	1.66%	8	3.03%	8	6.65%	13	1.02%	8	1.05%	8
Emerging Markets (Total)	4.68%	17	10.32%	17	15.81%	17	3.22%	17	3.26%	17
Equity Hedge	2.89%	13	5.45%	13	5.70%	11	1.36%	13	1.40%	13
Equity Market Neutral	0.98%	3	1.51%	2	1.52%	1	0.35%	1	0.38%	1
Equity Non-Hedge	4.40%	16	9.16%	15	10.60%	14	2.74%	14	2.78%	14
Event Driven	2.01%	10	3.65%	9	6.64%	12	1.19%	11	1.22%	11
Fixed Income (Total)	0.97%	2	1.55%	4	2.78%	5	0.52%	4	0.54%	4
Fixed Income Arbitrage	1.29%	7	2.52%	7	5.17%	9	0.96%	7	0.99%	7
Fixed Income Convertible Bonds	4.11%	14	8.86%	14	12.15%	16	2.77%	15	2.81%	15
Fund of Funds	1.89%	9	3.77%	10	5.47%	10	1.05%	9	1.10%	9
Macro	2.27%	12	4.46%	11	4.72%	8	1.16%	10	1.21%	10
Merger Arbitrage	1.13%	5	1.73%	5	3.93%	6	0.69%	6	0.72%	6
Relative Value	0.74%	1	0.98%	1	2.14%	3	0.39%	2	0.41%	2
Short Selling	7.08%	18	15.89%	18	16.55%	18	4.55%	18	4.60%	18
Statistical Arbitrage	1.14%	6	1.95%	6	2.09%	2	0.50%	3	0.54%	3
SSB WGBI	2.21%	11	4.58%	12	4.61%	7	1.24%	12	1.29%	12
MSCI	4.13%	15	9.19%	16	10.72%	15	2.91%	16	2.96%	16

Source: Data from Alexander Fabre-Bulle and Sebastien Pache, "The Omega Measure: Hedge Fund Portfolio Optimization," University of Lausanne, Ecole des HEC, 2003. Data from www.ssrn.com or Social Science Research Network and altered by the author.

Deviation						Omega: Probability-Weighted Loss in I_1					
0.63%	Ranking for 0.63%	0.00%	Ranking for 0.00%	0.10%	Ranking for 0.10%	0.63%	Ranking for 0.63%	Synchronized LIBOR	Ranking for Synchronized LIBOR	Synchronized FOF	Ranking for Fund of Funds
1.67%	6	0.62%	5	0.65%	5	0.86%	5	0.69%	5	0.33%	1
1.10%	3	0.29%	3	0.31%	3	0.45%	3	0.34%	3	0.58%	4
3.71%	11	2.00%	12	2.05%	12	2.34%	12	2.10%	12	2.82%	12
4.05%	12	1.91%	11	1.95%	11	2.20%	11	2.01%	11	1.66%	11
0.51%	1	0.09%	1	0.11%	1	0.26%	1	0.14%	1	0.52%	3
1.48%	4	0.36%	4	0.39%	4	0.55%	4	0.42%	4	0.35%	2
1.04%	2	0.24%	2	0.26%	2	0.40%	2	0.29%	2	0.66%	6
2.37%	8	0.95%	8	0.99%	8	1.18%	8	1.02%	8	0.89%	7
2.12%	7	0.85%	7	0.89%	7	1.10%	7	0.93%	7	0.60%	5
2.41%	9	1.04%	9	1.09%	9	1.37%	9	1.14%	9	1.54%	10
1.57%	5	0.62%	6	0.66%	6	0.91%	6	0.70%	6	1.19%	8
3.24%	10	1.52%	10	1.56%	10	1.80%	10	1.61%	10	1.43%	9
0.73%	3	0.16%	4	0.17%	4	0.30%	2	0.20%	4	0.48%	6
1.24%	8	0.33%	8	0.35%	8	0.54%	8	0.39%	8	0.41%	3
3.52%	17	1.60%	17	1.65%	17	1.89%	17	1.70%	17	1.35%	15
1.64%	13	0.61%	12	0.64%	12	0.85%	12	0.68%	12	0.40%	2
0.60%	2	0.12%	2	0.14%	2	0.32%	3	0.16%	2	0.64%	9
3.04%	14	1.35%	15	1.39%	15	1.61%	15	1.44%	15	1.12%	13
1.41%	10	0.41%	9	0.43%	9	0.61%	9	0.47%	9	0.38%	1
0.73%	4	0.15%	3	0.17%	3	0.34%	5	0.19%	3	0.47%	5
1.16%	7	0.29%	7	0.31%	7	0.50%	7	0.34%	7	0.83%	11
3.05%	15	1.24%	14	1.28%	14	1.51%	14	1.33%	14	1.05%	12
1.34%	9	0.46%	10	0.50%	10	0.72%	10	0.55%	10	NA	NA
1.46%	11	0.52%	11	0.56%	11	0.80%	11	0.61%	11	0.47%	4
0.87%	6	0.19%	5	0.21%	5	0.32%	4	0.23%	5	0.50%	7
0.56%	1	0.09%	1	0.10%	1	0.23%	1	0.13%	1	0.50%	8
4.89%	18	2.49%	18	2.54%	18	2.81%	18	2.58%	18	3.35%	17
0.79%	5	0.20%	6	0.23%	6	0.44%	6	0.27%	6	0.68%	10
1.57%	12	0.62%	13	0.66%	13	0.91%	13	0.70%	13	1.19%	14
3.24%	16	1.52%	16	1.56%	16	1.80%	16	1.61%	16	1.43%	16

TABLE AP I.14   Global Minimum Risk Portfolios

Statistics	Mean Variance	Mean-VaR	Mean Adjusted VaR	Mean Deviation 0%	Omega 0%
Hedge Funds CSFB					
Mean	0.74%	0.76%	0.76%	0.76%	0.76%
Standard Deviation	0.64%	0.65%	0.70%	0.70%	0.69%
Skewness	−0.5	−0.2	0.3	0.2	0.2
Kurtosis	3.4	2.9	2.5	2.4	2.6
5th Moment	−4.3	−1.5	2.2	1.9	2
6th Moment	19.3	12.9	10.3	8.9	10.6
7th Moment	−37.7	−9.9	16.3	13.6	15.4
8th Moment	139.5	70.2	56.1	44.4	58
Omega 0%	14.04	16.53	20.6	19.5	21.6
I_1	0.056%	0.048%	0.038%	0.040%	0.036%
I_2	0.779%	0.792%	0.782%	0.785%	0.780%
Hedge Fund Research (HFR)					
Mean	0.77%	0.82%	0.84%	0.82%	0.84%
Standard Deviation	0.62%	0.63%	0.72%	0.71%	0.69%
Skewness	−0.8	−0.6	0.6	0.7	0.6
Kurtosis	6.2	5.5	3.9	4.6	4.2
5th Moment	−12.7	−7.9	7.7	12.2	8.9
6th Moment	73.3	59.8	29.8	52.5	40.5
7th Moment	−200	125.5	86.3	194.3	132.3
8th Moment	1,024.6	805.7	305.6	792.5	537.3
Omega 0%	15.37	17.83	30.4	31.12	33.3
I_1	0.052%	0.047%	0.028%	0.027%	0.025%
I_2	0.802%	0.845%	0.849%	0.826%	0.845%

Source: Data from Alexander Fabre-Bulle and Sebastien Pache, "The Omega Measure: Hedge Fund Portfolio Optimization," University of Lausanne, Ecole des HEC, 2003. Data from www.ssrn.com or Social Science Research Network and altered by the author.

TABLE AP I.15 Global Minimum Risk Portfolios for Credit Suisse First Boston

Statistics	Mean Variance	Mean- VaR	Mean Adjusted VaR	Mean Deviation 0%	Omega 0%
Global CSFB (Credit Suisse First Boston)					
Mean	0.70%	0.74%	0.73%	0.74%	0.74%
Standard Deviation	0.61%	0.62%	0.66%	0.68%	0.67%
Skewness	−0.1	−0.1	0.2	0.2	0.2
Kurtosis	2.9	2.8	2.5	2.3	2.4
5th Moment	−0.5	−0.4	1.9	1.6	1.5
6th Moment	12.1	11.3	9.7	7.8	8.8
7th Moment	−0.1	−1.8	12.7	9.9	9.4
8th Moment	62	55.5	47.7	33	39.4
Omega 0%	15.2	17.58	21.72	21.25	23.28
I_1	0.048%	0.044%	0.035%	0.036%	0.033%
I_2	0.734%	0.769%	0.750%	0.762%	0.758%
Global Hedge Fund Research (GHFR)					
Mean	0.75%	0.80%	0.81%	0.82%	0.83%
Standard Deviation	0.58%	0.60%	0.65%	0.68%	0.67%
Skewness	−0.5	−0.4	0.7	0.7	0.7
Kurtosis	5.3	5.1	3.9	4.5	4.3
5th Moment	−9.5	−7.9	7.3	11.7	10.5
6th Moment	57.8	55.4	29.5	49.1	43.4
7th Moment	−158.9	−140.6	82.4	180.1	151.8
8th Moment	791	771.1	300.7	723.2	594.7
Omega 0%	18.66	21.76	38.22	40.73	43.98
I_1	0.041%	0.038%	0.021%	0.020%	0.019%
I_2	0.772%	0.818%	0.814%	0.821%	0.831%

Source: Data from Alexander Fabre-Bulle and Sebastien Pache, "The Omega Measure: Hedge Fund Portfolio Optimization," University of Lausanne, Ecole des HEC, 2003. Data from www.ssrn.com or Social Science Research Network and altered by the author.

TABLE AP I.16   Global Minimum Risk Portfolios

Statistics	Mean Dev 0%	Mean Dev 0.1%	Mean Dev 0.63%	Omega 0%	Omega 0.1%	Omega 0.63%
Global Hedge Fund Index (GHFI)						
Mean	0.71%	0.71%	0.72%	0.73%	0.74%	0.73%
Standard Deviation	1.66%	1.66%	1.67%	1.69%	1.71%	1.68%
Skewness	−0.1	−0.1	−0.1	−0.1	0	−0.1
Kurtosis	2.8	2.8	2.8	2.9	2.9	2.8
5th Moment	−0.3	−0.3	−0.4	−0.7	−0.7	−0.6
6th Moment	11.3	11.3	11.3	12.4	12.7	11.8
7th Moment	−1	−1.1	−2.5	−7.2	−7.7	−5.2
8th Moment	55	55.2	54.5	65.5	68.1	59.5
Omega 0%	2.72	2.34	1.08	2.77	2.41	1.1
I_1	0.391%	0.427	0.649%	0.390%	0.424%	0.646%
I_2	1.061%	0.997%	0.700%	1.078%	1.022%	0.708%
Global Fund of Funds (GFOF)						
Mean	0.60%	0.60%	0.60%	0.61%	0.61%	0.61%
Standard Deviation	1.40%	1.40%	1.40%	1.44%	1.44%	1.44%
Skewness	−0.1	−0.1	−0.1	−0.3	−0.3	−0.3
Kurtosis	3.4	3.4	3.5	4.8	4.8	4.8
5th Moment	−2.3	−2.3	−2.7	−8.5	−8.5	−8.5
6th Moment	21.9	21.9	23	51.2	51.2	51.2
7th Moment	−30.3	−30.3	−36.7	−161.3	−161.3	−161.3
8th Moment	181.2	181.2	199.5	739	739	739
Omega 0%	2.78	2.31	0.88	2.82	2.34	0.89
I_1	0.314%	0.351%	0.593%	0.310%	0.347%	0.589%
I_2	0.873%	0.810%	0.524%	0.874%	0.811%	0.526%

Source: Data from Alexander Fabre-Bulle and Sebastien Pache, "The Omega Measure: Hedge Fund Portfolio Optimization," University of Lausanne, Ecole des HEC, 2003. Data from www.ssrn.com or Social Science Research Network and altered by the author.

TABLE AP I.17   Global Minimum Risk Portfolios

Statistics	Mean Dev 0%	Mean Dev 0.1%	Mean Dev 0.63%	Omega 0%	Omega 0.1%	Omega 0.63%
Hedge Funds CSFB (Credit Suisse First Boston)						
Mean	0.76%	0.76%	0.76%	0.76%	0.77%	0.79%
Standard Deviation	0.70%	0.70%	0.70%	0.69%	0.69%	0.69%
Skewness	0.2	0.2	0.2	0.2	0.2	0
Kurtosis	2.4	2.4	2.4	2.6	2.7	3
5th Moment	1.9	1.9	1.9	2	1.4	0.3
6th Moment	8.9	8.9	9.4	10.6	11.2	12.9
7th Moment	13.6	13.6	14.1	15.4	10.6	3.7
8th Moment	44.4	44.4	48.4	58	58.5	66.1
Omega 0%	19.5	11.47	1.5	21.6	13.32	1.7
I_1	0.040%	0.062%	0.235%	0.036%	0.053%	0.207%
I_2	0.785%	0.706%	0.351%	0.780%	0.707%	0.352%
Hedge Funds HFR (Hedge Fund Research)						
Mean	0.82%	0.84%	0.87%	0.84%	0.84%	0.89%
Standard Deviation	0.71%	0.70%	0.70%	0.69%	0.69%	0.69%
Skewness	0.7	0.7	0.5	0.6	0.6	0.2
Kurtosis	4.6	4.3	3.9	4.2	4.5	3.8
5th Moment	12.2	10.1	7.4	8.9	10.5	3.1
6th Moment	52.5	42.6	32.1	40.5	48.8	25.2
7th Moment	194.3	144.4	95.2	132.3	171.9	38.8
8th Moment	792.5	566.9	361.1	537.3	716.9	219.9
Omega 0%	31.12	20.25	2.29	33.3	20.41	2.47
I_1	0.027%	0.037%	0.173%	0.025%	0.037%	0.165%
I_2	0.826%	0.757%	0.395%	0.845%	0.756%	0.406%

Source: Data from Alexander Fabre-Bulle and Sebastien Pache, "The Omega Measure: Hedge Fund Portfolio Optimization," University of Lausanne, Ecole des HEC, 2003. Data from www.ssrn.com or Social Science Research Network and altered by the author.

TABLE AP I.18   Global Minimum Risk Portfolios

Statistics	Mean Dev 0%	Mean Dev 0.1%	Mean Dev 0.63%	Omega 0%	Omega 0.1%	Omega 0.63%
Global CSFB (Credit Suisse First Boston)						
Mean	0.74%	0.74%	0.75%	0.74%	0.74%	0.77%
Standard Deviation	0.68%	0.67%	0.64%	0.67%	0.65%	0.66%
Skewness	0.2	0.2	0.1	0.2	0.2	0.1
Kurtosis	2.3	2.3	2.7	2.4	2.6	2.9
5th Moment	1.6	1.6	1.3	1.5	1.2	1.1
6th Moment	7.8	8.2	11.3	8.8	9.9	12
7th Moment	9.9	10.1	10.3	9.4	7.7	8.5
8th Moment	33	36.2	57.5	39.4	46.1	59.7
Omega 0%	21.25	13.08	1.51	23.28	14.62	1.62
I_1	0.036%	5.200%	0.211%	0.033%	0.046%	0.204%
I_2	0.762%	0.678%	0.318%	0.758%	0.672%	0.330%
Global Hedge Fund Research (Hedge Fund Research)						
Mean	0.82%	0.83%	0.85%	0.83%	0.83%	0.89%
Standard Deviation	0.68%	0.67%	0.66%	0.67%	0.66%	0.67%
Skewness	0.7	0.7	0.5	0.7	0.6	0.1
Kurtosis	4.5	4.4	3.6	4.3	3.9	3.6
5th Moment	11.7	11	5.4	10.5	7.1	0.5
6th Moment	49.1	45.7	23.4	43.4	30.7	22.4
7th Moment	180.1	163.3	56.3	151.8	87.9	3.4
8th Moment	723.2	646.2	208.2	594.7	336.3	179.6
Omega 0%	40.73	23.93	2.25	43.98	27.71	2.55
I_1	0.020%	0.031%	0.163%	0.019%	0.027%	0.156%
I_2	0.821%	0.742%	0.367%	0.831%	0.740%	0.398%

Source: Data from Alexander Fabre-Bulle and Sebastien Pache, "The Omega Measure: Hedge Fund Portfolio Optimization," University of Lausanne, Ecole des HEC, 2003. Data from www.ssrn.com or Social Science Research Network and altered by the author.

TABLE AP 1.19 Risk Management Excess Returns for Largest Databases: FRM, HFR, CSFR, Hennessee by Strategies, 1994–2001

		Excess Returns as of January 1994 up to December 2001			Autocorrelations as of January 1994 up to December 2001				Adjusted Returns as of December 2001			Autocorrelations as of December 2001			
		Mean	Standard Deviation	Information Ratio	First	Second	Third	Fourth	Mean	Standard Deviation	Information Ratio	First	Second	Third	Fourth
Convertible Arbitrage	FRM	0.682	1.065	0.640	0.399	0.249	-0.020	0.034	0.670	1.624	0.413	0	0	0	0
	HFR	0.524	1.033	0.507	0.508	0.198	-0.076	-0.094	0.503	0.594	0.315	0	0	0	0
	CSFR	0.494	1.371	0.361	0.604	0.470	0.147	0.126	0.485	2.618	0.185	0	0	0	0
	Hennessee	0.357	1.235	0.289	0.503	0.133	-0.026	-0.094	0.349	1.865	0.187	0	0	0	0
Fixed Income Arbitrage	FRM	0.470	1.370	0.343	0.527	0.358	0.069	0.087	0.439	2.574	0.171	0	0	0	0
	HFR	0.045	1.320	0.034	0.373	0.029	0.120	0.030	0.037	1.931	0.019	0	0	0	0
	CSFR	0.166	1.176	0.141	0.403	0.133	0.049	0.100	0.162	1.882	0.086	0	0	0	0
Credit Trading	FRM	0.415	1.572	0.264	0.319	0.150	-0.033	0.088	0.409	2.295	0.178	0	0	0	0
	HFR	0.103	1.447	0.071	0.309	0.144	-0.030	0.028	0.091	2.001	0.046	0	0	0	0
Distressed Securities	FRM	0.561	1.515	0.371	0.401	0.074	-0.085	-0.042	0.540	2.036	0.265	0	0	0	0
	HFR	0.476	1.656	0.287	0.410	0.089	-0.065	-0.001	0.444	2.364	0.188	0	0	0	0
	Zurich	0.437	1.731	0.253	0.320	0.174	-0.003	0.020	0.432	2.513	0.172	0	0	0	0
Merger Arbitrage	FRM	0.676	1.117	0.605	0.170	-0.040	-0.082	-0.125	0.675	1.130	0.597	0	0	0	0
	HFR	0.612	1.064	0.575	0.104	0.047	0.078	-0.170	0.616	1.135	0.543	0	0	0	0
	Hennessee	0.556	1.024	0.543	0.153	-0.053	-0.007	-0.178	0.556	0.986	0.564	0	0	0	0
	Zurich	0.555	1.079	0.514	0.235	0.034	-0.062	-0.102	0.548	1.237	0.443	0	0	0	0
Multiprocess (Event Driven)	FRM	0.891	1.585	0.562	0.210	0.115	0.004	-0.061	0.891	1.930	0.462	0	0	0	0
	HFR	0.792	1.904	0.416	0.215	-0.031	-0.040	0.010	0.784	2.120	0.370	0	0	0	0
	CSFB	0.563	1.804	0.312	0.326	0.126	0.009	-0.001	0.550	2.511	0.219	0	0	0	0
	Hennessee	0.645	1.700	0.379	0.396	0.098	-0.050	-0.108	0.620	2.129	0.291	0	0	0	0
	Zurich	0.469	1.223	0.384	0.242	0.098	-0.033	-0.080	0.463	1.488	0.311	0	0	0	0

Source: Data from John Okunev and Derek White, "The Hedge Fund Risk Factors and Value at Risk of Credit Trading Strategies," working paper, 2003. Data from www.ssrn.com or Social Science Research Network and altered by the author.

TABLE AP I.20 Hedge Fund Indexes Correlations from January 1994 to December 2001

	Convertible Arbitrage				Fixed Income Arbitrage			Credit Trading		Distressed
	FRM	HFR	CSFB	Hennessee	FRM	HFR	CSFB	FRM	HFR	FRM
Convertible Arbitrage										
FRM	1	0.785	0.706	0.742	0.451	0.265	0.336	0.489	0.48	0.429
HFR		1	0.719	0.812	0.539	0.152	0.3	0.588	0.656	0.643
CSFB			1	0.599	0.584	0.262	0.464	0.652	0.63	0.483
Hennessee				1	0.388	0.204	0.205	0.431	0.438	0.528
Fixed Income Arbitrage										
FRM					1	0.57	0.642	0.59	0.688	0.529
HFR						1	0.532	0.263	0.373	0.233
CSFB							1	0.436	0.474	0.312
Credit Trading										
FRM								1	0.717	0.572
HFR									1	0.77
Distressed Securities										
FRM										1
HFR										
Zurich										
Merger Arbitrage										
FRM										
HFR										
Hennessee										
Zurich										
Multiprocess (Event Driven)										
FRM										
HFR										
CSFB										
Hennessee										
Zurich										

Source: Data from John Okunev and Derek White, "Hedge Fund Risk Factors and Value at Risk of Credit Trading Strategies," working paper, 2003. Data from www.ssrn.com or Social Science Research network and altered by the author.

Securities		Merger Arbitrage				Multiprocess (Event Driven)				
HFR	Zurich	FRM	HFR	Hennessee	Zurich	FRM	HFR	CSFB	Hennessee	Zurich
0.434	0.432	0.322	0.329	0.398	0.43	0.436	0.45	0.47	0.418	0.427
0.623	0.628	0.502	0.497	0.575	0.62	0.595	0.61	0.649	0.598	0.628
0.455	0.447	0.407	0.446	0.489	0.528	0.513	0.506	0.562	0.496	0.553
0.502	0.488	0.29	0.271	0.391	0.421	0.531	0.54	0.513	0.483	0.46
0.517	0.475	0.35	0.319	0.383	0.475	0.455	0.516	0.599	0.462	0.483
0.226	0.113	0.093	0.071	0.161	0.158	0.143	0.212	0.22	0.161	0.138
0.318	0.274	0.166	0.096	0.208	0.297	0.324	0.348	0.309	0.321	0.272
0.566	0.575	0.421	0.419	0.446	0.557	0.537	0.566	0.631	0.5	0.54
0.727	0.715	0.579	0.559	0.608	0.709	0.628	0.721	0.784	0.701	0.72
0.947	0.864	0.667	0.632	0.725	0.795	0.803	0.872	0.847	0.858	0.854
1	0.872	0.632	0.582	0.687	0.774	0.77	0.838	0.85	0.827	0.831
	1	0.65	0.623	0.694	0.775	0.797	0.822	0.83	0.763	0.847
		1	0.902	0.939	0.9	0.746	0.739	0.704	0.746	0.805
			1	0.887	0.853	0.706	0.682	0.71	0.695	0.802
				1	0.91	0.773	0.768	0.731	0.794	0.855
					1	0.831	0.839	0.838	0.841	0.933
						1	0.909	0.811	0.806	0.844
							1	0.859	0.858	0.854
								1	0.819	0.873
									1	0.853
										1

TABLE AP 1.21 Index Factors: Excess Monthly Returns from January 1994 to December 2001

	Mean Return	Standard Deviation Return	Information Ratio	Standard Deviation				Autocorrelation	
				1994–1995	1996–1997	1998–1999	2000–2001	First	Second
S&P 500	0.795	4.402	0.181	2.614	3.792	4.941	5.144	-0.041	-0.079
DJIA	0.799	4.568	0.175	3.198	3.986	5.122	5.131	-0.048	-0.054
NASDAQ	0.936	8.526	0.11	3.329	5.345	8.442	12.558	0.047	-0.035
Russell 2000	0.423	5.572	0.076	3.049	4.304	6.534	7.269	0.038	-0.118
Wilshire 5000	0.576	4.524	0.127	2.692	3.618	5.255	5.382	0.011	-0.104
S&P Barra Growth	0.765	5.028	0.152	2.537	4.225	5.122	6.389	-0.027	-0.010
S&P Barra Value	0.499	4.285	0.117	2.879	3.480	5.172	4.909	-0.033	-0.137
MSCI World	0.370	4.041	0.092	2.859	3.222	4.517	4.553	-0.027	-0.094
Nikkei	-0.742	5.980	-0.124	6.509	5.161	5.551	6.017	-0.009	-0.026
FTSE	0.118	3.862	0.030	3.499	3.323	4.063	3.975	-0.006	-0.058
EAFE	-0.038	4.195	-0.009	3.582	3.456	4.566	4.294	-0.043	-0.122
Lipper Mutual Funds	0.626	4.362	0.144	2.515	3.673	4.957	5.352	-0.023	-0.117
MSCI AAA	-0.090	2.780	-0.032	2.505	2.113	2.611	3.489	0.177	-0.041
MSCI 10 Year+	0.237	2.322	0.102	2.586	2.535	1.860	2.148	0.177	-0.051
MSCI World Sov ex-USA	-0.084	2.342	-0.036	2.493	1.851	2.335	2.433	0.110	-0.061
UBS Warburg AAA/AA	0.680	3.616	0.188	1.282	2.982	4.815	4.12	0.021	-0.237
UBS Warburg Sub BBB/NR	0.765	5.946	0.129	2.834	2.754	6.970	7.975	0.060	0.063
UBS Warburg Conv Global	0.279	3.393	0.082	2.706	2.065	3.760	4.060	0.038	-0.035
CBT Municipal Bond	-0.422	2.234	-0.189	3.043	2.072	1.415	1.967	0.088	-0.065
Lehman U.S. Aggregate	-0.423	1.113	-0.38	1.383	1.150	0.865	0.913	0.253	-0.025
Lehman U.S. Credit Bond	-0.430	1.411	-0.305	1.734	1.491	1.150	1.086	0.165	0.009
Lehman Mortgage-Backed Securities	-0.416	0.918	-0.453	1.245	0.868	0.576	0.785	0.288	-0.003
Lehman U.S. High Yield	-0.571	2.130	-0.268	1.538	1.144	1.810	3.302	0.021	-0.085

Lehman Gov/Corp	0.134	0.910	0.147	1.052	0.956	0.761	0.786	0.262	-0.025
SSB High Yield Index	0.094	1.943	0.048	1.381	0.821	2.003	2.827	0.015	-0.104
U.S. Credit Bond	-0.439	1.410	-0.311	1.733	1.491	1.151	1.085	0.165	0.008
Salomon WGBI	-0.029	1.740	-0.017	1.692	1.317	1.812	1.967	0.195	0.050
JPM non-U.S. Govt Bond	-0.057	2.274	-0.025	2.322	1.818	2.282	2.432	0.116	-0.067
JPM Brady Bond	0.646	5.066	0.127	5.560	4.081	6.735	2.885	-0.01	-0.131
JPM Brady Fixed	0.650	4.935	0.132	6.099	4.686	5.412	2.713	0.031	-0.086
JPM Brady Bond Float	0.675	5.409	0.125	5.318	3.813	7.871	3.334	-0.023	-0.148
CME Goldman Commodity	-0.248	5.116	-0.049	2.950	4.332	6.262	6.080	-0.048	-0.143
Dow Jones Commodity	-0.739	5.056	-0.146	2.540	2.980	8.324	4.042	-0.001	-0.191
Philadelphia Gold/Silver	-0.789	10.559	-0.075	8.271	9.588	15.217	7.174	-0.239	-0.135
World ex-U.S. Real Estate	-0.166	6.111	-0.027	6.214	5.496	7.177	4.896	-0.035	0.046
U.S. Real Estate	0.338	4.952	0.068	3.973	4.248	6.011	4.604	-0.024	-0.010
CME Yen Futures	-0.487	4.040	-0.121	4.071	3.014	4.864	3.554	-0.020	0.058
NYBOT Dollar Index	-0.186	2.140	-0.087	1.968	2.019	1.868	2.419	-0.006	-0.092
NYBOT Orange Juice	-0.182	8.778	-0.021	7.845	8.363	10.636	7.747	-0.374	0.244
% Change VXN	1.764	15.202	0.116	13.334	9.698	18.992	16.873	-0.075	-0.193
% Change VIX	1.981	19.19	0.103	20.412	16.585	22.923	15.816	-0.153	-0.211
SMB	-0.334	4.036	-0.083	1.818	3.456	3.522	5.987	-0.007	-0.006
HML	-0.413	4.897	-0.084	2.126	2.624	4.492	7.638	0.097	0.023
Low	0.764	4.893	0.156	2.691	4.103	5.489	5.887	0.000	-0.059
High	0.728	4.051	0.18	2.729	2.929	4.575	5.278	0.110	-0.269
Big	0.765	4.527	0.169	2.585	3.698	5.132	5.457	-0.013	-0.083
Small	0.732	5.944	0.123	3.012	4.801	6.588	8.073	0.125	-0.198
Momentum	0.592	5.511	0.107	1.641	2.344	4.667	9.493	-0.108	-0.079
Europe High BM	0.908	5.354	0.170	3.382	4.147	6.286	6.500	-0.024	-0.052
Europe Low BM	0.412	4.672	0.088	3.092	3.489	5.106	5.737	-0.024	-0.011
Europe HML	0.105	3.321	0.032	1.716	2.412	3.748	4.520	0.222	0.062
UK High BM	0.504	4.693	0.107	4.203	2.728	4.946	6.004	0.024	-0.172
UK Low BM	0.422	3.943	0.107	3.993	2.935	3.594	4.314	-0.052	0.017
UK HML	-0.308	3.610	-0.085	1.787	2.024	4.325	5.008	0.083	0.104

(Continued)

TABLE AP I.21 (*Continued*)

	Mean Return	Standard Deviation Return	Information Ratio	Standard Deviation				Autocorrelation	
				1994–1995	1996–1997	1998–1999	2000–2001	First	Second
Pacific Rim High BM	0.104	7.520	0.014	4.862	5.659	10.439	6.891	0.050	-0.114
Pacific Rim Low BM	-0.785	5.787	-0.136	4.724	5.398	5.942	5.492	0.070	-0.018
Pacific Rim HML	0.498	5.210	0.096	1.649	3.180	7.425	5.962	0.025	0.010
Japan High BM	0.238	8.598	0.028	5.969	6.331	11.728	7.931	0.012	-0.136
Japan Low BM	-0.850	6.428	-0.132	5.671	5.886	6.267	6.087	0.089	-0.010
Japan HML	0.697	6.209	0.112	1.858	3.957	8.818	7.091	-0.026	-0.029
Nondurable	0.672	4.098	0.164	2.455	3.777	5.172	4.188	0.092	-0.115
Durable	0.926	5.737	0.161	3.683	4.370	6.049	7.370	-0.061	-0.013
Manufacturing	0.522	4.407	0.118	3.070	3.481	5.466	4.871	0.024	-0.095
Energy	0.664	5.085	0.130	3.352	3.680	6.516	5.912	-0.039	-0.069
High Tech	1.439	9.122	0.158	4.187	6.692	8.769	13.004	-0.027	-0.015
Telecom	0.392	6.554	0.060	3.015	4.678	7.225	7.890	0.068	-0.017
Shops	0.759	4.825	0.157	3.076	3.819	5.620	5.874	0.045	-0.269
Health	1.291	4.785	0.270	3.851	4.681	5.699	4.627	-0.176	-0.027
Utilities	0.430	4.369	0.098	3.280	3.267	4.322	5.929	0.001	-0.160
Other	0.858	4.868	0.176	3.123	3.810	6.097	5.581	-0.045	-0.094

Source: Data from John Okunev and Derek White, "The Hedge Fund Risk Factors and Value at Risk of Credit Trading Strategies," working paper, 2003. Data from www.sssrn.com or Social Science Research Network and altered by the author.

TABLE AP I.22 Index Factors and Value at Risk Approximations

Index Factors—50,000 Simulations	Six Months Analysis					One Year Analysis				
	Mean	Standard Deviation	Minimum	1 Percentile	5 Percentile	Mean	Standard Deviation	Minimum	1 Percentile	5 Percentile
S&P 500	4.68	11.09	-43.09	-21.25	-13.63	9.82	16.52	-48.37	-26.07	-16.42
DJIA	5.10	11.61	-42.78	-21.52	-13.96	10.37	17.11	-50.60	-26.62	-16.80
NASDAQ	5.26	21.85	-64.56	-39.97	-28.58	10.92	33.04	-74.62	-49.51	-36.57
Russell 2000	2.79	13.97	-49.46	-28.90	-19.72	5.48	20.37	-56.68	-36.42	-25.82
Wilshire 5000	3.54	11.33	-40.08	-23.16	-15.34	7.08	16.62	-51.46	-29.09	-19.43
Sp Barra Growth	4.48	12.64	-41.34	-24.27	-16.11	9.20	18.82	-49.25	-30.06	-20.06
Sp Barra Value	3.01	10.66	-44.46	-22.21	-14.77	6.22	15.68	-47.40	-27.91	-18.52
MSCI World	2.22	10.01	-37.22	-21.19	-14.32	4.53	14.58	-46.74	-27.06	-18.50
Nikkei	-4.00	14.20	-48.19	-32.45	-25.44	-7.64	19.43	-64.10	-44.07	-35.94
FTSE	0.82	9.44	-32.68	-21.02	-14.69	1.49	13.43	-47.44	-27.10	-19.75
EAFE	-0.10	10.27	-39.54	-23.10	-16.76	-0.33	14.58	-50.10	-30.89	-22.91
Lipper Mutual Funds	3.79	10.97	-41.25	-22.44	-14.57	7.66	16.16	-48.13	-27.91	-18.11
MSCI AAA	-0.61	6.71	-24.24	-14.46	-10.87	-1.29	9.41	-32.82	-20.46	-15.55
MSCI 10 Year+	1.30	5.82	-20.31	-11.81	-8.15	2.66	8.27	-28.70	-15.50	-10.42
MSCI World Sovereign ex-USA	-0.57	5.62	-23.91	-12.62	-9.32	-1.14	7.92	-30.17	-17.67	-13.34
UBS Warburg AAA/AA	4.18	9.10	-34.22	-15.58	-9.83	8.43	13.32	-38.14	-18.89	-11.78
UBS Warburg Sub BBB/NR	4.55	15.11	-48.50	-27.20	-18.69	9.18	22.28	-60.85	-34.57	-23.52

(Continued)

TABLE AP I.22 *(Continued)*

Index Factors—50,000 Simulations	Six Months Analysis					One Year Analysis				
	Mean	Standard Deviation	Minimum	1 Percentile	5 Percentile	Mean	Standard Deviation	Minimum	1 Percentile	5 Percentile
CBT Municipal Bond	-2.51	5.37	-28.16	-15.12	-11.33	-4.91	7.45	-39.01	-21.62	-16.99
Lehman Brothers Gov/Corp	0.80	2.25	-7.87	-4.34	-2.85	1.58	3.24	-10.82	-5.73	-3.66
U.S. Credit Bond	-2.64	3.38	-15.35	-10.43	-8.17	-5.10	4.67	-23.11	-15.54	-12.62
Salomon WGBI	-0.27	4.22	-17.71	-9.33	-6.92	-0.48	5.95	-22.67	-13.26	-5.74
CME Goldman Commodity	-0.33	12.91	-40.71	-25.81	-19.45	-0.56	18.28	-51.14	-35.15	-26.89
Dow Jones Commodity	-3.55	12.13	-66.89	-43.03	-33.19	-6.98	16.65	-80.39	-50.83	-41.07
Philadelphia Gold/Silver	-2.86	25.42	-65.95	-46.73	-37.16	-5.56	35.61	-79.38	-60.09	-49.90
World Ex-U.S. Real Estate	-0.86	14.72	-59.14	-36.17	-25.19	-1.76	20.66	-71.94	-45.60	-35.86
U.S. Real Estate	2.45	12.33	-40.28	-24.38	-17.02	4.93	17.91	-51.50	-31.16	-22.19
CME Yen Futures	-2.86	9.51	-32.80	-21.04	-16.49	-5.52	13.21	-45.55	-29.90	-26.24
NYBOT Dollar Index	-0.95	5.16	-21.07	-12.26	-9.11	-1.84	7.28	-27.15	-17.49	-15.22
NYBOT Orange Juice	-1.01	21.31	-64.08	-41.72	-31.82	-1.65	30.13	-74.32	-53.52	-42.77
SMB	-1.89	9.59	-35.49	-21.67	-16.30	-3.82	13.28	-42.80	-30.09	-23.37
HML	-2.39	11.67	-50.91	-31.44	-22.62	-4.74	16.12	-66.99	-40.62	-30.67
Low	4.60	12.31	-42.01	-23.61	-15.77	9.35	18.26	-54.23	-29.50	-19.47
High	4.32	10.06	-37.94	-17.89	-11.77	8.84	15.00	-45.03	-22.49	-14.36
Big	4.62	11.29	-43.58	-21.86	-14.00	9.33	16.80	-54.30	-27.19	-17.35
Small	4.32	14.91	-52.45	-29.24	-19.70	9.05	22.12	-60.07	-36.52	-24.73
Momentum	3.55	13.70	-55.56	-30.65	-19.40	7.09	20.16	-63.66	-37.10	-24.64
Europe High BM	5.46	13.53	-50.76	-25.95	-16.79	11.05	20.41	-55.74	-32.18	-20.57
Europe Low BM	2.42	11.51	-41.65	-23.11	-16.10	4.91	16.74	-57.93	-29.86	-20.97

Europe HML	0.60	8.07	-39.68	-18.68	-12.59	1.13	11.48	-45.80	-24.40	-17.18
UK High BM	2.93	11.56	-38.66	-22.80	-15.64	6.03	16.96	-48.87	-29.01	-20.08
UK Low BM	2.51	9.71	-33.17	-19.06	-13.15	5.00	14.20	-40.52	-25.02	-17.30
UK HML	-1.79	8.61	-35.12	-21.13	-15.36	-3.55	11.88	-42.54	-28.76	-22.04
Pacific Rim High BM	0.68	18.34	-46.53	-32.15	-24.71	1.17	26.39	-62.15	-43.12	-34.03
Pacific Rim Low BM	-4.53	13.51	-47.15	-31.39	-25.02	-8.80	18.37	-60.81	-43.30	-35.49
Pacific Rim HML	3.00	12.90	-48.59	-24.46	-16.73	5.79	18.92	-51.14	-31.40	-21.93
Japan High BM	1.24	21.16	-52.11	-34.89	-27.21	2.90	30.81	-62.41	-47.03	-36.83
Japan Low BM	-4.81	14.98	-48.91	-33.77	-26.97	-9.49	20.19	-62.51	-46.25	-38.14
Japan HML	4.21	15.61	-47.22	-27.01	-18.77	8.33	22.87	-53.33	-34.22	-23.98
Nondurable	3.94	10.29	-37.81	-19.69	-12.83	8.10	15.08	-46.03	-24.35	-15.67
Durable	5.48	14.46	-39.47	-24.55	-16.68	11.29	21.72	-56.39	-31.21	-20.88
Manufacturing	3.09	10.89	-46.44	-21.96	-14.57	6.23	15.98	-53.93	-28.02	-18.78
Energy	3.93	12.70	-33.89	-21.20	-14.94	7.95	18.73	-45.90	-27.42	-19.28
High Tech	8.69	23.79	-63.03	-39.99	-27.97	18.07	37.23	-75.36	-48.84	-34.86
Telecom	2.24	16.13	-52.43	-32.26	-22.97	4.63	23.54	-64.64	-41.67	-30.27
Shops	4.58	12.07	-38.96	-21.60	-14.44	9.18	18.02	-47.35	-27.34	-18.20
Health	7.71	12.30	-39.27	-19.35	-12.08	16.06	18.90	-46.20	-23.13	-13.14
Utilities	2.55	10.82	-34.46	-20.45	-14.35	5.12	15.71	-47.13	-26.47	-18.77
Other	5.19	12.26	-46.45	-24.34	-14.85	10.50	18.39	-57.02	-29.64	-18.51

Source: Data from John Okunev and Derek White, "The Hedge Fund Risk Factors and Value at Risk of Credit Trading Strategies," working paper, 2003. Data from www.ssrn.com or Social Science Research Network and altered by the author.

321

TABLE AP I.23 Value at Risk Estimation Excess Returns by Strategies and by Methodologies: Indexes, All and Historical as of 2003

Given Database Index	Assumed Methodology	Assumed Distribution	Six Months Analysis					One Year Analysis				
			Mean	Standard Deviation	Minimum	1 Percentile	5 Percentile	Mean	Standard Deviation	Minimum	1 Percentile	5 Percentile
Convertible Arbitrage												
FRM	Index, Ken French	Normal	4.09	4.14	−11.14	−5.20	−2.63	8.34	6.10	−17.37	−5.22	−1.40
		T-Distribution	4.10	5.63	−71.06	−9.12	−4.71	8.28	8.22	−50.33	−10.44	−4.68
	All: Interest rates, Index, Ken French, directional, trading strategies	Normal	4.08	4.14	−14.31	−5.98	−2.79	8.31	6.10	−18.32	−5.93	−1.65
		T-Distribution	4.04	5.53	−37.21	−9.55	−4.94	8.31	8.21	−52.34	−10.63	−4.68
	Historical		4.05	4.10	−15.82	−5.62	−2.63	8.33	6.05	−16.55	−5.45	−1.46
HFR	Index, Ken French	Normal	3.06	4.06	−13.64	−6.42	−3.64	6.19	5.91	−17.96	−7.25	−3.34
		T-Distribution	3.07	5.04	−43.26	−8.80	−5.04	6.25	7.33	−56.24	−10.38	−5.42
	All: Interest rates, Index, Ken French, directional, trading strategies	Normal	3.06	4.02	−16.26	−7.16	−3.86	6.19	5.89	−18.87	−7.94	−3.70
		T-Distribution	3.06	4.91	−31.81	−8.94	−5.08	6.17	7.16	−44.28	−10.57	−5.43
	Historical		3.11	3.87	−16.93	−7.32	−3.80	6.26	5.66	−21.35	−7.92	−3.42
CSFB	Index, Ken French	Normal	2.90	6.60	−24.06	−11.74	−7.67	5.95	9.66	−29.45	−14.88	−9.21
		T-Distribution	2.99	8.78	−99.61	−17.06	−10.72	6.07	12.76	−97.37	−21.67	−13.69
	All: Interest rates, Index, Ken French, directional, trading strategies	Normal	2.93	6.66	−29.81	−14.36	−8.56	5.99	9.66	−35.24	−17.17	−10.05
		T-Distribution	2.96	8.28	−72.27	−17.33	−10.60	5.90	12.03	−57.70	−21.66	−13.14
	Historical		2.93	7.27	−31.81	−16.42	−9.77	5.96	10.57	−44.07	−19.54	−11.67
Hennessee	Index, Ken French	Normal	2.07	4.68	−15.71	−8.32	−5.42	4.22	6.80	−20.40	−10.61	−6.60
		T-Distribution	2.15	5.98	−45.26	−11.68	−7.24	4.30	8.67	−99.74	−15.24	−9.27
	All: Interest rates, Index, Ken French, directional, trading strategies	Normal	2.09	4.68	−17.11	−8.86	−5.59	4.27	6.79	−21.95	−11.09	−6.71
		T-Distribution	2.09	5.81	−76.74	−11.56	−7.26	4.27	8.39	−49.07	−14.82	−9.03
	Historical		2.18	4.52	−18.58	−9.16	−5.48	4.40	6.48	−22.72	−10.95	−6.30

(Continued)

Fixed Income Arbitrage

Model	Strategy	Method										
FRM	Index, Ken French	Normal	2.66	6.55	-27.22	-12.81	-7.93	5.44	9.56	-32.68	-16.16	-9.96
		T-Distribution	2.65	8.24	-51.27	-16.70	-10.59	5.43	12.06	-95.22	-21.44	-13.37
	All: Interest rates, Index, Ken French, directional, trading strategies	Normal	2.69	6.55	-29.90	-14.10	-8.48	5.42	9.49	-36.07	-17.09	-10.22
		T-Distribution	2.68	8.19	-62.24	-17.13	-10.77	5.36	11.90	-73.17	-21.84	-13.66
	Historical		2.68	6.23	-32.24	-15.55	-9.22	5.40	9.02	-38.69	-18.30	-10.69
HFR	Index, Ken French	Normal	0.23	4.80	-19.26	-10.72	-7.55	0.45	6.82	-30.45	-14.75	-10.50
		T-Distribution	0.26	6.11	-43.01	-14.00	-9.47	0.47	8.58	-85.42	-18.61	-12.94
	All: Interest rates, Index, Ken French, directional, trading strategies	Normal	0.22	4.80	-23.14	-11.99	-7.96	0.43	6.82	-33.38	-15.96	-10.80
		T-Distribution	0.20	6.11	-73.96	-14.81	-9.76	0.42	8.63	-51.77	-19.58	-13.37
	Historical		0.18	4.59	-27.55	-12.30	-8.23	0.47	6.51	-32.03	-16.26	-10.75
CSFB	Index, Ken French	Normal	0.97	4.68	-16.16	-9.58	-6.60	1.97	6.77	-22.96	-12.87	-8.82
		T-Distribution	1.03	6.15	-47.45	-13.39	-8.75	1.95	8.77	-69.18	-17.77	-11.73
	All: Interest rates, Index, Ken French, directional, trading strategies	Normal	0.98	4.69	-20.42	-9.96	-6.75	1.94	6.69	-25.41	-13.14	-8.85
		T-Distribution	0.95	6.14	-50.84	-13.57	-8.81	1.98	8.71	-43.67	-17.71	-11.78
	Historical		0.95	4.13	-21.45	-10.82	-6.85	1.87	5.94	-25.13	-13.68	-8.64

Credit Trading

Model	Strategy	Method										
FRM	Index, Ken French	Normal	2.44	5.77	-19.80	-10.80	-6.96	5.02	8.43	-24.36	-13.45	-8.39
		T-Distribution	2.44	7.14	-54.16	-14.13	-8.92	5.04	10.45	-63.00	-17.84	-11.32
	All: Interest rates, Index, Ken French, directional, trading strategies	Normal	2.49	5.80	-28.28	-12.68	-7.46	5.02	8.36	-35.10	-15.44	-9.05
		T-Distribution	2.52	7.13	-51.46	-15.28	-9.17	5.03	10.31	-48.36	-19.05	-11.65
	Historical		2.42	5.32	-26.32	-12.24	-7.21	4.90	7.67	-30.68	-14.28	-8.16
HFR	Index, Ken French	Normal	0.56	4.95	-23.96	-11.88	-7.97	1.10	7.09	-32.71	-15.72	-10.66
		T-Distribution	0.56	5.48	-23.63	-13.07	-8.61	1.12	7.83	-45.20	-17.04	-11.66
	All: Interest rates, Index, Ken French, directional, trading strategies	Normal	0.56	4.93	-33.95	-13.00	-8.32	1.11	7.07	-32.75	-16.80	-11.11
		T-Distribution	0.53	5.36	-28.40	-13.68	-8.81	1.14	7.68	-34.05	-18.07	-11.95
	Historical		0.50	4.85	-27.67	-13.39	-8.67	1.04	6.91	-37.49	-17.28	-11.12

TABLE AP 1.23 *(Continued)*

Given Database Index	Assumed Methodology	Assumed Distribution	Six Months Analysis					One Year Analysis				
			Mean	Standard Deviation	Minimum	1 Percentile	5 Percentile	Mean	Standard Deviation	Minimum	1 Percentile	5 Percentile
Distressed Securities												
FRM	Index, Ken French	Normal	3.29	5.17	−19.52	−9.34	−5.41	6.69	7.55	−25.03	−11.16	−5.77
		T-Distribution	3.31	5.87	−29.91	−10.89	−6.35	6.70	8.49	−30.05	−12.67	−7.10
	All: Interest rates, Index, Ken French, directional, trading strategies	Normal	3.31	5.14	−26.86	−11.84	−6.30	6.65	7.57	−32.79	−13.56	−6.86
		T-Distribution	3.29	5.71	−52.91	−12.66	−7.03	6.69	8.31	−35.54	−14.49	−7.72
	Historical		3.29	4.91	−26.32	−11.70	−6.01	6.71	7.15	−29.03	−12.60	−6.24
HFR	Index, Ken French	Normal	2.67	5.99	−26.58	−10.98	−7.09	5.44	8.65	−36.79	−13.83	−8.39
		T-Distribution	2.68	6.99	−71.05	−13.38	−8.56	5.44	10.19	−42.66	−17.11	−10.70
	All: Interest rates, Index, Ken French, directional, trading strategies	Normal	2.65	5.97	−34.85	−15.21	−8.59	5.50	8.67	−41.38	−17.42	−9.94
		T-Distribution	2.68	6.67	−37.49	−15.77	−9.23	5.44	9.79	−71.59	−19.17	−11.36
	Historical		2.67	5.40	−33.59	−13.55	−7.38	5.43	7.87	−39.60	−15.44	−8.68
Zurich	Index, Ken French	Normal	2.65	6.33	−22.37	−11.78	−7.66	5.31	9.22	−30.63	−15.15	−9.43
		T-Distribution	2.68	7.33	−43.69	−14.16	−9.12	5.27	10.69	−82.58	−18.34	−11.61
	All: Interest rates, Index, Ken French, directional, trading strategies	Normal	2.68	6.32	−40.82	−15.12	−8.65	5.26	9.23	−41.73	−18.01	−10.70
		T-Distribution	2.64	7.01	−41.79	−16.26	−9.36	5.28	10.19	−51.65	−19.79	−11.99
	Historical		2.61	6.35	−31.17	−16.06	−9.65	5.34	9.22	−38.97	−19.03	−11.30
Merger Arbitrage												
FRM	Index, Ken French	Normal	4.14	2.89	−7.05	−2.50	−0.57	8.44	4.27	−9.87	−1.29	1.49
		T-Distribution	4.10	3.63	−20.01	−4.51	−1.70	8.43	5.36	−31.35	−3.97	−0.16
	All: Interest rates, Index, Ken French, directional, trading strategies	Normal	4.12	2.89	−12.64	−4.13	−1.02	8.40	4.28	−12.57	−2.81	0.97
		T-Distribution	4.13	3.52	−30.46	−5.17	−1.86	8.39	5.14	−17.72	−4.32	−0.25
	Historical		4.10	3.02	−17.83	−4.67	−1.66	8.39	4.48	−19.19	−3.83	0.33

Fund	Factor	Distribution										
HFR	Index, Ken French	Normal	0.77	-2.00	-8.86	4.26	7.67	-1.00	-2.87	-7.37	2.90	3.76
-0.99		T-Distribution	-4.75	-32.75	5.45	7.68	-2.21	-5.04	-32.51	3.72	3.74	
	All: Interest rates, Index, Ken French, directional, trading strategies	Normal	0.25	-3.40	-14.64	4.23	7.63	-1.40	-4.40	-12.83	2.88	3.76
Hennessee	Historical	Normal	-1.08	-5.36	-26.12	5.31	7.66	-2.40	-5.83	-24.77	3.63	3.75
		T-Distribution	-1.46	-6.14	-26.95	4.94	7.62	-2.98	-6.68	-16.20	3.36	3.71
	Index, Ken French	Normal	0.89	-1.42	-7.54	3.67	6.87	-0.75	-2.44	-7.45	2.50	3.37
		T-Distribution	-0.54	-3.90	-15.19	4.62	6.88	-1.68	-4.16	-21.71	3.17	3.39
	All: Interest rates, Index, Ken French, directional, trading strategies	Normal	0.58	-2.68	-11.42	3.67	6.89	-1.05	-3.50	-10.29	2.50	3.37
Zurich	Historical	Normal	-0.51	-4.00	-39.41	4.40	6.88	-1.80	-4.61	-14.27	3.04	3.38
		T-Distribution	-0.79	-4.78	-17.04	4.23	6.83	-2.16	-5.17	-13.75	2.88	3.38
	Index, Ken French	Normal	-0.75	-3.68	-11.55	4.59	6.76	-1.84	-4.04	-10.43	3.15	3.34
		T-Distribution	-2.23	-6.28	-33.75	5.65	6.77	-2.88	-5.86	-38.08	3.85	3.32
	All: Interest rates, Index, Ken French, directional, trading strategies	Normal	-1.20	-4.77	-20.12	4.58	6.78	-2.26	-5.38	-15.54	3.14	3.31
Multiprocess (Event Driven)	Historical	Normal	-2.04	-6.29	-23.25	5.27	6.83	-2.85	-6.14	-19.01	3.60	3.36
		T-Distribution	-2.03	-6.93	-21.75	4.83	6.80	-3.21	-6.86	-17.53	3.32	3.34
FRM	Index, Ken French	Normal	-0.96	-5.75	-18.30	7.48	11.19	-2.66	-6.04	-14.69	4.97	5.48
		T-Distribution	-2.16	-7.65	-26.78	8.38	11.18	-3.60	-7.28	-32.92	5.57	5.49
	All: Interest rates, Index, Ken French, directional, trading strategies	Normal	-1.12	-6.34	-20.37	7.41	11.26	-3.00	-7.10	-22.06	4.97	5.46
HFR	Historical	Normal	-2.43	-8.47	-40.35	8.36	11.20	-3.91	-8.27	-28.54	5.57	5.48
		T-Distribution	-2.04	-8.05	-27.34	8.05	11.30	-3.70	-8.88	-24.09	5.42	5.49
	Index, Ken French	Normal	-3.11	-8.16	-19.00	8.05	9.86	-4.15	-7.90	-16.85	5.46	4.83
		T-Distribution	-4.90	-10.85	-43.40	9.18	9.75	-5.27	-9.66	-37.58	6.21	4.77

(Continued)

TABLE AP I.23 (Continued)

Given Database Index	Assumed Methodology	Assumed Distribution	Six Months Analysis					One Year Analysis				
			Mean	Standard Deviation	Minimum	1 Percentile	5 Percentile	Mean	Standard Deviation	Minimum	1 Percentile	5 Percentile
	All: Interest rates, Index, Ken French, directional, trading strategies	Normal	4.80	5.44	-23.32	-9.25	-4.48	9.86	8.06	-25.68	-9.64	-3.65
		T-Distribution	4.81	6.02	-35.74	-10.09	-5.30	9.83	8.96	-50.27	-11.43	-4.87
	Historical		4.80	5.38	-23.33	-10.21	-4.61	9.84	8.05	-29.88	-10.51	-3.94
CSFB	Index, Ken French	Normal	3.35	6.42	-25.67	-12.26	-7.45	6.80	9.31	-31.45	-14.24	-8.34
		T-Distribution	3.33	7.38	-41.63	-14.23	-8.74	6.84	11.00	-58.39	-17.83	-10.70
	All: Interest rates, Index, Ken French, directional, trading strategies	Normal	3.42	6.32	-36.23	-17.44	-9.85	6.73	9.38	-42.40	-19.60	-11.78
		T-Distribution	3.33	6.96	-38.27	-18.28	-10.61	6.80	10.09	-45.44	-20.67	-12.11
	Historical		3.33	6.47	-36.21	-18.59	-12.45	6.85	9.41	-45.03	-20.38	-12.72
Hennessee	Index, Ken French	Normal	3.76	5.45	-19.05	-8.74	-5.14	7.68	7.98	-19.65	-10.07	-5.11
		T-Distribution	3.83	6.67	-51.35	-11.73	-6.86	7.67	9.87	-67.22	-14.10	-7.86
	All: Interest rates, Index, Ken French, directional, trading strategies	Normal	3.78	5.46	-21.96	-10.80	-5.56	7.67	8.05	-32.66	-11.52	-5.92
		T-Distribution	3.80	6.35	-39.64	-12.28	-6.86	7.70	9.29	-49.14	-14.34	-7.52
	Historical		3.79	6.05	-32.64	-13.44	-6.98	7.75	8.89	-33.75	-14.52	-7.58
Zurich	Index, Ken French	Normal	2.79	3.79	-13.20	-5.97	-3.42	5.69	5.49	-18.34	-6.65	-3.20
		T-Distribution	2.83	4.57	-56.39	-7.79	-4.55	5.68	6.61	-41.37	-9.31	-4.93
	All: Interest rates, Index, Ken French, directional, trading strategies	Normal	2.79	3.77	-20.86	-8.50	-4.23	5.70	5.49	-22.09	-8.54	-4.10
		T-Distribution	2.81	4.28	-46.74	-9.06	-4.77	5.67	6.25	-29.30	-10.46	-5.06
	Historical		2.80	4.04	-22.47	-9.89	-5.20	5.71	5.84	-23.12	-10.50	-5.14

T-distribution assumed degree of freedom t = 4; 50,000 simulations repeated.

Source: Data from John Okunev and Derek White, "The Hedge Fund Risk Factors and Value at Risk of Credit Trading Strategies," working paper, 2003. Data from www.ssrn.com = Social Science Research Network and altered by the author.

U.S. Regulatory Filings by Hedge Fund Managers

L isted in this appendix are regulatory filings (excluding tax-related, broker-dealer, and state "blue sky" filings) that hedge fund managers may be required to make in the United States depending on either their trading activity or their status as a regulated entity. The filings made to regulators by individual hedge fund managers vary depending on the type and volume of trading in which they engage, their business model, and the jurisdictions in which they operate. For example, like other market participants and institutional investors, hedge fund managers are required to make certain filings in the United States if the size of the positions they hold in certain markets reaches reportable levels. In addition, some hedge fund managers are regulated entities in the United States or are otherwise subject to a regulatory regime, and, like other similarly situated entities, are required to make certain filings in that capacity.

This appendix lists filings required in the United States where the aforementioned circumstances apply to a hedge fund manager. Hedge fund managers may also be subject to regulatory reporting and filing requirements in the foreign jurisdictions in which they conduct their business.

Reports and Filing Forms for the Federal Reserve

Large Position Reporting: Treasury security issues that exceed the large position U.S. Treasury Department threshold of $2 billion. Reports are filed in response to notices issued by the U.S. Department of the Treasury if such threshold is met. Reports are filed with the Federal Reserve Bank of New York and are not public.

Form FC-1: Report of weekly, consolidated data on the foreign exchange contracts and positions of major market participants.

Reports are to be filed throughout the calendar year by each foreign exchange market participant who had more than $50 billion equivalent in foreign exchange contracts on the last business day of any calendar quarter during the previous year. The report is filed with the appropriate Federal Reserve Bank acting as agent for the U.S. Department of the Treasury and is confidential.

Form FC-2: Report of monthly, consolidated data on the foreign exchange contracts and foreign currency–denominated assets and liabilities of major market participants. Reports are to be filed throughout the year by each foreign exchange market participant who had more than $50 billion equivalent in foreign exchange contracts on the last business day of any calendar quarter during the previous year. The report is filed with the appropriate Federal Reserve Bank acting as agent for the U.S. Department of the Treasury and is confidential.

Form FC-3: Report of quarterly, consolidated data on the foreign exchange contracts and foreign currency–denominated assets and liabilities of major market participants. Reports are to be filed throughout the calendar year by each foreign exchange market participant who had more than $5 billion equivalent in foreign exchange contracts on the last business day of any calendar quarter during the previous year and who does not file Form FC-2. The report is filed with the appropriate Federal Reserve Bank acting as agent for the U.S. Department of the Treasury and is confidential.

Reports for the Treasury Auction Filings

Treasury Auction: Treasury security report filed when it is compelled. Confirmation of filing has to be filed by a customer who is awarded a par amount of $500 million or more in U.S. government securities in a Treasury auction. The confirmation must include reportable net long position, if any. The confirmation is filed with the Federal Reserve Bank to which the bid was submitted and is not public.

Treasury International Capital Forms

Form CQ-1, CQ-2, and CM: Forms filed by U.S. persons who have claims on or financial liabilities to unaffiliated foreigners, have balances on deposit with foreign banks (in the U.S. or abroad), or otherwise engage in transactions in securities or other financial assets with foreigners.

Forms CQ-1 ("Financial Liabilities to, and Claims on, Unaffiliated Foreigners") and CQ-2 ("Commercial Liabilities to, and Claims on, Unaffiliated Foreigners") are quarterly reports that collect data on financial and commercial liabilities to, and claims on, unaffiliated foreigners held by nonbanking enterprises in the United States, which must be filed when the consolidated total of such liabilities is $10 million or more during that period.

Form CM ("Dollar Deposit and Certificate of Deposit Claims on Banks Abroad") is a monthly report whereby nonbanking enterprises in the United States report their total dollar deposit and certificate of deposit claims on foreign banks, which must be filed when the consolidated total of such claims is $10 million or more during that period. The forms are filed with the Federal Reserve Bank of New York and are nonpublic except for aggregate information.

Form S: Form is filed by any U.S. person who purchases or sells $2 million or more of long-term marketable domestic and foreign securities in a month in direct transactions with foreign persons. The form is filed with the Federal Reserve Bank of New York and is nonpublic except as to aggregate information.

Sale of Securities by an Issuer Exempt from Registration under Reg. D or 4(6)

Form D: Notice of sale filed after securities, such as interests in a private hedge fund, are sold in reliance on a Regulation D private placement exemption or a Section 4(6) exemption from the registration provisions of the 1933 Securities Act. The form is filed with the SEC and relevant states and is publicly available.

Secondary Sale of Restricted and Control Securities under Rule 144

Form 144: Form filed as notice of the proposed sale of restricted securities or securities held by an affiliate of the issuer in reliance on Rule 144 when the amount to be sold during any three-month period exceeds 500 shares or units or has an aggregate sales price in excess of $10,000. The form is filed with the SEC and the principal national securities exchange, if any, on which such security is traded and is publicly available.

Ownership of Equity Securities Publicly Traded in the United States

Schedule 13D: Disclosure report for any investor, including a hedge fund and its fund manager, who is considered beneficially to own more than 5 percent of a class of equity securities publicly traded in the United States. The report identifies the source and amount of the funds used for the acquisition and the purpose of the acquisition. This reporting requirement is triggered by direct or indirect acquisition of more than 5 percent of beneficial ownership of a class of equity securities publicly traded in the United States. Amendments must be filed promptly for material ownership changes. Some investors may instead report on short-form Schedule 13G if they are eligible. The report is filed with the SEC and is publicly available.

Schedule 13G: Short-form disclosure report for any passive investor, including a hedge fund and its fund manager, who would otherwise have to file a Schedule 13D but who owns less than 20 percent of the subject securities (or is in certain U.S. regulated investment businesses) and has not purchased securities for the purpose of influencing control. This reporting requirement is triggered by direct or indirect acquisition of beneficial ownership of more than 5 percent of a class of equity securities publicly traded in the United States. Amendments must be filed annually if there are any changes and either monthly (for U.S. regulated investment businesses) or promptly (for other passive investors) if ownership changes by more than 5 percent of the class. The report is filed with the SEC and is publicly available.

Forms 3, 4, and 5: Every director, officer, or owner of more than 10 percent of a class of equity securities of a domestic public company must file a statement of ownership. The initial filing is on Form 3, and changes are reported on Form 4. The annual statement of beneficial ownership of securities is on Form 5. The statements contain information on the reporting person's relationship to the company and on purchases and sales of the equity securities.

Form 3 reporting is triggered by acquisition of more than 10 percent of the equity securities of a domestic public company, the reporting person becoming a director or officer, or the equity securities becoming publicly traded as the case may be.

Form 4 reporting is triggered by any open market purchase or sale or an exercise of options of those reporting under Form 3.

Form 5 reporting is required annually for those insiders who have had exempt transactions and have not reported them previously on a Form 4. The statements are filed with the SEC and are publicly available.

Registered and Unregistered Institutional Investment Managers

Form 13F: Quarterly position report for registered and unregistered institutional investment managers (any person, other than a natural person, investing in or buying and selling securities for the person's own account, and any person exercising investment discretion with respect to the account of any other person) with investment discretion over $100 million or more in equity securities publicly traded in the United States. Reports contain position information about the equity securities under the discretion of the fund manager and the type of voting authority exercised by the fund manager. The reporting requirement is triggered by an institutional investment manager holding equity securities having an aggregate fair market value of at least $100 million on the last trading day of a calendar year and requires a report as of the end of that year and each of the next three quarters. The reports are filed with the SEC and are publicly available.

Material Associated Persons of Registered Broker-Dealers

Form 17-H: Material associated persons (MAP) reports, filed by registered broker-dealers. Some hedge fund managers are affiliated with registered broker-dealers. MAPs generally include material affiliates and parents and may therefore include an affiliated hedge fund manager or the related hedge fund. Broker-dealers must report four items:

1. Organizational chart of the broker-dealers.
2. Risk management policies of the broker-dealer.
3. Material legal proceedings.
4. Additional financial information, including aggregate positions, borrowing, and off-balance-sheet risk for each MAP.

The reporting requirement is triggered by status as broker or dealer registered under Section 15 of the Securities Exchange Act. This report is filed with the SEC quarterly and cumulatively at year-end and is not public. A variety of filings must be made with the SEC and the securities self-regulatory organizations by registered broker-dealers and their employees who are associated persons.

Commodity Futures Trading Commission (CFTC), National Futures Association (NFA), and Registration of Commodity Trading Advisors and Commodity Pool Operators

Commodity Pool Operator and Commodity Trading Advisor Registration: An individual or entity that operates or solicits funds for a commodity pool is generally required to register as a commodity pool operator (CPO). As a result, a hedge fund manager may be required to register as a commodity pool operator if the hedge fund trades futures or options on futures and the hedge fund manager operates the fund.

An individual or entity that, for compensation or profit, advises others as to the value of or advisability of buying or selling futures contracts or options on futures must generally register as a Commodity Trading Advisor (CTA) unless it has provided advice to 15 or fewer persons, including each person in an advised fund or pool, in the past 12 months and does not generally hold itself out to the public as a CTA. Providing advice indirectly includes exercising trading authority over a fund or account. A hedge fund manager is liable to register as a CTA if the related hedge fund trades futures or options on futures.

The documents required for registration as a commodity pool operator or Commodity Trading Advisor are a completed Form 7R providing CPO or CTA information; Form 8R providing biographical data and fingerprint card for each principal (defined to include executive officers, directors, and 10 percent owners), branch office manager, and associated person (defined to include persons soliciting fund interests or accounts or supervising persons so engaged); and proof of passage of the Series 3 examination for each associated person and proof of passage of the Series 3 and futures branch office manager exams for each branch office manager.

Applications for registration are filed with and approved by the NFA under authority granted to it by the CFTC, and the registration documents are generally public except for fingerprint cards, although confidentiality may be requested for certain information relating to the principals.

Form 3R: Form used to report any changes to information contained in the basic registration Form 7R. The requirement to file this form is triggered by changes in the information provided in Form 7R. The form is filed with the NFA and is public, though confidentiality may be requested for certain information relating to principals.

Form 8T Associated: Form that must be filed within 20 days of the termination of an associated person, principal, or branch manager. The form is filed with the NFA and is generally public.

Annual Report: Annual report of a fund must be filed pursuant to Reg. §4.22 (c) by that fund's CPO (unless the fund is exempt under §4.7). The annual report must contain certain information, such as actual performance information and fees, and must be distributed to each participant in the fund. The annual report must be filed by a registered CPO with the CFTC within 60 days of the fund's fiscal year-end and is generally publicly available; however, the CFTC is prohibited from disclosing information that would separately disclose the business transactions or market positions of any person, trade secrets, or names of any investors.

CPO/CTA: Annual compliance questionnaire concerning business activities for applicants registered as CPOs or CTAs. The questionnaire is filed with the NFA and is not public.

NFA Self-Audits: NFA members review operations on an annual basis using a self-examination checklist. The checklist focuses on a member's regulatory responsibilities and requests information on examinees' internal procedures. Registered CPOs and CTAs as members of the NFA are required to conduct such a self-audit annually. A written attestation affirming completion of the self-audit must be signed and dated by supervisory personnel. The attestation must be retained by the member for five years and provided to the NFA upon request.

Claims for Exemption: Filings made pursuant to Reg. §4.12 (b) (3) notice of claim for exemption from certain requirements by a CPO that complies with the Securities Act and manages a fund with limited trading in commodity futures and options or Reg. §4.7 (d) notice of claim for exemption by a CPO or CTA with "qualified eligible persons" as investors. Reg. §4.7 provides exemptions for qualifying CPOs and CTAs from most disclosure, recordkeeping, and reporting requirements applicable to CPOs and CTAs. These statements are filed with the CFTC and NFA and are public.

Disclosure Document: CPOs and CTAs are generally required to prepare detailed disclosure documents containing specified information.

Documents are filed with the CFTC and NFA and provided to investors but are not publicly available. CPOs and CTAs operating under Reg. §4.7 are exempt from the disclosure document requirement and are only required to provide all material disclosures and include specified legends on their materials. Under the exemption provided in Reg. §4.8, funds that would otherwise be treated as commodity pools with exemptions under Reg. §4.12 (b) compliance with the requirements of the Securities Act and certain limits on the trading of commodity futures and options, or that sell interests solely to accredited investors and rely on the safe harbor provisions of Rule 506 or 507 of Regulation D under the Securities Act, may begin soliciting, accepting, and receiving money upon providing the CFTC and the participants with disclosure documents for the fund; this requirement may be satisfied by a private placement memorandum.

Year-End Financial Reports for §4.7 Funds: Annual reports for §4.7 funds (funds that are limited to qualified eligible persons and are exempt from the normal disclosure requirements applicable to commodity pools) must contain a statement of financial condition, a statement of income (loss), appropriate footnote disclosure, and other material information, as well as legend as to any claim made for exemption. The annual report must be presented and computed in accordance with generally accepted accounting principles (GAAP) consistently applied, and if it is certified by an independent public accountant, it must be certified in accordance with Rule 1.16. The annual report is filed with the CFTC and NFA and distributed to each investor; the report is not public.

Positions Reports

Form 40: "Statement of Reporting Trader" for individuals who own or control reportable positions in futures. A hedge fund and/or hedge fund manager is required to file a Form 40 if it holds reportable positions in futures. A hedge fund and/or hedge fund manager is liable to file a Form 40 if it holds reportable positions upon special call by the CFTC or its designee. The form must be filed within 10 business days following the day that a hedge fund's position and/or its managers' position equals or exceeds specified levels. Such specified levels are set separately for each type of contract; for example, the reportable level for S&P 500 futures is 600 contracts. The Form 40 requires the disclosure of information about ownership and control of futures and options positions held by the reporting trader as well as the trader's use of the markets for hedging. Hedging exemptions from speculative position limits have to be reported. The form is filed with the CFTC and is not publicly available.

Form 102: Form filed by clearing members, futures commission merchants (FCMs), and foreign bankers. Form 102 identifies persons and entities, including hedge funds, having financial interest in or trading control of special accounts in futures and options; informs the CFTC of the type of account that is being reported; and gives preliminary information regarding whether positions and transactions are commercial in nature. The form must be filed when the account first becomes reportable or when it first contains reportable futures or options positions and must be updated when information concerning financial interest in or control of the special account changes. In addition, the form is used by exchanges to identify accounts reported through their large trader reporting systems for both futures and options. The form is filed with the CFTC and is nonpublic.

Application for Exemption from Speculative Position Limits

Speculative Position Limit Exemption: Application filed for exemption from speculative position limits. Exchanges generally have speculative position limits for physical commodities and stock index contracts, and the CFTC has speculative position limits for agricultural commodities. Exemptions from such limits are generally available for hedging transactions. Financial contracts, such as interest rate contracts, do not have such position limits. For example, under Rule 543 of the Chicago Mercantile Exchange (CME), persons intending to exceed speculative position limits on S&P 500 contracts must either file the required exemption application and receive approval prior to exceeding such limits or receive verbal approval prior to exceeding such limits and if approved file the required application promptly thereafter. Generally, an application for any speculative position limit exemption must show that such position is a bona fide hedging, risk management, arbitrage, or spread position. The filing is performed with the appropriate exchange in the case of physical commodities and stock index contracts and with the CFTC in the case of agricultural commodities.

Federal Trade Commission (FTC)

Hart-Scott-Rodino Notice: Notification filed prior to the consummation of certain mergers, acquisitions, and joint ventures. After notification is filed, there is a waiting period while the FTC and Department of Justice review the competitive effects of the transaction.

Acquisitions of voting securities are exempt from filing if they are made "solely for the purpose of investment" and if as a result of the acquisition, the securities held do not exceed 10 percent of the outstanding voting securities of the issuer. Securities are acquired solely for investment purposes if the person acquiring the securities has no intention of participating in the formulation, determination, or direction of the basic business decisions of the issuer. The notice is filed with the FTC and the Department of Justice.

Compliance Cases Involving Hedge Funds

The Securities and Exchange Commission passed a law to require all hedge funds to be registered in the United States effective in 2006. Also, it has undertaken at least 25 large cases in order to restore risk management controls and promote more transparency. These cases are described and commented on in the following section, taken from the SEC web site (www.sec.gov), and can be used as cases of reference for compliance officers and risk managers in hedge funds and funds of funds.

HEDGE FUND FRAUD CASE STUDIES

This section describes how hedge fund managers willfully behaved in alleged fraudulent activities. These documents are to be used as a basis for reference for risk managers and especially compliance officers to avoid being put into similar situations. These informational cases may also prompt other hedge fund managers to remedy any current internal problems that are similar to those described before they also are investigated for similar issues. These cases have been opened in recent years with the goal of producing regulations and enforcing them. The problems occurring in these hedge funds are similar to those of numerous other hedge funds that have not yet been investigated (but might be eventually) in their local and international markets. Each of these cases is described in detail as the enforced case occurred and a comment is provided if needed.

BALLYBUNION CAPITAL

Securities and Exchange Commission v. Michael T. Higgins, et al., United States District Court for the Northern District of California, No. 00-1657-MEJ

The Securities and Exchange Commission ("SEC") and the U.S. Attorney's Office for the Northern District of California announced the filing of separate civil and criminal actions against Michael T. Higgins, a hedge fund manager based in San Francisco, California. The actions allege that from December 1998 through March 2000, Higgins raised over $7.6 million by lying about the performance record of Ballybunion Capital Partners, L.P. (the "Fund"), and a hedge fund he ran. Higgins told investors that the Fund had impressive gains when in fact it had suffered severe losses. By March 2000, the Fund's assets had dwindled to approximately $750,000, barely one-tenth the amount Higgins continued to tell investors they had. Higgins also distributed false information to a website that posted the information on the Internet.

Named as defendants in the SEC's action are: Higgins; his wholly owned investment advisory firm, Ballybunion Capital Associates, LLC ("Ballybunion Capital"); and the Fund. Higgins is the sole defendant in the criminal action. Higgins, 36, resides in San Anselmo, California, while Ballybunion Capital and the Fund are located in San Francisco, California.

Higgins first solicited investors by grossly overstating the Fund's 1998 performance record. For example, Higgins told investors that the Fund had gross returns of nearly 54% and net returns of nearly 40% for 1998. In fact, the Fund had a net loss that year and by late 1998 had less than $11,000 under management. Based on these and other misrepresentations, in early 1999 Higgins raised approximately $6 million (out of an eventual total of $7.6 million raised) from investors.

By May 1999, the Fund had suffered trading losses of approximately $2.4 million, or 40% of the $6 million Higgins had raised to that point, according to the complaints. To conceal the losses and solicit additional investors, Higgins continued to distribute performance summaries that falsified the Fund's performance, and he forged "reports" of the Fund's clearing broker and auditors.

BAYOU MANAGEMENT LLC

Commission Seeks Freeze of Assets and Appointment of Receiver

The Securities and Exchange Commission ("Commission") filed a civil injunctive action against Samuel Israel III of New York and Daniel E. Marino of Connecticut, the managers of a group of hedge funds known as the Bayou Funds ("Funds"), based in Stamford, Connecticut. The Commission's complaint alleges that, beginning in 1996 and continuing through the present, Israel and Marino have defrauded investors in the Funds and misappropriated millions of dollars in investor funds for their personal use. The Commission is seeking permanent injunctions for violations of the antifraud provisions of the federal securities laws against Israel, the founder of and investment adviser to the Funds; Bayou Management, the investment adviser to the funds; and Marino, the chief financial officer of Bayou Management. Additionally, the Commission has requested that the court freeze the defendants' assets and appoint a receiver to marshal any remaining assets for the benefit of defrauded hedge fund investors. All of the defendants have consented to the freeze of assets and appointment of a receiver. The requested relief is subject to court approval.

The United States Attorney for the Southern District of New York announced that it has filed criminal fraud charges against Israel and Marino. The Commodity Futures Trading Commission (CFTC) has also announced that it has filed an action arising from the same conduct.

The Commission alleges in its complaint that from 1996 through 2005, investors deposited over $450 million into the Bayou Funds and a predecessor fund. During that period, Israel and Marino defrauded current investors, and attracted new investors, by grossly exaggerating the Funds' performance to make it appear that the Funds were profitable and attractive investments, when in fact, the Funds had never posted a year-end profit. The Commission's complaint further alleges that, in furtherance of their fraud, Israel and Marino concocted and disseminated to the Funds' investors periodic account statements and performance summaries containing fictitious profit and loss figures and forged audited financial statements in order to hide multimillion dollar trading losses from investors. Among other things, the complaint alleges that:

- Israel, Marino, and Bayou Management overstated the Funds' 2003 performance by claiming a $43 million profit in the four hedge funds, while trading records show that the Funds actually lost $49 million;
- In 1999, Marino created a sham accounting firm, "Richmond-Fairfield Associates," that he used to fabricate annual "independent" audits of the Funds and attest to the fake results that he and Israel had assigned to the Funds;
- Israel and Marino stole investor funds by annually withdrawing from the Funds "incentive fees" that they were not entitled to receive because the Funds never returned a year-end profit;
- By mid-2004, Israel and Marino had largely suspended trading securities on behalf of the Funds and transferred all remaining Fund assets, consisting of approximately $150 million, to Israel and other non-Bayou-related entities, for investment in fraudulent prime bank note

trading programs and venture capital investments in non-public startup companies; and

- Despite having abandoned their hedge fund strategy in 2004, Bayou Management continued to send periodic statements and financial statements to investors describing purportedly profitable hedge fund trading activities through mid-2005.

The Commission's complaint also seeks to permanently enjoin: Bayou Management, Israel, Marino, and the Bayou Funds from violating Section 17(a) of the Securities Act of 1933, Section 10(b) of the Securities Exchange Act of 1934 ("Exchange Act") and Exchange Act Rule 10b-5 thereunder, which are the general antifraud provisions of the federal securities laws; Bayou Management and Israel from violating the antifraud provisions of the Investment Advisers Act of 1940 ("Advisers Act"), Sections 206(1) and 206(2); and Marino from aiding and abetting violations of Sections 206(1) and 206(2) of the Advisers Act. The Commission also seeks disgorgement of ill-gotten gains, prejudgment interest, and civil money penalties from Israel, Marino, and Bayou Management.

The Commission acknowledges the assistance and cooperation of the White Plains Division of the United States Attorney's Office for the Southern District of New York, the Federal Bureau of Investigation, and the CFTC in this matter. The Commission's investigation continues.

BEACON HILL ASSET MANAGEMENT

The Securities and Exchange Commission ("Commission") deems it appropriate and in the public interest that public administrative proceedings be, and hereby are, instituted pursuant to Section 203(f) of the Investment Advisers Act of 1940 ("Advisers Act") against John D. Barry ("Barry"), Thomas P. Daniels ("Daniels"), John M. Irwin ("Irwin"), and Mark P. Miszkiewicz ("Miszkiewicz") (collectively, "Respondents").

In anticipation of the institution of these proceedings, Respondents have each submitted an Offer of Settlement ("Offers") which the Commission has determined to accept. Solely for the purpose of these proceedings and any other proceedings brought by or on behalf of the Commission, or to which the Commission is a party, and without admitting or denying the findings herein, except as to the Commission's jurisdiction over them and the subject matter of these proceedings, which are admitted, Respondents consent to the entry of this Order Instituting Administrative Proceedings

Pursuant to Section 203(f) of the Investment Advisers Act of 1940, Making Findings, and Imposing Remedial Sanctions ("Order"), as set forth below.

On the basis of this Order and Respondents' Offers, the Commission finds that:

Barry was the President and part-owner of Beacon Hill Asset Management LLC ("Beacon Hill"), Chairman of its Management Board, and was responsible for marketing, sales, client relationships and overall management of the firm. From at least the beginning of 2002 through October 2002, Barry was associated with Beacon Hill, which served as the investment advisor for certain hedge funds, including Beacon Hill Master Ltd. Barry, 53 years old, is a resident of New Jersey.

Daniels was the Chief Investment Officer and part-owner of Beacon Hill, and directed the firm's overall investment, securities valuations, and risk management. From at least the beginning of 2002 through October 2002, Daniels was associated with Beacon Hill. Daniels, 46 years old, is a resident of New Jersey.

Irwin was a part-owner of Beacon Hill and was the Senior Portfolio Manager in charge of the firm's credit sensitive mortgage portfolio, sharing portfolio management responsibilities and all trading decisions with respect to the funds' investments and security valuations with the Chief Investment Officer. From at least the beginning of 2002 through October 2002, Irwin was associated with Beacon Hill. Irwin, 47 years old, is a resident of New Jersey.

Miszkiewicz was the Chief Financial Officer and part-owner of Beacon Hill, and was responsible for Beacon Hill's financial, accounting and administrative operations. From at least the beginning of 2002 through October 2002, Miszkiewicz was associated with Beacon Hill. Miszkiewicz, 40 years old, is a resident of New Jersey.

On October 28, 2004, final judgments were entered by consent against each of the Respondents, permanently enjoining each of them from future violations of Sections 17(a) of the Securities Act of 1933 ("Securities Act"), Section 10(b) of the Exchange Act and Rule 10b-5 thereunder, and Sections 206(1), 206(2), and 206(3) of the Advisers Act, in the civil action entitled *Securities and Exchange Commission v. Beacon Hill Asset Management, et al.*, Civil Action Number 02-8855(LAK), in the United States District Court for the Southern District of New York.

The Commission's Amended Complaint alleged that from at least the beginning of 2002 through October 2002, the defendants in the civil action, including the Respondents, made material misrepresentations to investors about the valuation methodology Beacon Hill used for calculating Net Asset Values ("NAVs"); the hedging and trading strategy for its purportedly "market neutral" hedge funds; and the value and performance of these funds. In addition, the Amended Complaint alleged that the defendants manipulated the valuations to allow steady and positive growth to be reported, and to hide losses. The Amended Complaint also alleged that as the funds suffered losses during the summer of 2002, the defendants made an increasing and ultimately unsuccessful bet on interest rates rising in an attempt to cover Beacon Hill's hidden losses. The Amended Complaint further alleged that the defendants traded between the hedge funds and other accounts Beacon Hill managed at prices that defrauded the hedge funds to try to hide losses in the managed accounts. The Amended Complaint alleged that when the defendants realized that the losses would be discovered, three of them liquidated an account where they were the only investors by effecting trades with the hedge fund without disclosure to investors. The Amended Complaint further alleged that on or about October 7, 2002, when Beacon Hill's prime broker had challenged the valuation of the hedge funds and Beacon Hill was forced to admit it had sustained losses, the defendants misrepresented that the magnitude of the actual losses was only approximately 25 percent in an attempt to save Beacon Hill's operations and make the losses appear to be the result of market conditions. Finally, the Amended Complaint alleged that on October 17, 2002, the defendants finally announced the full extent of investor losses, admitting that, as of September 30, the NAVs of Beacon Hill's hedge funds had declined 54 percent from previously reported August 31, 2002 levels.

In view of the foregoing, the Commission deems it appropriate and in the public interest to impose the sanctions agreed to in Respondent Barry, Daniels, Irwin and Miszkiewicz Offers.

Accordingly, it is hereby ORDERED:

Pursuant to Section 203(f) of the Advisers Act, Respondents Barry, Daniels, and Irwin be, and hereby are barred from association with any investment adviser;

Pursuant to Section 203(f) of the Advisers Act, Respondent Miszkiewicz be, and hereby is barred from association with any investment adviser, with the right to reapply for association after 4 years to the appropriate self-regulatory organization, or if there is none, to the Commission;

Any reapplication for association by the Respondents will be subject to the applicable laws and regulations governing the reentry process, and reentry may be conditioned upon a number of factors, including, but not limited to, the satisfaction of any or all of the following: (a) any disgorgement ordered against the Respondents, whether or not the Commission has fully or partially waived payment of such disgorgement; (b) any arbitration award related to the conduct that served as the basis for the Commission order; (c) any self-regulatory organization arbitration award to a customer, whether or not related to the conduct that served as the basis for the Commission order; and (d) any restitution order by a self-regulatory organization, whether or not related to the conduct that served as the basis for the Commission order.

CHESTNUT FUND

The Securities and Exchange Commission ("Commission") announced that the Honorable Richard G. Stearns of the United States District Court for the District of Massachusetts has approved an Initial Distribution Plan to distribute $1.1 million to victims of former money manager Stevin R. Hoover. The distribution will be supervised by Keith D. Lowey, CPA, of Foxborough, Massachusetts, who was appointed by the court as receiver over the Chestnut Fund LP, a hedge fund once-managed by Hoover.

In its complaint, the Commission alleged that between 1995 and 2001, Hoover and his wholly-owned entities misappropriated funds from investment advisory clients, including the hedge fund. The Commission also alleged that Hoover solicited and obtained investments in the hedge fund by making fraudulent misrepresentations to prospective investors, and that Hoover attempted to conceal his misappropriations by distributing fictitious account statements to investors.

As previously announced, on February 11, 2003, the court entered a Final Judgment, by consent, ordering Hoover and/or his wholly-owned entities to pay disgorgement of ill-gotten gains and prejudgment interest in the amount of $1,011,007.48, and permanently enjoining them from future violations of the relevant provisions of the federal securities laws. On February 26, 2003, the Commission entered an administrative order, by consent that permanently bars Hoover from association with an investment adviser. In a related criminal proceeding, Hoover pleaded guilty to criminal charges that he defrauded investment advisory clients out of nearly $200,000 in violation of Section 206(2) of the Investment Advisers Act of 1940. Hoover is currently serving 3 years of supervised release, following an 18 month prison sentence.

For more information see Litigation Release Nos. 17981 (February 11, 2003), 17825 (November 1, 2002), 17666 (August 8, 2002), 17487 (April

24, 2002), 17284 (December 19, 2001), 17240 (November 19, 2001), 17236 (November 16, 2001) and 16983 (May 2, 2001).

DOBBINS CAPITAL

SEC v. J. Robert Dobbins, Dobbins Capital Corp., Dobbins Offshore Capital LLC, Dobbins Partners, L.P., and Dobbins Offshore, Ltd., Civ. Action No. 3-04-CV-605(H) (Northern District of Texas)

The Securities and Exchange Commission filed an action in the United States District Court for the Northern District of Texas and was granted emergency relief against J. Robert Dobbins, two unregistered investment advisers under his control, Dobbins Capital Corp. and Dobbins Offshore Capital LLC (collectively "Dobbins Investment Advisers"), and two unregistered hedge funds, Dobbins Partners, L.P. and Dobbins Offshore, Ltd. (collectively, "Dobbins Hedge Funds") for violations of the antifraud provisions of the federal securities laws.

The Commission alleges that Dobbins, since at least January 1, 2000, raised at least $50 million from over 50 investors from around the world. The complaint alleges that Dobbins made false statements to Dobbins Hedge Funds investors concerning the funds' performance by arbitrarily overvaluing investments in thinly-traded and non-publicly traded securities. The complaint also alleges that Dobbins provided the false valuations to Fund investors, in some circumstances, at the time of their investment, in e-mail correspondence, telephone conversations, meetings, and reports posted on Dobbins' Internet website. The complaint alleges that then, using the fraudulently inflated valuations, Dobbins caused the funds to pay management and incentive fees of over $5.3 million to Dobbins and the Dobbins Investment Advisers. Further, the complaint alleges that Dobbins caused the Dobbins Hedge Funds to fraudulently pay unnecessary commission payments to a broker, who then kicked back a significant portion of the commissions to Dobbins.

The Complaint alleges that all of the defendants violated Section 17(a) of the Securities Act of 1933 and Section 10(b) of the Securities Exchange Act of 1934 and Rule 10b-5 thereunder. The complaint also alleges that Dobbins and the Dobbins Investment Advisers violated Section 206(1) and (2) of the Investment Advisers Act of 1940. Without admitting or denying the Commission's allegations, Defendants Dobbins, Dobbins Capital, Dobbins Offshore Capital, and Dobbins Offshore consented to the emergency relief sought. The Court today issued a preliminary injunction as well as an order freezing assets, requiring an accounting of all assets and investor funds, and prohibiting the destruction of documents.

FANAM CAPITAL MANAGEMENT

The Securities and Exchange Commission ("Commission") deems it appropriate and in the public interest that public administrative and cease-and-desist proceedings be, and hereby are, instituted pursuant to Sections 203(e), 203(f), and 203(k) of the Investment Advisers Act of 1940 ("Advisers Act"), against Fanam Capital Management ("Fanam"), Richard J. Ennis ("Ennis"), and Seth Morgulas ("Morgulas").

1. Fanam was organized on June 30, 2000 as a Nevada limited liability company. Fanam was an unregistered investment adviser of a hedge fund and its assets under management never exceeded $25 million. Ennis, Morgulas, and Michael Beckford ("Beckford") were the Managing Members, officers, and principal owners of Fanam. Fanam managed Fanam Fund I LLC (the "Fund"). Fanam employed primarily three investment strategies for the Fund: (1) Fanam sought to identify covered call opportunities; it then bought stocks, held the positions for approximately one month, and wrote short-term call options against these stocks; (2) Fanam bought LEAPs, and wrote short-term call options against the LEAPs throughout the life of the positions; and (3) Fanam developed a statistical algorithm to identify temporarily mispriced stocks that were likely to revert to their statistical mean, and traded the stocks accordingly. Fanam ceased operations, and now only exists as a corporate shell.

2. Ennis, age 37, is a resident of Pace, Florida. He was the President and Chief Executive Officer of Fanam, and a Managing Member. He served as Fanam's marketer and principal client contact. Ennis solicited the majority of Fanam's third party investors, and issued periodic statements and sent periodic performance updates to investors. Ennis was also a Fanam investor who lost money as a result of Beckford's fraud, and he contacted the criminal authorities after learning of Beckford's fraud.

3. Morgulas, age 33, is a New York, New York resident. He was an Executive Vice President, Portfolio Manager, and Managing Member of Fanam. Morgulas' responsibilities included strategic planning, and market strategy and analysis. In addition, Morgulas performed company specific research, and directed Fanam's trading strategies, which were executed by Beckford, Fanam's trader. Morgulas was also a Fanam investor who lost money as a result of Beckford's fraud. Prior to joining Fanam, Morgulas was a securities lawyer and financial research analyst.

Other Relevant Persons or Entities

4. Beckford, age 35, is a Schaumburg, Illinois, resident. He was an Executive Vice President, Portfolio Manager, and Managing Member of Fanam. Beckford was responsible for executing Fanam's trades, and for managing Fanam's administrative operations, serving as both trader and accountant. Beckford was the only Managing Member who communicated with the initial clearing broker and Fanam's external accountant.

5. The Fund was organized as a Delaware limited liability company on October 11, 2000. The Fund had less than 100 investors and was liquidated in June 2003.

Beckford's Fraud

6. Beckford gambled with investor money, traded outside of the Fund's objectives, and paid himself money to which he was not entitled, resulting in investor losses of $4,828,129.

7. Beckford started gambling with investor money in February 2001. Beckford used the Fund's money for gambling activities in Lake Tahoe, Las Vegas, and Henderson, Nevada, at horseracing tracks and off-track betting parlors around the country, and on sporting events over the Internet. For example, on December 17, 2002, February 7, 2003, and March 7, 2003, Beckford wired $150,000, $243,000, and $307,000, respectively, to the Bellagio Hotel Casino in Las Vegas from Fanam's brokerage account. Beckford lost the majority of the money sent to the Bellagio by gambling at its casino and on its sports book, and he lost some of the remaining money gambling at other casinos. Beckford also used Fanam's money to finance his gambling trips. Investors paid for Beckford's airfare, rental cars, and hotel rooms. In total, Beckford lost $776,344 of investor money through his gambling losses and travel expenses.

8. Beckford also failed to follow Fanam's stated trading objectives. Beckford, among other things, held unhedged stocks, bought unhedged LEAPs, and traded unhedged equity and index options. For example, in February 2002, Beckford lost $46,500 in a single unhedged index option trade. Later that month, Beckford bought large unhedged quantities of March NASDAQ index puts for $126,000 and $392,000, respectively, and these puts expired worthless. Beckford continued to increase the size of his index option trades throughout 2002 to attempt to recoup Fanam's losses. On December 6, 2002, Beckford bought $505,000 worth of NASDAQ index calls, and these calls expired worthless. On January 14, 2003, Beckford placed a larger bet on the next month of the same options series for $1,976,000, and these calls also expired

worthless. In total, Beckford lost $3,876,775 trading outside of the Fund's objectives.

9. Beckford also misappropriated investor funds for his personal use. Beckford paid himself a monthly draw of approximately $5,000 from July 2001 through March 2003 and reimbursed himself for expenses. The Managing Members agreed that Beckford could take a monthly advance against his percentage of the 1.0% management fee and the 20% incentive fee (the "Fees"). Because Fanam failed to make any money during this time, Beckford was not entitled to a monthly draw or personal expense reimbursements. In total, Beckford misappropriated $175,010 of Fanam's money for his personal use.

10. Beckford issued false documents to Ennis, Morgulas, and Fanam's investors to cover-up his fraudulent conduct. He prepared and sent false spreadsheets to Ennis and Morgulas regarding Fanam's trading, holdings, and performance. Beckford also forged auditor statements and prepared false K-1's. He furnished copies of these documents to Ennis and Morgulas, fully aware that Ennis would use these documents to solicit investors. The returns Beckford listed in these documents did not include his gambling losses, trading losses, and improper draws. The investor statements issued to Fanam's investors, based on Beckford's misrepresentations, stated that the Fund's annual returns were approximately 25% to 30%. In reality, the Fund lost money during the entire time it operated.

Morgulas' Failure to Supervise

11. Beckford was subject to Morgulas' supervision. Morgulas was responsible for managing the Fund's positions, and he had the authority to direct Beckford's trading to manage the Fund's portfolio. Morgulas regularly communicated with Beckford regarding the Fund's portfolio. Beckford was Fanam's sole trader, and managed Fanam's administrative operations. Only Beckford communicated with Fanam's initial clearing broker and external accountant. Morgulas never independently reviewed Beckford's trading activity or independently confirmed the Fund's positions or distributions. Morgulas never contacted the initial clearing broker or the accountant to confirm the Fund's holdings. Instead, Morgulas relied on spreadsheets supplied by Beckford to monitor the trading, holdings, and performance of the Fund.

12. Morgulas failed reasonably to supervise Beckford with a view to preventing violations of the federal securities laws. Morgulas failed to take reasonable supervisory action, which could have included maintaining accurate records of the Fund's transactions, reviewing daily trading activity, valuing the Fund's positions, and separating trading and administrative

operations. Morgulas' reliance on Beckford's spreadsheets, without independently verifying their accuracy, enabled Beckford to continue his fraudulent activity.

Ennis Inflated Fanam's Assets under Management

13. Unrelated to Beckford's fraud, from November 2001 through November 2002, Ennis overstated Fanam's assets under management to institutional investors. In the fall of 2001, Fanam entered into negotiations with an international bank to manage certain holdings of the bank. Ennis and representatives of this bank discussed Fanam managing $13 million to $20 million of the bank's assets in an offshore account, but the money never came into Fanam's account. Nevertheless, Ennis told investors that Fanam managed $13 to $20 million in an offshore account. For example in November 2001, Ennis told a potential institutional investor that Fanam managed $13 million in an offshore account, and this investor subsequently invested $800,000. On November 30, 2001, Fanam's actual assets under management were only $139,565. In November 2002, Ennis solicited a large "fund of funds" to invest with Fanam, and he told this investor that Fanam had "total firm assets" of $25.25 million. The investor subsequently invested $8,000,000 with Fanam in December 2002. On October 31, 2002 and November 29, 2002, Fanam's actual "firm" assets under management were $1,282,112 and $1,545,945, respectively.

Legal Findings

14. As a result of the conduct described above, Fanam willfully violated Sections 206(1) and (2) of the Advisers Act, which prohibit an investment adviser from employing any device, scheme, or artifice to defraud or to engage in any transaction, practice, or course of business, which operates as a fraud or deceit upon any client or prospective client.

15. As a result of the conduct described above, Ennis willfully aided and abetted and caused Fanam's violations of Sections 206(1) and 206(2) of the Advisers Act by knowingly and substantially assisting Fanam in employing any device, scheme, or artifice to defraud or to engage in any transaction, practice, or course of business, which operates as a fraud or deceit upon any client or prospective client by overstating Fanam's assets under management.

16. As a result of the conduct described above, Morgulas failed to reasonably supervise Beckford, with a view to preventing violations of the federal securities laws while Beckford was subject to his supervision, within the meaning of Section 203(e)(6) of the Advisers Act. A person is a "supervisor" if, under the facts and circumstances of a particular case, that person has the requisite degree of responsibility, ability, or authority to affect the conduct of the other individual whose behavior is at issue. In the Matter of John H. Gutfreund, Thomas W. Strauss, and John W. Meriwether, Exchange Act Rel. No. 31554, 51 S.E.C. Docket 93 (December 3, 1992). A supervisor with an unregistered investment adviser has a duty to reasonably supervise individuals subject to his supervision with a view towards preventing violations of the federal securities laws.

FOUNTAINHEAD FUND, LP

Securities and Exchange Commission v. Anthony P. Postiglione, Jr., et al., Civil Action No. 04-CV-3604 (E.D. Pa.)

The Securities and Exchange Commission ("Commission") announced that on August 9, 2004, the Honourable Legrome D. Davis, U.S. District Court Judge for the Eastern District of Pennsylvania, issued a preliminary injunction against Anthony P. Postiglione, Jr. ("Postiglione"), of Malvern, PA, William J. Lennon ("Lennon"), of Media, PA, and two companies they owned and controlled, namely, Fountainhead Fund, LP ("the Fund"), a hedge fund located in Wayne, PA, and its general partner Fountainhead Asset Management, LLC ("FAM"). The Court's Order, which was entered upon the defendants' consent, preliminarily enjoins them from violating the antifraud provisions of the Securities Act of 1933, the Securities Exchange Act of 1934, and the Investment Advisers Act of 1940, and continues an asset freeze, appointment of a receiver, and other relief imposed by the Judge in the temporary restraining order issued July 30, 2004.

In its Complaint, originally filed July 30, 2004, the Commission alleges that, from November 2001 through the present, Postiglione and Lennon raised approximately $5 million for the Fund from at least 18 private investors. Through a series of fraudulent acts, defendants Postiglione and Lennon, acting through FAM, obtained assets fraudulently, lulled investors into keeping their assets in the Fund, and misused investor funds. The Complaint alleges that, from the inception of the Fund through the present, Postiglione and Lennon have sent false quarterly statements and newsletters to investors, consistently overstating the Fund's value and performance. In addition, they have overstated the amount of Postiglione's personal investment in the Fund and the Fund's performance in order to lure new investments. Further, in violation of their fiduciary duties to their clients, Postiglione and Lennon excessively traded several Fund securities accounts for the sole purpose of generating soft dollar credits, which they then withdrew as cash and used for, among other things, their own personal living expenses. The Complaint alleges that, during the course of this fraud, Postiglione and Lennon also misappropriated several hundred thousand dollars of Fund assets for their personal use. As of the date of filing, investor funds in the Fund totalled approximately $1.7 million.

The Complaint alleges that defendants Postiglione, Lennon, FAM, and the Fund have violated Section 17(a) of the Securities Act, Section 10(b) of the Exchange Act, and Rule 10b-5 hereunder, and that Postiglione, Lennon, and FAM have violated Sections 206(1) and 206(2) of the Advisers Act. The Complaint seeks permanent injunctions, disgorgement together with prejudgment interest, and civil penalties.

FRIEDLANDER MANAGEMENT CORPORATION

1. In May 2001, the SEC brought this action to stop a massive fraud perpetrated by Defendants Friedlander, Friedlander Management Limited ("FML"), Friedlander Capital Management Corporation ("FCMC"), Opal International Fund ("Opal") and Friedlander Limited Partnership ("FLP") in connection with an investment entity known as Friedlander International Limited ("the Hedge Fund"). Since August 2000, or earlier, Defendants Friedlander, FML, and FCMC had misrepresented and inflated the net asset value ("NAV") of the Hedge Fund to its shareholders by overstating the value of certain assets of the Hedge Fund, had induced investments in the Hedge Fund based upon misrepresented and inflated statements of performance results, and had redeemed their own interests in the Hedge Fund at misrepresented and inflated values, to the detriment of the Hedge Fund's other investors. In perpetrating their fraudulent scheme, Friedlander and FCMC had used the assets of Opal and FLP, other investment funds managed by Friedlander and FCMC, to make month-end purchases of a security, in order to manipulate the price upward and thereby artificially inflate the value of securities held by the Hedge Fund.

2. The SEC hereby amends its Complaint to include an additional and separate fraudulent scheme involving the management of a pooled investment fund ("pooled fund") by Friedlander and FCMC, including the generation and distribution of false and misleading reports regarding the investors' returns in this pooled fund, the fraudulent use of an accounting firm's letterhead and signature, and the conversion by Friedlander and FCMC of investor funds for Friedlander's personal use.

3. By engaging in the conduct set forth in paragraphs 1 and 2, Friedlander, the Hedge Fund, FML, FCMC, Opal and FLP have violated, and unless enjoined will continue to violate, Section 17(a) of the Securities Act of 1933 ("Securities Act"), 15 U.S.C. § 77q(a), and Section 10(b) of the

Securities Exchange Act of 1934 ("Exchange Act"), 15 U.S.C. § 78j(b), and Rule 10b-5 hereunder, 17 C.F.R. § 240.10b-5. In addition, Friedlander, FML and FCMC have violated, and unless enjoined will continue to violate, Section 206(1) and (2) of the Investment Advisors Act of 1940 ("Adviser's Act"), 15 U.S.C. § 80b-6.

    4. The SEC seeks permanent injunctions against the Defendants from engaging in the wrongful conduct alleged in this Complaint. The SEC also seeks a final judgment ordering the Defendants to account for and to disgorge any ill-gotten gains and to pay prejudgment interest thereon, and ordering the Defendants to pay civil money penalties pursuant to Section 20(d) of the Securities Act, 15 U.S.C. § 77t(d), and Section 21(d)(3) of the Exchange Act, 15 U.S.C. § 78u(d)(3).

Jurisdiction and Venue

5. This court has jurisdiction over this action pursuant to Section 22(a) of the Securities Act, 15 U.S.C. § 77v(a), Sections 21(e) and 27 of the Exchange Act, 15 U.S.C. §§ 77u(e) and 78aa, and Section 214 of the Advisors Act, 15 U.S.C. § 80b-14.

    6. Venue in this Court is proper because certain of the transactions, acts, practices and courses of business alleged occurred within the Southern District of New York, including the purchase of investments on behalf of the Hedge Fund by Friedlander, FML, FCMC, Opal and FLP through accounts at Bear Stearns Securities Corp. ("Bear Stearns") as well as other brokerage and bank accounts located in this District. Substantially all of the assets of the Hedge Fund are located in an account at Bear Stearns, which is located in this District. In addition, the primary bank account for FCMC, into which pooled fund deposits were made, was located in this District at Citibank, NA.

Defendants

7. BURTON G. FRIEDLANDER, age 64, is an unregistered investment advisor who lives and works in Greenwich, Connecticut. Friedlander is a director of Friedlander International Limited (the Hedge Fund), and is a director of and controls both Friedlander Management Limited (FML) and Friedlander Capital Management Corporation (FCMC), which act as the investment advisor for the Hedge Fund.

    8. FRIEDLANDER INTERNATIONAL LIMITED (the Hedge Fund) is a hedge fund incorporated as an International Business Company in the Commonwealth of the Bahamas, with its registered office in Nassau, Bahamas. The Hedge Fund is managed by Friedlander Management Limited (FML).

9. FRIEDLANDER MANAGEMENT LIMITED (FML) is an International Business Company incorporated in the Bahamas. FML manages the Hedge Fund through subcontracts with other entities, including Friedlander Capital Management Corporation (FCMC). FML is also a shareholder in the Hedge Fund.

10. FRIEDLANDER CAPITAL MANAGEMENT CORPORATION (FCMC) is a Connecticut corporation in the business of investment management and based in Greenwich, Connecticut. Friedlander controls FCMC and is solely responsible for the day-to-day operations and investment advice rendered by FCMC. FCMC was retained by FML to manage the assets of the Hedge Fund. In addition, FCMC was the entity through which Friedlander managed the pooled investment fund.

11. OPAL INTERNATIONAL FUND (Opal) is an investment vehicle incorporated in the Cayman Islands. The assets of Opal are managed by Friedlander and FCMC, who make all investment decisions for Opal.

12. FRIEDLANDER LIMITED PARTNERSHIP (FLP) is an investment vehicle formed as a Limited Partnership in the State of Connecticut. Friedlander and FCMC also manage and make investment decisions regarding the assets of FLP.

Other Involved Entities

13. Morning Star Management Limited ("MSML"), is an International Business Company formed under the laws of the Bahamas, and controlled by Dean W. Lodmell ("Lodmell"), a resident of Connecticut. FML used MSML to perform the Hedge Fund's administrative functions, including a month end calculation of the net asset value (NAV) using information supplied by Friedlander, FCMC, Bear Stearns, and public resources. On August 4, 2000, MSML resigned as administrator effective November 2, 2000. However, Lodmell continued to perform administrative services for the Hedge Fund, including calculation of the NAV through at least January 2001.

14. Lion Investor Services (Bahamas) ("Lion"), an entity organized under the laws of the Bahamas, began providing administrative services to the Hedge Fund in January 2001, replacing MSML.

15. eNote.com Inc. ("eNote") is a Delaware corporation with its principal place of business in Williston, Vermont. The stock of eNote is traded over-the-counter and quoted on the OTC Bulletin Board system. eNote purports to be in the business of developing a system to allow access to electronic mail through a television set. According to its most recent filing with the SEC, as of September 30, 2000, the liabilities of eNote exceeded its assets. eNote has not generated any substantial revenue from operations since its inception in April 1999, and has relied upon loans from Friedlander, FCMC and others to meet its operating expenses.

16. KPMG, LLP ("KPMG"), formerly known as KPMG Peat Marwick LLP, is an accounting firm that Friedlander retained in or around January 1995 to prepare compilation reports for pooled fund investors for the fiscal year 1994. The letterhead of the firm was used for subsequent compilation reports without its knowledge or consent.

17. Gruntal & Co., Inc. ("Gruntal") was a broker-dealer at which Friedlander maintained a securities account for the pooled fund.

The First Fraudulent Scheme

18. Since October 2000, or earlier, the defendants distributed false and misleading account statements to investors in the Hedge Fund, and, by means of these misrepresentations, induced additional investors to invest in the Hedge Fund. While directing and assisting in the calculation of the Net Asset Value (NAV) of the Hedge Fund, Friedlander overstated the value of certain unmarketable warrants in eNote held by the Hedge Fund and failed to account for the dilution of the common stock that would occur if the warrants were exercised and additional stock issued by eNote. In the calculation of the NAVs for October, November and December 2000, Friedlander valued the warrants at a price higher than the market price of the underlying common stock and continued to ignore the dilutive effect that the exercise of the warrants would cause.

19. In addition, at the end of each month from August 2000 to December 2000, Friedlander manipulated the stock price of eNote upward to be included in the month-end NAV. FCMC and Friedlander used the assets of Opal and FLP to purchase eNote stock in the month-end manipulations. On the last day of trading in August, September, October, November, and December 2000, Friedlander caused those two funds to purchase large amounts of eNote stock, which resulted in a price increase for each of those months. The price of eNote stock doubled on the last trading days of October 2000 and December 2000. At no other time during those five months did Friedlander (through FLP and Opal) purchase stock except at month's end.

20. Friedlander continued to sell shares in the Hedge Fund to investors through December 2000, using the Fund's inflated NAV. Between September 2000 and February 2001, Friedlander caused FML to redeem approximately $2.4 million in the Hedge Fund shares at inflated asset values for his benefit and that of FML and FCMC.

The Operations of the Hedge Fund, MSML and FCMC

21. Defendant Friedlander controlled FML and FCMC and was solely responsible for overseeing their day-to-day operations. Through these entities, he exercised de facto control over the investment program of the Hedge Fund and had the authority and discretion to effect securities transactions for the Hedge Fund. Friedlander effected transfers of monies belonging to the Fund, had sole discretion in managing the Fund's assets, had the ability to hire or remove the Fund's administrator, and had the sole ability to modify the terms of the Hedge Fund's "explanatory memorandum," which served as the Hedge Fund's offering memorandum. As compensation for managing and advising the Hedge Fund, FML received a monthly management fee based upon a percentage of the total NAV of the Hedge Fund as well as a quarterly performance fee based upon the net profits of the Hedge Fund. FML then distributed the fee proceeds to FCMC and Friedlander as compensation for their role in the management of the Hedge Fund.

22. The Hedge Fund was not "transparent" in that its investors were not provided with the identity of the securities held in the Hedge Fund. The sole disclosure made to Hedge Fund investors was a statement of the per-share NAV of the Hedge Fund as of the last trading day of each month. The Hedge Fund was not registered with the SEC and did not make public filings of its holdings or financial condition.

23. Since the Fund's inception in 1998 through January 2001, MSML and Lodmell calculated the NAV of the Hedge Fund on a monthly basis under Friedlander's direction. MSML then sent monthly account statements based on the NAV to the Hedge Fund's investors. In performing the NAV calculation, MSML and Lodmell first determined the value of the total assets of the Hedge Fund, and then divided that value by the number of shares outstanding.

24. MSML and Lodmell used published closing prices for the last trading day of the month when assigning value to publicly traded Hedge Fund assets. However, from April 2000, or earlier, through January 2001, MSML or Lodmell requested the prices of unlisted securities from Friedlander and FCMC and relied on the value provided by Friedlander to calculate the Fund's NAV. MSML and Lodmell provided the NAV to Friedlander and FCMC for approval before MSML transmitted it to the Hedge Fund's investors in their monthly account statements.

The Fund's Holdings of eNote Securities

25. In April 1999, Friedlander caused the Hedge Fund to invest $5 million in eNote, which had recently become a public company through a reverse merger. In exchange, the Hedge Fund received 5 million shares of preferred convertible stock (the "Preferred Stock"), becoming the sole holder of preferred stock in eNote.com. The fund also received a warrant that entitled the Hedge Fund to obtain an additional 2 million shares of eNote common stock at an exercise price $1.00 per share (the "Original Warrant") through April 2004.

26. Between August 2000 and March 2001, FCMC has been the main source of funding for eNote, lending a total of approximately $1.5 million in exchange for convertible debt instruments given by eNote to FCMC. For no further consideration, eNote also gave additional warrants for the purchase of 11,666,667 shares of eNote common stock to FCMC between August 2000 and November 2000, which were purportedly "gifted" to the Hedge Fund by FCMC. These warrants varied as to exercise price and expiration date.

27. A warrant is a security that entitles the buyer to buy a quantity of common stock at a specified exercise price for a stated period of time. If a warrant has an exercise price of $2.50, a rational investor would exercise the warrant only if the price of the common stock was above $2.50. If that price were below $2.50, a rational investor would buy the stock on the open market rather than exercise the warrant and take a loss. The eNote warrants were not publicly traded on an exchange or over-the-counter, and prices for these securities were not quoted in any market. As a result, the "price" or "value" of the warrants was not publicly available from a ticker or computer service.

28. As of December 31, 2000, these eNote holdings (the warrants and the Preferred Stock) constituted approximately 40 percent of the NAV represented to investors.

29. From March 2000 to the present, the market price for eNote's common stock has declined from $6.00 to $0.08 per share. The Hedge Fund continues to hold the Preferred Stock, the Original Warrant, and the additional warrants obtained without consideration, as a significant portion of its holdings.

The Defendants Overstated the Value of the Fund's eNote Warrants

30. From April 2000, or earlier through October 2000, FCMC and Friedlander valued the warrants by utilizing the Bloomberg Standard Option Valuation Program, a computer service for the valuation of options. An FCMC employee entered five variables into this program and used the results to establish a value for the eNote warrants. The option program did not take into account either the exercise price of the warrants (it would cost the Hedge Fund $1.00 to purchase a share of eNote common stock were it to exercise the option) nor did it account for the dilutive effect on the eNote common stock if the warrants were exercised and additional shares issued.

31. FCMC's valuation of the warrants also conflicted with the value assigned to those warrants by eNote. In August and September 2000, FCMC obtained warrants for 2.8 million shares of common stock in partial consideration for loans of $350,000 to eNote. In December 2000, FCMC assigned a value of over $4,000,000 to these warrants, while eNote valued the warrants at $325,500 in a filing with the SEC, stating that that the value was "determined by their proportionate share of value based upon the ratio of the warrant value, as determined by using Black-Scholes, to the aggregate value of the note and the warrant multiplied by the total proceeds received."

32. When calculating the NAVs for the periods ending November 30, 2000, and December 31, 2000, FCMC and Friedlander departed from the use of the computer program to value the warrants. Instead, FCMC and Friedlander arbitrarily assigned a value to the eNote warrants which had no relationship to the market price of eNote common stock, and in fact valued the warrants at a higher price than the market price for the underlying common stock.

33. On or about February 15, 2001, FCMC sent a letter to the new administrator of the Hedge Fund, Lion Corporate Services, in which FCMC represented the values of the preferred/convertible stock and warrants remained the same as those values misrepresented by Friedlander in connection with the NAV valuation for the end of January 2000.

34. The overstatement of the value of eNote warrants by Friedlander and FCMC caused continuing and substantial overvaluations of the Hedge Fund's net asset value, which resulted in new investors paying more for shares in the fund than the shares were worth. The overvaluation also caused the Hedge Fund to pay redemptions to shareholders, including FML and Friedlander, for more than their shares were worth, to the detriment of remaining shareholders, whose interest in the Fund was diminished.

Friedlander and FCMC Manipulated the Price of eNote Common Stock

35. In addition to the overvaluation of the warrants, which resulted in an inflated NAV for the Hedge Fund, Friedlander and FCMC also knowingly

or recklessly manipulated the price of eNote common stock to overstate the Hedge Fund NAV.

36. At the end of each month from August through December 2000, Friedlander and FCMC purchased substantial quantities of eNote common stock through various brokerage accounts held for the benefit of FLP and Opal, with the intent to raise the market price of eNote stock and thereby inflate the value of the eNote holdings in the Hedge Fund for the calculation of NAV. To effect these purchases, Friedlander placed a series of orders, at increasing prices, on the last trading day of each month.

37. On the last trading day of November and December 2000, Friedlander also "marked the close" of trading in eNote common stock. "Marking the close" is a manipulative device by which a trader conducts the last trade of the day at a higher price than the prior trade, with the intent of affecting the reported closing price of the stock for that day.

38. In December of 2000, Friedlander purchased 140,000 shares of eNote common stock from an individual who wished to sell them to incur a tax loss. Friedlander only paid $1.00 for all of these shares to prevent those shares from entering the open market and thereby interfering with his manipulative scheme. His manipulative conduct pushed up the closing price of eNote common stock to $.50 per share at the end of that same month.

39. The end-of-the-month transactions by Friedlander between August 2000 and December 2000 were made with the intent to create actual or apparent active trading in eNote stock, raise the price of eNote stock, and maintain the price at an artificial level for the purpose of calculation of the Hedge Fund's NAV. The ultimate goal was to induce the purchase of shares in the Hedge Fund, and to inflate the value of the redemption or sale of shares in the Hedge Fund for the benefit of Friedlander and FML.

40. Friedlander directly benefited from the manipulative conduct. FCMC used the closing stock price of eNote on the last trading day of each month to determine the value to be assigned to the Hedge Fund's holdings of eNote Preferred Stock. Through October 2000 Friedlander used this month-end price to value the warrants held by eNote as well. These values were used to calculate the Hedge Fund's NAV, which increased the value of shares held by FML in the Hedge Fund for the benefit of FCMC and Friedlander. The overstated value also attracted additional investors to the Hedge Fund resulting in increased compensation paid to the FML for the benefit of FCMC and Friedlander, since the compensation of FML by the Hedge Fund was based on the net asset value and the performance of the Hedge Fund.

41. Friedlander was successful in manipulating the price of eNote stock upward at the end of each month, as follows:

Date	8/31/2000	9/29/2000	10/31/2000	11/30/2000	12/29/2000
Closing Price	$3	$2.50	$1.09375	$0.50	$0.50
Previous Day's Close	$1.68750	$1.75	$0.40625	$0.40625	$0.18750
Percentage Increase	78%	43%	169%	23%	167%

42. The table below sets forth the details of Friedlander's trading, which was not disclosed to the investors in the Hedge Fund:

Purchase Date	08/31/2000	09/29/2000	10/31/2000	11/30/2000	12/29/2000
No. of Shares	49,000	31,000	208,500	10,000	45,000
Purchasing Entity	Opal	Opal	Opal	FLP	FLP

Friedlander dominated and controlled the market for eNote common stock on each of those days, where his purchases accounted for 80% or more of the retail purchase volume.

Friedlander, FML and FCMC Misappropriated $2.3 Million of the Fund's Assets

43. FML receives shares in the Hedge Fund on a monthly basis as partial compensation for managing the Hedge Fund, and holds those shares for the benefit of FCMC. The number of shares received is based upon the NAV of the Hedge Fund.

44. Between August 2000 and February 2001, redemptions in the amount of approximately $2.4 million were wired from the Hedge Fund account at Bear Stearns to a Citibank account in the name of FCMC, including a $1M transfer on February 5, 2001, which was used solely for Friedlander's personal expenses. The remainder of these proceeds has been used for his personal expenses, to fund loans made by FCMC to eNote, and conduct the business of FCMC.

45. The redemptions made by FML for the benefit of FCMC were based upon inflated NAV caused by the misrepresentation of the value of eNote securities and by the manipulative devices set forth above, and have benefited FCMC and Friedlander to the detriment of the remaining shareholders in the Hedge Fund. Friedlander personally profited by increasing the rate and amount of the share redemptions during the period of the fraud.

46. In May 2000, Friedlander sent letters and memoranda to some investors in the Hedge Fund, which state that there was an earlier overvaluation of the eNote holdings and that the SEC was conducting an investigation. Friedlander announced his intention to liquidate the Hedge Fund. He failed to inform the investors of the inflated and preferential redemptions earlier received by himself and FCMC, and gave no assurances that such preferential treatment would not continue during the liquidation process. He also represented that the SEC investigation was focused on eNote, rather than on himself, and his entities, including the Hedge Fund. Friedlander was involved in another fraudulent scheme:

47. From 1994 through at least 2000, Friedlander solicited money from individuals and entities to invest for the benefit of those individuals and entities. In doing so, Friedlander represented that he would manage such funds as a "pooled" investment or pooled fund, combining the investors' money in one or more securities accounts, for the purpose of buying and selling securities.

48. From 1994 through 2000, at least seven individuals and three entities gave money to Friedlander to invest in the pooled fund pursuant to an investment advisory services agreement ("investment agreement"). According to these investment agreements, the investors in the pooled fund would share in the fund's returns on a pro rata basis, with certain management and/or performance fees deducted. The investment agreements also required Friedlander to maintain the pooled fund assets in one or more brokerage accounts and to provide periodic reports of the investor's return.

49. From 1994 through 2001, Friedlander represented to investors in the pooled fund that he was investing their money in accordance with the investment agreements by buying and selling securities for the benefit of all investors in the pooled fund.

50. From at least 1995 through 2001, Friedlander represented to investors in the pooled fund that their returns were positive and that their principal was secure. He did so even after two investors questioned him about the Commission's original complaint filed in this action in May 2001.

51. Until at least 2000, Friedlander continued to solicit investments in the pooled fund, making false representations—both written and oral—about profitable returns and increasing account balances. At the times he made such representations, Friedlander knew or was reckless in not knowing that investors would rely upon his representations in deciding whether to stay invested in the pooled fund and/or whether to invest additional funds.

52. Based upon Friedlander's representations, existing pooled fund investors and other individuals made additional investments in the pooled fund from 1998 through 2000. During this period, investors also relied upon Friedlander's false representations in deciding not to redeem their interests in the pooled fund.

53. In 2002, Friedlander informed investors in the pooled fund that their investments were worth nothing and that the total loss was due to investments he had made for their benefit in eNote.com, a company in which he had a controlling interest.

54. The pooled fund investors were surprised by this apparent turn of events. In early 2001, Friedlander had forwarded a compilation report showing another profitable year and, throughout 2001, he had assured some investors that their principal was secure and that they had lost no money.

False and Misleading Compilation Reports

55. In or around January 1995, Friedlander retained the Stamford, Connecticut office of KPMG to prepare compilation reports of the gains or losses of each pooled fund investor for investor portfolio and tax purposes. In undertaking this engagement, KPMG reviewed the brokerage account statements for the pooled account, as well as other documents provided by Friedlander, and calculated each investor's return.

56. In early 1995, KPMG prepared the compilation reports for each investor for 1994. In these compilation reports, KPMG set forth year-end investment results, including information on the management fee and instructions on tax reporting. The compilation reports were five pages in length, several pages of which were on "KPMG Peat Marwick" letterhead. The reports were also signed "KPMG Peat Marwick LLP."

57. In or around March 1995, KPMG forwarded the compilation reports for 1994 to Friedlander, who forwarded the reports to the investors in the pooled fund. These reports were consistent with the assets held in FCMC'S securities account at Gruntal at the end of 1994.

58. Following the engagement in early 1995, KPMG performed no further services for Friedlander or any entity controlled by Friedlander.

59. During 1995, the FCMC account at Gruntal suffered significant losses.

60. In the early months of each year from 1996 through 2001, Friedlander directed the preparation of year-end compilation reports for the pooled fund investors for the prior year, and caused the compilation reports to be forwarded to the investors.

61. The compilation reports prepared each year from 1996 through 2001 were in the same form, were the same length, and used the same wording as those prepared by KPMG in 1995. The compilation reports prepared each year from 1996 through 2001 were also on "KPMG Peat Marwick" letterhead and, at least for the years ended 1999 and 2000, were signed "KPMG Peat Marwick LLP."

62. KPMG did not prepare or assist in preparing the compilation reports forwarded by Friedlander between 1996 and 2001. KPMG also did not authorize the use of its letterhead, nor did it sign or approve any of these compilation reports. In fact, KPMG had ceased using "Peat Marwick" in its name, including on its letterhead, in late 1998.

63. Prior to forwarding the compilation reports to investors in the pooled fund, Friedlander reviewed the reports. At the time he forwarded or caused the post-1995 reports to be forwarded, Friedlander knew or was reckless in not knowing that KPMG had not prepared or assisted in preparing these reports. Nevertheless, Friedlander caused the reports to be transmitted on "KPMG Peat Marwick" letterhead to pooled fund investors, who believed that the reports had been compiled and reviewed by KPMG.

64. From 1996 through 2001, the compilation reports for the prior fiscal years that Friedlander provided to investors in the pooled fund were false and misleading because they had not been prepared by, at the direction of, or with the knowledge of KPMG. Friedlander knew, or was reckless in not knowing, that the pooled fund investors would rely upon the implicit representation that KPMG had prepared the reports.

65. From at least 1999 through 2001 (for the fiscal years 1998 through 2000), the compilation reports that Friedlander provided to the investors were false and misleading because they overstated the value of investors' assets and returns, and were not based upon the actual assets held in FCMC securities accounts. Specifically:

a. The compilation reports forwarded to investors by Friedlander in 1999 (for the year ended 12/31/98) represented total pooled fund assets of more than $3.29 million. However, based upon brokerage and bank statements, the pooled fund had assets of less than $1.86 million.

b. The compilation reports forwarded to investors by Friedlander in 2000 (for the year ended 12/31/99) represented total pooled fund assets of more than $4.75 million. Based upon brokerage and bank statements, the pooled fund had assets of less than $245,000.

c. The compilation reports forwarded to investors by Friedlander in 2001 (for the year ended 12/31/00) represented total pooled fund assets of more than $5.74 million. Based upon brokerage and bank statements, the pooled fund had assets of less than $269,000.

66. Friedlander knew or was reckless in not knowing that the amount of assets and the investment returns reflected in the compilation reports were false and misleading. Friedlander also knew or was reckless in not knowing that the pooled fund investors would rely on the compilation reports and make investment decisions accordingly.

Friedlander Converted the Pooled Fund Assets for His Personal Use

67. Starting by at least January 1996, Friedlander commingled the assets of the pooled fund with those of defendant corporation FCMC.

68. From at least January 1998 through 2000, Friedlander failed to deposit all new investments from pooled account investors into securities accounts for the benefit of those investors. Instead, as a general rule, Friedlander left the investors' money in the non-interest bearing bank account of FCMC at Citibank, NA, where those funds were commingled with money derived from other activities of Friedlander and FCMC. Friedlander used the commingled money to pay for personal expenses, including country club dues, legal fees associated with a prior divorce, maintenance and dockage fees for a sailboat, and monthly condominium fees. Friedlander also used money from new investments in the pooled fund to repay pooled fund investors who wished to redeem, to pay other individuals for whom he claimed to be managing money, and to fund loans to family members and/or friends.

69. From 1998 through 2001, Friedlander used at least $1.4 million from commingled money in the FCMC bank account for personal expenses, and an additional $879,000 to pay for the operations of FCMC.

70. From at least 1998 through 2001, Friedlander failed to maintain any system or process for tracking the money deposited by pooled fund investors from 1998 through 2000. In most cases, Friedlander made no effort to invest this money. Further, he represented to investors that he had invested their money profitably during this time. Friedlander knew that these representations were false and knew that the investors relied on these representations.

GLOBAL MONEY MANAGEMENT, L.P.

Commission Files Action to Halt Ongoing Fraud by Operators of Unregistered Hedge Fund in San Diego

The Securities and Exchange Commission announced the filing, on March 11, 2004, of an emergency action to halt an alleged ongoing multi-million dollar securities fraud, naming San Diego–based Global Money Management, L.P. (GMM), an unregistered private hedge fund, LF Global Investments, LLC (LF Global), which operated GMM, and Marvin I. Friedman, 65, of La Jolla, California, who is alleged in the Commission's complaint to have controlled both entities. The Commission's complaint alleges that the defendants grossly overstated the assets of GMM to investors.

Acting on the Commission's lawsuit, the Honorable Barry T. Moskowitz, United States District Judge for the Southern District of California, yesterday issued a temporary restraining order against GMM, LF Global, and Friedman, appointed a receiver over GMM and LF Global, and issued orders freezing the assets of the defendants, prohibiting the destruction of documents, and ordering accountings from the defendants. A hearing on whether a preliminary injunction be issued against the defendants is scheduled for March 25, 2004.

The Commission's complaint alleges that since 1993, the defendants have sold, in an unregistered offering, limited partnership interests in GMM, a purported private hedge fund that invested in securities, such as stock and stock options. While the amount of money actually raised is not known, Friedman has told investors at various times over the last several months that the hedge fund held assets ranging from $60 million to over $100 million. GMM's brokerage records, however, show that, since at least December 2002, the securities it holds have been worth no more than $11 million. In addition, Friedman touted his investment experience but failed to inform investors about his disciplinary history, including that he has been barred from association with any member of the National Association of Securities Dealers.

The Commission's complaint alleges that GMM, LF Global, and Friedman violated the antifraud provisions of the federal securities laws, Section 17(a) of the Securities Act of 1933, Section 10(b) of the Securities Exchange Act of 1934 and Rule 10b-5 thereunder, and, as to LF Global, Sections 206(1) and 206(2) of the Investment Advisers Act of 1940, and, as to Friedman, that he aided and abetted those violations of the Advisers Act, seeking, in addition to the emergency relief described above, from each defendant, preliminary and permanent injunctions, disgorgement with prejudgment interest, and a civil penalty.

HOUSE ASSET MANAGEMENT, L.L.C.

On June 20, 2002, the Commission obtained an Order of Permanent Injunction and Other Equitable Relief ("Order of Permanent Injunction") against defendants House Edge, L.P. (the "Hedge Fund"), House Asset Management, L.L.C. (the "Adviser"), Paul J. House ("House"), and Brandon R. Moore ("Moore"), enjoining them from violating the antifraud and registration provisions of the securities laws. The Order of Permanent Injunction also freezes the assets of the Hedge Fund, the Adviser, House, and Moore pending the resolution of the appropriate amount of disgorgement and civil penalties, requires the defendants to give an accounting, prohibits document destruction and permits expedited discovery. The defendants consented to the Order of Permanent Injunction without admitting or denying the allegations of the Commission's complaint.

In its complaint, which was filed on June 20, 2002, the Commission alleged that, from at least March 2000 to the present, the defendants raised approximately $2.9 million from at least 60 investors through an unregistered offering of units in the Hedge Fund. The Commission alleged in its complaint that House and Moore controlled the Hedge Fund, which is located in Mt. Zion, Illinois. The complaint alleged that the defendants solicited investors and potential investors to invest their retirement savings in the Hedge Fund by making false and misleading statements in offering materials and on the Hedge Fund's website. The Commission's complaint alleged that the defendants told investors that the Hedge Fund had generated cumulative returns of 148% since its inception because it used investor proceeds to engage in a sophisticated securities trading strategy. The Commission alleged that the Hedge Fund had, in fact, suffered losses totalling at least $850,000 since its inception. Further, the complaint alleged that from at least May 2001 to June 2002, House and Moore borrowed approximately $425,000 from the Hedge Fund to purchase their personal residences and the Adviser's office building. The complaint alleged that the defendants failed to disclose to investors that they had used investor proceeds in this manner and that House and Moore had each emerged from personal bankruptcy in the last two years. The complaint also alleged that the defendants made false and misleading statements about House's background in the offering materials. The offering materials touted House's six years of experience in the securities industry, but failed to disclose that House was terminated as a registered representative for unauthorized sales of Hedge Fund units and that he was barred by the NASD for making unauthorized sales of Hedge Fund units and for providing the NASD with false information.

The complaint alleged that, by the above conduct, the Hedge Fund violated Sections 5(a), 5(c) and 17(a) of the Securities Act of 1933 ("Securities Act"), Section 10(b) of the Securities Exchange Act of 1934 ("Exchange Act") and Rule 10b-5 thereunder, and Section 7(a) of the Investment Company Act of 1940. The complaint also alleged the Adviser, House, and Moore violated Sections 5(a), 5(c) and 17(a) of the Securities Act, Section 10(b) of the Exchange Act and Rule 10b-5 thereunder, and that the Adviser violated Sections 206(1) and 206(2) of the Investment

Advisers Act of 1940 ("Advisers Act") and that House and Moore aided and abetted the Adviser's violation of Sections 206(1) and 206(2) of the Advisers Act.

IDT GROUP, INC.

The Securities and Exchange Commission sues Darren Silverman and Matthew Brenner in connection with $33 million securities fraud that affected hundreds of investors nationwide. The case is described as follows:

The Securities and Exchange Commission (SEC) announced that on February 19, 2004, it filed a complaint for injunctive and other relief against Darren Silverman ("Silverman") and Matthew Brenner ("Brenner") to enjoin them from violating the antifraud provisions and the securities registration provisions of the federal securities laws. Silverman and Brenner both reside in Boca Raton, Florida. The SEC alleges that from August 1999 through May 2002, Silverman and Brenner defrauded hundreds of investors out of approximately $33 million through the offer and sale of unregistered securities marketed as purported hedge funds. The hedge funds, IDT Fund A Ltd., IDT Fund B Ltd., IDT Fund C Ltd., The Millennium IDT Fund Ltd., and IDT Venture (collectively, IDT Funds) were later rolled into IDT Group, Inc. (IDT Group). During the relevant time period, Silverman and/or Brenner were instrumental in operating, managing and supervising IDT Funds and IDT Group.

According to the SEC's Complaint, Silverman and Brenner used deceptive offering materials and fictitious statements, among other things, to entice persons to invest in the hedge funds. The Complaint alleges that they then lulled investors into keeping their funds invested—and making additional investments—by sending account statements falsely stating the IDT Funds were profitable and outperforming major market indicators.

The Complaint also alleges that Silverman and Brenner misrepresented the safety of the investments and lied to investors about the compensation paid to the hedge fund day traders. Further, the Complaint alleges that Silverman and Brenner also misled investors by paying investors what they claimed were "dividends" but, in truth, were new investor funds paid to earlier investors, in a Ponzi-like fashion. Finally, the Complaint alleges that Silverman and Brenner directed both IDT Funds, and its successor IDT

Group, to employ unlicensed sales representatives who raised millions of dollars from investors, including more than $3 million from religious non-profit organizations.

As a result, the SEC alleges that Silverman and Brenner violated Sections 5(a), 5(c), and 17(a) of the Securities Act of 1933, Section 10(b) of the Securities Exchange Act of 1934 (Exchange Act) and Rule 10b-5, thereunder; and violated Sections 206(1) and 206(2) of the Investment Advisers Act of 1940. In addition, the Complaint alleges that Silverman and Brenner acted as "control persons" of IDT Funds under Section 20(a) of the Exchange Act for its violations of Section 10(b) of the Exchange Act and Rule 10b-5, thereunder. The SEC is also seeking in its lawsuit, among other things, a permanent injunction, disgorgement and civil penalties.

INTEGRAL INVESTMENT MANAGEMENT LP

Securities and Exchange Commission Brings Action Alleging Hedge Fund Fraud

On June 16, 2004, the Securities and Exchange Commission filed a complaint alleging hedge fund fraud perpetrated by Conrad Seghers, age 36, a resident of Garland, Texas, and James Dickey, age 37, a resident of Flower Mound, Texas. The commission's complaint, filed in federal court in Dallas, alleges that from June 2000 through September 2001, Seghers and Dickey fraudulently offered and sold securities in three Texas-based hedge funds, Integral Equity, LP, Integral Hedging, LP, and Integral Arbitrage, LP (collectively, the Funds). During this period, the Funds raised over $71.6 million from approximately 30 investors.

The Commission alleges that Seghers controlled and made investment decisions for the Funds through Integral Investment Management, LP, and that Dickey marketed the Funds to investors. As alleged in the complaint, Seghers and Dickey fraudulently offered the Funds' securities by failing to disclose to investors the substantial losses the Funds incurred and that Seghers was overstating the Funds' assets. Seghers caused the Funds' assets to be overstated by amounts ranging from 13% to 77% per month. The Commission further alleges that Seghers misrepresented to a potential investor, The Art Institute of Chicago, that certain brokerage firm errors did not affect one of the hedge funds, Integral Arbitrage, LP, when, in fact, they did. Based on this statement, The Art Institute invested $22.5 million in Integral Arbitrage, LP.

The Commission also alleges that Seghers and Dickey misrepresented to investors that the Funds had prominent brokerage firms at various times as their "prime broker," when the Funds never had a prime broker. In a prime brokerage relationship, the prime broker is a broker-dealer that, among other things, clears and finances customer trades made at other brokerage firms at the customer's request.

JTI GROUP FUND, LP

Fine and Boyle have used their company, KS Advisors, to raise approximately $10 million from about 100 investors nationwide and abroad through investments in two hedge funds, KS Condor Partners, Ltd., II ("Condor II") and Damian Partners, LLC ("Damian Partners").

On February 27, 2004, Judge Steele, U.S. District Judge for the Middle District of Florida, issued various emergency orders against the defendants, including temporary restraining orders, asset freezes against KS Advisors, Condor II, and Damian Partners, the appointment of a receiver, and other emergency relief.

The Commission's Complaint alleges that the representations made by KS Advisors, Boyle and Fine to the hedge funds' investors about the ever-increasing profits and net asset values of Condor II and Damian Partners were completely false.

According to the Commission's Complaint, the investments made by Boyle and Fine on behalf of the hedge funds, consisting mostly of speculative options trading, have lost millions of dollars. The Commission's Complaint also alleges that Fine and Boyle charged investors fraudulent fund performance fees based on the fictitious gains in the values of the two hedge funds and additional undisclosed "advisory fees."

The Commission's complaint charges KS Advisors, Condor II, Damian Partners, Fine and Boyle with violating Section 17(a) of the Securities Act of 1933, Section 10(b) of the Securities Exchange Act of 1934 and Rule 10b-5 thereunder, and KS Advisors, Fine and Boyle with violating Sections 206(1) and 206(2) of the Investment Advisers Act of 1940 (Advisers Act).

MacQUEEN CAPITAL MANAGEMENT CORPORATION

The Securities and Exchange Commission ("Commission") deems it appropriate and in the public interest to enter an order in this public administrative proceeding, previously instituted on September 23, 2004, against Kenneth B. MacQueen ("Respondent" or "MacQueen") pursuant to Section 203(f) of the Investment Advisers Act of 1940 ("Advisers Act").

MacQueen has submitted an Offer of Settlement ("Offer"), which the Commission has determined to accept. Solely for the purpose of these proceedings and any other proceedings brought by or on behalf of the Commission, or to which the Commission is a party, and without admitting or denying the findings herein, except as to the Commission's jurisdiction over Respondent, the subject matter of these proceedings and the findings contained in paragraph III.E below, which are admitted, Respondent consents to the issuance of this Order Making Findings and Imposing Remedial Sanctions ("Order") as set forth below.

On the basis of the Order Instituting Administrative Proceedings Pursuant to Section 203(f) of the Investment Advisers Act of 1940 and the Offer submitted by MacQueen, the Commission makes the following findings:

A. MacQueen, age 47, was a resident of Orland Park, Illinois, during the relevant time frame. From at least 1993 until March 2003, MacQueen was a principal of MacQueen Capital Management Corp. ("MacQueen Capital"). He was not registered with the Commission in any capacity.

B. MacQueen Capital was an unregistered investment adviser and was an Illinois corporation during the relevant time. MacQueen operated MacQueen Capital's advisory business. MacQueen Capital was the adviser to the Dividend Reinvestment Fund, L.L.C. ("Dividend Fund"), and an unregistered hedge fund.

C. On February 29, 2003, the Commission filed a Complaint in the United States District Court for the Northern District of Illinois against MacQueen, MacQueen Capital, and the Dividend Fund captioned *SEC v. Kenneth B. MacQueen, et al.*, No. 03 C 1423.

D. The Complaint alleges that MacQueen, through MacQueen Capital and the Dividend Fund, raised at least $1.325 million from five investors in an ongoing fraudulent investment scheme. According to the Complaint, MacQueen misrepresented the Dividend Fund's investment objectives by telling investors that the Dividend Fund would generate annual returns of approximately 25% through a low risk, dividend reinvestment arbitrage investment strategy, even though the Dividend Fund generated little or no returns from its stated investment strategy. The Complaint also alleges that MacQueen misrepresented the use of investor proceeds by claiming that proceeds would be used by the Dividend Fund for its dividend reinvestment arbitrage trading strategy, when

MacQueen actually used the proceeds to pay existing investors and to pay personal expenses such as the purchase of a vacation home. The Complaint also alleges that, to conceal his fraud and to obtain additional investments, MacQueen made numerous misrepresentations to investors regarding the value of their interests in the Dividend Fund. Based on these allegations, the Complaint asserts that MacQueen violated Sections 17(a)(1), 17(a)(2) and 17(a)(3) of the Securities Act of 1933 ("Securities Act"), Section 10(b) of the Securities Exchange Act of 1934 ("Exchange Act") and Rule 10b-5 thereunder, and Sections 206(1) and 206(2) of the Advisers Act.

E. On July 8, 2003, the Court entered an order permanently enjoining MacQueen, MacQueen Capital and the Dividend Fund from violating Sections 17(a)(1), 17(a)(2) and 17(a)(3) of the Securities Act, Section 10(b) of the Exchange Act and Rule 10b-5 thereunder, and Sections 206(1) and 206(2) of the Advisers Act. In a written consent, MacQueen and MacQueen Capital admitted the allegations of the Complaint and agreed to the entry of the order of permanent injunction.

In view of the foregoing, the Commission deems it appropriate and in the public interest to impose the sanctions specified in Respondent's Offer.

Pursuant to Section 203(f) of the Advisers Act, that Respondent MacQueen be, and hereby is, barred from association with any investment adviser.

Any reapplication for association by the Respondent will be subject to the applicable laws and regulations governing the re-entry process, and re-entry may be conditioned upon a number of factors, including, but not limited to, the satisfaction of any or all of the following: (a) any disgorgement ordered against the Respondent, whether or not the Commission has fully or partially waived payment of such disgorgement; (b) any arbitration award related to the conduct that served as the basis for the Commission order; (c) any self-regulatory organization arbitration award to a customer, whether or not related to the conduct that served as the basis for the Commission order; and (d) any restitution order by a self-regulatory organization, whether or not related to the conduct that served as the basis for the Commission order.

MANHATTAN INVESTMENT FUND, LTD.

Securities and Exchange Commission v. Michael W. Berger, Manhattan Investment Fund Ltd. and Manhattan Capital Management, Inc., Civ. Action No. 00 Civ. 0333 (DLC), Southern District of New York

The Securities and Exchange Commission announced that on January 18, 2000, it filed an emergency enforcement action charging Michael W. Berger, a hedge fund adviser, with securities fraud. Also charged were Manhattan Investment Fund Ltd., a hedge fund organized and managed by Berger, and Manhattan Capital Management Inc., an investment adviser owned by Berger. Berger is an Austrian citizen who lives in New York City, where Manhattan Capital is located. Manhattan Investment Fund is a British Virgin Islands corporation. The fund has approximately 280 investors.

The Honourable Denise L. Cote, United States District Judge, entered an order freezing the assets of Manhattan Investment Fund and Manhattan Capital Management. The Judge's order also included a temporary restraining order barring further violations against Manhattan Investment Fund and preliminary injunctions against Berger and Manhattan Capital Management. Currently pending before the judge is the Commission's request for appointment of a receiver for Manhattan Investment Fund Ltd. and for Manhattan Capital Management. Berger and Manhattan Capital consented to the relief imposed.

The Commission charged that beginning in September 1996, Manhattan Investment Fund began to sustain market losses that ultimately totalled more than $300 million. At the same time the fund was sustaining these huge losses, Berger was reporting to investors that the fund had returns of between 12 and 27 percent annually. By August 1999, Berger told investors that Manhattan Investment Fund had a net market value of more than $426 million in assets. In fact, the fund was never that large, and by August, its net value had been reduced to less than $28 million.

The Complaint alleges the following: Berger organized Manhattan Investment Fund in April 1996. Since then, he has raised more than $350 million from investors. Berger's investment strategy for the fund was based on the proposition that the stock market generally, and stocks of Internet-related companies particularly, were overvalued, and that there would be a market correction in which the prices of many Internet-related stocks would decline sharply. Berger sold these securities short, in order to profit from the anticipated decline. However, because the prices of most Internet-related stocks have instead increased dramatically, the Manhattan Investment Fund has consistently suffered losses. Those losses now total in excess of $300 million.

To hide the fund's losses from investors, beginning in September 1996, Berger created phony account statements that materially overstated the performance and value of Manhattan Investment Fund. The information contained in the false account statements was provided to investors in the fund, and was shared with potential investors. The false account statements were provided to the fund's administrator, and to the fund's auditors. Earlier this month, both the administrator and the auditors resigned.

Throughout the relevant period, Berger had a close professional and personal relationship with Respondent James Rader, and the Fund maintained a brokerage account at Financial Asset Management (FAM). By virtue of its role as an executing broker for the Fund, FAM collected substantial commission income from the Fund's trades. In fact, between 1996 and 1999, the commissions generated by the Fund's trades accounted for at least 10–33% of FAM's annual revenues.

As an executing broker, FAM never held any of the Fund's securities or other assets, nor did it generate any account statements for the Fund. During the relevant period, all the transactions of the Fund were cleared through Bear Stearns Securities Corporation in New York City. Bear Stearns held the vast majority of the Fund's cash and securities, and generated the only genuine monthly account statements and daily trading summaries for the Fund.

As part of his ongoing fraud, Berger falsely represented to the Fund's administrator, the Fund's auditor, and the Fund's investors that FAM held the vast majority of the Fund's cash and securities. Berger also fabricated phony account statements purportedly from FAM, which detailed the fictitious trading the Fund was supposedly conducting through FAM.

The Respondents' Unlawful Conduct: Contributing to Berger's Scheme to Mislead the Fund's Auditors

The Fund engaged Deloitte and Touche (Bermuda) ("Deloitte") to audit its financial statements for the years ended December 31, 1996, 1997 and 1998. Each year, as part of its audit process, Deloitte, through the Fund's administrator, Fund Administration Services (Bermuda) Limited (the "Fund administrator"), sent audit confirmation requests to FAM. Debra Kennedy responded to these requests on behalf of FAM. Each request sought a list of any investments that the Fund held at FAM, and requested FAM to furnish its response to Deloitte.

In each of the three years in question, just before the audit confirmation letters were sent out, Berger requested that Kennedy send FAM's responsive information directly to him, rather than to Deloitte, because he was purportedly "collecting responses" for the auditors. Notwithstanding the unusual nature of Berger's request, and without consulting Deloitte about its propriety, Kennedy complied with Berger's request. Thus, each year Kennedy, with Rader's approval, prepared cover letters on FAM letterhead addressed to Deloitte, attached copies of the requested Fund account statements that FAM had received from Bear Stearns, and forwarded the package to Berger without any notification to Deloitte.

This circumvention of the audit confirmation process, in addition to the acts discussed below, made it possible for Berger to perpetrate his fraudulent scheme. Each year, upon receipt of FAM's audit response package, Berger removed the attached Bear Stearns account statements, substituted fictitious year-end account statements designed to appear as if generated by FAM, and sent them (sometimes via facsimile from a fax machine reprogrammed to appear to be from FAM) to Deloitte. In two of the three years in question, the fictitious year-end account statements were sent along with a forged cover letter purportedly coming from Kennedy. One year, a FAM employee provided Berger with an Airborne Express envelope addressed to Deloitte (which Berger used to send the fictitious FAM statements) that inaccurately showed FAM in Ohio as the sender/return addressee of the envelope.

The fabricated FAM account statements materially overstated the assets and investment performance of the Fund. In reliance on these statements, Deloitte issued unqualified audit reports on the Fund's financial statements for its 1996, 1997 and 1998 fiscal years. These audited financial statements were erroneous and misleading and were sent to investors in the Fund. Had the Respondents sent FAM's audit confirmation responses directly to Deloitte in any of the three years in question, Berger's fraudulent scheme would likely have been instantly exposed.

MARQUE MILLENNIUM GROUP, LTD.

The Securities and Exchange Commission ("Commission") deems it appropriate and in the public interest that public administrative and cease-and-desist proceedings be, and hereby are, instituted pursuant to Sections 203(f) and 203(k) of the Investment Advisers Act of 1940 ("Advisers Act") against Wilfred Meckel ("Meckel") and Robert T. Littell ("Littell").

In anticipation of the institution of these proceedings, Meckel and Littell have each submitted an Offer of Settlement (the "Offers") which the Commission has determined to accept. Solely for the purpose of these proceedings and any other proceedings brought by or on behalf of the Commission, or to which the Commission is a party, and without admitting or denying the findings herein, except as to the Commission's jurisdiction over them and the subject matter of these proceedings, Meckel and Littell consent to the entry of this Order Instituting Administrative and Cease-and-Desist Proceedings, Making Findings, and Imposing Remedial Sanctions pursuant to Sections 203(f) and 203(k) of the Investment Advisers Act of 1940 ("Order"), as set forth below.

On the basis of this Order and the Offers, the Commission finds that:

Robert T. Littell, age 40 and a resident of New York, New York, from October 1997 through June 2000 was employed by Marque Millennium Group, Ltd. ("MMG") as Manager of Investments. Until March 2000, Littell was primarily responsible for operating Marque Partners I ("MPI"), Marque Partners II ("MPII") and Marque Fund II Limited ("MFIILtd") (collectively the "Hedge Funds"), including making all investment decisions, entering trades, and communicating with investors. From August 1987 through August 1997, Littell was a registered representative associated with broker-dealers registered with the Commission.

Wilfred Meckel, age 57 and a resident of New York, New York, is the founder and Senior Managing Director of MMG.

Related Party

MMG, a Delaware corporation with offices in New York, New York, was the General Partner of MPI and MPII and listed investment adviser of MFIILtd.[1] MMG was a holding company for Marque Millennium Capital Management, Ltd. ("MMCM"), an investment adviser registered with the Commission since January 1, 1991 and Marque Millennium Financial Services, Ltd., an inactive broker-dealer.[2] MPI began operations in October 1997. MPII and MFIILtd (an offshore fund which invested in MPII) began operations in May 1999 using a variation of the same trading system as MPI. From their inception through March 2000, a total of 112 limited partners invested $53,140,466 into MPI, 71 limited partners invested $43,650,260 into MPII and 14 limited partners invested $30,620,000 into MFIILtd. Throughout the relevant time, MMG was an unregistered investment adviser.[3]

---

[1]MMG ceased operations in March 2001 and has no assets. Any assets that existed in March 2001 were used to satisfy creditors and pay investors.

[2]MMCM and Marque Millennium Financial Services, Ltd. were not involved in the matters giving rise to this proceeding or Order.

[3]Section 203(b)(3) of the Advisers Act exempts an investment adviser from registration if over the previous twelve months it had fewer than fifteen clients and neither holds itself out as an investment adviser to the general public nor acts as an investment adviser to an investment company.

Summary

From at least December 1998 through March 2000, MMG, through Littell, communicated materially inaccurate performance information to limited partners and potential investors in the Hedge Funds. In addition, from MPI's inception in October 1997 through March 2000, MMG, through Littell, made various misrepresentations to investors and potential investors about the Hedge Funds' management structure, retention of an accountant and auditor, and risk management techniques. They also provided these misrepresentations to brokers and third party promoters hired by MMG to solicit investments for the Hedge Funds. Littell also improperly redeemed the full amount of investments by two large investors at a time when the Hedge Funds had incurred substantial undisclosed losses, and he took numerous steps to conceal the losses from investors and from Meckel. Meckel failed reasonably to supervise Littell's activities with a view to preventing violations of the federal securities laws.

MMG and Littell Defrauded Hedge Fund Investors

Meckel hired Littell as the investment manager for MMG in 1997. MPI, a hedge fund designed to utilize a trading system invented by Littell, officially began operations on October 1, 1997.

According to the MPI and MPII private offering memoranda, MMG, as general partner, received a quarterly management fee equal to one quarter of one percent of each limited partner's opening quarterly balance and the possibility of receiving a yearly incentive fee equal to 20% of net profits if the funds achieved positive returns. MMG also received compensation as the listed investment adviser for MFIILtd. From October 1997 to March 2001, MMG collected $828,078.35 in management and incentive fees from the Hedge Funds.

MMG and Littell made misrepresentations to investors, potential investors, brokers, and third party solicitors concerning the Hedge Funds' performance, management oversight, and independent verification of performance by an accountant and/or auditor, and risk management practices. MMG and Littell made these misrepresentations orally in informal conversations and pitch meetings, and in writing through handwritten facsimiles, K-1 tax documents, advertisements (also known as "Primers"), newsletters, and/or solicitation letters. These materials were written by Littell and some were reviewed by Meckel.

Littell performed substantially all trading and back office operations of the Hedge Funds.

Littell provided all of the performance information contained in the

Primers, solicitation letters, newsletters and other materials disseminated by MMG. Littell had little or no experience calculating performance results and did not retain an accountant for MPI until March 2000. Furthermore, even though MPII had an accountant throughout its operation Littell did not provide investors with performance information from the accountant, but rather reported performance based on his own calculations. Therefore, much of this performance information was incorrect and materially overstated the performance returns achieved by the Hedge Funds during the relevant periods. For example, for MPI in August 1998, Littell reported a gain of 0.9% instead of an actual loss of 13.21%.[4] In Newsletters for November and December 1998, Littell reported performance as positive 0.28% and negative 3.86%, respectively, when in fact MPI lost 16.08% and another 27.55% for those months. Moreover, from November 1998 forward, in addition to the other misrepresentations, all Primers contained November 1998's materially overstated performance numbers. In March 1999, Littell reported that MPI had earned a monthly gain of 0.73%, when in fact MPI lost 16.1%. Littell also reported a year-to-date gain of 4.9%, when the actual year-to-date performance was a loss of 28.3%. For July 1999, Littell reported conflicting numbers in two separate Newsletters, one representing that the July 1999 performance was a gain of 3.05% and another stating that it was a loss of 0.17%. In fact, MPI's actual July 1999 performance was a loss of 4.66%. The actual performance information was calculated in the spring of 2000 by an accountant, but was never disclosed to investors.

In addition to providing investors with inflated performance information, MMG and Littell failed to disclose material information to all investors and potential investors concerning trading losses suffered by the Hedge Funds in November and December 1999. In November 1999, MPI lost 35.86%, MPII lost 24.04%, and MFIILtd lost 24.16%. In December 1999, MPI lost 58.95%, MPII lost 43.51%, and MFIILtd lost 42.60%. Although some investors received partial information within weeks of the losses, other investors received little or no information until several months later.

Two investors who learned the true extent of the November and December losses insisted on redemptions from MFIILtd. In February 2000, in contravention of the distribution procedures established by MFIILtd's administrator and outlined in MPII and MFIILtd's partnership agreements, Littell authorized transfers totalling $15 million from MPII to these in-

---

[4]The actual performance numbers are based on calculations by the Hedge Funds' independent accountant.

vestors. MPII and MFIILtd's offering memoranda provide that net profits or losses will be allocated to limited partners in proportion to their capital accounts. As a result, these two investors received approximately $6.8 million in excess of their investment value in MFIILtd at the time of their redemptions. Littell falsely claimed that he authorized the distributions as a result of threats made by representatives for the investors, failed to inform Meckel of the distributions until May 2000, and misleadingly blamed others for the improper distributions.

In addition to the two redemptions described above, Littell permitted other redemptions at inflated values from January 1999 through May 2000. These excess distributions to partners totaled at least $3,338,385. As a result, those partners who remained invested after May 2000 suffered both from the large devaluation of their assets due to trading losses and the dilution of their remaining assets resulting from the improper distributions. The MPI accounting records show that total partners' capital on December 31, 2000 has been $3,473,547, but because of the excess distributions, the remaining partners' capital was only $291,041. These excess distributions conflict with the Hedge Funds' offering memoranda, which state that net profits or losses will be allocated to limited partners in proportion to their capital accounts.

The Hedge Funds' offering memoranda also state those portfolio securities will be valued as of the last sale price on the exchange or market where the security is primarily traded. Therefore, Littell did not have a reasonable basis to believe that the performance information he supplied to investors conformed with the valuation method outlined in the offering memoranda. From October 1997 through March 2000, Littell did not maintain any record of his trades, such as a trade blotter, and did not check his trades against confirmations or account statements received from the brokerage firms where the Hedge Funds maintained accounts. Therefore, Littell could not have reasonably believed that the performance information he provided accurately reflected the Hedge Funds' value. Moreover, MMG and Littell did not maintain accurate records of investments into and distributions from the Hedge Funds or a complete set of subscription agreements. As a result, Littell recklessly identified capital contributions as gains in the trading accounts.

Prior to the devastating losses of the 1999 year end, Littell received $590,000 in incentive fees from MFIILtd. Littell later turned all of those incentive fees as well as sizeable trading profits from the investment of those fees over to MMG.

Upon discovering Littell's fraud, Meckel and the other principal of MMG engaged in a year-long effort to keep MPI and MPII afloat and to restore investor losses. Their efforts proved unsuccessful and MPI and

MPII ceased operations on March 31, 2001 with no money left to distribute to their remaining investors.

On March 26, 2001, Meckel and the other principal of MMG sold their interests in MMCM. Most of the proceeds from the sale of MMCM were used to satisfy outstanding obligations to creditors of MMG. Meckel and the other principal of MMG provided the remaining proceeds to MPI and MPII for the benefit of their investors. Meckel paid $593,882 and the other principal paid $535,172 to MPI and MPII, for a total of $1,129,054, which exceeded the $828,078.35 of management and incentive fees MMG collected from the Hedge Funds.

Meckel Failed Reasonably to Supervise Littell

Throughout the relevant period, Littell was subject to Meckel's supervision. Meckel and Littell both worked in MMG's small suite of offices. Meckel investigated Littell's background and trading strategy before Littell was hired. Meckel then helped Littell establish the Hedge Funds, attended some pitch meetings for the Hedge Funds, and reviewed the initial Primers, which included Meckel in the description of the "management" of the Hedge Funds. Meckel restricted the marketing of Littell's trading strategy until the third quarter of 1998 when he and an assistant used a common performance measurement software system to review performance information provided by Littell. Meckel communicated with Littell regularly about the Hedge Funds and their investments.

Meckel failed reasonably to supervise Littell with a view to preventing violations of the federal securities laws. Meckel failed to take reasonable supervisory actions, which could include maintaining accurate records of investments into and distributions from the Hedge Funds, review of daily trading activity, valuation of the Hedge Funds' positions, and separation of the Hedge Funds' trading and back office functions. Instead, Meckel relied on Littell's reporting and did not independently verify the performance information and other representations Littell made to the Hedge Funds' investors. Meckel's reliance on Littell's reports without independently verifying their accuracy delayed his discovery of Littell's misconduct and enabled Littell to continue his fraudulent activities. Legal findings are such:

As a result of the conduct described above, Littell wilfully violated Section 17(a) of the Securities Act of 1933 ("Securities Act"), Section 10(b) of the Securities Exchange Act of 1934 ("Exchange Act"), and Rule 10b-5 thereunder, which prohibit fraudulent conduct in the offer and sale of securities and in connection with the purchase or sale of securities.

As a result of the conduct described above, MMG wilfully violated, and Littell wilfully aided and abetted and caused MMG's violations of, Sections 206(1) and 206(2) of the Advisers Act, which prohibit an investment adviser from employing any device, scheme, or artifice to defraud or to engage in any transaction, practice, or course of business which operates as a fraud or deceit upon any client or prospective client.

Section 203(f) of the Advisers Act authorizes the Commission to sanction any person associated with an investment adviser where such person has failed reasonably to supervise as set forth in Section 203(e)(6), with a view to preventing violations of the federal securities laws, another person who commits a violation, if such other person is subject to his supervision. The Commission repeatedly has emphasized that the duty to supervise is a critical component of the federal regulatory scheme. *In re Rhumbline Advisers*, Advisers Act Rel. No. 1765 (September 29, 1998); *In re Western Asset Management Co.*, Advisers Act Rel. No. 1980 (September 28, 2001).

Meckel was Littell's supervisor and an associated person of MMG, an investment adviser. Meckel failed reasonably to supervise Littell with a view toward preventing Littell's violations of the federal securities laws. Furthermore, Meckel does not have a defense for a failure to supervise charge because he failed to establish procedures and a system for applying such procedures, which would reasonably be expected to prevent and to detect any such violation by Littell. Meckel did not create or implement procedures to detect violations by Littell; such procedures could have included reviewing confirmations and statements, valuing positions, and properly calculating fund performance. It is essential that advisers implement policies reasonably designed, under the circumstances of the particular investment strategies employed by the firms, to detect and prevent violations of the federal securities laws by even their most experienced employees. *Oechsle International Advisors, L.L.C.*, Advisers Act Rel. No. 1966 (August 10, 2001). The Commission has recognized that the "delicate fiduciary relationship" between an investment adviser and a client imposes an obligation on an adviser to review and to monitor its activities and the activities of its employees. *Shearson Lehman Brothers, Inc. and Stein Roe & Farnham*, Exchange Act Rel. No. 23640, 36 SEC Docket 1075 (September 24, 1996). Accordingly, an investment adviser that does not reasonably supervise its associated persons with a view towards preventing violations of the federal securities laws may be subject to sanction by the Commission. See *Nicholas-Applegate Capital Management*, Advisers Act Rel. No. 1741, 67 SEC Docket 2312 (August 12, 1998). Similarly, associated persons of an investment adviser in supervisory positions may be subject to sanctions for failing reasonably to supervise any person subject to their supervision. *Quest Capital Strategies, Inc.,* 76 SEC Docket 102 (October 15, 2001).

As a result of the conduct described above, Meckel failed reasonably to supervise Littell, with a view to preventing violations of the federal securities laws while Littell was subject to his supervision, within the meaning of Sections 203(e)(6) and 203(f) of the Advisers Act.

Disgorgement and Civil Penalties

Littell has submitted a sworn Statement of Financial Condition dated August 21, 2002 and other evidence and has asserted his inability to pay a civil penalty.

Remedial Efforts

In determining to accept the Offers, the Commission considered remedial acts promptly undertaken by Meckel and the cooperation he afforded the Commission staff.

In view of the foregoing, the Commission deems it appropriate and in the public interest to impose the sanctions specified in the Offers.

Pursuant to Section 203(k) of the Advisers Act, Littell shall cease and desist from committing or causing any violations and any future violations of Section 17(a) of the Securities Act, Section 10(b) of the Exchange Act and Rule 10b-5 thereunder, and Sections 206(1) and 206(2) of the Advisers Act.

Littell shall, within ten days of the entry of this Order, pay a civil money penalty in the amount of $15,000 to the United States Treasury. Such payment shall be: (A) made by United States postal money order, certified check, bank cashier's check or bank money order; (B) made payable to the Securities and Exchange Commission; (C) hand-delivered or mailed to the Office of Financial Management, Securities and Exchange Commission, Operations Center, 6432 General Green Way, Stop 0-3, Alexandria, VA 22312; and (D) submitted under cover letter that identifies Littell as a Respondent in these proceedings, the file number of these proceedings, a copy of which cover letter and money order or check shall be sent to Caren N. Pennington, Assistant Regional Director, Division of Enforcement, Securities and Exchange Commission, 233 Broadway, New York, NY 10279.

Pursuant to Section 203(f) of the Advisers Act, Littell shall be, and hereby is, barred from association with any investment adviser.

Pursuant to Section 203(f) of the Advisers Act, Meckel shall be censured.

Pursuant to Section 203(f) of the Advisers Act, Meckel shall be, and hereby is, suspended from association in any supervisory capacity with any investment adviser for a period of six months effective on the second Monday following the entry of this Order.

PARAMOUNT FINANCIAL PARTNERS, L.P.

The Securities and Exchange Commission ("Commission") deems it appropriate and in the public interest that public administrative proceedings be, and hereby are, instituted pursuant to Section 15(b) of the Securities Exchange Act of 1934 ("Exchange Act") against Respondents James Curtis Conley ("Conley"), Michael L. Vogt ("Vogt") and John E. Hawley, Jr. ("Hawley") and Section 203(f) of the Investment Advisers Act of 1940 ("Advisers Act") against Respondents Von Christopher Cummings ("Cummings"), John A. Ryan ("Ryan"), Kevin L. Grandy ("Grandy") and Conley (collectively Cummings, Ryan, Grandy, Conley, Vogt and Hawley are referred to as "Respondents").

In anticipation of the institution of these proceedings, Respondents have submitted Offers of Settlement (the "Offers") which the Commission has determined to accept. Solely for the purpose of these proceedings and any other proceedings brought by or on behalf of the Commission, or to which the Commission is a party, and without admitting or denying the findings herein, except as to the Commission's jurisdiction over them and the subject matter of these proceedings, and the findings contained in Section III.A(2) with respect to Cummings, Section III.B(2) with respect to Ryan, Section III.C(2) with respect to Grandy, Section III.D(2) with respect to Conley, Section III.E(2) with respect to Vogt and Section III.F(2) with respect to Hawley, which are admitted, Respondents consent to the entry of this Order Instituting Administrative Proceedings Pursuant to Section 15(b) of the Securities Exchange Act of 1934 and Section 203(f) of the Investment Advisers Act of 1940, Making Findings, and Imposing Remedial Sanctions ("Order"), as set forth below.

On the basis of this Order and Cumming's Offer, the Commission finds that Cummings held himself out as an investment adviser and represented Paramount Financial Partners, L.P. ("Paramount Financial") as a registered investment adviser when he solicited and induced clients and other associates to invest. Cummings claimed to investors that Paramount Financial was a hedge fund that generated large returns for clients. Paramount Financial and Cummings were not registered with the Commission as investment advisers. Cummings is licensed by the National Association of Securities Dealers (NASD). Cummings, age 34, resides in Dublin, Ohio.

On September 27, 2004, a final judgment was entered by consent against Cummings, permanently enjoining him from future violations of Section 17(a) of the Securities Act of 1933 ("Securities Act"), Section 10(b) of the Exchange Act and Rule 10b-5 thereunder, and Sections 206(1) and 206(2) of the Advisers Act, in the civil action entitled *Securities and Exchange Commission v. Von Christopher Cummings, et al.*, Civil Action No. C2-02-629, in the United States District Court for the Southern District of Ohio (*"SEC v. Cummings, et al."*).

The Commission's complaint alleged that Cummings solicited and induced clients to participate in Paramount Financial investments. Cummings claimed to be a registered investment adviser in order to further Paramount Financial's activities. Cummings and Paramount Financial were not registered with the Commission as investment advisers. Cummings did not invest the investors' funds as promised. On the basis of this Order and Ryan's Offer, the Commission finds that between January 1, 2001 and July 5, 2001, Ryan was associated with Paramount Financial, a purported hedge fund that was falsely represented to investors as generating large returns for clients. Unbeknownst to Ryan at the time, Paramount Financial was in fact not a hedge fund and did not buy or sell securities for clients' accounts. Ryan, however, at the direction of Cummings, acted as an unregistered investment adviser who used investor funds to repay prior investors and for personal and business expenses.

On September 27, 2004, a final judgment was entered by consent against Ryan, permanently enjoining him from future violations of Section 17(a) of the Securities Act, Section 10(b) of the Exchange Act and Rule 10b-5 thereunder, and Sections 206(1) and 206(2) of the Advisers Act, in the civil action entitled *SEC v. Cummings, et al.*

The Commission's complaint alleged, among other things, that Ryan solicited and induced clients to participate in Paramount Financial investments; that Ryan and Paramount Financial were not registered with the Commission as investment advisers; and that Paramount Financial did not invest the investors' funds as promised. On the basis of this Order and Grandy's Offer, the Commission finds that Grandy was associated with Paramount Financial when he solicited and induced clients and other associates to invest. Grandy claimed to investors that Paramount Financial was a hedge fund that generated large returns for clients. Paramount Financial and Grandy were not registered with the Commission as investment advisers. Grandy, age 34, resides in Columbus, Ohio.

On September 27, 2004, a final judgment was entered by consent against Grandy, permanently enjoining him from future violations of Section 17(a) of the Securities Act, Section 10(b) of the Exchange Act and Rule 10b-5 thereunder, and Sections 206(1) and 206(2) of the Advisers Act, in the civil action entitled *SEC v. Cummings, et al.*

The Commission's complaint alleged that Grandy solicited and induced clients to participate in Paramount Financial investments. Grandy and Paramount Financial are not registered with the Commission as investment advisers. On the basis of this Order and Conley's Offer, the Commission finds that Conley was a Paramount Financial employee from July 1999 through at least August 2001. Conley opened and conducted transactions in various bank accounts as part of the Paramount Financial scheme. Conley also falsely claimed to be president of a New York broker-dealer in connection with one of Paramount Financial's fraudulent schemes. Conley is a licensed broker with Series 7 and 24 securities licenses. Conley, age 33, resides in Columbus, Ohio.

On September 27, 2004, a final judgment was entered by consent against Conley, permanently enjoining him from future violations of Section 17(a) of the Securities Act, Section 10(b) of the Exchange Act and Rule 10b-5 thereunder, and Sections 206(1) and 206(2) of the Advisers Act, in the civil action entitled *SEC v. Cummings, et al.*

The Commission's complaint alleged that Conley opened and conducted transactions in various bank accounts used to deposit investor funds and wrote checks to investors which did not clear in furtherance of Paramount Financial's fraudulent schemes. Conley also falsely claimed to be president of a New York broker-dealer in connection with one of Paramount Financial's fraudulent schemes. Conley had Series 7 and 24 licenses.

On the basis of this Order and Vogt's Offer, the Commission finds that Vogt is a licensed broker and registered representative who solicited and induced clients and other associates to invest in Paramount Financial, a purported hedge fund that was falsely represented to investors as generating large returns for clients. In fact, Paramount Financial was not a hedge fund and did not buy or sell securities for clients' accounts but used investor funds to repay prior investors and for personal and business expenses. Vogt, age 31, is a resident of Clearwater, Florida.

On September 27, 2004, a final judgment was entered by consent against Vogt, permanently enjoining him from future violations of Section 15(a) of the Exchange Act in the civil action entitled *SEC v. Cummings, et al.*

The Commission's complaint alleged that Vogt solicited and referred clients to participate in Paramount Financial investments. Vogt did not disclose to his registered broker-dealer employer that he had solicited investors for Paramount Financial in exchange for fees and commissions from Paramount Financial in the approximate amount of $104,000. Vogt agreed to use nominee accounts to disguise the use of investor funds to pay his commissions.

On the basis of this Order and Hawley's Offer, the Commission finds that Hawley is a licensed broker and registered representative who solicited and induced clients to invest in Paramount Financial, a purported hedge fund that was falsely represented to investors as generating large returns for clients. In fact, Paramount Financial was not a hedge fund and did not buy and sell securities for clients' accounts, but used investor funds to repay prior investors and for personal and business expenses. Hawley, age 33, is a resident of Mount Vernon, New York.

On September 27, 2004, a final judgment was entered by consent against Hawley, permanently enjoining him from future violations of Section 15(a) of the Exchange Act, in the civil action entitled *SEC v. Cummings, et al.*

The Commission's complaint alleged that Hawley solicited and referred clients to participate in Paramount Financial investments. Hawley did not disclose to his registered broker-dealer employer that he had solicited investors for Paramount Financial in exchange for fees and commissions from Paramount Financial in the approximate amount of $80,000. Hawley agreed to use nominee accounts to disguise the use of investor funds to pay his commissions.

In view of the foregoing, the Commission deems it appropriate and in the public interest to impose the sanctions agreed to in Respondents' Offers.

Accordingly, it is hereby ORDERED:

Pursuant to Section 203(f) of the Advisers Act, that Respondents Cummings, Ryan, Grandy and Conley be, and hereby are barred from association with any investment adviser;

Pursuant to Section 15(b)(6) of the Exchange Act, that Respondent Conley be, and hereby is barred from association with any broker or dealer;

Pursuant to Section 15(b)(6) of the Exchange Act, that Respondents Vogt and Hawley be, and hereby are barred from association with any broker or dealer, with the right to reapply for association after one year to the appropriate self-regulatory organization, or if there is none, to the Commission.

Any reapplication for association by the Respondents will be subject to the applicable laws and regulations governing the re-entry process, and re-entry may be conditioned upon a number of factors, including, but not limited to, the satisfaction of any or all of the following: (a) any disgorgement ordered against the Respondent, whether or not the Commission has fully or partially waived payment of such disgorgement; (b) any arbitration award related to the conduct that served as the basis for the Commission order; (c) any self-regulatory organization arbitration award to a customer, whether or not related to the conduct that served as the basis for the Commission order; and (d) any restitution order by a self-regulatory organization, whether or not related to the conduct that served as the basis for the Commission order.

PORTUS ALTERNATIVE ASSET MANAGEMENT INC.

Ontario Securities Commission Information regarding hedge fund:

WHEREAS it appears to the Ontario Securities Commission (the "Commission") that:

Portus Alternative Asset Management Inc. ("Portus") is a registered Investment Counsel/Portfolio Manager and Limited Market Dealer. The most accurate information provided to date indicates that Portus has approximately $730 million under management. The majority of these funds are from Ontario clients.

At present, Portus has opened managed client accounts for approximately 26,000 clients across Canada. The majority of these clients are resident in Ontario. Portus appears to be offering clients the same portfolio of Canadian equities and assets. Each portfolio appears to contain securities and assets which are held and/or traded to mimic the performance of BancNote Trust mutual funds, non-prospectus mutual funds which Portus also manages.

The structure of the investment provided by Portus appears to be such that clients' funds flow through bank accounts held by Portus on behalf of Portus's off-shore counterparties, and eventually flow to an account held by Portus. Portus deposits sufficient client funds into five to seven year term notes issued by Société Générale (Canada) (the "Notes") to guarantee a minimum return of the principal invested with Portus. Société Générale then promises to return to the holder of the Note (BancNote Trust) the higher of the principal invested with Portus or the return achieved by a fund of funds selected by Portus. This appears to be the basis for Portus's representation to clients that their investments are guaranteed.

At the same time, Portus transacts with two off-shore counterparties to achieve a position whereby the Canadian equities appear to be held in client name by one of the off-shore counterparties. Portus transacts in two derivatives which provide the client with the return on the Notes in exchange for the return on the Canadian equities.

The Notes are presently held in an account at RBC Dominion Securities Inc. ("RBCDS") over which Boaz Manor ("Manor") has trading authority. At maturity, the Notes will have a value of at least the principal invested by the clients.

Withdrawals of clients' funds prior to maturity of the Notes could result in a loss to certain clients and preferential treatment for some clients to the detriment of others.

Manor is the owner and Managing Director of Portus. Manor is registered as an Associate Investment Counsel/Portfolio Manager. Manor has trading authority with respect to the RBCDS account.

BancNote Trust buys the Notes on behalf of investors. Manor is the adviser to BancNote Trust. Portus appears to have contravened sections 113 and 123 of Ontario Regulation 1015, R.R.O. 1990 of the Securities Act, and subsections 2.1(1) and 1.5(1)(b) of OSC Rule 31-505 and, to date, has failed to take adequate steps to remedy these breaches.

The conduct referred to above appears to be contrary to the public interest.

And whereas the Commission is of the opinion that it is in the public interest to make this Order; and whereas the Commission is of the opinion that the time required to conclude a hearing could be prejudicial to the public interest; and whereas by Commission order made March 15, 2004 pursuant to section 3.5(3) of the Act, any one of David A. Brown, Paul M. Moore and Susan Wolburgh Jenah acting alone, is authorized to make orders under section 127 of the Act;

It is hereby ordered that, pursuant to subsections 127(1)1 and 2 and 127(5) of the Act:

Trading in any securities by Portus cease, except with respect to the pre-authorized periodic withdrawals permitted pursuant to paragraph 2(b) below; and

The following terms and conditions are imposed on Portus's and Manor's registration (the "Terms"):

a. Effective immediately, Portus shall not pay out, redeem or otherwise return any funds or other assets from any existing client accounts, except as provided in paragraph (b), below.

b. Notwithstanding the restrictions imposed under paragraph 2(a), above, Portus may continue to make periodic payments from any existing client account in respect of which a client has entered into a pre-authorized periodic withdrawal plan with Portus, provided (a) such plan was entered into before February 10, 2005, (b) such payments are made in compliance with the provisions of the plan, and (c) the amount of such future payments may not be increased from the amount of the most recent previous payment.

c. Effective immediately, Manor shall not undertake any action that directly or indirectly constitutes a trade or act in furtherance of a trade in the Notes.

d. Without limiting the generality of the foregoing, Manor shall not authorize, direct or execute trades in the Notes or appoint, authorize or direct any other party to make trades in the Notes.

It is further ordered that the Terms supplement and do not replace any other specific terms and conditions that currently apply to Portus and Manor, including but not limited to the terms and conditions imposed on Portus's registration pursuant to the Temporary Order issued by the Commission on February 2, 2005, and Portus and Manor continue to be subject to all applicable general terms, conditions and other requirements contained in the Act and any Regulations made thereunder; and

It is further ordered that, pursuant to subsection 127(6) of the Act, this Order shall take effect immediately and shall expire on February 17, 2005, unless extended by the Commission

Dated at Toronto this "10th" day of February, 2005.

STRATEGIC INCOME FUND, L.L.C.

On February 5, 2004, a federal criminal jury found Edward Thomas Jung guilty on 8 counts of wire fraud and two counts of securities fraud in a case brought by the United States Attorney for the Northern District of Illinois. U.S. District Judge Joan Humphrey Lefkow set sentencing for June 4, 2004. According to the indictment against him, Jung was previously the manager of a hedge fund known as the Strategic Income Fund, L.L.C., and also the controlling general partner of ETJ Partners, Ltd., a broker-dealer through which Jung traded stock options on the Chicago Board Options Exchange.

The indictment alleged that from July 1994 to September 1998, Jung engaged in a fraudulent scheme in which he falsely represented to prospective investors and investors that their pledged securities and cash would be used solely to conduct stock options trading on behalf of the Strategic Income Fund. Instead, Jung misappropriated the investors' assets to collateralize his own securities trading, and other securities trading unrelated to the Strategic Income Fund. Beginning no later than January 1995, Jung also misappropriated pledged securities and cash for other purposes, including paying the expenses of ETJ Partners.

In addition, the indictment alleged that Jung misrepresented his trading performance record to prospective investors by distributing written trading track records that inflated the success of his trading for the fund and failed to disclose the adverse financial impact of his misappropriations. The indictment further alleged that Jung distributed false quarterly statements to investors to retain their investments and to lull them into a false sense of security. The indictment alleged that Jung's scheme caused approximately 55 investors to lose more than $21 million.

On June 19, 2001, the Securities and Exchange Commission filed a civil complaint against Jung and ETJ Partners in connection with the scheme described above. The Commission's complaint charged that Jung and his broker-dealer, ETJ Partners, violated the antifraud provisions of the federal securities laws, including Section 17(a) of the Securities Act of 1933, Section 10(b) of the Securities Exchange Act of 1934, and Rule 10b-5 thereunder, and Sections 206(1) and 206(2) of the Investment Advisers Act of 1940. On March 14, 2002, the United States District Court for the Northern District of Illinois entered a final judgment order against Jung and ETJ Partners, pursuant to their consent, which enjoined Jung and ETJ Partners from future violations of the above antifraud provisions of the federal securities laws.

In addition, on March 28, 2002, the Commission entered an order in an administrative proceeding filed against Jung and ETJ Partners which barred Jung from association with any broker or dealer or investment adviser and which revoked ETJ Partners registration with the Commission as a broker-dealer.

For further information, see Litigation Releases 17995 (February 25, 2003), 17041 (June 20, 2001), 17417 (March 15, 2002), and Matter of Edward Thomas Jung and E. Thomas Jung Partners, Ltd., d/b/a ETJ Partners, Ltd., 77 SEC Docket 656 (March 28, 2002).

TRADEWINDS INTERNATIONAL, LP

The U.S. Securities and Exchange Commission announced that on September 1, 2004, a federal district court in Chicago entered an order freezing the assets of Charles L. Harris, of Winnetka, Illinois, Tradewinds International II, LP and Tradewinds International, L.L.C. based on their fraudulent offer and sale of securities in violation of federal securities laws. The Court also ordered the Defendants to preserve all documents. The Commission's Complaint and Motions further request the entry of orders of temporary, preliminary and permanent injunction, disgorgement, civil penalties and other relief against the Defendants. The Court set a hearing for Tuesday, September 7 on the other relief sought.

The Commission coordinated its investigation with the Commodity Futures Trading Commission. The CFTC simultaneously filed an action in the same court and has obtained an order of similar relief against Harris and Tradewinds L.L.C. for fraud under the Commodity Exchange Act.

The Commission's Complaint alleges that Defendants fraudulently raised at least $10 million from at least 30 investors for Tradewinds II, a private investment "hedge fund," since July 2001. The Complaint further alleges that the Defendants made false and misleading statements to investors regarding Tradewinds II's past rates of return, net asset value and the use of investor funds.

The Complaint alleges that, in July 2004, Harris sent certain investors e-mails and a DVD in which he confessed that he had falsely reported a 12% annual profit to investors in Tradewinds II for 2003, when in reality, Tradewinds II lost a significant amount of money. Harris also claimed to have fled the country and to have taken the claimed remaining investor assets offshore.

The Complaint also alleges that, while Harris told investors in 2003 that Tradewinds II's net asset value was between $18 and $23 million, trading account statements reflect a total value of at most $1.1 million during 2003, and approximately $30,000 at the end of the year.

The Complaint further alleges that, contrary to representations to investors, Harris used investor funds for purposes other than trading. The Complaint alleges that, in 2003 and 2004, at least $2.4 million of investor funds were never transferred to the trading accounts, but were used instead for Harris' personal and business expenses and to repay investors at artificially inflated rates, while Tradewinds II secretly incurred losses.

The Court's Order finds that there is good cause to believe that Defendants have violated and will continue to engage in violations of Section 17(a) of the Securities Act of 1933, and Section 10(b) of the Securities Exchange Act of 1934 and Rule 10b-5 thereunder unless immediately restrained and enjoined.

TRUEHEDGE ADVISORS, L.L.C.

Suit Alleges That Wichita-Based Hedge Fund Manager Committed Securities Fraud by Stealing Investor Funds

On August 23, 2004, the Commission filed an emergency action in United States district court in Wichita, Kansas against a Wichita-based hedge fund and its manager, alleging that the hedge fund manager fraudulently promoted the hedge fund by lying to investors and then spent their money on his personal expenses, including the construction of his new private residence in Wichita. The Commission simultaneously filed in the civil action, and the court granted, a motion seeking an asset freeze and other emergency relief against the defendants, in order to prevent the dissipation or concealment of assets that the Commission claims are paid as civil money penalties and disgorgement of illegal profits.

In its complaint, the Commission alleged that Scott B. Kaye, of Wichita, Kansas, is the sole managing member of TrueHedge Advisors, L.L.C. ("TrueHedge Advisors"), the unregistered investment adviser of True-Hedge Capital Partners, L.P. ("TrueHedge Capital"), a hedge fund based in Wichita. From June 2002 through February 2003, according to the Commission's complaint, Kaye and TrueHedge Advisors raised $1.9 million for TrueHedge Capital by selling limited partnership interests to 18 investors. The Commission further alleges that, whereas the private placement memorandum claimed TrueHedge Advisors and Kaye would use the funds to operate a hedge fund, investing in stocks and options, Kaye misappropriated more than a third of the offering proceeds.

In its action, the Commission charged Kaye, TrueHedge Advisors, and TrueHedge Capital with violating Section 17(a) of the Securities Act of 1933, Section 10(b) of the Securities Exchange Act of 1934 and Rule 10b-5 thereunder, as well as Sections 206(1) and 206(2) of the Investment Advisers Act of 1940. The Commission is seeking permanent injunctions, an order requiring the defendants to disgorge any illicit profits from their fraudulent scheme, plus prejudgment interest, and civil money penalties. The Commission also filed a motion on August 23, seeking, against each of the defendants, ex parte emergency relief, including an accounting, an asset freeze, and an order prohibiting the destruction or alteration of documents and expediting discovery. The court granted all relief sought by the Commission in its motion. The Commission gratefully acknowledges the assistance and cooperation of the Kansas Securities Commission.

ZION CAPITAL MANAGEMENT, LLC

Zion Capital Management LLC ("Zion"), formerly a registered investment adviser, and Ricky A. Lang, Zion's president and sole owner, appeal from an initial decision by an administrative law judge. The law judge found that the Respondents wilfully violated Section 17(a) of the Securities Act of 1933, Section 10(b) of the Securities Exchange Act of 1934 and Exchange Act Rule 10b-5, and Sections 206(1) and 206(2) of the Investment Advisers Act of 1940, by favoring an account in which Lang had a financial interest over Zion's advisory client, a hedge fund, in the allocation of securities trades, contrary to representations that any conflicts that occurred in the future would be resolved in a manner fair to all interests. The law judge further found that the Respondents wilfully violated Section 207 of the Advisers Act by making, in Zion's Form ADV filed with the Commission, material misrepresentations and omissions regarding the existence of an actual conflict of interest and that Lang wilfully aided and abetted and was a cause of Zion's violations of Advisers Act Section 204 and Advisers Act Rules 204-2(a)(3) and 204-2(a)(7) by failing to maintain copies of memoranda of orders given by the adviser for the purchase or sale of a security and all written communications relating to the execution of securities trades.

The law judge barred Lang from association with any investment adviser or investment company, ordered Respondents, jointly and severally, to pay a $220,000 civil money penalty, ordered Respondents to disgorge, jointly and severally, $211,827, with prejudgment interest, and imposed cease-and-desist orders.

Dominion Asset Management ("DAM")

In April 1996, Lang, Jay Glickman, Doug Mallach, Terry Vickery, and David Dambro formed Jayhead Investments LLC to trade capital contributed by Glickman, Mallach, Vickery, and Dambro. Although Lang did not contribute capital to Jayhead, as did the other participants, he received an equity interest, initially set at 9-11/12%.

Jayhead maintained an account at Salomon Smith Barney ("Smith Barney"), identified by Lang as the "master account." The master account had several sub-accounts. Shortly after the formation of Jayhead, Lang organized Dominion Asset Management ("DAM"), a subchapter S corporation. Lang was DAM's sole owner. Through DAM, Lang traded one of the Jayhead sub-accounts, entitled "Jayhead Investments LLC/Dominion Asset Management" ("DAM sub-account"). Pursuant to an oral agreement, Jayhead promised to pay Lang each month 50% of the trading profits that Lang generated in the DAM sub-account, but Lang would be responsible for 100% of the trading losses. For example, if Lang profited in April, but lost money in May, he would not be paid again until his trading recouped the May losses. Jayhead paid Lang's share of the trading profits to DAM.

Lang testified that his trading strategy for the DAM sub-account involved short-term trading of mostly NASDAQ-listed equities and their derivatives. He stated that he sought to make small and frequent trades throughout the day, and to carry, on average, less than 20% of the account's positions overnight.

According to the Smith Barney account statement for the DAM sub-account in March 1998, the sub-account's starting balance was $220,241. However, Lang asserted that Jayhead made available to him $500,000 in trading capital and the margin of the Jayhead master account.

Zion and the Dominion Fund

In 1998, Lang organized Zion to be the investment adviser and general partner of the Dominion Fund II L.P. ("Dominion Fund"), a hedge fund organized as a limited partnership. The Dominion Fund was Zion's only advisory client. Lang, the president and sole owner of Zion, was responsible for Zion's investment decisions.

Lang retained Jim Hicks and his partner Brian McGuane of J. Edgar Capital to solicit investors for the Dominion Fund. Lang, on Zion's behalf, prepared and provided Hicks and McGuane with marketing materials, an "Investment Summary" dated August 1997, an updated "Investment Summary" dated January 1998, and an "Offering Circular."

The Offering Circular included Zion's Form ADV filed with the Commission. Although an adviser must disclose conflicts of interest that would render such adviser not disinterested, none of the disclosure documents explained that Lang was an owner of and would continue to trade for the DAM sub-account and share in the profits and losses of the DAM sub-account. Indeed, the Form ADV represented that Lang's association with DAM had ended in December 1997.

Although Lang continued to trade for DAM, the Offering Circular stated merely that Zion "is or may in the future sponsor, manage or participate in other securities investment activities and programs unrelated to the Partnership's business" and "[t]he other activities of [Zion] may create conflicts of interest with the [Dominion Fund]." The Respondents further represented in the Offering Circular that Zion "will attempt to resolve all such conflicts in a manner that is fair to all such interests."

The disclosure documents also stated that Zion's personnel would refrain from trading a security for personal accounts for a period of one day after any transaction in that same security had been made for a Zion client account. Lang testified that he thought this restriction applied to trading only for an account of an individual person and did not restrict his trading for the DAM sub-account because DAM was a separate entity.

The Investment Summaries described Lang's previous trading strategy for DAM, stated that this strategy had produced an 88% return since inception, and included a chart that illustrated how DAM outperformed the Dow Jones Industrial Average and the Standard & Poor's Index. The Investment Summaries represented that Zion and Lang would pursue the same strategy for the Dominion Fund, claiming that the strategy "has been tested in real time market conditions" and "can be duplicated and actually improved upon with a larger capital base," for the Dominion Fund.

Although Lang wanted to raise $20 million for the Dominion Fund, and at least $5 million before he started trading for it, only three individuals invested in the Dominion Fund: James Robert Anderson invested $962,611; Patrick L. Tigue invested $150,000; and Alan Westman invested $57,053.

Lang's Trading for DAM and the Dominion Fund

From April 1998 through December 1998, Lang traded securities for both the Dominion Fund and the DAM sub-account. Lang opened an omnibus account at Smith Barney. The omnibus account allowed Lang to buy shares of a security in a single transaction and allocate shares of that security between the DAM sub-account and the Dominion Fund, instead of entering two separate buy orders.

Lang traded for both DAM and the Dominion Fund through several broker-dealers. All of these trades, however, cleared through Smith Barney. A majority of the trades (68%) were executed through Market Wise Securities, Inc. ("Market Wise"), and its predecessor. Market Wise assigned Zion separate computer terminal log-on identifications to place trades for the Dominion Fund and DAM. However, Lang often placed trades for both entities while logged onto DAM's Market Wise account. He claimed this was easier than having to log on and off while trading for the two accounts.

Lang testified that he kept records throughout the day of which trades were for the DAM sub-account and which were for the Dominion Fund. At the end of each trading day, Lang prepared from these contemporaneous notes a handwritten summary of the trades. Lang would aggregate the trades that he made in a given security. For example, if he made five separate purchases of a security at various prices, he would record these orders as a single purchase and compute an average price. At the end of the day,

Lang provided instructions to Smith Barney to allocate the securities cleared through the omnibus account between the DAM sub-account and the Dominion Fund.

Respondents did not keep the contemporaneous handwritten notes that Lang made while trading for the DAM sub-account and the Dominion Fund or the written allocation instructions sent to Smith Barney. Respondents could not produce the trade blotter for DAM and produced only a photocopy of the Dominion Fund's trade blotter. Comparing this Dominion Fund trade blotter to Smith Barney account statements shows that Dominion Fund's trade blotter was incomplete and inaccurate.

Lang produced profit-and-loss reports for the Dominion Fund and for DAM that he claimed reflected every trade he made. These reports show securities purchased and sold in a given month as well as the amount paid for the purchases and the amount received for the sales. There is no indication on the face of the reports when they were created. When compared against the Smith Barney account statements, they do not include all of the trades made on behalf of the two entities. The reports show positions only on an aggregated basis and do not show the time of each transaction. Moreover, the reports do not show which transactions offset previously held positions in a given stock.

Despite Lang's representations that he would pursue the same trading strategy for the Dominion Fund that he had used in the past for the DAM sub-account and that he would resolve any conflicts of interest fairly, the result of his contemporaneous trading for both entities was quite different. An analysis of Lang's trading and allocations for both accounts for the period April to December 1998 showed that, for day trades (in which Lang opened and closed a position in the same day by buying and selling a like amount of the same security in one day), 197 of the profitable day trades were allocated to the DAM account and only 39 to the Dominion Fund account. For so-called "partial day trades" (in which Lang opened and then closed a portion of a position in the same day), while approximately half of the 181 partial day trades were allocated to each entity, the allocations resulted in a net gain of $75,307 for DAM and a net loss of $103,997 for the Dominion Fund. With respect to positions that were opened and not offset the same day, Lang allocated $67,789 in net unrealized gains from 347 trades to DAM and allocated $510,652 in net unrealized losing trades from 458 transactions to the Dominion Fund. As of December 31, 1998, the DAM account achieved profits of $236,411 while the Dominion Fund suffered losses of $699,180. The staff, while conducting its routine examination of Zion as a registered investment adviser, discovered this allocation scheme.

From April 1, 1998, through December 31, 1998, Lang received $138,498.08 in compensation from DAM, his 50% share of Dam's trading profits. Jayhead was dissolved on March 31, 2000. Although Jayhead had approximately $600,000 in assets at the time of its dissolution and Lang had an ownership in the dissolved entity, Lang did not receive a distribution of assets at dissolution.

A. Antifraud Violations

Securities Act Section 17(a), Exchange Act Section 10(b), and Exchange Act Rule 10b-5 prohibit fraudulent and deceptive acts and practices in connection with the offer, purchase, or sale of a security, including making a material misrepresentation or omission. Advisers Act Section 206(1) prohibits an investment adviser from employing "any device, scheme, or artifice to defraud any client or prospective client."

Advisers Act Section 206(2) further prohibits an investment adviser from engaging in a course of business that operates as a fraud or deceit. The Supreme Court has held that this provision establishes "'the delicate fiduciary nature of an investment advisory relationship.'" The Court found that Section 206(2) requires an investment adviser "to eliminate, or at least to expose, all conflicts of interest which might incline an investment adviser—consciously or unconsciously—to render advice which was not disinterested." Thus, an investment adviser has "an affirmative duty of 'utmost good faith, and full and fair disclosure of all material facts,' as well as an affirmative obligation 'to employ reasonable care to avoid misleading' his clients."

The Respondents misrepresented and omitted material facts with respect to the conflicts of interest in Lang's involvement with the Dominion Fund and the DAM sub-account. They did not disclose that Lang continued to trade for the DAM sub-account, that he had an interest in the sub-account, and that Lang's trading created an actual conflict of interest between the Dominion Fund and DAM. Instead, the Investment Summaries and the Offering Circular, including the Form ADV attached to the Offering Circular, discussed only potential conflicts of interest. Zion's Form ADV represented that Lang ceased working for DAM in December 1997.

Zion and Lang further represented that they would employ a trading strategy for the Dominion Fund similar to that Lang had purportedly employed for DAM in the past. In fact, Lang continued to trade for DAM and used different trading strategies for DAM and the Dominion Fund. Lang repeatedly assigned better trades to DAM and worse trades to the Dominion Fund. Thus, the Dominion Fund received only 39 of the 197 profitable day trades. Lang also assigned most of the unrealized losses to the Dominion Fund.

Lang's favoring of the DAM account is especially telling given the differences in how his compensation was determined for each account. The fact that Lang received from DAM 50% of the trading profits payable on a monthly basis (rather than 25% of the trading profits payable on an annual basis from the Dominion Fund) created an incentive for Lang to favor DAM over the Dominion Fund.

The Respondents further represented that Lang would engage in quick in-and-out trades and that he would not expose more than 20% of capital, on average, to overnight risk. However, Lang admitted that he held positions much longer in the Dominion Fund. By the end of 1998, he had subjected much more than 20% of the Dominion Fund's capital to overnight risk.

The Respondents represented that Zion personnel would refrain from effecting a trade of a security in any personal account for at least one day after that security was traded in the Dominion Fund account. In fact, Lang effected trades for securities in the DAM sub-account on the same days that he effected trades in those securities for the Dominion Fund. Lang claims that he thought the Form ADV language that prohibited same day trading referred to his "personal" account, not DAM. However, Lang admitted that he was DAM's sole owner and that DAM was organized to receive his profits from trading the DAM sub-account.

Although, under Advisers Act Section 206(2), the Respondents had an obligation to eliminate or, at a minimum, to disclose conflicts between DAM and the Dominion Fund, the Respondents' method of trading for DAM and the Dominion Fund aggravated and disguised these conflicts. Lang generally used a single computer account at Market Wise to trade for both accounts. These commingled trades were sent to a single Smith Barney omnibus account. Zion failed to keep either Lang's trading records or their allocation instructions to Smith Barney.

As a result of Lang's trading allocations, during the eight months that Lang traded for both the Dominion Fund and the DAM sub-account, the sub-account was profitable for six months of the period. Even by Lang's reckoning, the Dominion Fund was profitable in only two months, April and September 1998.

The Respondents claim that they did not favor DAM in their allocations. Instead, they assert that "market factors" resulted in the disparate results between the Dominion Fund and the DAM sub-account. Like the law judge, we find this claim to be "unpersuasive." The Respondents contend that volatile and illiquid markets affected DAM and the Dominion Fund differently because of the position size and holding period.

However, during this period, DAM and the Dominion Fund generally engaged in similarly sized trades in similar and often in the same securities.

The Respondents further suggest that the difference in the size of DAM and the Dominion Fund accounts for the different trading outcomes. The Respondents do not explain why the difference between $220,241 versus $1,169,665 (the value of the DAM sub-account and the Dominion Fund at the beginning of the trading period at issue) was significant to their trading. Moreover, Lang asserted repeatedly that the DAM sub-account had access to $500,000 of Jayhead's capital. Thus, the alleged disparity in the sizes of the accounts appears less than the Respondents now claim. We also note that Lang had represented that his strategy for the DAM sub-account would be even more successful with greater capital.

The Respondents also assert that changes in NASD's rules governing the Small Order Execution System ("SOES") reducing the size of transactions that could be effected through SOES hampered Lang's ability to liquidate positions after October 1998. However, the average size of sale trades for the Dominion Fund account in fact increased slightly after the rule change—from 3,668 shares in July 1998 to 4,137 in November 1998. We conclude that SOES policies do not explain the different outcomes of the two accounts.

Lang, as president and sole owner of Zion, controlled Zion. We find that Respondents wilfully violated Securities Act Section 17(a), Exchange Act Section 10(b) and Rule 10b-5, and Advisers Act Sections 206(1) and 206(2).

Section 207 of the Advisers Act   Advisers Act Section 207 makes it unlawful for any person wilfully to make material misstatements or omissions in registration applications or reports, such as the Form ADV, filed with the Commission. In Zion's Form ADV, Respondents omitted disclosure of the actual conflicts of interest between DAM and the Dominion Fund. Moreover, Respondents represented that Lang had ceased his association with DAM in 1997. The Respondents represented that any potential conflicts of interest would be resolved fairly. They misstated that Lang had been employed by Rockmont and misrepresented that in 1991 he had been unemployed for one month, when in fact, he had been unemployed for one year. By making these material misstatements in Zion's Form ADV, the Respondents wilfully violated Advisers Act Section 207.

B. Books and Records Violations

Section 204 of the Advisers Act requires that investment advisers "make and keep" appropriate records in the course of conducting their business.

Advisers Act Rule 204-2(a)(3) requires investment advisers to keep "[a] memorandum of each order given by the investment adviser for the purchase or sale of any security," and Advisers Act Rule 204-2(a)(7) requires investment advisers to maintain originals of all written communications received and sent by the investment adviser relating to the placement or execution of any order to purchase or sell any security.

Zion did not maintain memoranda of the orders made on behalf of the Dominion Fund or Lang's allocation instructions. Neither the Dominion Fund's "trade blotter" nor Lang's profit and loss reports record every trade Lang made on behalf of the Dominion Fund. We find that Zion's failure to maintain these records constituted willful violations of Advisers Act Section 204 and Rules 204-2(a)(3) and 204-2(a)(7) thereunder.

Lang willfully aided and abetted these violations. Lang concedes that he did not retain his contemporaneous trading notes that purportedly memorialized the trades he placed on behalf of the Dominion Fund. Lang also concedes that Zion did not retain copies of the written communications sent to Smith Barney directing the allocation of trades in the omnibus account to the DAM and the Dominion Fund brokerage accounts. Lang's failure to comply with these important legal requirements was at least reckless. Lang continued to assert before us that these violations are merely "technical" and that the trading notes he discarded— the only complete record of the orders placed—were "not essential for any record keeping purpose." We disagree. His failure to keep these records disguised his fraudulent allocations. Because we find Lang aided and abetted these recordkeeping violations, he necessarily was a cause of the violations.

C. Bar and Cease-and-Desist Orders

In order to determine appropriate sanctions, we consider factors such as: the egregiousness of the violations, the isolated or recurrent nature of the violations, the sincerity of the respondents' assurances against future violations, the respondents' recognition of the wrongful nature of their conduct, and the respondents' opportunity to commit future violations. In determining whether to impose cease-and-desist orders, we also consider the risk of future violations.

The Respondents made material misrepresentations and omissions about the Dominion Fund and Lang's relationship with the DAM sub-account. They repeatedly favored the DAM sub-account over their client, the Dominion Fund, in the allocation of securities trades. The Respondents harmed the Dominion Fund investors, who incurred substantial losses. Their conduct was egregious, and took place over several months. Accordingly, pursuant to Section 9(b) of the Investment Company Act and Section 203(f) of the Advisers Act, we find that it is in the public interest to bar Lang from association with any investment adviser or investment company.

We also find that, because of the nature of the Respondents' conduct and because the Respondents are in a position to commit such violations in the future, there is a risk that they will engage in violations in the future. We therefore order them to cease and desist from committing or causing any violations or future violations of Exchange Act Section 10(b) and Rule 10b-5, Securities Act Section 17(a), and Advisers Act Sections 204, 206(1), 206(2), 207 and Rules 204-2(a)(3) and 204-2(a)(7).

D. Disgorgement

Disgorgement is an equitable remedy designed to deprive wrongdoers of unjust enrichment and to deter others from violating the securities laws. The Respondents' failure to maintain complete and accurate trading records makes the task of determining an appropriate amount of disgorgement difficult. Particularly since the uncertainty of the disgorgement amount was caused by the Respondents' illegal conduct, the amount of disgorgement "need only be a reasonable approximation of profits causally connected to the violation."

The law judge denied the Division's request for disgorgement of all of the Dominion Fund's losses and all of Lang and DAM's profits. Based on Lang's representation that he would use the same investment strategy for the Dominion Fund and DAM, the law judge determined that it was appropriate to allocate the sum of DAM's profits and Dominion Fund's profits in proportion to their starting values in March 1998. The law judge therefore ordered the Respondents to disgorge $211,827, the sum of (1) $138,498, Lang's 50% share of DAM's trading profits for the relevant period, plus (2) $73,329, an apportionment of the net of Dominion's losses and DAM's profits.

We believe that the law judge's calculation is a reasonable approximation of Respondents' unjust enrichment. Lang's allocations of profitable trades to the DAM sub-account ensured that Lang received monthly compensation from DAM. Lang also avoided having to recoup losses before he could receive a share in further trading profits. We believe the law judge's formula was a reasonable effort to undo Lang's allocations. If Lang had not made the allocations and had, as he represented, traded the accounts using the same strategy, the profits or losses would have been roughly proportional. Adding this amount to his trading profits from DAM approximates his total benefit from both his share of the trading profits and his avoiding having to make up the trading losses in the DAM sub-account.

Respondents claim that there "is no mathematical or factual basis" for this calculation of disgorgement. They, however, bear the burden of demonstrating why that figure is not a reasonable approximation. Other than Lang's testimony that he did not make allocations that favored the DAM sub-account, they have not produced any evidence to support their assertion. Accordingly, we order Respondents to pay, jointly and severally, disgorgement in the amount of $211,821.

E. Civil Money Penalty

Investment Company Act Section 9(d) and Advisers Act Section 203(i) authorize the Commission to impose a civil money penalty when such penalty is in the public interest. Once a public interest determination is made, Investment Company Act Section 9(d)(2) and Advisers Act Section 203(i)(2) establish a three-tier system for assessing the amount of the penalty to be imposed. The third tier provides for a maximum of $110,000 for each act or omission by a natural person ($550,000 for any other person) if the conduct (a) involved fraud, deceit, manipulation, or deliberate or reckless disregard of a regulatory requirement and (b) resulted in, or created a significant risk of, substantial loss to others or resulted in substantial pecuniary gain to the person who committed the act or omission.

As set forth in this opinion, we find that the Respondents' conduct involved fraud, deceit, and a deliberate or reckless disregard of the antifraud provisions of the securities laws, and the conduct caused substantial loss to the three Dominion Fund investors. Lang was the sole owner of Zion and used it as a vehicle for his violations. We therefore find that the third-tier joint and several penalty of $220,000 imposed by the law judge are appropriate in the public interest.

Section 308(a) of the Sarbanes-Oxley Act permits the Commission to direct that a civil money penalty be added to a disgorgement fund for the benefit of the victims of violations of the securities laws. We deem it appropriate that the funds paid to satisfy the civil money penalty be added to the disgorgement fund to be distributed to victims of the Respondents' fraud, pursuant to Section 308 (Fair Funds for Investors) of the Sarbanes-Oxley Act of 2002.

MARKET TIMING CASES

The following cases are from Xingua Consulting on Hedge Funds. They
are also in www.sec.gov.

H&R BLOCK—H&R BLOCK FINANCIAL
ADVISORS, INC.

The company was fined $500,000 in order to disgorge $325,000 in profits by clients. Two brokers were aiding hedge funds to market time. According to the National Association of Securities Dealers (NASD), H&R
Block recruited and hired the two brokers in question in September
2002 knowing they were going to open accounts for hedge funds that intended to actively trade or market time in mutual funds that limited such
trading. H&R Block Financial Advisors was headed by Brian Nygaard,
and they settled with the SEC. The NASD's initial press release paints
a completely different picture than the settlement does. The political
activity of H&R Block Financial Advisors is evident here. The NASD
also hid the names of the two brokers engaging in this scheme in its
press release.

JEMMCO CAPITAL

Jemmco was identified in a Securities and Exchange Commission lawsuit
as a participant in market timing along with several other hedge funds.
Jemmco acknowledged in its statement it undertook market timing strategies but said it did so briefly and with a small portion of its assets.
Jemmco has not been accused of wrongdoing, according to the statement
by David Muschel. Muschel was the head principal of Jemmco and no
charges or fines have been levied on Jemmco. Jemmco's political activity
can be found here. Several mutual fund companies blocked Jemmco's account from trading their mutual fund shares, but Druffner concocted new
ways of bypassing these blocks, and the statement from the SEC shows
you the correspondence between each mutual fund and the group headed
up by Druffner at Prudential Securities.

KAPLAN & CO. SECURITIES

The Securities and Exchange Commission separately announced a $750,000 civil settlement against two brokers, Delano Sta.Ana, 29, and Lawrence Powell, 40. They each faced one to four years in prison for alleged felony securities fraud under New York's Martin Act. The brokers agreed to pay a total of $750,000, split evenly, as a partial settlement, New York attorney general Eliot Spitzer said. The two men were accused of illegal late trading of mutual funds for Kaplan and specific hedge fund clients. Kaplan is a privately held financial services firm based in Boca Raton, Florida. One of its clients was Canary Capital Partners, a hedge fund operator.

According to the SEC:

> *The Commission's Order finds that Powell and Sta.Ana willfully violated Section 10(b) of the Securities Exchange Act of 1934 and Rule 10b-5 thereunder, and willfully aided and abetted and caused Kaplan & Co.'s violations of Section 15(c)(1) of the Exchange Act and Rule 22c-1 promulgated under Section 22(c) of the Investment Company Act, and requires Powell and Sta.Ana to cease and desist from violating these provisions. The Order also bars Powell and Sta.Ana from association with any broker, dealer or investment adviser.*

CANARY CAPITAL PARTNERS

This was the fund that started it all, or at least when the SEC and Eliot Spitzer took action. Canary Capital was run by Edward Stern of Secaucus, New Jersey, the son of Leonard Stern, whose name graces New York University's School of Business. The late trading by Canary was uncovered by an employee named Noreen Harrington after she overheard a few guys on the trading desk gloating about trading mutual funds after hours. The Penalties handed out were $30 million dollars in restitution and a $10 million dollar fine.

One of the people who paid for Edward Stern's fraud was a guy named Theodore Sihpol at Banc of America (BOA). Sihpols' lawyer said Sihpol, 36, was supervised by older, more experienced employees after he went to work at Banc of America in December 2000. Yet, the lawyer said, his client is the only person from that office who has been charged.

Banc of America Capital Management, BACAP Distributors, and Banc of America Securities were involved in the Banc of America–Canary Capital mutual fund late trading scandal. The SEC and Spitzer settled with Banc of America, and the following punishments were handed out: Under a specific provision of the agreement, eight members of the board of directors of Nations Funds, BOA' s mutual fund complex, will resign or otherwise leave the board in the course of the next year for their role in approving a controversial measure that enabled a hedge fund to conduct company-sanctioned market timing of BOA funds.

In addition to requiring the board members to retire or resign, the agreement also included a provision that restricts BOA's ongoing involvement in the securities clearing business.

The agreement provides for payments of $250 million in restitution and $125 million in penalties by BOA. Fleet will pay $70 million in restitution and $70 million in penalties. In a separate agreement with Spitzer's office, BOA and Fleet agreed to reduce the fees they charge investors by $160 million over a five-year period.

In May 2002, Robert Gordon, an executive in the bank's mutual fund division, briefed directors of Nations Funds on a proposal to charge a 2 percent fee to investors who held the company's international funds for less than 90 days, according to a person briefed on the investigation. Gordon also told the directors that one hedge fund would be exempt from the redemption fee. That fund was Canary Capital Partners, Stern's hedge fund, said a spokesperson for Spitzer, and Canary subsequently made short-term trades in two of the bank's international funds. Gordon left Banc of America soon after the fund investigation became public.

COMPLIANCE CASES WITH COMMODITY POOL OPERATORS

Hedge fund cases often relate to commodity pools, hedge fund trading activities with regard to commodities and futures contracts, and commodity pool operators (CPOs). The following is a list of the legal and compliance cases involving commodity pools, hedge funds, and CPOs undertaken by the Commodity Futures Trading Commission (CFTC) from 1993 to 2003.

In 1993:

- *In re Daniel Clothier and Collins Commodity Brokerage Company Inc.*, CFTC administrative action.

- *CFTC v. De Gol Enterprises Inc., De Gol Financial Group Inc., and Dennis J. Golubowski,* civil injunctive action filed in federal district court in Florida.
- *In re Oliver Burnham Ecles,* CFTC administrative action.
- *CFTC v. Buff Aaron Hofberg,* civil injunctive action filed in federal district in Illinois.
- *In re Thomas Kolter, Philipp C. Zarcone, and Coopers & Lybrand,* CFTC administrative action.
- *CFTC v. Christian Schindler, Falcon Investment Corp. Inc., FIC Inc., Investment Banker's Brokerage, and IBB Inc.,* civil injunctive action filed in federal district court in New York.
- *In re George Cole Smith,* CFTC administrative action.
- *In re Spear, Leeds & Kellogg, Charles N. Sweeney, and Franklin Errol Douet,* CFTC administrative action.

In 1994:

- *CFTC v. Richard Conroy Bell, Barrett Bell Investment Corp., Manticore Resources, and Zia Investments,* civil injunctive action filed in federal district court in Oklahoma.
- *CFTC v. William Steel Bowen and Michael J.Goldberg,* civil injunctive action filed in federal district court in Tennessee.
- *CFTC v. Edward M. Collins, Thomas W. Collins, and Lake States Commodities Inc.,* civil injunctive action filed in federal district court in Illinois.
- *CFTC v. Keith Dominick and Main Street Investment Group Inc.,* civil injunctive action filed in federal district court in Florida.
- *In re J. Gary Fritts and Gary Lyn McCorkell,* CFTC administrative action.
- *In re Jerry W. Slusser, First Republic Financial Corp., First Republic Trading Corp., Hans J. Brinks, Edward T. Hamlet, and Cantor Fitzgerald & Co.,* CFTC administrative action.

In 1995:

- *CFTC v. Charles Nicholas Barth,* civil injunctive action filed in federal district court in Kentucky.
- CFTC and Ohio Division of Securities versus Allied Financial Group Inc.; Robert G. Bobo; and Jeffrey A. Smith; civil injunctive action filed in federal court in Ohio.

In 1996:

- *CFTC v. Gary Berus, Meca International Inc., and Patricia Gale*, civil injunctive action filed in federal district court in Michigan.
- *CFTC v. Donald B. Chancey and Southeastern Venture Partners Group*, civil injunctive action filed in federal district court in Georgia.
- *CFTC versus Thomas J. Deniz*, civil injunctive action filed in federal district court in California.
- *In re Fenchurch Capital Management, Ltd*, CFTC administrative action.
- *CFTC v. Everett Scott Hobbs*, civil injunctive action filed in federal district court in California.
- *CFTC v. Michael Indihar, Robert P. Hoffman, Computer Warehouse Inc., and Automated Trading Systems, Inc.*, civil injunctive action filed in federal district court in Florida.
- *CFTC v. Richard E. Maseri, Ronald Bruce Romberg, AIM International Inc., Bulleye International Inc., and Private Research Inc.*, civil injunctive action filed in federal district court in Florida.
- *CFTC v. Prism Financial Corp., Brian Prandergast, Joel DeAngelis, Amerinational Financial*, civil injunctive action filed in federal district court in Colorado.
- *In re Refco Inc.*, CFTC administrative action.
- *In re Sanjay Saxena and Select Sector Research and Management Inc.*, CFTC administrative action.
- *CFTC v. Christopher C. Schaffer, ARS Financial Services, Alchemy Financial Group Inc., and Peter J. Urbani*, civil injunctive action filed in federal district court in Texas.
- *CFTC v. Edward W. Schroeder, Edward W. Schroeder Living Trust, and Andre D. Fite*, civil injunctive action filed in federal district in California.
- *CFTC v. Michael Tropiano*, civil injunctive action filed in federal district court in New Jersey.
- *CFTC v. United Metals Trading Corp., Western National Trading, Anthony F. Andrews, and Marvin C. Pendergraft*, civil injunctive action filed in federal district court in Arizona.
- *CFTC v. Ken Willey*, civil injunctive action filed in federal district court in Washington.

In 1997:

- *CFTC v. AC Trading Group, Inc., AC Trading Group Fund LP, Alexis Carles, and Fred Eric Dejong*, civil injunctive action filed in federal district court in California.

- *In re Curtis McNair Arnold and London Financial Inc.*, CFTC administrative action.
- *CFTC v. James V. Dowler & Beekman Trading Co. Ltd.*, civil injunctive action filed in federal district court in Florida.
- *CFTC v. Carl J. Hermans*, civil injunctive action filed in federal district court in California.
- *In re Willy Kerzinger*, CFTC administrative action.
- *CFTC v. Oscar A. Klitin and Klitin Associates II*, civil injunctive action filed in federal district court in New York.
- *CFTC v. L.A. Forex Inc., Gabor Urban, and Marta Ban*, civil injunctive action filed in federal district court in California.

In 1998:

- *In re Abraham and Sons Capital Inc., and Brett Brubaker*, CFTC administrative action.
- *CFTC versus James Bonney*, civil injunctive action filed in federal district court in Wisconsin.
- *CFTC v. Chateauforte Consortium Inc., Richard E. Busch, John La-Tourette, James Michael Hanks, William Amos, Financial Planning Alliance International, and WorldEx S.A.*, civil injunctive action filed in federal district court in Alabama.
- *CFTC v. Jack Dwight Cullen*, civil injunctive action filed in federal district court in Texas.
- *CFTC v. S. David Friedman, Intercap International Inc., and Whitehall Trust*, civil injunctive action filed in federal district court in New York.
- *CFTC v. FTI Financial Group, Samuel H Foreman, Mark G. Steven, and Carolyn F. Munn*, civil injunctive action filed in federal district court in Illinois.
- *CFTC v. Thomas Lamar*, civil injunctive action filed in federal district court in Michigan.
- *CFTC v. Market Capital Growth Inc., Carmen Field, Mona Smith, Steven Hudkins, Bart Bemiller, and Robert Riethman*, civil injunctive action filed in federal district court in Indiana.
- *In re New York Currency Corporation*, CFTC administrative action.
- *CFTC v. Thomas O'Connell*, civil injunctive action filed in federal district court in Vermont.
- *CFTC v. John Larry Schenk, Douglas Foster, and Robert Moncur*, civil injunctive action filed in federal district court in Utah.
- *CFTC v. Brian Sullivan*, civil injunctive action filed in federal district court in Hawaii.

- *CFTC v. James M. Zoller and Tech-Comm Limited Partnerships*, civil injunctive action filed in federal district court in Minnesota.

In 1999:

- *CFTC v. Richard Belz, Andrew E. Cafferty, and Blue Chip Information Corp.*, civil injunctive action filed in federal district court in Tennessee.
- *CFTC v. Morris Benun*, civil injunctive action filed in federal district court in New York.
- *CFTC v. Peter Berzins*, civil injunctive action filed in federal district court in Virginia.
- *CFTC v. Mark Chulik*, civil injunctive action filed in federal district court in California.
- *CFTC v. Michael Colton*, civil injunctive action filed in federal district court in Florida.
- *CFTC v. Europacific Equity and Capital Management Ltd, Tortola Corporation Ltd, International Investment Group Ltd., and David Michael Loyd*, civil injunctive action filed in federal district court in Florida.
- *In re Ross Godres*, CFTC administrative action.
- *In re David Green*, CFTC administrative action.
- *CFTC v. David T. Marantette III and Troubadour, Inc.*, civil injunctive action filed in federal district court in Hawaii.
- *CFTC v. Joseph McGivney, Edwin Koziol Jr., Capital Strategies Inc., JPM 2 Inc., JPM Commodities Inc., JPM Investments Inc., and JPM Inc.*, civil injunctive action filed in federal district court in Illinois.
- *CFTC v. Princeton Global Management Ltd., Princeton Economic International Ltd., and Martin Armstrong*, civil injunctive action filed in federal district court in New York.

In 2000:

- *In re William G. Billings and Billfund, Inc.*, CFTC administrative action.
- *CFTC v. Stephen W. Brockbank, Carol J. Love, and Birma Ltd.*, civil injunctive action filed in federal district court in West Virginia.
- *CFTC v. Robert Dormagen and Delta Financial Corporation*, civil injunctive action filed in federal district court in West Virginia.
- *CFTC v. Phillip Ferguson, Ferguson Fund, B and F Trading, and First Investors Group Inc.*, civil injunctive action filed in federal district court in Indiana.

- *In re Suengho Kim, John Ki Park, Houston System Trading, LLC,* CFTC administrative action.
- *CFTC v. Michael James Konkel, Ad Astra Inc., and the Inscape Funds,* civil injunctive action filed in federal district court in Alabama.
- *CFTC v. David Mobley Sr., Maricopa Index Investment Fund Ltd, Maricopa Financial Corp., Ensign Trading Corp., and Maricopa International Investment Corp.,* civil injunctive action filed in federal district court in New York.
- *CFTC v. Pension America Inc., Selective Futures Management, Futures Profit Making, Specialized Commodities Timing, Commodity Timing Specialists, Edward Stevenson Kirris III, Leonard Nauman, and William Reif,* civil injunctive action filed in federal district court in Minnesota.
- *In re George Velissaris and ACG Partners LP,* CFTC administrative action.

In 2001:

- *CFTC v. Jeffrey T. Bailey and JMK Capital Management Inc.,* civil injunctive action filed in federal district court in Ohio.
- *CFTC v. Andrew Duncan and The Aurum Society,* civil injunctive action filed in federal district court in Illinois.
- *In re Isaac Fleyshmakher,* CFTC administrative action.
- *In re Harvey T. Gilkerson,* CFTC administrative action.
- *CFTC v. Edward Knipping and Time Traders Inc.,* civil injunctive action filed in federal district court in Maine.
- *CFTC v. John O'Herron and O'Herron Asset Management,* civil injunctive action filed in federal district court in Michigan.
- *CFTC v. Rothlin and Windsor Capital Management Inc. and Peter Scott,* civil injunctive action filed in federal district court in Maryland.

In 2002:

- *CFTC v. Thomas Chilcott, Ted Whidden, and Leona Westbrook,* civil injunctive action filed in federal district court in Florida.
- *CFTC v. Gahma Corporation, Stephen Brockbank, John Garrett, Allen Andersen, and Robert Heninger,* civil injunctive action filed in federal district court in Utah.

- *CFTC v. John Lofgren and Melrose Asset Management Corporation*, civil injunctive action filed in federal district court in Illinois.

In 2003:

- *In re Beacon Hill Asset Management LLC*, CFTC administrative action.
- *CFTC v. Paulino Rene Bias Jr., Victor Smith, and Krute Corporation*, civil injunctive action filed in federal district court in California.

References

Ackermann, C., R. McEnally, and D. Ravenscraft. 1999. The performance of hedge funds: Risk, return, and incentives. *Journal of Finance* 54: 833–874.

Ackermann, C., and D. Ravenscraft. 1998. The impact of regulatory restrictions on fund performance: A comparative study of hedge funds and mutual funds. Dissertation, University of North Carolina.

Adkisson, J. A., and D. R. Fraser. 2003a. Reading the stars: Age bias in Morningstar ratings. *Financial Analysts Journal* 59, no. 5 (September/October): 24–27.

Adkisson, J. A., and D. R. Fraser. 2003b. Realigning the stars. Working paper.

Adkisson, J. A., and D. R. Fraser. 2004. Is there still an age bias in the Morningstar ratings? Working paper, January.

Agarwal, V., N. Daniel, and N. Naik. 2003. Risk-taking incentives and hedge fund volatility. Working paper, Georgia State University and London Business School.

Agarwal, V., N. Daniel, and N. Naik. 2004. Flows, performance, and managerial incentives in the hedge fund industry. Georgia State University, working paper presented at the Gutmann Center Symposium on Hedge Funds, University of Vienna, November 29.

Agarwal, V., and N. Naik. 2000a. Generalized style analysis of hedge funds. *Journal of Asset Management* 1: 93–109.

Agarwal, V., and N. Naik. 2000b. Multi-period performance persistence analysis of hedge funds source. *Journal of Financial and Quantitative Analysis* 35: 327–342.

Agarwal, V., and N. Naik. 2000c. On taking the alternative route: Risks, rewards, and performance persistence of hedge funds. Working paper, London Business School; *Journal of Alternative Investments* 2–4, 6–23.

Agarwal, V., and N. Naik. 2000d. Performance evaluation of hedge funds with buy-and-hold and option-based strategies. Hedge Fund Centre Working Paper HF-003, London Business School.

Agarwal, V., and N. Naik. 2002. Risks and portfolio decisions involving hedge funds. *Review of Financial Studies* 17 (Spring): 63–98.

Agarwal, V., and N. Naik. 2004. Risk and portfolio decisions involving hedge funds. *Review of Financial Studies* 17: 63–98.

Agresti, A. 2002. *Categorical data analysis*, 2nd Ed. New York: John Wiley & Sons.

Alexander, C., and A. Dimitriu. 2003a. Optimizing passive investments. ISMA Centre Discussion Paper Series in Finance DP2003-08.

Alexander, C., and A. Dimitriu. 2003b. Regimes of index out-performance: A Markov switching model of index dispersion. ISMA Centre Discussion Paper Series in Finance DP2002-08.

Alexander, C., and A. Dimitriu. 2004. The art of investing in hedge funds: Fund selection and optimal allocations. ISMA Centre, University of Reading, working paper.

Amenc, N., and V. Le Sourd. 2003. *Portfolio theory and performance analysis.* West Essex, England: John Wiley & Sons.

Amenc, N., and L. Martellini. 2002a. The brave new world of hedge fund indexes. EDHEC/MISYS multi-style/multi-class program and CIBEAR Program.

Amenc, N., and L. Martellini. 2002b. Portfolio optimization and hedge fund style allocation decisions. *Journal of Alternative Investments:* 5–2, 7–20. EDHEC/ACT multi-style/multi-class program.

Amenc, N., and L. Martellini. 2003a. The alpha and omega of hedge fund performance measurement. Discussion paper, EDHEC Business School, www.edhec-risk.com.

Amenc, N., and L. Martellini. 2003b. The brave new world of hedge fund indices. Working paper, EDHEC-MISYS Risk and Asset Management Research Center.

Amenc, N., and L. Martellini. 2003c. Optimal mixing of hedge funds with traditional investment vehicles. Discussion paper, EDHEC Business School, www.edhec-risk.com.

Amenc, N., L. Martellini, and M. Vaissié. 2004. Indexing hedge fund indexes. In *Intelligent Hedge Fund Investing,* ed. B. Schachter. London: Risk Books.

Amin, G., and H. Kat. 2002. "Portfolio of hedge funds: What investors really invest in. ISMA Centre Discussion Paper 07/2002.

Amin, G., and H. Kat. 2003a. Hedge fund performance 1990–2000: Do the "money machines" really add value? Working paper, ISMA Centre, University of Reading, 2001; *Journal of Financial and Quantitative Analysis* 38: 251–274.

Amin, G., and H. Kat. 2003b. Stocks, bonds, and hedge funds. *Journal of Portfolio Management* 29, no. 4: 113–119.

Amin, G., and H. Kat. 2003c. Welcome to the dark side: Hedge fund attrition and survivorship bias over the period 1994–2001. Working paper, Case Business School; *Journal of Alternative Investments* 6: 57–73.

Anjilvel, S. I., B. E. Boudreau, M. W. Peskin, and M. S. Urias. 2000. Why hedge funds make sense. Morgan Stanley Quantitative Strategies.

Anson, M. 2002. *Handbook of alternative assets,* New York: John Wiley & Sons.

Anson, M. 2003. Benchmarking the hedge fund market place. *Journal of Indexes* (Third Quarter).

Aragon, G. 2004. Share restrictions and asset pricing: Evidence from the hedge fund industry. Working paper, Boston College.

Armistead, L. 2004. Dalman stakes his own cash on hedge fund. UK *Sunday Times,* Business Section, October 10.

Artzner, P., F. Delbaen, J. Eber, and D. Heath. 1999. Coherent risk measures. *Mathematical Finance* 9, no. 3.

Arzac, E. R., and V. S. Bawa. 1977. Portfolio choice and equilibrium in capital markets with safety-first investors. *Journal of Financial Economics* 4: 277–288.

Asness, C. 2004a. An alternative future: Part I. *Journal of Portfolio Management*, 30th Anniversary Issue: 94–103.

Asness, C. 2004b. An alternative future: Part II. *Journal of Portfolio Management* 30, Fall: 8–23.

Asness, C., R. Krail, and J. Liew. 2001. Do hedge funds hedge? *Journal of Portfolio Management* 28: 6–19; AQR Capital Management LLC.

Atkins, P. S., and C. A. Glassman. 2004. Dissent of Commissioners Glassman and Atkins to proposing release no. IA-2266. www.sec.gov/rules/proposed/ia-2266 .htm#dissent.

Atkins, T., and S. Hays. 2004. Worries rise about indebted funds of hedge funds. Reuters, October 15.

Bacmann, J.-F., and G. Gregor. 2004. Fat tail risk in portfolios of hedge funds and traditional investments. Working paper, RMF Investment Management, a member of the Man Group, 1–28.

Bacmann, J.-F., and S. Pache. 2003. Optimal hedge fund style allocation under higher moments. RMF Research Paper.

Bacmann, J.-F., and S. Scholz. 2003. Alternative performance measures for hedge funds. *AIMA Journal* (June).

Bailey, J. 1992. Are manager universes acceptable performance benchmarks? *Journal of Portfolio Management* 18 (Spring): 3, 9–13.

Bansal, R., D. Hsieh, and S. Viswanathan. 1993. A new approach to international arbitrage pricing. *Journal of Finance* 48: 1719–1747.

Bansal, R., and S. Viswanathan. 1993. "A new approach to international arbitrage pricing. *Journal of Finance* 48, 1231–1262.

Baquero, G., J. Horst, and M. Verbeek. 2002. Survival, look-ahead bias and the performance of hedge funds. Working paper, Erasmus University, Rotterdam, and Tiburg University, Netherlands.

Baquero, G., J. Ter Horst, and M. Verbeek. 2004. Survival, look-ahead bias, and the persistence in hedge fund performance. *Journal of Financial and Quantitative Analysis.*

Barès, P., R. Gibson, and S. Gyger. 2003. Style consistency and survival probability in the hedge funds industry. Swiss Federal Institute of Technology, Lausanne, and University of Zurich, working paper.

Barry, R. 2003. Hedge funds: A walk through the graveyard. Working paper, Applied Finance Centre, Macquarie University, Sydney, Australia.

Berenyi, Z. 2002. Measuring hedge fund risk with multi-moment risk measures. University of Munich.

Berk, J., and R. Green. 2004. Mutual fund flows and performance in rational markets. *Journal of Political Economy.*

Bernardo, A., and O. Ledoit. 2000. Gain, loss and asset pricing. *Journal of Political Economy* 8: 144–172.

Bernatzi, S., and R. Thaler. 1995. Myopic loss aversion and the equity premium puzzle. *Quarterly Journal of Economics* 110: 73–92.

Best, M., and R. Grauer. 1991. On the sensitivity of mean-variance-efficient portfolios to changes in asset means: Some analytical and computational results. *Review of Financial Studies* 4: 315–342.

Bettis, J. C., J. M. Bizjack, and M. L. Lemmon. 2001. Managerial ownership, incentive contracting, and the use of zero-cost dollars and equity swaps by corporate insiders. *Journal of Financial and Quantitative Analysis* 36: 345–370.

Bienstock, S., and E. Sorensen. 1992. Segregating growth from value: It's not always either/or. Salomon Brothers, *Quantitative Equities Strategy* (July).

Billingsley, R., and D. M. Chance. 1996. Benefits and limitations of diversification among commodity trading advisors. *Journal of Portfolio Management* 23: 65–80.

Black, F. 1976a. The pricing of commodity contracts. *Journal of Finance* 3: 167–179.

Black, F. 1976b. Studies of stock price volatility changes. *Proceedings of the 1976 Meetings of the American Statistical Association*, Business and Economical Statistics Section, 177–181.

Blake, C., and M. Morey. 2000. Morningstar rating and mutual fund performance. *Journal of Financial and Quantitative Analysis* 35, no. 3: 451–483.

Blum, P., M. Dacorogna, and L. Jaeger. 2003. Performance and risk measurement challenges for hedge funds: Empirical considerations. In *The new generation of risk management for hedge funds and private equity investments*, L. Jaeger. ed. Euromoney Books.

Bollen, N. P. B., and J. A. Busse. 2001. On the timing ability of mutual fund managers. *Journal of Finance* 56: 1075–1094.

Bollen, N. P. B., and M. Cohen. 2004. Mutual funds attributes and investor behavior. Working paper, Vanderbilt University.

Bollen, N. P. B., and V. Krepely. 2005. Red flags for fraud in the hedge fund industry. Working paper, Vanderbilt University, 2–23.

Bookstaber, R. 1999. A framework for understanding market cisis. In *Risk Management: Principles and Practices*. Charlottesville, VA: Association for Investment Management and Research.

Bookstaber, R. 2000. Understanding and monitoring the liquidity crisis cycle. *Financial Analysts Journal*: 17–22.

Boudoukh, J., M. Richardson, M. Subrahmanyam, and R. Whitelaw. 2002. Stale prices and strategies for trading mutual funds. *Financial Analysts Journal* 58: 53–71.

Boyson, N. 2002. How are hedge fund manager characteristics related to performance, volatility and survival. Working Paper, Ohio State University.

Breeden, D., and R. Litzenberger. 1978. Prices of state contingent claims implicit in option prices. *Journal of Business* 51: 612–651.

Brooks, C., and H. Kat. 2002. The statistical properties of hedge fund index returns and their implications for investors. Working paper, Case Business School; ISMA Centre, University of Reading; also, *Journal of Alternative Investments* 5, no. 2: 25–44.

Brown, K. C., W. V. Harlow, and L. T. Starks. 1996. Of tournaments and temptations: An analysis of managerial incentives in the mutual fund industry. *Journal of Finance* 51: 85–110.

Brown, S. J. 1989. The number of factors in security returns. *Journal of Finance* 44: 1247–1262.

Brown, S. J., D. R. Gallagher, O. W. Steenbeek, and P. L. Swan. 2004. Double or nothing: Patterns of equity fund holdings and transactions. Working paper, New York University.

Brown, S. J., and W. N. Goetzmann. 2003. Hedge funds with style. *Journal of Portfolio Management* 29: 101–112. Working paper, Yale School of Management.

Brown, S. J., W. N. Goetzmann, and R. G. Ibbotson. 1999. Offshore hedge funds: Survival and performance 1989–1995. *Journal of Business* 72, no. 1 (January): 91–118.

Brown, S. J., W. N. Goetzmann, R. G. Ibbotson, and S. Ross. 1992. Survivorship bias in performance studies. *Review of Financial Studies* 5: 553–580.

Brown, S. J., W. N. Goetzmann, and B. Liang. 2002. Fees on fees in funds of funds. Yale ICF Working paper No. 02-33. Working paper, New York University.

Brown, S. J., W. N. Goetzmann, and J. Park. 2000 & 2002. Hedge funds and the Asian currency crisis. *Journal of Portfolio Management* 26 (Summer), 6, no. 4: 95–101.

Brown, S. J., W. N. Goetzmann, and J. Park. 2001a. Careers and survival: Competition and risks in the hedge fund and CTA industry. *Journal of Finance* 56: 1869–1886.

Brown, S. J., W. N. Goetzmann, and J. Park. 2001b. Conditions for survival: Changing risk and the performance of hedge fund managers and CTAs. Yale School of Management Working Paper F-59.

Brunnermeier, M. K., and S. Kagel. 2004. Hedge funds and the technology bubble. *Journal of Finance* 59, no. 5 (October): 2013–2040.

Buetow, G. W., R. R. Johnson, and D. E. Runkle. 2000 The inconsistency of return-based style analysis. *Journal of Portfolio Management* (Spring): 61–77.

Busse, J. A. 2001. Another look at mutual fund tournaments. *Journal of Financial and Quantitative Analysis* 36: 53–73.

Cacson, A., C. Keating, and W. F. Shadwick. 2002. The omega function. London: Finance Development Centre.

Caldwell, T. 1995. Introduction: The model of superior performance. In *Hedge Funds*, ed. Lederman, Jess, and Klein. New York: Irwin Professional Publishing.

Cantrell, A. 2005. Hedge funds headed for a fall? *CNN/Money* (November 15).

Capocci, Daniel P. J., A. Corhay, and G. Hubner. 2004. Hedge fund performance and persistence in bull and bear markets. Working paper.

Carpenter, J., and A. Lynch. 1999. Survivorship bias and attrition effects in measures of performance persistence. *Journal of Financial Economics* 54: 337–374.

Casey, Quirk, and Acito and Bank of New York. 2004. Institutional demand for hedge funds: New opportunities and standards. White paper, CQA and Bank of New York, www.cqallc.com.

Chan, L. K. C., J. Karceski, and J. Lakonishok. 1999. On portfolio optimization: Forecasting covariances and choosing the risk model. *Review of Financial Studies* 12: 937–974.

Chan, N., M. Getmansky, S. Haas, and A. Lo. 2004. Systemic risk and hedge funds. In *The risks of financial institutions and the financial sector*, ed. M. Carey and R. Stulz. Chicago: University of Chicago Press.

Chandar, N., and R. Bricker. 2002. Incentives, discretion, and asset valuation in closed end mutual funds. *Journal of Accounting Research* 40: 1037–1070.

Chen, G., M. Firth, and O. M. Rui. 2001. The dynamic relation between stock returns, trading volume, and volatility. *Financial Review* 38: 153–174.

Chen, N., R. Roll, and S. Ross. 1986. Economic forces and the stock market. *Journal of Business* 59: 383–403.

Chevalier, J., and G. Ellison. 1997. Risk taking by mutual funds as a response to incentives. *Journal of Political Economy* 105: 1167–1200.

Chevalier, J., and G. Ellison. 1999. Are some mutual fund managers better than others? Cross-sectional patterns in behavior and performance. *Journal of Finance* 54 (June): 875–899.

Chiang, K. C. H., K. Kozhevnikov, and C. H. Wisen. 2003. The ranking properties of the Morningstar risk-adjusted rating. Working paper.

Christie, A. A. 1982. The stochastic behavior of common stock variances—Value, leverage, and interest rate effects. *Journal of Financial Economics* 10: 407–432.

Christie-David, R., and M. Chaudhry. 2001. Coskewness and cokurtosis in futures markets. *Journal of Empirical Finance* 8: 55–81.

Christoffersen, S. K., C. C. Geczy, D. K. Musto, and A. V. Reed. 2004. How and why do investors trade votes, and what does it mean? Working paper, Wharton.

Chunhachinda, P., K. Dandapani, S. Hamid, and A. K. Prakash. 1997. Portfolio selection and skewness: Evidence from international stock markets. *Journal of Banking & Finance* 21, no. 2: 143–167.

Coles, S., J. Hefernan, and J. Tawn. 1999. Dependence measures for extreme value analyse. *Extremes* 3.

Committee on the Global Financial System. 1999. A review of financial market events in Autumn 1998 (The Johnson Report). Bank for International Settlements, www.bis.org/publ/cgfs12.pdf.

Conine, T. E., Jr., and M. J. Tamarkin. 1981. On diversification given asymmetry in returns. *Journal of Finance* 36, no. 5 (December): 1143–1155.

Cornish, E. A., and R. A. Fisher. 1937. Moments and cumulants in the specification of distributions. *Review of the International Statistical Institute*: 307–320.

Credit Suisse First Boston. 2002. Index construction rules.

Dacorogna, M., U. Muller, O. Pictet, and C. De Vries. 2001. The distribution of external foreign exchange rate returns in extremely large data sets. *Extremes* 4, no. 2.

Darst, E. M. 2000. Performance evaluation for alternative investments: The effects of firm characteristics and fund style on the performance of hedge funds. Harvard University, senior thesis.

Das, N. 2003. Development of an analytical framework for hedge fund investment. Working paper.

Dauthine, J. P. and J. B. Donaldson. 2002. The intermediate financial theory. Upper Saddle River, NJ: Prentice Hall.

Davidson, A. C., and R. L. Smith. 1990. Models for exceedances over high thresholds. *Journal of the Royal Statistical Society*, Series B: 52.

Del Guercio, D., and P. A. Tkac. 2002. The determinants of the flow of funds of managed portfolios: Mutual funds versus pension funds. *Journal of Financial and Quantitative Analysis* 37, no. 4, 523–557.

diBartolomeo, D., and E. Witkowski. 1997. Mutual fund misclassification: Evidence based on style analysis. *Financial Analysts Journal* 53, no. 5 (September/October): 32–43.

Dimson, E. 1979. Risk measurement when shares are subject to infrequent trading. *Journal of Financial Economics* 7, no. 2, 197–226.

Duc, F. 2004a. Hedge fund indices: Status review and user guide. Alternative Asset Advisors.

Duc, F. 2004b. Investable hedge fund indices: Illusion or reality? Alternative Asset Advisors.

Edwards, F. R., and M. O. Caglayan. 2000 and 2001. An analysis of hedge fund performance: Excess returns, common risk factors, and manager skill. Working paper, Columbia Business School; *Journal of Futures Market* 21, no. 11: 1003–1028.

Edwards, F. R., and M. O. Caglayan. 2001a. Hedge fund and commodity fund investment styles in bull and bear markets. *Journal of Portfolio Management* 27, no. 4: 97–108.

Edwards, F. R., and M. O. Caglayan. 2001b. Hedge fund performance and manager skill. *Journal of Futures Markets* 21, no. 11: 1003–1028.

Edwards, F. R., and J. Liew. 1999a. Hedge funds versus managed futures as asset classes. *Journal of Derivatives* 6: 45–64.

Edwards, F. R., and J. Liew. 1999b. Managed commodity funds. *Journal of Futures Markets* 19: 377–411.

Eichengreen, B., D. Mathieson, B. Chadha, A. Jansen, L. Kodres, and S. Sharma. 1998. Hedge fund and financial market dynamics. (Occasional Paper No. 166). Washington, DC: International Monetary Fund.

Elton, E. J., and M. J. Gruber. 1977. Risk reduction and portfolio size: An analytical solution. *Journal of Business* 50 (October): 415–437.

Elton, E. J., and M. J. Gruber. 1995. *Modern portfolio theory and investment analysis*, 5th ed. New York: John Wiley & Sons.

Elton, E. J., M. J. Gruber, and J. C. Rentzler. 1987. Professionally managed, publicly traded commodity funds. *Journal of Business* 60: 175–199.

Embrechts, P., C. Kuppelberg, and T. Mikosch. 1997. *Modelling external events for insurance and finance*. Berlin: Springer Verlag.

Ennis, M., and M. D. Sebastian. 2003. A critical look at the case for hedge funds. *Journal of Portfolio Management* (Summer): 103–112.

Fabre-Bulle, A., and P. Sebastien. 2003. The omega measure: Hedge fund portfolio optimization. University of Lausanne, Ecole des HEC.

Fama, E., and K. French. 1992. The cross-section of expected stock returns. *Journal of Finance* 47, no. 2 (June): 427–465.

Fama, E., and K. French. 1993. Common risk factors in the returns on stocks and bonds. *Journal of Financial Economics* 33, no. 1: 3–56.

Farmer, D. 2002. Market force, ecology and evolution. *Industrial and Corporate Change* 11: 895–953.

Farmer, D., and A. Lo. 1999. Frontiers of finance: Evolution and efficient markets. *Proceedings of the National Academy of Sciences* 96: 9991–9992.

Favre, L., and J. A. Galeano. 2000. Portfolio allocation with hedge funds—Case study of a Swiss institutional investor. MBF Master's Thesis, University of Lausanne.

Favre, L., and J. A. Galeano. 2002. Mean-modified value at risk optimization with hedge funds. *Journal of Alternative Investments* 5, no. 2.

Feffer, S., and C. Kundro. 2003. Understanding and mitigating operational risk in hedge fund investments. Working paper, Capital Markets Company Ltd.

Focardi, S., and F. Fabozzi. 2003. Fat tails, scaling and stable laws. *Journal of Risk Finance* 5, no. 1.

Frost, P. A., and J. E. Savarino. 1986. Empirical Bayes approach to efficient portfolio selection. *Journal of Financial and Quantitative Analysis* 31: 293–305.

Frost, P. A., J. E. Savarino. 1988. For better performance: Constrain portfolio weights. *Journal of Portfolio Management*: 29–34.

Fung, W. and D. A. Hsieh. 1997a. Empirical characteristics of dynamic trading strategies: The case of hedge funds. *Review of Financial Studies* 10: 275–302.

Fung, W., and D. A. Hsieh. 1997b. The Information content of performance track records: Investment style and survivorship bias in the historical returns of commodity trading advisors. *Journal of Portfolio Management* 24 (Fall): 30–41.

Fung, W., and D. A. Hsieh. 1997c. Survivorship bias and investment style in the returns of CTAs: The information content of track records. *Journal of Portfolio Management* 24: 30–41.

Fung, W., and D. A. Hsieh 1999a. On the performance of hedge funds. *Financial Analysts Journal* 55 (July/August): 72–85.

Fung, W., and D. A. Hsieh. 1999b. A primer on hedge funds. *Journal of Empirical Finance* 6: 309–331.

Fung, W., and D. A. Hsieh. 2000. Performance characteristics of hedge funds and commodity funds: Natural versus spurious biases. *Journal of Financial and Quantitative Analysis* 35, no. 3 (September) 291–307.

Fung, W., and D. A. Hsieh. 2001. The risk in hedge fund strategies: Theory and evidence from trend followers. *Review of Financial Studies* 14, no. 2: 313–341.

Fung, W., and D. A. Hsieh. 2002a. Asset-based style factors for hedge funds. *Financial Analysts Journal* 58, no. 5 (September/October): 16–27.

Fung, W., and D. A. Hsieh. 2002b. Benchmarks of hedge fund performance: Information content and measurement biases. *Financial Analysts Journal*; and *Journal of Alternative Investments* 58, no. 1 (January/February): 22–34.

Fung, W., and D. A. Hsieh. 2003. Benchmarks for alternative investments. Security Analysts Association of Japan.

Fung, W., and D. A. Hsieh. 2004. Hedge fund benchmarks: A risk based approach. *Financial Analysts Journal* 60, no. 5 (September/October): 65–80.

Gehin, W., and M. Vaissié. 2004. Hedge fund indices: Investable, non-investable and strategy benchmarks. EDHEC Risk and Asset Management Research Centre: 1–31.

Geltner, D. 1991. Smoothing in appraisal-based returns. *Journal of Real Estate Finance and Economics* 4: 327–345.

Geltner, D. 1993. Estimating market values from appraisal values without assuming an efficient market. *Journal of Real Estate Research* 8: 325–345.

Getmansky, M. 2004. The life cycle of hedge funds: Fund flows, size and performance. Unpublished working paper, MIT Laboratory for Financial Engineering.

Getmansky, M., and A. Lo. 2003. A system dynamics model of the hedge fund industry. Unpublished working paper, MIT Laboratory for Financial Engineering.

Getmansky, M., A. Lo, and I. Makarov. 2004. An econometric analysis of serial correlation and illiquidity in hedge fund returns. *Journal of Financial Economics* 74: 529–609. Working paper, MIT Sloan School of Management.

Getmansky, M., A. Lo, and S. Mei. 2004. Sifting through the wreckage: Lessons from recent hedge-fund liquidations. Working paper, MIT and University of Massachusetts.

Glosten, L., and R. Jagannathan. 1994. A contingent claim approach to performance evaluation. *Journal of Empirical Finance* 1: 133–160.

Goetzmann, W., J. Ingersoll, and S. Ross. 2003. High water marks and hedge fund management contracts. *Journal of Finance* 58: 1685–1718.

Goltz, F., L. Martellini, and V. Mathieu. 2004. Hedge fund indices from an academic perspective: Reconciling investability and representation. Working paper, EDHEC Risk and Asset Management Research Centre.

Greene, W. 2003. *Econometric analysis*, 5th ed. Upper Saddle River, NJ: Prentice Hall.

Greenspan, A. 1998. Statement before the Committee on Banking and Financial Services, U.S. House of Representatives. *Federal Reserve Bulletin* 84: 1046–1050.

Greer, R. J. 1997. What is an asset class, anyway?" *Journal of Portfolio Management* 23, no. 2: 86–91.

Gregoriou, G. 2002. Hedge fund survival lifetimes. *Journal of Asset Management* 3, vol. 2, no. 3: 237–252.

Grinblatt, M., and S. Titman. 1989. Portfolio performance evaluation: Old issues and new insights. *Review of Financial Studies* 2: 393–421.

Grosvenor Capital Management. 2004. Composite hedge fund and fund of funds indices performance benchmark review. (February).

Guner, A. B. 2002. Asset pricing and portfolio optimization with non-normal returns: An application to hedge funds.

Gutpa, A., and B. Liang. 2003. Risk analysis and capital adequacy of hedge funds. Working Paper.

Hamilton, J. D. 1994. Modelling time series with changes in regime. In *Time series analysis*, 677–703. Princeton, NJ: Princeton University Press.

Harlow, W. V. 1991. Asset allocation in a downside-risk framework. *Financial Analysts Journal* (September-October): 28–40.

Harvey, C., and A. Siddique. 2000. Conditional skewness in asset pricing tests. *Journal of Finance* 55: 1263–1295.

Haslem, J. A., and C. A. Scheraga. 2001. Morningstar's classification of large-cap mutual funds. *Journal of Investing* (Spring) 79–84.

Hendricks, D., J. Patel, and R. Zeckhauser. 1997. The J-shape of performance persistence given survivorship bias. *Review of Economics and Statistics* 79: 161–170.

Henker, T. 1998. Naïve diversification for hedge funds. *Journal of Alternative Investments* 1, no. 3 (Winter): 33–38.

Henricksson, R. D., and R. C. Merton. 1981. On market timing and investment performance II: Statistical procedures for evaluating forecasting skills. *Journal of Business* 54: 513–533.

Hill, B. M. 1975. A simple general approach to inference about the tail of a distribution. *Annals of Statistics* 3.

Horst, J., T. Nijman, and M. Verbeek. 2001. Eliminating look-ahead bias in evaluating persistence in mutual fund performance. *Journal of Empirical Finance* 8: 345–373.

Howell, M. J. 2001. Fund age and performance. *Journal of Alternative Investments* 4 (2): 57–60.

Hubermann, G., S. Kandel, and R. F. Stambaugh. 1987. Mimicking portfolios and exact arbitrage pricing. *Journal of Finance* 42, no. 1: 1–9.

Huisman, R., K. G. Koedijk, and R. A. J. Pownall. 1999. Asset allocation in a value-at-risk framework. Erasmus University, Rotterdam.

Ibbotson Associates. 2004. *Stocks, bonds, bills, and inflation 2004 yearbook*. Chicago, IL: Ibbotson Associates.

Ibbotson Associates. 2005. *Stocks, bonds, bills, and inflation 2005 yearbook*. Chicago, IL: Ibbotson Associates.

Ibbotson R., and P. Chen. 2005. Sources of hedge funds' returns: Alphas, betas, and costs. Working paper.

Ineichen, A. 2001. The myth of hedge funds: Are hedge funds the fireflies ahead of the storm? *Journal of Global Financial Markets* 2, no. 4: 34–46.

International Monetary Fund. 2004. Global financial stability report. (April): 146–148.

Investment Company Institute. 2004. *2004 Mutual fund fact book*. Washington, DC: Investment Company Institute.

Jagannathan, R., and R. A. Korajczyk. 1986. Assessing the market timing performance of managed portfolios. *Journal of Business* 59: 217–235.

Jagannathan, R., and T. Ma. 2003. Risk reduction in large portfolios: Why imposing the wrong constraints helps. *Journal of Finance* 58: 1651–1683.

Jen, P., C. Heasman, and K. Boyatt. 2001. Alternative asset strategies: Early performance in hedge fund managers. Internal document, Lazard Asset Management, London. www.aima.org.

Jensen, M. C. 1968. The performance of mutual funds in the period 1945–1964. *Journal of Finance* 23: 389–416.

Jin, X.-J., and X.-L. Yang. 2004. Empirical study on mutual fund objective classification. *Journal of Zhejiang University SCIENCE* 5, no. 5.

Jorion, P. 1985a. Bayes-Stein estimation for portfolio analysis. *Journal of Financial and Quantitative Analysis* 21, no. 3: 279–292.

Jorion, P. 1985b. International portfolio diversification with estimation risk. *Journal of Business* 58: 259–278.

Jorion, P. 2000. Risk management lessons from long-term capital management. *European Financial Management* 6: 277–300.

Kahan, M., and E. B. Rock. 2005. Hedge funds in corporate governance and corporate control. Unpublished manuscript, September 28.

Kahnemann, D., and A. Tversky. 1979. Prospect theory: An analysis of decision under risk. *Econometrica* 47, no. 2.

Kalbfleisch, J. D., and R. L. Prentice. 2002. *The statistical analysis of failure time data.* 2nd ed. New York: John Wiley & Sons.

Kao, D. 2000. Estimating and pricing credit risk: An overview. *Financial Analysts Journal* 56: 50–66.

Kao, D. 2002. Battle for alphas: Hedge funds versus long-only portfolios. *Financial Analysts Journal* 58: 16–36.

Karmel, R. S. 2004. Should a duty to the corporation be imposed on institutional investors? *Business Law* 60: 1.

Kat, H. M. 2001. Hedge fund mania—Some words of caution. ISMA Centre, University of Reading.

Kat, H. M. 2002. Managed futures and hedge funds: A match made in heaven. Working paper.

Kat, H. M. 2003a. The dangers of using correlation to measure dependence. *Journal of Alternative Investment* 6, no. 2.

Kat, H. M. 2003b. 10 things investors should know about hedge funds. Working paper, Case Business School.

Kat, H. M., and S. Lu. 2002. An excursion into the statistical properties of hedge fund returns. Working paper, University of Reading.

Kazemi, H., G. Martin, and T. Schneeweiss. 2001 & 2002. Understanding hedge fund performance: Research issues and results and rules of thumb for institutional investor. Lehman Brothers; *Journal of Alternative Investments* 5, no. 3: 6–22.

Keating, C., and W. F. Shadwick. 2002a. *An introduction to omega.* London: Finance Development Centre.

Keating, C., and W. F. Shadwick. 2002b. *A universal performance measure.* London: Finance Development Centre.

Kempf, A., and C. Memmel. 2003. On the estimation of the global minimum variance portfolio. Discussion paper, Social Sciences Research Network.

Kim, M., R. Shukla, and M. Thomas. 2000. Mutual fund objective misclassification. *Journal of Economics and Business* (July/August).

King, G., and L. Zeng. 1999. Logistic regression in rare events data. Working paper, Department of Government, Harvard University.

Knepper, Z. T. 2004. Future-priced convertible securities and the outlook for "death-spiral" securities-fraud litigation. *ExpressO Preprint Series.* Working Paper 363 (August 29). http://law.bepress.com/expresso/eps/363.

Ko, F., W. T. H. Ko, and M. Teo. 2003. Asian hedge funds: Return persistence, style, and fund characteristics. Working paper.

Kohler, A. 2003. Hedge fund indexing: A square peg in a round hole? State Street Global Advisors.

Korana, A., and E. Nelling. 1998. The determinants and predictive ability of mutual fund ratings. *Journal of Investing.*

Koshi, J., and J. Pontiff. 1999. How are derivatives used? Evidence from the mutual fund industry. *Journal of Finance* 54: 791–816.

Kramer, D. 2001. Hedge fund disasters: Avoiding the next catastrophe. *Alternative Investment Quarterly* 1.

Kundig, O., S. Lodeiro, P. Meier, and A. Ruckstuhl. 2004. Funds of hedge funds indices: Properties, purpose and representativeness. Institut Banking & Finance.

Kurdas, Ch. 2004. Benchmarking: What hedge fund indices can and cannot do. Tremont Capital Management Inc.

Lai, T. 1991. Portfolio selection with skewness. *Review of Quantitative Finance and Accounting* 1: 293–305.

Lamm, R. McF. 1999. Portfolios of alternative assets: Why not 100% hedge funds? *Journal of Investing* 8, no. 4.

Lamm, R. McF. 2002. How reliable are hedge fund performance indexes? Deutsche Bank.

Ledford, A., and J. Tawn. 1996. Statistics for near independence in multivariate extreme values. *Biometrika* 83, no. 1.

Ledford, A., and J. Tawn. 1997. Modelling dependence within joint tail regions. *Journal of the Royal Statistical Society*, Series B: 49.

Ledoit, O., and M. Wolf. 2003. Improved estimation of the covariance matrix of stock returns with an application to portfolio selection. *Journal of Empirical Finance* 10: 603–621.

Lerner, L. M. 2003. Disclosing toxic pipes: Why the SEC can and should expand the reporting requirements surrounding private investments in public equities. *Business Law* 58 (February): 655.

Lhabitant, F. S. 2001a. Assessing market risk for hedge funds and hedge fund portfolios. *Journal of Risk Finance* (Spring): 1–17.

Lhabitant, F. S. 2001b. Hedge funds investing: A quantitative look inside the black box. *Journal of Financial Transformation* 1, no. 1: 82–90; Union Bancaire Privée.

Lhabitant, F. S. 2003. Hedge funds: A look beyond the sample. Working paper.

Lhabitant, F. S., and M. Learned. 2002. Hedge fund diversification: How much is enough? Research Paper 52, FAME—International Center for Financial Asset Management and Engineering.

Li, D. 1999. Value at risk based on the volatility, skewness and kurtosis. Working paper, Riskmetrics Group.

Liang, B. 1999. On the performance of hedge funds. *Financial Analysts Journal* 55, Weatherhead School of Management, Case Western Reserve University: 72–85.

Liang B. 2000. Hedge funds: The living and the dead. *Journal of Financial and Quantitative Analysis* 35, no. 3 (September): 309–336.

Liang B. 2001. Hedge fund performance: 1990–1999. *Financial Analysts Journal* 57, no. 1: 11–18.

Liang, B. 2002. Hedge fund returns: Auditing and accuracy. *Journal of Portfolio Management*, Weatherhead School of Management, Case Western Reserve University: 1–30.

Liang B. 2003. The accuracy of hedge fund returns. *Journal of Portfolio Management* 29: 111–122.

Liew, J. 2003. Hedge fund index investing examined. *Journal of Portfolio Management* 29, no. 2: 113–123.

Liu, J., and F. A. Longstaff. 2004. Losing money on arbitrages: Optimal dynamic portfolio choice in markets with arbitrage opportunities. *Review of Financial Studies* 17: 611–641.

Lo, A. 1999. The three P's of total risk management. *Financial Analysts Journal* 55: 87–129.

Lo, A. 2001. Risk management for hedge funds: Introduction and overview. *Financial Analysts Journal* 57: 16–33.

Lo, A. 2002. The statistics of Sharpe ratios. *Financial Analysts Journal* 58: 36–50.

Lo, A. 2004. The adaptive markets hypothesis: Market efficiency from an evolutionary perspective. *Journal of Portfolio Management* 30: 15–29.

Lo, A., H. Mamaysky, and J. Wang. 2004. Asset prices and trading volume under fixed transactions costs. *Journal of Political Economy* 112: 1054–1090.

Lobosco, A., and D. diBartolomeo. 1997. Approximating the confidence intervals for Sharpe style weights. *Financial Analysts Journal* (July/August): 80–85.

Lochoff, R. 2002. Hedge funds and hope. *Journal of Portfolio Management* 28: 92–99.

MacKenzie, D. 2003. Long-Term Capital Management and the sociology of arbitrage. *Economy and Society* 32: 349–380.

Mahdavi, M. 2004. Risk-adjusted return when returns are not normally distributed: Adjusted Sharpe ratio. *Journal of Alternative Investments* 6, no. 4: 47–57.

Malkiel, B. G. 1999. Returns from investing in equity mutual funds 1971 to 1991. *Journal of Finance* 50 (June): 549–572.

Malkiel, B. G., and A. Saha. 2004. Hedge funds: Risk and return. Working paper, Princeton Paper.

Markowitz, H. M. 1952. Portfolio selection. *Journal of Finance* 7, no. 1: 77–91.

McDonough, W. 1998. Statement before the Committee on Banking and Financial Services, U.S. House of Representatives. *Federal Reserve Bulletin* 84: 1050–1054.

McGuire P., E. Remolona, and K. Tsatsaronis. 2005. Time-varying exposures and leverage in hedge funds. *Bis Quarterly Review*, March 2005: 59–72.

Merton, R. 1980. On estimating the expected return on the market: An exploratory investigation. *Journal of Financial Economics* 8: 323–361.

Merton, R. 1981. On market timing and investment performance I: An equilibrium theory of value for market forecasts. *Journal of Business* 54: 363–406.

Metzger, L., and the IAFE Investor Risk Committee. 2004. Valuation concepts for investment companies and financial institutions and their stakeholders. Investor Risk Committee White Paper, International Association of Financial Engineers.

Michaud, R. 1989. The Markowitz optimization enigma: Is "optimized" optimal? *Financial Analysts Journal* 45: 31–42.

Michaud, R. 1998. Efficient asset management. Boston: Harvard Business School Press.

Mirabaud, P. G. 2003. Is traditional long-term investment a thing of the past? Address to Fourth International Sustainability Forum, University of Zurich, October 15.

Mitchell, M., and T. Pulvino. 2001. Characteristics of risk and return in risk arbitrage. *Journal of Finance* 56, no. 6: 2135–2175.

Moix, P. Y., and C. Schmidhuber. 2001. Fat tail risk: The case of hedge funds. AIMA Newsletter (September/December); Working paper.

Morey, M. R. 2003a. The kiss of death: A 5-star Morningstar mutual fund rating? *Financial Analysts Journal* 54 (March–April).

Morey, M. R. 2003b. Should you carry the load? A comprehensive analysis of load and no-load out-of-sample performance. *Journal of Banking and Finance* 27: 1245–1271.

Morgan Stanley Capital International Inc. 2002a. Hedge fund index methodology.

Morgan Stanley Capital International Inc. 2002b. Hedge fund indexes: Manager guide to classification.

Morley, I. 2004. Hedge fund indices: A measure of performance or the hangman's noose for hedge funds? *AIMA Journal*.

Muhtaseb, M. R. 2003. Hedge funds, asset allocation and investable benchmarks. *Journal of Wealth Management* 6, no. 1: 64–67.

Newey, W., and K. West. 1987. A simple, positive, semi-definite, heteroskedasticity and autocorrelation consistent covariance matrix. *Econometrica* 55: 703–708.

Oberhofer, G., and L. B. Ross. 2002. What the indexes don't tell you about hedge funds. EFMA London Meetings.

Okunev, J., and D. White. 2003. Hedge fund risk factors and value at risk of credit trading strategies. Working paper: 41–63.

Pérold, A. 1999. *Long-Term Capital Management, L.P. (A–D)*. Harvard Case Study. Boston: Harvard Business School Press.

Pickands, J. 1975. Statistical inference using extreme order statistics. *Annals of Statistics* 3.

Plerou, V., P. Gopikrishnan, B. Rosenow, N. Amaral, T. Guhr, and E. Stanley. 2002. Random matrix approach to cross correlations in financial data. *Physical Review E* 65: 1–18.

PlusFunds. 2002. Hedge fund indexing: The next industry evolution.

Poon, S. H., M. Rockinger, and J. Tawn. 2003. Extreme value dependency in international stock markets. *Review of Financial Studies*, working paper.

Posthuma, N., and P. J. Van der Sluis. 2003. A reality check on hedge fund returns. Working paper, ABP Investments. In *Intelligent hedge fund investing*, ed. B. Schachter. London: Risk Books, 2004.

Posthuma, N., and P. J. van der Sluis. 2004a. A critical examination of historical hedge fund returns. Chapter 13 in *Intelligent hedge hund investing: Successfully avoiding pitfalls through better risk evaluation*, ed. by B. Schachter. London: Risk Books.

Posthuma, N., and P. J. van der Sluis. 2004b. *A reality check on hedge fund returns*. VU Research Memorandum 2003–17.

Posthuma, N., and P. J. van der Sluis. 2004c. Unveiling hedge funds. *Fiducie* 13, no. 2: 17–24.

Prakash, A. J., C.-H. Chang, and T. E. Pactwa. 2003. Selecting a portfolio with skewness: Recent evidence from U.S., European, and Latin American equity markets. *Journal of Banking & Finance* 27, no. 7: 1375–1390.

Pratt, J., and R. Zeckhauser. 1987. Proper risk aversion. *Econometrica* 55, no. 1.

President's Working Group on Financial Markets. 1999. Hedge funds, leverage, and the lessons of Long-Term Capital Management. President's Working Group on Financial Markets, Washington, DC.

Rouah, F. 2005. Competing risks in hedge fund survival. Working paper, McGill University, Montreal; Foundation for Managed Derivatives Research (FMDR), Institut de Finance Mathématique de Montréal (IFM2), and Centre de Recherche en E-finance (CREF).

Schmidhuber, C., and P. Y. Moix. 2001. Fat tail risk: The case for hedge funds. *AIMA Newsletter* (September–Dececember).

Schneeweis, T., and R. Spurgin. 1996. Survivorship bias in commodity trading advisor performance. *Journal of Futures Markets* 16: 757–772.

Schneeweis, T., and R. Spurgin. 1998a. Alternative investments in the institutional portfolio. Working paper, CISDM Isenberg School of Management, University of Massachusetts.

Schneeweis, T., and R. Spurgin. 1998b. Multifactor analysis of hedge funds, managed futures and mutual fund return and risk characteristics. *Journal of Alternative Investments* 1, no. 2 (Fall): 1–24.

Schneeweis, T., and R. Spurgin. 1999. The benefits of hedge funds. Working paper, CISDM Isenberg School of Management, University of Massachussetts.

Schneeweis, T., and R. Spurgin. 2000 and 2001. The benefits of index option-based strategies for institutional portfolios. *Journal of Alternative Investments* (Spring): 44–52.

Scholes, M., and J. Williams. 1977. Estimating betas from non-synchronous data. *Journal of Financial Economics* 5: 309–327.

Schupp, O. 2004. Appetite for alternatives. *Professional Wealth Management* 18, Credit Suisse First Boston.

Schupp, O., and H. Xia. 2003. Take the index high road. *Risk*.

Scott, R. C., and P. A. Horvath. 1980. On the direction of preference for moments of higher order than the variance. *Journal of Finance* 35, Issue 4: 915–919.

Securities and Exchange Commission. 2003. Implications of the growth of hedge funds, staff report to the United States Securities and Exchange Commission. United States Securities and Exchange Commission, Washington, DC (September). www.sec.gov.

Securities and Exchange Commission. 2004. Registration under the advisers act of certain hedge fund advisers. File No. S7-30-04, United States Securities and Exchange Commission, Washington, DC.

Sender, H. 2005. Hedge-fund flows become more fickle. *Wall Street Journal* (December 23–26).

Sharpe, W. 1963. A simplified model for portfolio analysis. *Management Science* 9: 277–293.

Sharpe, W. F. 1964. Capital asset prices: A theory of market equilibrium under conditions of risk. *Journal of Finance* 19: 425–442.

Sharpe, W. F. 1988. Determining a fund's effective asset mix. *Investment Management Review* (December): 59–69.

Sharpe, W. F. 1992. Asset allocation: Management style and performance measure. *Journal of Portfolio Management* 18, no. 2 (Winter): 7–19.

Sharpe, W. F. 1997. *Morningstar's performance measures.*

Shleifer, A., and R. Vishny. 1997. The limits of arbitrage. *Journal of Finance* 52: 35–55.

Siegmann, A., and A. Lucas. 2002. Explaining hedge fund investment styles by loss aversion: A rational alternative. Vrije Universiteit.

Signer, A., and L. Favre. 2002. The difficulties of measuring the benefits of hedge funds. *Journal of Alternative Investments* 5, no. 1.

Sortino, F., and L. Price. 1994. Performance measurement in a downside risk framework. *Journal of Investing.* Working Paper.

Spurgin, R. 1999. A benchmark for commodity trading advisor performance. *Journal of Alternative Investments.*

Stutzer, M. 2001. A portfolio performance index and its implications. University of Iowa.

Sun, Q., and Y. Yan. 2003. Skewness persistence with optimal portfolio selection. *Journal of Banking & Finance* 27, no. 6: 1111–1121.

Teitelbaum, R. 2006. Hedge fund hotshots. *Bloomberg Markets.*

Treynor, J., and K. Mazuy. 1966. Can mutual funds outguess the market? *Harvard Business Review* 44: 131–136.

UBS Warburg. 2000. In search of alpha: Investing in hedge funds.

Vaissié, M. 2003. A detailed analysis of the construction methods and management principles of hedge fund indices: Are all hedge fund indices created equal? EDHEC-MISYC Risk and Asset Management Research Center.

Watts, D. 1999. Small worlds: The dynamics of networks between order and randomness. Princeton, NJ: Princeton University Press.

Watts, D., and S. Strogatz. 1998. Collective dynamics of small world networks. *Nature* 393: 440–442.

Weber, J. 2006a. Credit risk—In Europe, Hedge Funds compete for assets while dealers compete for hedge funds. Global Association of Risk Professionals.

Weber, J. 2006b. Market risk—Climbing cost of compliance for hedge funds. Global Association of Risk Professionals.

WEB SITES

www.xhedgefund.com
This is the web site of operational due diligence consulting firm Xagua.

www.hedgefundresearch.com
This web site offers information on the monthly performance by strategy at no charge but access to detailed analysis of trends and more detailed information on performance is available by subscription only.

www.hedgeworld.com
This web site offers information performance data on more than 3,900 funds covered by Lipper TASS, a source of performance data.

www.msci.com
This database has information on 2,500 funds representing $270 billion and a sliding scale of fees.

www.hedgeindex.com
This web site offers performance data for CSFB/Tremont Hedge Fund index, specific sector indexes, and an investable index.

Index